T0156142

Communications
in Computer and Information Science   2002

Rationale

The CCIS series is devoted to the publication of proceedings of computer science conferences. Its aim is to efficiently disseminate original research results in informatics in printed and electronic form. While the focus is on publication of peer-reviewed full papers presenting mature work, inclusion of reviewed short papers reporting on work in progress is welcome, too. Besides globally relevant meetings with internationally representative program committees guaranteeing a strict peer-reviewing and paper selection process, conferences run by societies or of high regional or national relevance are also considered for publication.

Topics

The topical scope of CCIS spans the entire spectrum of informatics ranging from foundational topics in the theory of computing to information and communications science and technology and a broad variety of interdisciplinary application fields.

Information for Volume Editors and Authors

Publication in CCIS is free of charge. No royalties are paid, however, we offer registered conference participants temporary free access to the online version of the conference proceedings on SpringerLink (http://link.springer.com) by means of an http referrer from the conference website and/or a number of complimentary printed copies, as specified in the official acceptance email of the event.

CCIS proceedings can be published in time for distribution at conferences or as post-proceedings, and delivered in the form of printed books and/or electronically as USBs and/or e-content licenses for accessing proceedings at SpringerLink. Furthermore, CCIS proceedings are included in the CCIS electronic book series hosted in the SpringerLink digital library at http://link.springer.com/bookseries/7899. Conferences publishing in CCIS are allowed to use Online Conference Service (OCS) for managing the whole proceedings lifecycle (from submission and reviewing to preparing for publication) free of charge.

Publication process

The language of publication is exclusively English. Authors publishing in CCIS have to sign the Springer CCIS copyright transfer form, however, they are free to use their material published in CCIS for substantially changed, more elaborate subsequent publications elsewhere. For the preparation of the camera-ready papers/files, authors have to strictly adhere to the Springer CCIS Authors' Instructions and are strongly encouraged to use the CCIS LaTeX style files or templates.

Abstracting/Indexing

CCIS is abstracted/indexed in DBLP, Google Scholar, EI-Compendex, Mathematical Reviews, SCImago, Scopus. CCIS volumes are also submitted for the inclusion in ISI Proceedings.

How to start

To start the evaluation of your proposal for inclusion in the CCIS series, please send an e-mail to ccis@springer.com.

Nur Haryani Zakaria · Nur Suhaili Mansor ·
Husniza Husni · Fathey Mohammed
Editors

Computing and Informatics

9th International Conference, ICOCI 2023
Kuala Lumpur, Malaysia, September 13–14, 2023
Revised Selected Papers, Part II

 Springer

Editors
Nur Haryani Zakaria ⓘ
Universiti Utara Malaysia
Sintok, Malaysia

Nur Suhaili Mansor ⓘ
Universiti Utara Malaysia
Sintok, Malaysia

Husniza Husni ⓘ
Universiti Utara Malaysia
Sintok, Malaysia

Fathey Mohammed ⓘ
Sunway University
Selangor, Malaysia

ISSN 1865-0929 ISSN 1865-0937 (electronic)
Communications in Computer and Information Science
ISBN 978-981-99-9591-2 ISBN 978-981-99-9592-9 (eBook)
https://doi.org/10.1007/978-981-99-9592-9

This Springer imprint is published by the registered company Springer Nature Singapore Pte Ltd.
The registered company address is: 152 Beach Road, #21-01/04 Gateway East, Singapore 189721, Singapore

Paper in this product is recyclable.

Preface

This year's International Conference on Computing and Informatics (ICOCI 2023) conference proceedings, centered around the theme "Nurturing an inclusive digital society for a sustainable nation," reflect the ever-evolving intersection of technology and society. The exploration of how we can harness digital innovation to foster sustainability, unity, and growth underscores our shared commitment to shaping a better digital landscape for our nations and the world.

The dedication and enthusiasm demonstrated by contributors from various countries highlight the significance of the addressed topics. Congratulations and appreciation are extended to all authors and presenters for their valuable contributions to this intellectual discourse.

As these proceedings find their place in our esteemed publication venues, they mark the continuation of the journey of knowledge dissemination. The enriched understanding and insights contained within these works pave the way for future research and innovations, contributing to a positive ripple effect that extends beyond the confines of this conference and into our societies.

The sub-themes of this year's conference proceedings are Digital Entrepreneurship and Innovation, Digital Healthcare and Well-Being, Digital Media and Information Literacy, Education Transformation through Technology, Ensuring Cybersecurity and Privacy, Harnessing Technology for Sustainable Development, and Navigating AI Development and Deployment. All these sub-themes serve as focal points for the exploration of diverse facets within the digital landscape.

This comprehensive exploration reflects the global perspective embedded in our discussions, showcasing the collaborative effort of minds from various corners of the world. The rich diversity of ideas and experiences brought forward by our contributors enriches the depth of understanding in each sub-theme.

We received a total of 134 paper submissions, a testament to the widespread interest and engagement in the topics under consideration. Through a rigorous double-blind review process, each paper was meticulously evaluated by at least 3 reviewers. Out of the submissions, 55 papers were selected for inclusion in these proceedings, representing the highest standards of academic rigor and relevance.

We sincerely hope that the knowledge shared within the pages of these conference proceedings serves as a robust foundation for future advancements and positive change in our ever-evolving digital societies. May the insights contained herein inspire further exploration, innovation, and collaboration, leading us towards a more inclusive, sustainable, and digitally connected future.

Warm regards,

Nur Haryani Zakaria

ICOCI 2023 Committee

Patron

Mohd. Foad Sakdan   Universiti Utara Malaysia

Advisor

Osman Ghazali   Universiti Utara Malaysia

Conference Chair

Norliza Katuk   Universiti Utara Malaysia

Vice-chair

Nur Azzah Abu Bakar   Universiti Utara Malaysia

Treasurer

Aniza Mohamed Din   Universiti Utara Malaysia

Secretary

Alawiyah Abd Wahab   Universiti Utara Malaysia

Finance and Sponsorship

Mazni Omar   Universiti Utara Malaysia
Norliza Katuk   Universiti Utara Malaysia

Secretariat

Alawiyah Abd Wahab   Universiti Utara Malaysia
Nur Azzah Abu Bakar   Universiti Utara Malaysia

Logistics and Accommodation

Suwannit Chareen Chit Sop Chit   Universiti Utara Malaysia

Paperwork and Proceedings

Nur Haryani Zakaria   Universiti Utara Malaysia
Husniza Husni   Universiti Utara Malaysia
Fathey Mohammed   Sunway University, Malaysia
Nur Suhaili Mansor   Universiti Utara Malaysia

Promotion and Publicity

Syamsul Bahrin Zaibon   Universiti Utara Malaysia
Azizi Abas   Universiti Utara Malaysia

International Technical Committee

Mario Jose Divan Koller   Intel, Argentina
Bakr Ahmed Taha   Universiti Kebangsaan Malaysia, Malaysia
Fateh Seghir   University Ferhat Abbas Setif 1, Algeria
Boubakeur Annane   University Ferhat Abbas Setif 1, Algeria
Adel Alti   University Ferhat Abbas Setif 1, Algeria
Shahzad Qaiser   Flextronics International (Flex), Austria
Safaet Hossain   City University, Bangladesh
Yong Wu   Institute of Applied Physics and Computational
                             Mathematics, China
Lo Man Fung   University of Hong Kong, China
Sunil Kumar   Amity University, Noida, India
G. S. Pradeep Ghantasala   Chitkara University, India
Chetna   Chitkara University, India
Sanjoy Kumar Debnath   Chitkara University, India
Ankit Bansal   Chitkara University, India

Nazeer Unnisa Qurishi	Muffakham Jah College of Engineering and Technology, India
Ali M. Abdulshahed	Misurata University, India
Pooja Gupta	Parul University, India
Prateek Agrawal	Lovely Professional University, India
Gulfam Ahamad	Baba Ghulam Shah Badshah University, India
Prashant Johri	Galgotias University, India
M. A. Ansari	Gautam Buddha University, India
Swagata Dey	Bhairab Ganguly College, India
Venkatesh Gauri Shankar	Manipal University Jaipur, India
Bali Devi	Manipal University Jaipur, India
Vikas Kamra	Krishna Institute of Engineering and Technology, India
Lalit Kumar	Galgotias University, India
R. Raja Subramanian	Kalasalingam Academy of Research and Education, India
Shrddha Sagar	Galgotias University, India
Vikram Kumar	Indian Institute of Information Technology Una, India
Susama Bagchi	Chitkara University, India
P. Sardar Maran	Sathyabama Institute of Science and Technology, India
Amit Kumar Mishra	Jain University, India
Ade Novia Maulana	Islamic State University of Sulthan Thaha Saifuddin Jambi, Indonesia
Apri Siswanto	Universitas Islam Riau, Indonesia
Abdullah	Universitas Islam Indragiri, Indonesia
Tito Sugiharto	Universitas Kuningan, Indonesia
Rio Andriyat Krisdiawan	Universitas Kuningan, Indonesia
Erlan Darmawan	Universitas Kuningan, Indonesia
Evizal Abdul Kadir	Universitas Islam Riau, Indonesia
Yeffry Handoko Putra	Universitas Komputer Indonesia, Indonesia
Waleed Khalid Al-Hadban	Charmo University, Iraq
Athraa Jasim Mohammed	University of Technology, Iraq
Suhaib Kh. Hamed	Universiti Kebangsaan Malaysia, Malaysia
Mohammed Rashad Baker	Kirkuk University, Iraq
Firas Mahmood Mustafa Zakho	Duhok Polytechnic University, Iraq
Khalid Shaker	University of Anbar, Iraq
Arwa Alqudsi Ramadi	Universiti Kebangsaan Malaysia, Malaysia
Hussein K. Almulla	University of Anbar, Iraq
Roberto Vergallo	University of Salento, Italy
Mohd Nor Akmal Khalid	Japan Advanced Institute of Science and Technology, Japan

Mustafa Ali Abuzaraida	Misurata University, Libya
Bhagyashree S. R.	ATME College of Engineering, Libya
Mohd Hasbullah Omar	Universiti Utara Malaysia, Malaysia
Rubijesmin Abdul Latif	Universiti Tenaga Nasional, Malaysia
Mohd Helmy Abd Wahab	Universiti Tun Hussein Onn Malaysia, Malaysia
Husna Sarirah Husin	Universiti Kuala Lumpur Malaysian Institute of Information Technology, Malaysia
Aida Zamnah Zainal Abidin	Asia Pacific University of Technology & Innovation, Malaysia
Mohammed Gamal Alsamman	Universiti Utara Malaysia, Malaysia
Quah Wei Boon	Ministry of Higher Education, Malaysia
Ihsan Ali	University of Malaya, Malaysia
Abdulrazak Yahya Saleh	Universiti Malaysia Sarawak, Malaysia
Rajina R. Mohamed	Universiti Tenaga Nasional, Malaysia
Dalilah Binti Abdullah	Universiti Kuala Lumpur, Malaysia
Shahrinaz Ismail	Albukhary International University, Malaysia
Ruhaya Ab. Aziz	Universiti Tun Hussain Onn Malaysia, Malaysia
Syahrul Fahmy	University College TATI, Malaysia
Nooraida Samsudin	University College TATI, Malaysia
Norhafizah Ismail	Politeknik Mersing, Malaysia
Noormadinah Allias	Tunku Abdul Rahman University of Management and Technology, Malaysia
Zainab Attar Bashi	International Islamic University Malaysia, Malaysia
Ashikin Ali	Universiti Tun Hussein Onn Malaysia, Malaysia
Roziyani Setik	Universiti Selangor, Malaysia
Siti Fairuz Nurr Sadikan	Universiti Teknologi MARA, Malaysia
Safyzan Salim	Universiti Kuala Lumpur British Malaysian Institute, Malaysia
Marwan Nafea	University of Nottingham Malaysia, Malaysia
Irny Suzila Ishak	Universiti Selangor, Malaysia
Abdul Majid Soomro	Universiti Tun Hussein Onn Malaysia, Malaysia
Nor Masharah Husain	Universiti Pendidikan Sultan Idris, Malaysia
Nur Intan Raihana Ruhaiyem	Universiti Sains Malaysia, Malaysia
Nik Zulkarnaen Khidzir	Universiti Malaysia Kelantan, Malaysia
Nadilah Mohd Ralim	Universiti Kuala Lumpur, Malaysia
Kavikumar Jacob	Universiti Tun Hussein Onn Malaysia, Malaysia
Fawad Salam Khan	Universiti Tun Hussein Onn Malaysia, Malaysia
Muhammad Abdulrazaaq Thanoon	Universiti Kebangsaan Malaysia, Malaysia
Mohammad Jassim Mohammad	Universiti Kebangsaan Malaysia, Malaysia
Muazam Ali	Universiti Tun Hussein Onn Malaysia, Malaysia

Khairol Amali Ahmad	Universiti Pertahanan Malaysia, Malaysia
Juliana Aida Abu Bakar	Universiti Utara Malaysia, Malaysia
Mohd Nizam Omar	Universiti Utara Malaysia, Malaysia
Waqas Ahmed	Universiti Kuala Lumpur, Malaysia
Shakiroh Khamis	Universiti Utara Malaysia, Malaysia
Habiba Akter	Universiti Kuala Lumpur, Malaysia
Noris Mohd Norowi	Universiti Putra Malaysia, Malaysia
Siti Munirah Mohd	Universiti Sains Islam Malaysia, Malaysia
Sulaiman Mahzan	Universiti Teknologi MARA, Malaysia
Shahidatul Arfah Baharudin	Universiti Kuala Lumpur, Malaysia
Pantea Keikhosrokiani	Universiti Sains Malaysia, Malaysia
Renugah Rengasamy	Social Institute of Malaysia, Malaysia
Khalid Hussain	Albukhary International University, Malaysia
Massudi Mahmuddin	Unversiti Utara Malaysia, Malaysia
Mahmood Abdullah Bazel	Unversiti Utara Malaysia, Malaysia
Masitah Ghazali	Malaysia-Japan International Institute of Technology, Malaysia
Norhanisha Yusof	Politeknik Balik Pulau, Malaysia
Saiful Bakhtiar Osman	PNB Commercial Sdn. Berhad, Malaysia
Azliza Mohd Ali	Universiti Teknologi MARA, Malaysia
Norhasyimatul Naquiah Ghazali	Universiti Utara Malaysia, Malaysia
Yusmadi Yah Jusoh	Universiti Utara Malaysia, Malaysia
Jasni Ahmad	Universiti Utara Malaysia, Malaysia
Azlin Nordin	International Islamic University Malaysia, Malaysia
Abdullah Al-Sakkaf	Universiti Utara Malaysia, Malaysia
Kamsiah Mohamed	Universiti Selangor, Malaysia
Mudiana Mokhsin	Universiti Teknologi MARA, Malaysia
Suhaimi Abd-Latif	Otago Polytechnic, New Zealand
Sani Salisu	Federal University Dutse, Nigeria
Ijaz Ahmad	Majan University College, Oman
Ghaith Abdulsattar Al-Kubaisi	University of Technology and Applied Sciences, Oman
Qamar Ul Islam	Dhofar University, Oman
Abdulrazak F. Shahatha Al-Mashhadani	Sohar University, Oman
Muhammad Kashif Shaikh	Sir Syed University of Engineering and Technology, Pakistan
Mir Jamal Ud Din	Abbottabad University of Science & Technology, Pakistan
Najia Saher	Islamia University Bahawalpur, Pakistan
Tasneem Mohammad Ameen Duridi	Palestine Technical University, Palestine

Krzysztof Marian Tomiczek	Silesian University of Technology, Poland
Abdullah Hussein Al-Ghushami	Community College of Qatar, Qatar
Abayomi Abdultaofeek	Mangosuthu University of Technology, South Africa
Fathima Musfira Ameer	South Eastern University of Sri Lanka, Sri Lanka
Mohammed Ahmed Taiye	Linnaeus University, Sweden
Sasalak Tongkaw	Songkhla Rajabhat University, Thailand
Abdulfattah Esmail Hasan Abdullah Ba Alawi	Ataturk University, Turkey
Mehmet Nergiz	Dicle University, Turkey
Huseyin First	Dicle University, Turkey
Ismail Rakip Karas	Karabuk University, Turkey
Mehmet Sirac Ozerdem	Dicle University, Turkey
Evi Indriasari Mansor	Abu Dhabi School of Management, UAE
Hamzah Alaidaros	Al-Ahgaff University, Yemen
Munya Saleh Ba Matraf	Hadhramout University, Yemen
Abdullah Almogahed	Taiz University, Yemen
Abdulaziz Yahya Yahya Al-Nahari	UNITAR International University, Malaysia
Ridhima Rani	Chitkara University, India
Hani Mizhir Magid	Al Furat Al Awsat Technical University, Iraq
Rohaida Romli	Universiti Utara Malaysia, Malaysia
Shaymah Akram Yasear	Al-Qasim Green University, Iraq
Mohd Hafizul Afifi Abdullah	Universiti Teknologi Petronas, Malaysia

Contents – Part II

Digital Healthcare and Well-Being

Air Quality Index Prediction Using Support Vector Regression Based
on African Buffalo Optimization 3
    Yuhanis Yusof and Inusa Sani Maijama'a

The Factors Influencing Blockchain Adoption in Hospitals: A Pilot Study 15
    Mahmood A. Bazel, Mazida Ahmad, Fathey Mohammed,
    Nabil Hasan Al-Kumaim, Wasef Mater, and Azman Yasin

Exploring the Relationship Between Protection Motivation and Addiction
Severity Towards Secure Intention Behavior in Online Game Addiction
Among Adolescents 30
    Wan Mohd Yusoff Wan Yaacob, Nur Haryani Zakaria,
    and Zahurin Mat Aji

Designing and Developing M-Thyroid Care for Mobile Virtual Consultation ... 43
    Ahmad Hanis Mohd Shabli, Noorulsadiqin Azbiya Yaacob,
    and Noor Rafhati Adyani Abdullah

CNN-Based Covid-19 Detection from Two Distinct Chest X-Ray Datasets:
Leveraging TensorFlow and Keras for Novel Results 56
    Yaser Mohammed Al-Hamzi and Shamsul Bin Sahibuddin

Eye-Tracking Usability Data of BacaDisleksia for an Informed
Dyslexia-Friendly Design Decision 69
    Husniza Husni, Nurul Ida Syaheera Mohd Nasri, and Mohamed Ali Saip

Hexa-Net Framework: A Fresh ADHD-Specific Model for Identifying
ADHD Based on Integrating Brain Atlases 81
    Dalia A. Al-Ubaidi, Azurah A. Samah, and Mahdi Jasim

An Automated Enhancement System of Diabetic Retinopathy Fundus
Image for Eye Care Facilities 95
    Nurul Atikah Mohd Sharif, Nor Hazlyna Harun,
    Nur Azmielia Muhammad Sharimi, Juhaida Abu Bakar, Hapini Awang,
    and Zunaina Embong

Persuading People to Fight Dengue and Sustaining It via Mobile
Application   110
    Masitah Ghazali, Nur Zuraifah Syazrah Othman, Zatul Alwani Shaffiei,
    Suriati Sadimon, Zuraini Ali Shah, and Zuriahati Mohd Yunos

Usability Study of UUM Student Portal Using Eye Tracker   123
    Nur Farah Amalina Azmi, Mohamed Ali Saip, and Husniza Husni

Education Transformation Through Technology

University Student Dashboard: Enhancing Student Trend Analysis
and Decision-Making Processes   139
    Teh Soon Li, Mohamad Sabri bin Sinal, Mazni Omar,
    and Muhammad Nur Adilin bin Mohamad Anuardi

Fostering Cyber-Resilience in Higher Education: A Pilot Evaluation
of a Malware Awareness Program for College Students   154
    Norliza Katuk, Nur A.' fyfah Zaimy, Suren Krishnan,
    Raj Kumar Kunhiraman, Hwee-Hsiung Lee, and Derar Eleyan

Analysis of the Effectiveness of Feedback Provision in Intelligent Tutoring
Systems   168
    Nur Hafiza Jamaludin and Rohaida Romli

Unlocking the Potential of Enhancing User Experience in Portal GREaT:
Cultivating Great Ideas Through Brainwriting Method   180
    Fauziah Baharom, Rohaida Romli, Wan Hussain Wan Ishak,
    Haslina Mohd, Yuhanis Yusof, Mohamed Ali Saip, Osman Ghazali,
    Rahayu Ahmad, Mohd Hasbullah Omar, Suzilah Ismail,
    Juhaida Abu Bakar, and Salwati Badroddin

The Effectiveness of Conducting STEM Projects Using Design Thinking
Approach in Rural Schools in Kedah, Malaysia: A Smart Farming Project   190
    Suwannit Chareen Chit, Ahmad Hanis Mohd Shabli,
    and Massudi Mahmuddin

Enhancing Supervisor Response Time: An Exploration of the Social
Representation Theory of Shame in ELISTA   204
    Jefri Marzal, Edi Elisa, Pradita Eko Prasetyo Utomo,
    and Suwannit Chareen Chit

Early Detection of School Disengagement Using *MyBuddy* Application   217
    Noraziah ChePa, Ahmad Hanis Mohd Shabli, Azizi Ab Aziz,
    Wan Hussain Wan Ishak, and Laura Lim Sei Yi

Digital Entrepreneurship and Innovation

E-commerce Carbon Footprint Contribution: A Preliminary Investigation
Framework 231
  Siti Sakira Kamruddin, Farzana Kabir Ahmad, Alawiyah Abd Wahab,
  Zahurin Mat Aji, and Noradila Nordin

Designing an Expert System for Personal Financial Management 244
  Brandon Chua Choon Kit and Nor Farzana Abd Ghani

Improving Rice Yield Prediction Accuracy Using Regression Models
with Climate Data 258
  Mohamad Farhan Mohamad Mohsin, Muhammad Khalifa Umana,
  Mohamad Ghozali Hassan, Kamal Imran Mohd Sharif,
  Mohd Azril Ismail, Khazainani Salleh, Suhaili Mohd Zahari,
  Mimi Adilla Sarmani, and Neil Gordon

The Application of UTAUT Theory to Determine Trust Among Women
in E-Hailing Apps Adoption 268
  Karrar Ali Abdullah and Musyrifah Mahmod

Design and Development of Housing Interview Management System
for Managing Housing Application 282
  Asvinitha Muniandy, Mazida Ahmad, and Mohamad Adli Desa

A Descriptive Study of Factors Influencing Online Purchasing Behavior:
Malaysian Consumer Perspective 296
  Nurul Ain Mustakim, Shuzlina Abdul-Rahman, Maslina Abdul Aziz,
  and Zuhairah Hasan

The Effects of Perceived Usefulness and Perceived Ease of Use
on Intention to Use ICT Services Among Agribusiness Practitioners
in Somalia 309
  Husein Osman Abdullahi and Murni Mahmud

Adoption of Machine Learning by Rural Farms: A Systematic Review 324
  Sayed Abdul Majid Gilani, Ansarullah Tantry, Soumaya Askri,
  Liza Gernal, Rommel Sergio, and Leonardo Jose Mataruna-Dos-Santos

Estate Planning Model for Sustaining Economic Values of Digital Assets 336
  Norliza Katuk, Peck-Yong Tey, Mohamad Sabri Sinal,
  Wan Aida Nadia Wan Abdullah, Norazlina Abd Wahab, Erik Kurniadi,
  and Heru Budianto

Author Index 351

Contents – Part I

Ensuring Cybersecurity and Privacy

Key Issues in Cybersecurity Implementation in Government Agencies:
A Case Study in Jakarta Smart City 3
   R. G. Guntur Alam, Huda Ibrahim, and Ismail Rakip Karas

Large Scale Web Crawling and Distributed Search Engines: Techniques,
Challenges, Current Trends, and Future Prospects 17
   Asadullah Al Galib, Md Humaion Kabir Mehedi,
   Ehsanur Rahman Rhythm, and Annajiat Alim Rasel

Data Archiving Model on Cloud for Video Surveillance Systems
with Integrity Check 30
   Norliza Katuk, Mohd Hasbullah Omar, Muhammad Syafiq Mohd Pozi,
   and Ekaterina Chzhan

Blockchain-Based Supply Chain for a Sustainable Digital Society:
Security Challenges and Proposed Approach 44
   Norshakinah Md Nasir, Khuzairi Mohd Zaini, Suhaidi Hassan,
   and Noradila Nordin

An Exploratory Study of Automated Anti-phishing System 58
   Mochamad Azkal Azkiya Aziz, Basheer Riskhan, Nur Haryani Zakaria,
   and Mohamad Nazim Jambli

Remote Public Data Auditing to Secure Cloud Storage 70
   Muhammad Farooq and Osman Ghazali

A Systematic Literature Review of Ransomware Detection Methods
and Tools for Mitigating Potential Attacks 80
   Mujeeb ur Rehman, Rehan Akbar, Mazni Omar, and Abdul Rehman Gilal

A Systematic Literature Review of Intrusion Detection System in Network
Security 96
   Guntoro Guntoro and Mohd. Nizam Bin Omar

Cross-layer Based Intrusion Detection System for Wireless Sensor
Networks: Challenges, Solutions, and Future Directions 108
   Noradila Nordin and Muhammad Syafiq Mohd Pozi

Digital Media and Information Literacy

A Feature-Based Optimization Approach for Fake News Detection
on Social Media Using K-Means Clustering 125
  Farzana Kabir Ahmad, Siti Sakira Kamaruddin, Adnan Hussein Ali,
  and Farah Lia Ibrahim

Sentiment Analysis of Arabic Dialects: A Review Study 137
  Abdullah Habberrih and Mustafa Ali Abuzaraida

Charting Inclusive Digital Society Research Trends: A Bibliometric
Analysis of E-Participation Through Social Media 154
  Hapini Awang, Nur Suhaili Mansor, Maslinda Mohd Nadzir,
  Osman Ghazali, Abderrahmane Benlahcene,
  Fadhilah Mat Yamin, Isyaku Uba Haruna, Shakiroh Khamis,
  and Abdulrazak F. Shahatha Al-Mashhadani

Systematic Literature Review and Bibliometric Analysis on Addressing
the Vanishing Gradient Issue in Deep Neural Networks for Text Data 168
  Shakirat Oluwatosin Haroon-Sulyman, Mohammed Ahmed Taiye,
  Siti Sakira Kamaruddin, and Farzana Kabir Ahmad

A Test Dataset of Offensive Malay Language by a Cyberbullying Detection
Model on Instagram Using Support Vector Machine 182
  Nurulhuda Ismail, David Enrique Losada, and Rahayu Ahmad

TikTok Video Cluster Analysis Based on Trending Topic 193
  Juhaida Abu Bakar, Nur Azmielia Muhammad Sharimi,
  Mohd Azrul Edzwan Shahril, Nur Syafiqah Azmi, Nor Hazlyna Harun,
  Hapini Awang, and Nur Syafiqah Abu Bakar

Navigating AI Development and Deployment

A Video Summarization Method for Movie Trailer-Genre Classification
Based on Emotion Analysis 209
  Wan En Ng, Muhammad Syafiq Mohd Pozi, Mohd Hasbullah Omar,
  Norliza Katuk, and Abdul Rafiez Abdul Raziff

E-Nose: Spoiled Food Detection Embedded Device Using Machine
Learning for Food Safety Application 221
  Wan Nur Fadhlina Syamimi Wan Azman,
  Ku Nurul Fazira binti Ku Azir, and Adam bin Mohd Khairuddin

An Analysis of Objective Function Modification Approaches in Routing
Protocols for Low Power and Lossy Networks: A Fuzzy Logic-Based
Perspective 235
    Laila Al-Qaisi, Suhaidi Hassan, and Nur Haryani Zakaria

An Empirical Study of Label Size Effect on Classification Model Accuracy
Using a Derived Rule from the Holy Quran Verses 248
    *Ghaith Abdulsattar A. Jabbar Alkubaisi, Siti Sakira Kamruddin,
    and Husniza Husni*

Anomalies in Mooring (Thin) Lines: Causes, Risk Mitigations, and Real
Time Consequences of Failure – A Comprehensive Review 260
    *Tarwan Kumar Khatri, Manzoor Ahmed Hashmani, Hasmi Taib,
    Nasir Abdullah, and Lukman Ab. Rahim*

Data Analytics Modelling System for Short Courses at Seberang Jaya
Community College 274
    Zuriana Zamberi and Nur Intan Raihana Ruhaiyem

Examining the Software Developers' Perception in Open-Source Software
of Blockchain Project Using Association Rules Mining 287
    *Alawiyah Abd Wahab, Huda Hj. Ibrahim, Shehu M. SarkinTudu,
    and Bilyaminu A. Romo*

Support Vector Machine for Satellite Images Classification Using Radial
Basis Function Kernel Method 301
    *Nur Suhaili Mansor, Hapini Awang, Sarkin Tudu Shehu Malami,
    Amirulikhsan Zolkafli, Mohammed Ahmed Taiye, and Hanhan Maulana*

Harnessing Technology for Sustainable Development

A Regression Test Case Prioritization Framework for Software
Sustainability 315
    Bakr Ba-Quttayyan, Haslina Mohd, and Yuhanis Yusof

Towards a Sustainable Digital Society: Supporting Producer Mobility
in Named Data Networking Through Immobile Anchor-Based Mechanism 330
    *Ahmad Abrar, Khuzairi Mohd Zaini, Ahmad Suki Che Mohamed Arif,
    and Mohd Hasbullah Omar*

Enabling a Sustainable and Inclusive Digital Future with Proactive
Producer Mobility Management Mechanism in Named Data Networking 343
    *Nurul Hidayah Ahmad Zukri, Ahmad Suki Che Mohamed Arif,
    Mohammed AlSamman, and Ahmad Abrar*

The Recent Trends of Research on GitHub Copilot: A Systematic Review 355
Zhamri Che Ani, Zauridah Abdul Hamid, and Nur Nazifa Zhamri

Blockchain Over Named Data Networking Architecture: A Review 367
*Mohammed Alsamman, Suhaidi Hassan, Fathey Mohammed,
and Yousef Fazea*

A Review of Policy on Creative Industry for Sustainable Nation:
A Malaysian Perspective 380
*Syamsul Bahrin Zaibon, Asmidah Alwi, Ahmad Hisham Zainal Abidin,
Adzrool Idzwan Ismail, Nur Kareelawati Abd Karim,
and Shamsul Arrieya Ariffin*

Author Index 395

Digital Healthcare and Well-Being

Air Quality Index Prediction Using Support Vector Regression Based on African Buffalo Optimization

Yuhanis Yusof[1]([⊠]) (iD) and Inusa Sani Maijama'a[1,2] (iD)

[1] School of Computing, Institute for Advanced and Smart Digital Opportunities,
Universiti Utara Malaysia, UUM Sintok, 06010 Bukit Kayu Hitam, Kedah, Malaysia
yuhanis@uum.edu.my
[2] Department of Computer Science, Hussaini Adamu Federal Polytechnic Kazaure, Kazaure,
Nigeria
inusa.sani.mjm@hafedpoly.edu.ng

Abstract. Support Vector Regression (SVR) is one of the machine learning models widely used in regression analysis. As an alternative for fitting a line to the data points like typical linear regression algorithms, it finds a hyperplane that is effective in fitting data points in a continuous space. The kernel type and hyperparameters significantly influence the performance and effectiveness of SVR. Determination of the optimal values is crucial in ensuring the success of prediction, regardless of the application domain. This study adapts the African Buffalo Optimization (ABO) algorithm to determine SVR's regularization and kernel parameters. The ABO algorithm mirrors African buffaloes' hunting and defensive behavior, offering ability to track the best position and extensive memory capacity to discover the best solution for problems under analysis. Evaluation is then performed on the air quality index benchmark dataset, and the prediction results of SVR-ABO are compared against other optimized SVR prediction models. The results show that SVR-ABO is a better algorithm because it produces smaller errors and best fits the data. Such an outcome indicates that the proposed SVR optimized by ABO is a competitive prediction model in data analytics.

Keywords: Support Vector Regression · African Buffalo Optimization · sustainable environment

1 Introduction

Air quality prediction can be realized by forecasting the concentration of pollutants in the air at a particular location and time using various data-driven techniques. With the increasing concerns about air pollution and its impacts on human health and the sustainability of the environment, accurate air quality prediction has become essential for government agencies, policymakers, and the public [1]. One of the main sources of air pollution is human activities, such as transportation, industry, and agriculture. Air quality prediction models use various input data sources, including meteorological data, emission inventories, satellite data, and ground-level air quality measurements, to forecast the concentration of pollutants in the air.

N. H. Zakaria et al. (Eds.): ICOCI 2023, CCIS 2002, pp. 3–14, 2024.
https://doi.org/10.1007/978-981-99-9592-9_1

Statistical methodologies, machine learning algorithms [2–5], and artificial neural networks [6–8] are just a few methods for air quality prediction. With the aid of these methods, air quality prediction models that can precisely estimate the quantity of pollutants, including particulate matter, nitrogen oxides, and ozone, have been created. Even though machine learning algorithms (such as Support Vector Regression (SVR)) have shown promising outcomes as prediction models, determining the model parameter's optimal values is crucial in ensuring prediction success, regardless of the application domain. The use of swarm optimization algorithms to optimize machine learning models, including in air quality prediction, is gaining some attention. Swarm optimization is a computational intelligence method inspired by the actions of social animals, for instance bees, ants, and birds. The goal of swarm optimization is to resolve challenging optimisation issues by simulating the collective actions of a group of individuals, known as a swarm, working together towards a common objective.

The basic premise of swarm optimization is that simplified local communications between individuals in the swarm can direct to advancing overall actions that optimizes the objective function. Every individual in the swarm is represented as a potential solution in the optimisation problem, and the swarm explores the search area to find the best solution. Swarm optimization algorithms can be used for many optimization problems, including continuous, discrete, and combinatorial problems. They have been positively applied in several application domains, including engineering [9–11], education [12], and health [13]. Among the swarm optimization algorithms includes Particle Swarm Optimization, which is known as PSO [14], Ant Colony Optimization, which is termed ACO [15], and an algorithm from the bees which is termed Artificial Bee Colony (ABC) [16]. These algorithms differ in their mechanisms for updating the positions of individuals in the swarm, and their strengths and weaknesses are made into use depending on the characteristics of the optimization problem.

This study investigates the adaption of African Buffalo Optimization (ABO) algorithm in optimizing the SVR model to predict the air quality index. The African Buffalo Optimization is an alternative nature-inspired optimization algorithm first proposed in 2015 [17]. The algorithm was established on the actions of African buffaloes, where the buffaloes gather in a herd and move towards a common goal. The goal of ABO is to discover the best result based on available resources by simulating the social activities of the buffaloes. Due to ABO's capability, the algorithm, has been deployed in various optimization problems that includes the Travelling Salesman Problem [18], network traffic analysis [19], and various benchmark datasets [20]. Owing to its quick convergence, ability to follow each buffalo's optimal location and pace, and progress of the best buffalo towards better exploration, ABO reported success in optimization scenarios when compared to similar algorithms. However, the ability of ABO to simultaneously optimise three mutual parameters, as with SVR, has not been documented in the literature. In order to discover the optimal value for SVR parameters, this study proposes the hybridization between SVR and ABO.

This paper is structured as follows: Sect. 2 presents some conveyed studies on the deployed models and application domain. This is followed by Sect. 3 that details the procedures undertaken to complete the study, while the obtained experimental results are examined in Sect. 4. Lastly, Sect. 5 concludes the discussion and provides direction for future studies.

2 Related Work

2.1 Particulate Matter Prediction Models

Air pollution is a major environmental concern that significantly impacts public health and the economy. Various techniques have been employed to mitigate air pollution and its related impacts. One approach uses Particulate Matter (PM2.5) prediction models, mathematical and statistical tools to forecast the intensity of fine particulate matter in the air [21]. These models utilize data from various sources, such as satellite imagery, meteorological information, and ground-based measurements of PM2.5 concentrations, to create a spatial and temporal understanding of air pollution. PM2.5 can be emitted from primary sources, such as transportation and industrial activities, or form through secondary sources through chemical reactions with gaseous pollutants.

Machine learning models have also been used for PM2.5 prediction, showing promising results. Some of the popular machine learning models employed for PM2.5 prediction are Artificial Neural Networks (ANNs) [1, 8], Support Vector Machines (SVMs) [22, 23], Random Forests (RFs) [24, 25], and Gradient Boosting Machines (GBMs). These models utilize data inputs such as meteorological observations, land use patterns, and satellite images that can help predict PM2.5 concentrations more accurately. It's worth noting that selecting a model to use in a specific case should be based on the nature of available data and specific prediction goals.

Traditional statistical and Machine learning models (ML) have been used in PM2.5 prediction, but they differ in their approaches and assumptions. Conventional statistical models are typically based on predefined algorithms developed using regression analysis or other statistical techniques. These models require that the data meet certain statistical assumptions such as linearity, homoscedasticity, and normal distribution. In contrast, ML models are built on machine learning algorithms that do not involve explicit statistical assumptions. Instead, they learn from data, identifying patterns and relationships without being specifically programmed. They can handle higher-dimensional data, non-linear relationships, and complex data structures.

Unlike traditional statistical models, ML models perform better in PM2.5 prediction because they can learn non-linear relationships and assumptions [26]. However, ML models may be considered black-box models that often provide no explanation of how the result was derived and may be difficult to interpret and diagnose. Traditional models are more straightforward, better understand the underlying statistical assumptions, and can be useful in interpreting the nature of the relationship between the predictor and response variable.

2.2 Support Vector Regression

Support Vector Regression is a widely held machine learning algorithm to analyze regression based on the Support Vector Machine (SVM) algorithm. It was introduced by Vapnik et al. in 1996 [27], and since then, it has been a powerful tool for predicting continuous output values from a given set of input data. The goal of SVR is to decrease the difference between the predicted and actual values, subject to a certain margin of error. SVR has several advantages over traditional regression techniques, such as its capability to lever non-linear relationships that exits between the input and output variables, its robustness to outliers, and its ability to generalize well to unseen data. Additionally, SVR can be easily extended to handle multi-dimensional input data and can be applied to various regression problems, including time series forecasting, image processing [28, 29], and financial prediction [30, 31]. Despite the generalisation ability of SVR, it has two concerns; SVR hyper-parameters (punishment factor (C), tube size (ε) and if RBF kernel is chosen, the kernel parameter (γ)) needs to be optimised. Determining optimal values of these three parameters proves to be a difficult task. However, regardless of the type of kernel selected, the value of C and ε significantly affects the final model. The value of ε determines the number of support vectors the model will use for the forecasting. Intuitively, a small value of ε results into large number of support vectors which could lead to high complexity and high degree of allowed deviation in the process of optimisation formulation.

The optimisation technique primarily aims to help the SVR algorithm to avoid under-fitting or over-fitting during training, consequently affecting the algorithm's generalisation ability. The most common methods found in the literature for SVR hyper-parameter optimisation are Cross-validation [32, 33] and the grid search method [32]. However, cross-validation optimisation methods are computationally expensive and easily fall into local optimum [33]. Hence researchers opt for a better approach that uses swarm algorithms.

2.3 Optimized Support Vector Regression

Due to inadequacy and problems associated with grid and cross-validation approaches of optimisation, swarm optimization approaches were deployed in SVR studies. Zhang, Kuang, and Hu [34] use artificial bee colony (ABC) to optimise SVR parameters to predict annual total electricity usage in China. The authors argued that population initialisation is one of the crucial tasks when using evolutionary algorithms. Hence, they deploy tent chaotic strategy and tournament selection procedure to initialise the ABC population and determine the value of each bee in their research. Their approach that was termed as ABC-SVR, recorded a substantial MAPE values compared to the ones produced by PSO-SVR, GA-SVR, GRNN, normal regression, and SVR with its default parameters.

· A study in forecasting grid electric load [36] claimed SVR requires a large computational cost, especially when the dataset is large (high number of instances and features/attributes). To overcome this issue, the study investigated the use of Fruitfly Optimisation Algorithm (FOA) in determining the optimal values for SVR parameters. However, it was learned that FOA has some shortcomings of premature convergence and a high possibility of being stuck in local optima. Hence, the study optimised the deployed FOA using Quantum Computing mechanism (QCM) and cat chaotic mapping function.

The QCM was used to enhance FOA searching ability and prevent premature convergence. While the cat chaotic mapping function was deployed to avoid the algorithm from being caught in local optima when there is little variation in the population.

In 2021, another optimized SVR was introduced in the engineering application domain. The GA-SVR [35] was deployed to forecast driven piles' ability to support vertical loads in cohesionless soil. The model's performance was compared against SVR and linear regression models. By achieving a lower error rate and larger coefficient of determination than the SVR and linear regression models, the GA-SVR [35] model has outperformed the benchmark models. Nevertheless, the complexity of GA does not scale well. That is, the size of the search space frequently grows exponentially in regions where the number of elements subject to mutation is high.

2.4 African Buffalo Optimization

The African Buffalo Optimisation [17] represents African buffaloes' defense and foraging strategies. This group of animals is distinguished by their exceptional memory capacity, social organisation, and democratic way of life. They make the sound "waaa" to indicate threat and "maaa" to denote that it is safe. Therefore, their organisational lifestyle might be connected to these distinctive traits [35, 36]. The "waaa" sound is represented by the symbolization "w_k," "maa" by the representation "m_k," and the learning parameters by the representations "l_1" and "l_2." The personal best ($bp_{max(k)}$) and global best (bg_{max}) positions are additional parameters that are relevant in exploring the search area. The algorithm subtracts the "waaa" value (w_k), where it requires the buffaloes to travel the search space from the largest vector (bg_{max} and $bp_{max(k)}$). Then, it is times by the learning parameters (l_1 and l_2). ABO's outcome is represented via "maaa" (m_k) notation that signals buffalo herds should npt move and remain grazing at the same location.

3 Materials and Methods

3.1 Dataset Description

The Beijing Air Quality Index (AQI) dataset used for this experiment is compiled from US Embassy in Beijing data and meteorological data from Beijing Capital International Airport obtained from UCI repository over five (5) years from 01/01/2010 to 31/12/2014. The dataset consists of 43,824 instances with 11 descriptive features that include 1) year, 2) month, 3) day, 4) hour, 5) Dew Point (â„ƒ), 6) Temperature (â„ƒ), 7) Pressure (hPa), 8) Combined wind direction, 9) Cumulated wind speed (m/s), 10) Cumulated hours of snow and 11) Cumulated hours of rain. The predicted feature is the Particulate Matter (PM2.5) in the air, which indicates poor air quality. PM2.5 are very small elements in the air that decrease visibility and initiate the air to appear blurred when elevated levels.

3.2 Data Preparation

The main reason behind selecting the SVR algorithm instead of other prediction models is due to the non-linearity properties of the deployed dataset. In this study, the linearity properties were analyzed using SPSS, and it was learned that the descriptive features are not linear with the target feature. Following this, the data was also normalized using MinMax scaler due to skewness of the target feature.

3.3 Optimized SVR-ABO

Figure 1 illustrates the adapted algorithm for predicting the dataset's air quality. The input for the deployment is the training data, while the output is the optimal values for SVR and the values of the evaluation measures.

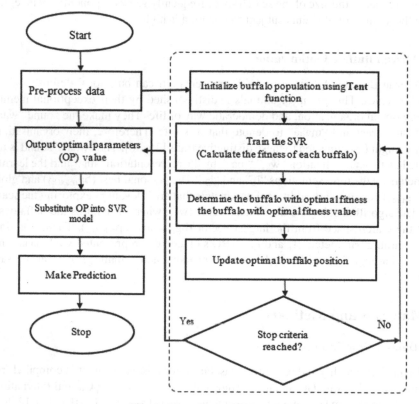

Fig. 1. Flow Chart of SVR-ABO

3.4 Experiment Setup

This experiment's next-hour forecast was based on the previous twenty-four (24) hours of data. The dataset was divided into 3 portions which includes training, validation, and testing. The data proportion is seventy (70%), fifteen (15%), and fifteen (15%), respectively. The range of regularization constant C, gamma (γ), and epsilon (ε) were set as (1–20), (0.001–1.00), and (0.1–10), respectively. The ABO, GA, and PSO algorithms were executed based on parameter values presented in Table 1.

Table 1. ABO, GA, and PSO parameters.

ABO		GA		PSO	
Parameters	Value	Parameters	Value	Parameters	Value
Population	100	Swarm size	100	Population	100
Maximum Iterations	1,000	Maximum Iterations	1,000	Maximum Iterations	1000
	0.4	Elite chromosomes	5	Cognitive parameter C_1	0.5
Democratic parameter (l_1)	0.6	Selection method	Roulette wheel	Social parameter C_2	0.5
Location update		Crossover function	Partially matched crossover (PMX)	Inertia weight	0.9
Lambda	1	Mutation function	Uniform		
		Mutation rate	0.1		

3.5 Evaluation Metrics

In this experiment, three evaluation metrics have been used: Mean Absolute Error (MAE) [36], Root Mean Square Error (RMSE) [36], Mean Squared Error (MSE) [36], and R2. The equations for the metrics are presented in Eqs. (1), (2), and (3).

$$MAE = \frac{1}{N} \sum_{n=1}^{N} |x_n - \breve{x}_n| \tag{1}$$

$$RMSE = \sqrt{\frac{\sum_{n=1}^{N} \left(x_i - \breve{x}_n\right)^2}{N}} \tag{2}$$

$$MSE = \frac{1}{N} \sum_{n=1}^{N} (x_n - \breve{x}_n)^2 \tag{3}$$

4 Results

The comparative performance of the algorithms and the actual values of PM2.5 is illustrated in Fig. 2. The figure reveals that all the algorithms find it difficult when the value of the actual PM2.5 is below fifty (50). However, as can be observed from the figure, the algorithm's performance did increase with the increase of the value of PM2.5, especially towards the peak values.

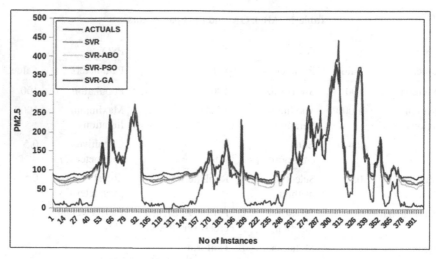

Fig. 2. Comparison of PM2.5 predicted values.

Upon the algorithm's training termination, the best parameters obtained by each algorithm with the least training error are denoted in Table 2. Table 3 presents the comparative outcomes of the four compared algorithms, SVR, SVR-ABO, SVR-PSO, and SVR-GA, based on the mentioned evaluation metrics.

Table 2. Optimal parameters determined by swarm-based algorithms.

	ALGORITHMS			
	SVR	SVR-PSO	SVR-ABO	SVR-GA
Regularisation Parameter (*C*)	–	20.0000	19.9860	18.0014
Gamma (γ)	–	0.6340	0.4950	0.8034
Epsilon (ε)	–	0.0927	0.8909	0.0929
Kernel type	rbf	rbf	rbf	rbf

Table 3. Performance of algorithms based on evaluation metrics.

	RMSE	MAE	MSE	R2
SVR	50.7254	41.9235	2573.0650	0.75
SVR-ABO	**45.1617**	**36.7451**	**2039.5810**	**0.80**
SVR-PSO	48.8515	40.0876	2386.4703	0.77
SVR-GA	50.5921	41.5541	2559.5584	0.76

From the values depicted in Table 3, it is learned that the performance of SVR-ABO based on RMSE metric is the best, with a value of 45.1617, while the least performance algorithm is the non-optimized model (SVR) with RMSE value of 50.7254. The SVR-PSO and SVR-GA each have an RMSE value of 48.8515 and 50.5921, respectively. Regarding algorithms performance based on MAE, the SVR-ABO obtained the least value of 36.7451, while SVR-PSO, SVR-GA, and SVR obtained 40.0876, 41.5541 and 41.9235, respectively. Regarding the R2 score, which determines how best the algorithm can fit the data, the metric shows that SVR-ABO is a better model where it obtained the highest value of 0.8, followed by SVR-PSO with an R2 value of 0.77. The model optimized by SVR-GA and non-optimized model (i.e., SVR) scored 0.76 and 0.75, respectively.

African Buffalo Optimization (ABO) and Particle Swarm Optimization (PSO) are metaheuristic optimization algorithms commonly used in various optimization problems. While both algorithms effectively find solutions, ABO has performed better than PSO and GA. One reason why ABO may perform better than PSO is that it exhibits coordinated behavior in herds. The ABO algorithm simulates this behavior by dividing the population into subgroups or "herds" and allowing them to interact with each other in a coordinated manner. This helps to avoid premature convergence and encourages exploration of the search space, leading to a better chance of finding the global optimum. In contrast, PSO is based on the behavior of a swarm of particles that randomly move through the search space and adjust their velocities based on the best solutions found so far. However, this random movement can sometimes lead to premature convergence or the particles getting caught in local optima. This is similar to the GA operations that are based on the principle of natural selection and evolution. GA randomly generates a population of candidate solutions and then applies selection, crossover, and mutation operators to evolve the population towards an optimal solution. Such an approach may also cause a stagnant search for the optimal value.

The undertaken experiments support the advantages of ABO that includes the followings:

- Improved convergence: ABO has shown to congregate faster and more reliable as compared to other optimization algorithms, such as Genetic Algorithm (GA) [35] and Particle Swarm Optimization (PSO) [37].
- Robustness: ABO is less sensitive to initial conditions and parameter settings than other optimization algorithms, making it more robust and reliable.

5 Conclusion

Swarm optimization has several advantages over traditional optimization techniques, such as gradient-based methods, as it can handle complex, non-linear, and multi-modal optimization problems without getting trapped in local optima. Additionally, swarm optimization algorithms are easy to implement, scalable, and can be parallelized to exploit modern computing architectures. The adaption of ABO in predicting air quality has shown to be superior to several optimized SVR. On another note, the study can further be improved by analyzing the means of initializing the ABO's population. Rather than deploying simple random distribution, ways and means to ensure population diversity is required, especially for non-linear data.

To ensure a sustainable environment, it is important to manage air quality to balance economic growth and social well-being with environmental protection. Hence, by providing swarm-based digital solutions alternatives, the air quality prediction model can be a valuable tool for policymakers and stakeholders requiring critical air quality information.

Acknowledgement. This work has been partially funded by the School of Computing, Universiti Utara Malaysia.

References

1. Yadav, V., Nath, S.: Prediction of air quality using artificial neural network techniques: a review. Pollut. Res. **36**, 623–625 (2017)
2. Corani, G., Scanagatta, M.: Air pollution prediction via multi-label classification. Environ. Model. Softw. **80**, 259–264 (2016). https://doi.org/10.1016/j.envsoft.2016.02.030
3. Tejbeer, S., Arya, N.: Analysis of various air pollution predictions methods. Int. J. Sci. Technol. Res. **9**, 2622–2625 (2020)
4. Delavar, M.R., et al.: A novel method for improving air pollution prediction based on machine learning approaches: a case study applied to the capital city of Tehran. ISPRS Int. J. Geo-Inf. **8**, 99 (2019). https://doi.org/10.3390/ijgi8020099
5. Gu, Y., Li, B., Meng, Q.: Hybrid interpretable predictive machine learning model for air pollution prediction. Neurocomputing. **468**, 123–136 (2022). https://doi.org/10.1016/j.neu com.2021.09.051
6. Drewil, G.I., Al-Bahadili, R.J.: Air pollution prediction using LSTM deep learning and metaheuristics algorithms. Meas. Sensors. **24**, 100546 (2022). https://doi.org/10.1016/j.measen. 2022.100546
7. Huang, G., et al.: Large scale air pollution prediction with deep convolutional networks. Sci. China Inf. Sci. **64**, 1–11 (2021). https://doi.org/10.1007/s11432-020-2951-1
8. Xayasouk, T., Lee, H.: Air pollution prediction system using deep learning. WIT Trans. Ecol. Environ. **230**, 71–79 (2018). https://doi.org/10.2495/AIR180071
9. El-Sherbeny, N.A.: Vehicle routing with time windows: an overview of exact, heuristic and metaheuristic methods. J. King Saud Univ. **22**, 123–131 (2010). https://doi.org/10.1016/j. jksus.2010.03.002
10. Ahn, C.W., Ramakrishna, R.S.: A genetic algorithm for shortest path routing problem and the sizing of populations. IEEE Trans. Evol. Comput. **6**, 566–579 (2002). https://doi.org/10. 1109/TEVC.2002.804323
11. Chakraborty, B.: GA-based multiple route selection for car navigation. In: Manandhar, S., Austin, J., Desai, U., Oyanagi, Y., Talukder, A.K. (eds.) AACC 2004. LNCS, vol. 3285, pp. 76–83. Springer, Heidelberg (2004). https://doi.org/10.1007/978-3-540-30176-9_10
12. Rizal, M.T., Yusof, Y.: Application of data mining in forecasting graduates employment. J. Eng. Appl. Sci. **12**, 4202–4207 (2017). https://doi.org/10.3923/jeasci.2017.4202.4207
13. Mustaffa, Z., et al.: An application of barnacle mating optimizer in infectious disease prediction: a dengue outbreak cases. Iraqi J. Sci. **61**, 2132–2141 (2020). https://doi.org/10.24996/ ijs.2020.61.8.28
14. Kennedy, J., Eberhart, R.: Particle swarm optimization. In: Proceedings of ICNN 1995-International Conference on Neural Networks, pp. 1942–1948 (1995)
15. Chen, C.-C., Liu, Y.-T.: Enhanced Ant Colony Optimization with dynamic mutation and ad hoc initialization for improving the design of TSK-type fuzzy system. Comput. Intell. Neurosci. **2018**, 9485478 (2018). https://doi.org/10.1155/2018/9485478

16. Wang, H., Wang, W., Xiao, S., Cui, Z., Xu, M., Zhou, X.: Improving artificial Bee colony algorithm using a new neighborhood selection mechanism. Inf. Sci. (Ny). **527**, 227–240 (2020). https://doi.org/10.1016/j.ins.2020.03.064

17. Odili, J.B., Kahar, M.N.M., Anwar, S.: African Buffalo Optimization: a swarm-intelligence technique. Procedia Comput. Sci. **76**, 443–448 (2015)

18. Odili, J.B., Kahar, M.N.M., Noraziah, A., Zarina, M., Haq, R.U.: Performance analyses of nature-inspired algorithms on the Traveling Salesman's Problems for strategic management. Intell. Autom. Soft Comput. (2017). https://doi.org/10.1080/10798587.2017.1334370

19. Mishra, S.: An optimized gradient boost decision tree using enhanced African Buffalo Optimization method for cyber security intrusion detection. Appl. Sci. **12**, 12591 (2022). https://doi.org/10.3390/app122412591

20. Panhalkar, A.R., Doye, D.D.: Optimization of decision trees using modified African Buffalo Algorithm. J. King Saud Univ. - Comput. Inf. Sci. **34**, 4763–4772 (2022). https://doi.org/10.1016/j.jksuci.2021.01.011

21. Biliaiev, M.M., Rusakova, T.I.: Determining zones of chemical pollution in the cities and assesment of chronic diseases risks. Sci. Transp. Progress. Bull. Dnipropetr. Natl. Univ. Railw. Transp. **0**(1(79)), 7–16 (2019). https://doi.org/10.15802/stp2019/159508

22. Shafii, N.H.B., Alias, R., Zamani, N.F., Fauzi, N.F.: Forecasting of air pollution index PM2.5 using Support Vector Machine (SVM). J. Comput. Res. Innov. **5**, 43–53 (2020). https://doi.org/10.24191/jcrinn.v5i3.149

23. Leong, W.C., Kelani, R.O., Ahmad, Z.: Prediction of air pollution index (API) using support vector machine (SVM). J. Environ. Chem. Eng. **8**, 103208 (2020). https://doi.org/10.1016/j.jece.2019.103208

24. Kianian, B., Liu, Y., Chang, H.H.: Imputing satellite-derived aerosol optical depth using a multi-resolution spatial model and random forest for PM2.5 prediction. Remote Sens. **13**, 126 (2021). https://doi.org/10.3390/rs13010126

25. Siwek, K., Osowski, S.: Data mining methods for prediction of air pollution. Int. J. Appl. Math. Comput. Sci. **26**, 467–478 (2016). https://doi.org/10.1515/amcs-2016-0033

26. Palanichamy, N., Haw, S.-C., Subramanian, S., Govindasamy, K., Murugan, R.: Prediction of PM2.5 concentrations in Malaysia using machine learning techniques: a review. F1000Research **10**, 1279 (2021). https://doi.org/10.12688/f1000research.73163.1

27. Vapnik, V.N.: The Nature of Statistical Learning Theory. Springer, New York (1995). https://doi.org/10.1007/978-1-4757-3264-1

28. Misra, T., et al.: Leaf area assessment using image processing and support vector regression in rice. Indian J. Agric. Sci. **91**, 388–392 (2021). https://doi.org/10.56093/ijas.v91i3.112496

29. Yang, R., et al.: Detection of abnormal hydroponic lettuce leaves based on image processing and machine learning. Inf. Process. Agric. **10**, 1–10 (2023). https://doi.org/10.1016/j.inpa.2021.11.001

30. Henrique, B.M., Sobreiro, V.A., Kimura, H.: Stock price prediction using support vector regression on daily and up to the minute prices. J. Financ. Data Sci. **4**, 183–201 (2018). https://doi.org/10.1016/j.jfds.2018.04.003

31. Astudillo, G., Carrasco, R., Fernández-Campusano, C., Chacón, M.: Copper price prediction using support vector regression technique. Appl. Sci. **10**, 6648 (2020). https://doi.org/10.3390/APP10196648

32. Bing, Q., Qu, D., Chen, X., Pan, F., Wei, J.: Short-term traffic flow forecasting method based on LSSVM model optimized by GA-PSO hybrid algorithm. Discret. Dyn. Nat. Soc. **2018**, 1–10 (2018). https://doi.org/10.1155/2018/3093596

33. Mustaffa, Z., Sulaiman, M.H., Ernawan, F., Yusof, Y., Mohsin, M.F.M.: Dengue outbreak prediction: hybrid meta-heuristic model. In: Proceedings - 2018 IEEE/ACIS 19th International Conference on Software Engineering, Artificial Intelligence, Networking and Parallel/Distributed Computing, SNPD 2018 (2018)

34. Zhang, S., Kuang, F., Hu, R.: Support vector regression with multi-strategy artificial bee colony algorithm for annual electric load forecasting. In: Advances in Intelligent Systems and Computing (2019)
35. Luo, Z., Hasanipanah, M., Bakhshandeh Amnieh, H., Brindhadevi, K., Tahir, M.M.: GA-SVR: a novel hybrid data-driven model to simulate vertical load capacity of driven piles. Eng. Comput. **37**, 823–831 (2021). https://doi.org/10.1007/s00366-019-00858-2
36. Seo, Y., Kim, S., Singh, V.P.: Estimating spatial precipitation using Regression Kriging and Artificial Neural Network Residual Kriging (RKNNRK) hybrid approach. Water Resour. Manag. **29**, 2189–2204 (2015). https://doi.org/10.1007/s11269-015-0935-9
37. Wang, D., Tan, D., Liu, L.: Particle swarm optimization algorithm: an overview. Soft Comput. **22**, 387–408 (2018). https://doi.org/10.1007/s00500-016-2474-6

The Factors Influencing Blockchain Adoption in Hospitals: A Pilot Study

Mahmood A. Bazel[1]([✉]) [iD], Mazida Ahmad[1] [iD], Fathey Mohammed[1,2] [iD],
Nabil Hasan Al-Kumaim[3] [iD], Wasef Mater[4], and Azman Yasin[1]

[1] School of Computing, University Utara Malaysia, Sintok, 06010 Bukit Kayu Hitam, Kedah,
Malaysia
mahmood_abdullah_@ahsgs.uum.edu.my
[2] Sunway Business School, Sunway University, 47500 Subang Jaya, Selangor, Malaysia
[3] Faculty of Technology Management and Technopreneurship, Universiti Teknikal Malaysia
Melaka (UTeM), 76100 Durian Tunggal, Melaka, Malaysia
[4] E-Business Department, University of Petra, Petra, Jordan

Abstract. Blockchain technology has gained popularity as a secure and efficient data storage and sharing method, with potential benefits for patient data management, cost reduction, and data security in the healthcare sector. However, the adoption rate of blockchain in healthcare organizations is significantly low. This pilot study aims to verify the validity and reliability of the instrument developed to determine the factors that may be impacting the adoption of blockchain technology by Malaysian hospitals. A small sample of decision-makers in Malaysian hospitals was targeted to collect the preliminary data using an online survey instrument developed based on the Technology-Organizational-Environment (TOE) framework and related studies constructs' items. The data was analyzed using Partial least squares structural equation modeling (PLS-SEM). The findings confirmed the reliability and validity of the measurement scales. This study contributes to ongoing research on BCT adoption in healthcare organizations and offers insights that can be useful to practitioners and researchers in this field.

Keywords: Blockchain adoption · Healthcare · Malaysia

1 Introduction

In recent years, blockchain technology (BCT), or distributed ledger technology, has garnered considerable interest [1]. BCT is considered a decentralized, cryptographically secure distributed ledger system that comprises a series of transaction lists with identical copies shared and sustained by multiple parties [2, 3] The more widespread adoption of this technology was observed after the proposal of the Bitcoin cryptocurrency [4]. Numerous benefits accrue from BCT, including increased transaction speed, decreased data replication, decreased risk of failure, and increased confidence and governance [5]. Governments and businesses are examining approaches to leverage this technology's disruptive potential in a variety of sectors, resulting in solutions that are impervious to change, transparent, secure, reliable, and trustworthy in public and private environments [6]. The healthcare sector is recognized as one of the sectors that is a possible beneficiary of BCT adoption [7].

Current healthcare systems confront numerous issues, including security, interoperability, privacy, lengthy processes, delays in diagnosis and treatment, difficulties in sharing information, high operational expenses, data control, and data ownership [8, 9]. Health information is fragmented and challenging to exchange due to diverse standards and formats [10]. Institutions often resist sharing data due to privacy concerns and fears of providing competitors with an advantage. The healthcare data ecosystem is excessively fragmented to meet modern patients' pressing needs [11]. As stakeholders are encouraged to retain their records, verifying their authenticity and accuracy becomes difficult. This situation leads to substantial server maintenance and security costs [10, 12, 13]. BCT offers a promising solution to these problems [14, 15]. It can address the exchange, integrity, confidentiality, privacy, and interoperability issues inherent in healthcare systems [10, 16]. BCT enables sharing a patient's medical data with international parties while granting patients control over their information [8, 17]. Due to the high sensitivity of medical data, the use of BCT in healthcare facilitates the secure transfer of patient medical records and enhances healthcare data security and transparency [14, 18]. If BCT is developed appropriately, it can lead to a revolution in healthcare and reshape it to make a stable, trustworthy, protected, and sustainable digital ecosystem for better-quality health data management [19, 20]. BCT is considered one of the top technology trends for health IT, notwithstanding the widespread notion that it is still in its infancy [21].

Despite the great potential that BCT brings to the healthcare industry, the adoption rate is significantly low, with a lack of empirical evidence [19, 22, 23]. However, little research has been done to discover the factors influencing BCT adoption in healthcare organizations [24]. Current academic literature on BCT adoption found that there are research shortages in terms of the factors impacting healthcare decision-makers to adopt BCT, and these factors require additional exploration [7, 14, 15, 25]. Therefore, to deliver the maximum benefit of BCT applications in the healthcare context, more research is required to identify the factors influencing hospitals' adoption of BCT, which motivated our study.

This pilot study aims to verify the validity and reliability of the instrument developed to identify the factors influencing BCT adoption in Malaysian hospitals. The questionnaire was developed by adapting Technology-Organizational-Environment (TOE) framework and related studies constructs' items. To the best of our knowledge, this study represents one of the earliest attempts to investigate the adoption of BCT in Malaysian hospitals at an organizational level. The healthcare sector in Malaysia is subject to rigorous regulations and stands out for its unique approach to providing services. With a vision to become a digital-first nation, Malaysia's healthcare industry is experiencing rapid growth, with an emphasis on transferring and developing technology to foster innovations, and BCT is one of the leading technologies driving this growth [26, 27] The government of Malaysia is interested in capitalizing on the assets of the country's current healthcare system to develop a long-term system that is equitable, effective, and efficient as well as adaptive to the quickly changing environment [27, 28]. Consequently, the healthcare industry must closely monitor changing technology adoption patterns to understand BCT's possible effects [29].

This paper is planned as follows: The theoretical foundation and proposed model are described in Sect. 2; the methodology used is explained in Sect. 3. The results are presented and discussed in Sect. 4. Lastly, the conclusion is given in Sect. 5.

2 Theoretical Foundation and Proposed Model

In this study, a theoretical lens approach, as recommended by [30] has been employed. This approach is particularly appropriate for studying BCT adoption in Malaysia, where literature on the subject is scarce and the phenomenon is relatively unknown. The theoretical lens approach involves utilizing a well-confirmed theory as a foundation for more exploration of the phenomenon. An extensive review of relevant literature that focused on BCT adoption at the organizational level was conducted to identify a suitable theory for investigating the adoption of BCT in the Malaysian healthcare sector. The most organizational-level theory proposed in this regard includes the Technology-Organizational-Environment (TOE) framework [31]. The TOE framework suggests that the decision to adopt new technology at the organizational level is influenced by three contextual factors: technology, organization, and environment.

In comparison to other organizational theories, such as the Diffusion of Innovation (DOI) theory [32], the TOE framework provides a more robust underpinning for explaining new technology adoption at an organizational level, as it supplements or overcomes the limitations of other theories [33]. Due to its comprehensiveness and robustness, the TOE framework has been widely used by researchers to understand the adoption of BCT technology in a range of sectors such as automotive [34], construction [35], retail Market [36], energy management [37], supply chain [38, 39], and elderly care [40]. Consequently, based on the empirical evidence, the TOE framework was chosen as a foundational framework for investigating the factors that impact BCT adoption within Malaysia's healthcare organizations.

A theoretical model for this study was developed from the TOE framework. The proposed model posits that the technological, organizational, and environmental contexts may influence BCT adoption in Malaysian hospitals. The technology context encompasses factors such as technology trust and cost-effectiveness, while the organizational context includes organization readiness and top management support. The environmental context consists of competitor pressure and government support (Fig. 1).

Technology Trust (TT): It refers to what extent to which a BCT-based system's availability and performance can be trusted. TT is becoming considered a crucial factor, as the majority of transactions and activities are conducted via the Internet. BCT can strengthen people's trust in the system's functioning. In contrast, their trust in a centralized authority can be undermined due to BCT's technical trust in ensuring the system's regular operation [41]. Integrating BCT into the healthcare systems can improve transparency, accountability, and the trustworthiness of healthcare organizations [42]. Regarding BCT adoption, trust in technology has been highlighted as an important factor [43].

Cost-Effectiveness (COEF): Cost is a critical issue in determining whether or not senior management will adopt or not adopt the technology [44, 45]. Cost is quantified in

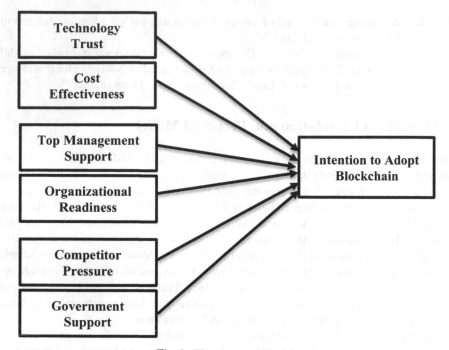

Fig. 1. The proposed Model.

terms of cost-effectiveness, suggesting that the advantages of adopting new technology outweigh the costs [46]. BCT involves an organization's investment, which implies that a cost is required for its acquisition. The primary benefits of BCT are cost savings and increased efficiency and security of corporate activities [47]. Since using BCT can produce faster and more accurate results while saving time and money [16], it is important of realizing the effect of COEF on adoption's decision-making.

Top Management Support (TMS) is defined as the degree to which a top manager recognizes and participates in technology adoption [48]. In the case of new technologies, long-term vision and support from top managers are crucial due to their high cost and complexity and the need for collaboration among partners [31]. Top management commitment can aid in the new technology adoption [49]. The studies [50, 51] have emphasized the beneficial function of TMS in fostering BCT adoption.

Organizational Readiness (OR): It refers to an organization's capacity to allocate financial resources, technological resources (which includes physical IT infrastructure), human resources with IT skills, and intangible resources, such as know-how and culture, to particular technology adoption [52, 53]. Generally, businesses that have a more thorough organizational structure are more likely to adopt novel technologies [54]. Organizational readiness is recognized as one of the most critical organizational factors impacting BCT adoption [40, 50].

Competitive Pressure (COM) is defined as the extent to which an organization experiences pressure from its rivals in the market [55]. Such pressure compels organizations to quickly adopt new technologies to increase their business performance and gain a competitive advantage [37, 56]. A study conducted [57] demonstrated the significant influence of competitive pressure on adopting HIS within Malaysian hospitals. BCT's improved efficiency and transparency give the organization an advantage over the competition [58, 59]. Competitive pressure was identified to be a significant factor influencing BCT adoption within Malaysian organizations [60].

Government Support (GOV): Governmental support is widely recognized as a crucial driving force in the organizational adoption of new technologies [31, 61, 62]. Governments play a crucial role in developing policies, regulations, and facilities aimed at encouraging the adoption of new technologies by organizations [63]. Koster & Borgman [64] stated that government pressure has a significant role in accelerating the adoption of BCT. According to [65]. Healthcare organizations are predominantly public or private healthcare firms regulated and controlled by the government [40]. Thus, government assistance and policies may influence BCT's development and adoption, either directly or indirectly [66, 67].

3 Research Methodology

3.1 Instrument Design

To evaluate the validity and reliability of the proposed model, preliminary data were collected using a survey questionnaire, which was developed based on concepts found in prior research on the adoption of BCT and the TOE framework, a theory related to technology adoption. Based on the available literature, the survey questionnaire was designed to assess respondents' perceptions of the six factors outlined in the proposed model, all of which are believed to impact the adoption of BCT within hospitals. Thus, it was necessary to establish the scales for these factors. The description of each construct was assessed based on the studies and theory employed to create the instrument scales, and the dimensions of each construct were determined. The items were revised to measure each dimension according to the specific context of inquiry (BCT in healthcare). Table 1 provides a list of the constructs, their number of items, and the relevant references. All items related to the constructs in the proposed model were rated using a five-point Likert scale, where 1 represented "strongly disagree" and 5 represented "strongly agree."

Table 1. Measurement of constructs

Variable	No of items	Source
Technology Trust	5	[42]
Cost-Effectiveness	6	[38, 68]
Organizational Readiness	4	[35]
Top managers support	6	[58, 69]
Competitor Pressure	5	[69]
Government Support	5	[35]
Intention to adopt Blockchain	4	[69]

3.2 Validation

Validation of the survey instrument is essential to guarantee clarity and lack of ambiguity in the questions. Before conducting the pilot study, this study's survey instrument was validated by five academic experts, who provided feedback on the structure of some questions and suggested changes to eliminate any ambiguity. Based on the experts' recommendations, modifications were made to the instrument, and its content validity was recognized.

3.3 Pilot Study

A pilot study surveyed a smaller subset of respondents to provide feedback on the final data-collecting process [70]. The pilot study allows for assessing the instrument's reliability and identifies any measures that may need to be removed to improve the scale's reliability. In this study, a pilot survey was administered online to top/mid-level managers, including senior managers, IT managers, executive managers, and CIOs, working in Malaysian hospitals, who are the intended audience for this research. The online survey is advantageous as respondents be able to complete it at their appropriateness. IT expert from each targeted hospital was contacted by email and provided with the questionnaire link, requesting that they distribute it to their colleagues. Twenty-five responses were received in one month. The collected data was analyzed using Smart PLS 4.0. Cronbach's alpha, composite reliability tests, and indicator reliability for each item were used to determine the instrument's level of reliability. The measure's validity was further tested by conducting convergent and discriminant validity analyses.

4 Results and Discussion

4.1 Reliability of Constructs

Two crucial criteria can assess the reliability of constructs in the research framework. The first criterion is internal consistency reliability, usually evaluated using Cronbach's alpha and composite reliability (CR). Cronbach's alpha implies that all indicators measuring each construct should be reliable and evaluates reliability based on the correlations between the observed indicator variables. In contrast, CR considers the various outer loadings of the indicator variables [71]. The second criterion is indicator reliability. It considers the significance of all the indicators' outer loadings, which are recommended to be above 0.70 to be deemed acceptable [72].

The CR and Cronbach's alpha coefficients range from 0 to 1, with higher values demonstrating more reliability. Specifically, in exploratory research, a range of 0.60 to 0.70 is considered acceptable, while a range of 0.70 to 0.90 is considered satisfactory [73]. However, a coefficient value below 0.60 is deemed unacceptable, indicating a lack of reliability of internal consistency [72]. As shown in Table 2, all constructs in the survey exhibited both Cronbach's alpha and CR coefficients that exceeded the suggested minimum level of 0.70. The analysis revealed that the constructs had CR values ranging from 0.871 to 0.909, and Cronbach's alpha values ranging from 0.807 to 0.882, indicating satisfactory and acceptable internal consistency reliability.

For assessing the indicator reliability, the outer loading value of items should be greater than 0.708 [72]. Values between 0.4 and 0.7 should be eliminated, as their removal may increase the average variance extracted (AVE) or CR values. As shown in Table 2, the outer loadings of all constructs are well above the threshold value of 0.7, except for one item TMS1 under the threshold value of 0.533. However, this indicator loading below the threshold was not removed from the final model because its removal did not affect the AVE's value of that construct. The result implies that all items exceeded the predefined level. Hence, construct reliability is assumed considering the internal consistency and indicator reliability.

Table 2. Internal consistency reliability, indicator reliability, and convergent validity

Construct	Items	Outer loadings	Cronbach's alpha	CR	AVE
Cost Effectiveness (COEF)	COEF1	0.782	0.882	0.909	0.624
	COEF2	0.823			
	COEF3	0.822			
	COEF4	0.828			
	COEF5	0.750			
	COEF6	0.731			
Competitor Pressure (COM)	COM1	0.798	0.856	0.897	0.638
	COM2	0.887			
	COM3	0.770			
	COM4	0.862			
	COM5	0.755			
Government Support (GOV)	GOV1	0.735	0.839	0.886	0.612
	GOV2	0.701			
	GOV3	0.897			
	GOV4	0.853			
	GOV5	0.736			
Intention to Adopt Blockchain (INT)	INT1	0.834	0.878	0.916	0.732
	INT2	0.861			
	INT3	0.908			
	INT4	0.816			
Organizational Readiness (OR)	OR1	0.739	0.807	0.871	0.628
	OR2	0.824			
	OR3	0.801			
	OR4	0.802			

(continued)

Table 2. (*continued*)

Construct	Items	Outer loadings	Cronbach's alpha	CR	AVE
Top Managers Support (TMS)	TMS1	0.533*	0.858	0.897	0.596
	TMS2	0.854			
	TMS3	0.778			
	TMS4	0.727			
	TMS5	0.874			
	TMS6	0.818			
Technology Trust (TT)	TT1	0.727	0.841	0.886	0.611
	TT2	0.725			
	TT3	0.800			
	TT4	0.864			
	TT5	0.783			

4.2 Validity of Constructs

The constructs' validity has been evaluated using the two most widely recognized forms of validity, which are convergent and discriminant validity [72, 73]. The convergent validity was measured by examining the AVE values for each construct. As presented above in Table 2, the AVE values for all constructs exceeded the minimum threshold of 0.5 [72], confirming the convergent validity of the constructs in the proposed model.

The discriminant validity describes a construct's ability to be differentiated from other constructs using measurable standards [72, 73]. To establish discriminant validity, this study employed the cross-loadings matrix, the Fornell-Larker criterion, and the Heterotrait Monotrait ratio of correlations (HTMT) [72, 73].

The loading value of a construct should exceed all other loadings in different constructs to ensure discriminant validity [72, 73]. This criterion can help minimize the presence of multicollinearity among latent variables by ensuring that the AVE value of the latent variable is higher than all other variables [74]. If the loading value for other constructs exceeds that of the construct in question, it suggests a potential problem with discriminant validity [72, 73]. Table 3 displays the cross-loading matrix, with bolded values indicating the items' loading on its assigned construct. The findings demonstrate that each item has a higher loading on its assigned construct than on any other constructs in the model.

The Fornell-Larcker criterion is a method of analysis that compares the square root of the AVE value with the correlation value of the construct exhibiting the highest value in any row or column to the highest correlation value of any other construct [72, 73]. This method is based on the premise that latent variables should account for more variance in the item measure than other latent variables. Table 4 validates that the AVE

Table 3. Discriminant validity based on cross-loadings matrix

	COEF	COM	GOV	INT	OR	TMS	TT
COEF1	**0.782**	0.368	0.406	0.177	0.537	0.358	0.259
COEF2	**0.823**	0.389	0.468	0.256	0.476	0.265	0.168
COEF3	**0.822**	0.334	0.237	0.164	0.548	0.230	0.261
COEF4	**0.828**	0.325	0.311	0.281	0.713	0.337	0.288
COEF5	**0.750**	0.404	0.522	0.322	0.532	0.379	0.217
COEF6	**0.731**	0.417	0.350	0.368	0.682	0.600	0.332
COM1	0.375	**0.798**	0.553	0.598	0.431	0.697	0.365
COM2	0.407	**0.887**	0.773	0.672	0.537	0.496	0.537
COM3	0.570	**0.770**	0.590	0.420	0.569	0.587	0.461
COM4	0.398	**0.862**	0.743	0.649	0.489	0.451	0.468
COM5	0.202	**0.655**	0.309	0.403	0.026	0.440	0.166
GOV1	0.365	0.404	**0.735**	0.481	0.471	0.374	0.377
GOV2	0.569	0.616	**0.670**	0.373	0.345	0.320	0.327
GOV3	0.574	0.695	**0.897**	0.618	0.653	0.560	0.537
GOV4	0.354	0.760	**0.853**	0.649	0.409	0.517	0.544
GOV5	0.147	0.501	**0.736**	0.520	0.334	0.295	0.497
INT1	0.289	0.629	0.556	**0.834**	0.651	0.690	0.503
INT2	0.216	0.542	0.554	**0.861**	0.479	0.553	0.478
INT3	0.295	0.642	0.643	**0.908**	0.469	0.493	0.275
INT4	0.440	0.596	0.611	**0.816**	0.482	0.583	0.151
OR1	0.824	0.317	0.309	0.366	**0.739**	0.458	0.062
OR2	0.607	0.344	0.351	0.420	**0.824**	0.420	0.296
OR3	0.392	0.383	0.307	0.457	**0.801**	0.408	0.427
OR4	0.622	0.571	0.714	0.631	**0.802**	0.564	0.527
TMS1	0.428	0.533	0.698	0.575	0.552	**0.533**	0.360
TMS2	0.469	0.366	0.255	0.465	0.551	**0.854**	0.158
TMS3	0.312	0.457	0.213	0.561	0.443	**0.778**	−0.009
TMS4	0.262	0.581	0.263	0.352	0.234	**0.727**	0.073
TMS5	0.251	0.556	0.441	0.608	0.368	**0.874**	0.331
TMS6	0.547	0.534	0.534	0.482	0.528	**0.818**	0.388
TT1	0.412	0.530	0.332	0.355	0.404	0.399	**0.727**
TT2	−0.007	0.350	0.435	0.208	0.144	0.110	**0.725**

(*continued*)

Table 3. (*continued*)

	COEF	COM	GOV	INT	OR	TMS	TT
TT3	0.216	0.392	0.598	0.299	0.316	0.376	**0.800**
TT4	0.210	0.444	0.501	0.338	0.230	0.124	**0.864**
TT5	0.333	0.291	0.474	0.392	0.561	0.132	**0.783**

squared values are greater than the correlation values for each other construct. Thus, the discriminant validity of the constructs based on the Fornell-Larcker criterion was confirmed.

Table 4. Discriminant validity based on Fornell-Larker criterion

	COEF	COM	GOV	INT	OR	TMS	TT
COEF	**0.790**						
COM	0.485	**0.799**					
GOV	0.501	0.768	**0.783**				
INT	0.360	0.707	0.690	**0.855**			
OR	0.757	0.534	0.572	0.616	**0.792**		
TMS	0.494	0.661	0.542	0.684	0.596	**0.772**	
TT	0.330	0.515	0.595	0.422	0.453	0.297	**0.781**

To further identify any lack of discriminant validity, this study also evaluated HTMT. Based on the findings presented in Table 5, it can be confirmed that this study has achieved discriminant validity. This is a result of the poor correlation found between the constructs, as indicated by the HTMT values below 0.90 [72, 73].

Table 5. Discriminant validity based on HTMT

	COEF	COM	GOV	INT	OR	TMS	TT
COEF							
COM	0.548						
GOV	0.592	0.883					
INT	0.383	0.791	0.792				
OR	0.881	0.605	0.638	0.690			
TMS	0.525	0.782	0.610	0.756	0.686		
TT	0.353	0.602	0.702	0.462	0.506	0.404	

Based on the results obtained from the three methods described above, compelling evidence supports the discriminant validity of the research constructs proposed in the model. Consequently, the measurements have been successfully validated by analyzing construct reliability and validity.

5 Conclusion

Blockchain technology has the possibility to improve the privacy, security, and authenticity of data, and solve the main issues in the current healthcare sector. However, its adoption is low and several factors may influence the decision. Encouraging healthcare institutions in Malaysia to implement and promote BCT requires an understanding of the factors influencing hospitals' adoption of BCT. This study validated the instrument developed to examine the impact of technology trust, cost-effectiveness, organization readiness, top management support, competitor pressure, and government support on hospitals' intention to adopt BCT. Measurements were modified from previous studies to fit the present investigation better. The instrument's content validity was assessed by obtaining feedback from five academic staff and information system researchers. A pilot test was conducted to examine the reliability and validity of the instrument. The results have provided preliminary support for the model constructs and instruments utilized to evaluate the adoption of BCT in Malaysian hospitals. The reliability of the model constructs was established, with all constructs exhibiting composite reliability and Cronbach's alpha coefficients that exceeded the recommended threshold. The convergent and discriminant validity analysis exhibited that all constructs have a satisfactory level of validity. As a result, the questionnaire is valid for use in large-scale data collection. In the context of hospitals' adoption of BCTs, this study is one of the few to evaluate the reliability and validity of a questionnaire based on a TOE framework. This might contribute to a better understanding of BCT adoption in developing countries' healthcare institutions, specifically Malaysia.

References

1. Frizzo-Barker, J., Chow-White, P.A., Adams, P.R., Mentanko, J., Ha, D., Green, S.: Blockchain as a disruptive technology for business: a systematic review. Int. J. Inf. Manage. **51**, 102029 (2020). https://doi.org/10.1016/j.ijinfomgt.2019.10.014
2. Engelhardt, M.A., Espinosa, D.: Hitching healthcare to the chain : an introduction to blockchain technology in the healthcare sector an introduction to blockchain technology in the healthcare sector. Technol. Innov. Manag. Rev. **7**(10), 22–35 (2017)
3. Hölbl, M., Kompara, M., Kamišali, A.: A systematic review of the use of blockchain in healthcare (2018). https://doi.org/10.3390/sym10100470
4. Nakamoto, S.: Bitcoin: a peer-to-peer electronic cash system. Decentralized Bus. Rev. 21260 (2008)
5. Esmaeilzadeh, P., Mirzaei, T.: The potential of blockchain technology for health information exchange: experimental study from patients' perspectives. J. Med. Internet Res. **21**(6), e14184 (2019). https://doi.org/10.2196/14184
6. Mackey, T., Bekki, H., Matsuzaki, T., Mizushima, H.: Examining the potential of blockchain technology to meet the needs of 21st-century Japanese health care: viewpoint on use cases and policy. J. Med. Internet Res. **22**(1), e13649 (2020). https://doi.org/10.2196/13649

7. Tandon, A., Dhir, A., Islam, A.K.M.N., Mäntymäki, M.: Computers in industry blockchain in healthcare : a systematic literature review, synthesizing framework and future research agenda. Comput. Ind. **122**, 103290 (2020). https://doi.org/10.1016/j.compind.2020.103290

8. Bazel, M.A., Mohammed, F., Ahmed, M.: Blockchain Technology in Healthcare Big Data Management : Benefits, Applications and Challenges (2021)

9. Dubovitskaya, A., Novotny, P., Xu, Z., Wang, F.: Applications of blockchain technology for data-sharing in oncology: results from a systematic literature review. Oncology **98**(6), 403–411 (2020). https://doi.org/10.1159/000504325

10. Ismail, L., Materwala, H.: Blockchain paradigm for healthcare: performance evaluation. Symmetry (Basel) **12**(8), 1200 (2020). https://doi.org/10.3390/SYM12081200

11. Katuwal, .J., Pandey, S., Hennessey, M., Lamichhane, B.: Applications of blockchain in healthcare: current landscape & challenges, December 2018. https://arxiv.org/abs/1812.027 76v1. Accessed 15 November 2021

12. Syafiqa, I., Mudaris, M.: Electronic Health Records : Planning the Foundation for Digital Healthcare in Malaysia, August 2021

13. Alabboodi, A.S.: Review on security and privacy issues in health information systems adoption and usage. Ijar **6**(11), 96–102 (2020). https://scholar.google.com/scholar?oi=bibs&cluster=10513046276192991222&btnI=1&hl=en

14. Bazel, M.A., Ahmad, M., Mohammed, F.: Hospital information systems in Malaysia: current issues and blockchain technology as a solution. In: 2022 2nd International Conference on Emerging Smart Technologies and Applications (eSmarTA), pp. 1–7 (2022)

15. Hira, F.A., Khalid, H., Abdul, S.Z.: A conceptual framework to investigate health professionals' blockchain technology adoption readiness in Malaysia, vol. 9, no. 2, pp. 58–66 (2021)

16. Tanwar, S., Parekh, K., Evans, R.: Blockchain-based electronic healthcare record system for healthcare 4.0 applications. J. Inf. Secur. Appl. **50**, 102407 (2020). https://doi.org/10.1016/J.JISA.2019.102407

17. Gökalp, E., Gökalp, M.O., Çoban, S., Eren, P.E.: Analysing opportunities and challenges of integrated blockchain technologies in healthcare. In: Eurosymposium on Systems Analysis and Design, pp. 174–183 (2018)

18. Hira, F.A., Khalid, H., Rasid, S.Z.A., Baskaran, S., Moshiul, A.M.: Blockchain technology implementation for medical data management in Malaysia: potential, need and challenges (2022)

19. Mamun, Q.: Blockchain technology in the future of healthcare. Smart Heal. **23**, 100223 (2022)

20. Sharma, M., Joshi, S.: Barriers to blockchain adoption in healthcare industry: an Indian perspective. J. Glob. Oper. Strateg. Sourc. **14**(1), 134–169 (2021). https://doi.org/10.1108/JGOSS-06-2020-0026

21. Ullah, N., Al-Rahmi, W.M., Alzahrani, A.I., Alfarraj, O., Alblehai, F.M.: Blockchain technology adoption in smart learning environments. Sustainability **13**(4), 1–18 (2021). https://doi.org/10.3390/su13041801

22. O. C. D. Models: Global blockchain technology market in the healthcare industry, 2018–2022 healthcare industry assesses blockchain potential to optimize healthcare workflows and improve, October 2019, pp. 2018–2022 (2022)

23. Alzahrani, A.G., Alhomoud, A., Wills, G.: A framework of the critical factors for healthcare providers to share data securely using blockchain. IEEE Access **10**, 41064–41077 (2022). https://doi.org/10.1109/access.2022.3162218

24. Bazel, M.A., Mohammed, F., Ahmad, M.: A systematic review on the adoption of blockchain technology in the healthcare industry. EAI Endorsed Trans. Pervasive Heal. Technol. **9**, e4 (2023)

25. Shukla, R.G., Agarwal, A., Shekhar, V.: Leveraging blockchain technology for Indian Health-care system: an assessment using value-focused thinking approach. J. High Technol. Manag. Res. **32**(2), 100415 (2021). https://doi.org/10.1016/j.hitech.2021.100415
26. Economic Planning Unit Prime Minister's Department, "Malaysia Digital Economy Blueprint," Econ. Plan. Unit Prime Minist. Dep., p. 104 (2021)
27. T. M. Plan: A Prosperous, Inclusive, Sustainable Malaysia (2021)
28. M. D. Division: Strategic Framework of the Medical Programme, Ministry of Health 2021–2025, vol. 20 (2020)
29. Milik, O.H.: National Blockchain Roadmap (2021)
30. Creswell, J.W., Creswell, J.D.: Research Design: Qualitative, Quantitative, and Mixed Methods Approaches. Sage Publications, Thousand Oaks (2017)
31. Tornatzky, L.G., Fleischer, M., Chakrabarti, A.K.: Processes of Technological Innovation. Lexington Books, Lexington (1990)
32. Everett, M.R.: Diffusion of innovations, vol. 12, New York (1995)
33. Oliveira, T., Martins, M.F.: Literature review of information technology adoption models at firm level. Electron. J. Inf. Syst. Eval. **14**(1), 110–121 (2011)
34. Supranee, S., Rotchanakitumnuai, S.: The acceptance of the application of blockchain technology in the supply chain process of the Thai automotive industry. In: Proceedings of the International Conference on Electronic Business (ICEB), vol. 2017-December, pp. 252–257 (2017). https://www.scopus.com/inward/record.uri?eid=2-s2.0-85057736431& partnerID=40&md5=cf2bf8d539187392ff51b7f5d23afabb
35. Badi, S., Ochieng, E., Nasaj, M., Papadaki, M.: Technological, organisational and environmental determinants of smart contracts adoption: UK construction sector viewpoint. Constr. Manag. Econ. **39**, 1–19 (2020). https://doi.org/10.1080/01446193.2020.1819549
36. Miraz, M.H., et al.: Factors affecting implementation of blockchain in retail market in Malaysia. Int. J. Supply Chain Manag. **9**(1), 385–391 (2020). http://excelingtech.co.uk/. Accessed 5 July 2021
37. Wamba, S.F., et al.: Dynamics between blockchain adoption determinants and supply chain performance: an empirical investigation. Int. J. Prod. Econ. **2021**, 1–17 (2020). https://doi.org/10.1080/00207543.2020.1803511
38. Wong, L.-W., Tan, G.W.-H., Lee, V.-H., Ooi, K.-B., Sohal, A.: Unearthing the determinants of Blockchain adoption in supply chain management. Int. J. Prod. Res. **58**(7), 2100–2123 (2020). https://doi.org/10.1080/00207543.2020.1730463
39. Malik, S., Chadhar, M., Chetty, M.: Factors affecting the organizational adoption of blockchain technology: an Australian perspective. In: Proceedings of the Annual Hawaii International Conference on System Sciences, vol. 2020-January, pp. 5597–5606 (2021). https://www.scopus.com/inward/record.uri?eid=2-s2.0-85108362939&partne rID=40&md5=222b484da728b74c098e74e162bfcd90
40. Lu, L., Liang, C., Gu, D., Ma, Y., Xie, Y., Zhao, S.: What advantages of blockchain affect its adoption in the elderly care industry? A study based on the technology–organisation–environment framework. Technol. Soc. **67**, 101786 (2021)
41. De Filippi, P., Mannan, M., Reijers, W.: Blockchain as a confidence machine: the problem of trust & challenges of governance. Technol. Soc. **62**, 101284 (2020). https://doi.org/10.1016/j.techsoc.2020.101284
42. Queiroz, M.M., Fosso Wamba, S., De Bourmont, M., Telles, R.: Blockchain adoption in operations and supply chain management: empirical evidence from an emerging economy. Int. J. Prod. Res. **59**, 6087–6103 (2020). https://doi.org/10.1080/00207543.2020.1803511
43. Wanitcharakkhakul, L., Rotchanakitumnuai, S.: Blockchain technology acceptance in electronic medical record system. In: Proceedings of the International Conference on Electronic Business (ICEB), 2017, vol. 2017-December, pp. 53–58 (2017). https://www.scopus.com/

inward/record.uri?eid=2-s2.0-85057753091&partnerID=40&md5=ce47128cdf34f6c268
656ea80e6d4277

44. Mousa, M.A.S.: Determinants of cloud based E-Government in Libya. J. Crit. Rev. **7**(13), 2239–2248 (2020). http://www.jcreview.com/fulltext/197-1596886870.pdf

45. Mohammed, F., Bin Ibrahim, O.: Drivers of cloud computing adoption for e-government services implementation. Int. J. Distrib. Syst. Technol. **6**(1), 1–14 (2015)

46. Premkumar, G., Ramamurthy, K.: The role of interorganizational and organizational factors on the decision mode for adoption of interorganizational systems. Decis. Sci. **26**(3), 303–336 (1995)

47. Sciarelli, M., Prisco, A., Gheith, M.H., Muto, V.: Factors affecting the adoption of blockchain technology in innovative Italian companies: an extended TAM approach. J. Strateg. Manag. **15**, 495–507 (2021). https://doi.org/10.1108/JSMA-02-2021-0054

48. Lian, J.-W., Yen, D.C., Wang, Y.-T.: An exploratory study to understand the critical factors affecting the decision to adopt cloud computing in Taiwan hospital. Int. J. Inf. Manage. **34**(1), 28–36 (2014)

49. Wong, L.-W., Leong, L.-Y., Hew, J.-J., Tan, G.W.-H., Ooi, K.-B.: Time to seize the digital evolution: adoption of blockchain in operations and supply chain management among Malaysian SMEs. Int. J. Inf. Manage. **52**, 101997 (2020). https://doi.org/10.1016/j.ijinfomgt.2019.08.005

50. Clohessy, T., Acton, T.: Investigating the influence of organizational factors on blockchain adoption: an innovation theory perspective. Ind. Manag. Data Syst. **119**(7), 1457–1491 (2019). https://doi.org/10.1108/IMDS-08-2018-0365

51. Kumar Bhardwaj, A., Garg, A., Gajpal, Y.: Determinants of blockchain technology adoption in supply chains by Small and Medium Enterprises (SMEs) in India. Math. Probl. Eng. **2021**, 1–14 (2021). https://doi.org/10.1155/2021/5537395

52. Grant, M.J., Booth, A.: A typology of reviews: an analysis of 14 review types and associated methodologies. Heal. Inf. Libr. J. **26**(2), 91–108 (2009)

53. Iacovou, C.L., Benbasat, I., Dexter, A.S.: Electronic data interchange and small organizations: adoption and impact of technology. MIS Q. **19**, 465–485 (1995)

54. Gangwar, H., Date, H., Ramaswamy, R.: Understanding determinants of cloud computing adoption using an integrated TAM-TOE model. J. Enterp. Inf. Manag. **28**, 107–130 (2015)

55. Zhang, N., Lu, S.F., Xu, B., Wu, B., Rodriguez-Monguio, R., Gurwitz, J.: Health information technologies: which nursing homes adopted them? J. Am. Med. Dir. Assoc. **17**(5), 441–447 (2016)

56. El-Haddadeh, R., Osmani, M., Hindi, N., Fadlalla, A.: Value creation for realising the sustainable development goals: fostering organisational adoption of big data analytics. J. Bus. Res. **131**, 402–410 (2021)

57. Ahmadi, H., Nilashi, M., Ibrahim, O.: Organizational decision to adopt hospital information system: an empirical investigation in the case of Malaysian public hospitals. Int. J. Med. Inform. **84**(3), 166–188 (2015)

58. Malik, S., Chadhar, M., Vatanasakdakul, S., Chetty, M.: Factors Affecting the Organizational Adoption of Blockchain Technology : Extending the Technology – Organization – Environment (TOE) Framework in the Australian Context (2021)

59. Aslam, J., Saleem, A., Khan, N.T., Kim, Y.B.: Factors influencing blockchain adoption in supply chain management practices: a study based on the oil industry. J. Innov. Knowl. **6**(2), 124–134 (2021). https://doi.org/10.1016/j.jik.2021.01.002

60. Wong, L.W., Leong, L.Y., Hew, J.J., Tan, G.W.H., Ooi, K.B.: Time to seize the digital evolution: adoption of blockchain in operations and supply chain management among Malaysian SMEs. Int. J. Inf. Manage. **52**, 101997 (2020). https://doi.org/10.1016/j.ijinfomgt.2019.08.005

61. Mangla, S.K., Kazancoglu, Y., Ekinci, E., Liu, M., Özbiltekin, M., Sezer, M.D.: Using system dynamics to analyze the societal impacts of blockchain technology in milk supply chainsrefer. Transp. Res. Part E Logist. Transp. Rev. **149**, 102289 (2021). https://doi.org/10.1016/j.tre.2021.102289

62. Holotiuk, F., Moormann, J.: Organizational adoption of digital innovation: the case of blockchain technology (2018). https://www.scopus.com/inward/record.uri?eid=2-s2.0-850 61297687&partnerID=40&md5=6b10ef3a43b01d9aa50886748ee1bb99

63. Bag, S., Viktorovich, D.A., Sahu, A.K., Sahu, A.K.: Barriers to adoption of blockchain technology in green supply chain management. J. Glob. Oper. Strateg. Sourc. **14**(1), 104–133 (2021). https://doi.org/10.1108/JGOSS-06-2020-0027

64. Koster, F., Borgman, H.P.: New Kid on the block! Understanding blockchain adoption in the public sector. In: Proceedings of the Annual Hawaii International Conference on System Sciences, vol. 2020-January, pp. 1770–1779 (2020). https://www.scopus.com/inward/record.uri?eid=2-s2.0-85090763721&partnerID=40&md5=0efb864d96c8f905ddfdb32df4501f8b

65. De Castro, P., Tanner, M., Johnston, K.: Perceived factors influencing blockchain adoption in the asset and wealth management industry in the Western Cape, South Africa. In: International Development Informatics Association Conference, pp. 48–62 (2020)

66. Liang, H., Saraf, N., Hu, Q., Xue, Y.: Assimilation of enterprise systems: the effect of institutional pressures and the mediating role of top management. MIS Q. **31**, 59–87 (2007)

67. Fosso Wamba, S., Queiroz, M.M., Trinchera, L.: Dynamics between blockchain adoption determinants and supply chain performance: an empirical investigation. Int. J. Prod. Econ. **229**, 107791 (2020). https://doi.org/10.1016/j.ijpe.2020.107791

68. Choi, D., Chung, C.Y., Seyha, T., Young, J.: Factors affecting organizations' resistance to the adoption of blockchain technology in supply networks. Sustain. **12**(21), 1–37 (2020). https://doi.org/10.3390/su12218882

69. Choi, D., Chung, C.Y., Seyha, T., Young, J.: Factors affecting organizations' resistance to the adoption of blockchain technology in supply networks. Sustainability **12**(21), 1–37 (2020). https://doi.org/10.3390/su12218882

70. Mohammed, F., Ibrahim, O., Nilashi, M., Alzurqa, E.: Cloud computing adoption model for e-government implementation. Inf. Dev. **33**(3), 303–323 (2017). https://doi.org/10.1177/026 6666916656033

71. Sarstedt, M., Hair, J.F., Ringle, C.M., Liengaard, B.D.: Progress in partial least squares structural equation modeling use in marketing research in the last decade. Psychol. Mark. **39**, 1035–1064 (2022). https://doi.org/10.1002/mar.21640

72. Query ID="Q4" Text="" Hair Jr., J.F., Sarstedt, M., Ringle, C.M., Gudergan, S.P.: Advanced Issues in Partial Least Squares Structural Equation Modeling. Sage Publications, London (2017)

73. Sarstedt, M., Ringle, C.M., Hair, J.F.: Partial least squares structural equation modeling. In: Homburg, C., Klarmann, M., Vomberg, A. (eds.) Handbook of market research, pp. 587–632. Springer, Cham (2022). https://doi.org/10.1007/978-3-319-57413-4_15

74. Chin, W.W.: The partial least squares approach to structural equation modeling. Mod. Methods Bus. Res. **295**(2), 295–336 (1998)

Exploring the Relationship Between Protection Motivation and Addiction Severity Towards Secure Intention Behavior in Online Game Addiction Among Adolescents

Wan Mohd Yusoff Wan Yaacob[1]([✉]) [iD], Nur Haryani Zakaria[2] [iD], and Zahurin Mat Aji[2] [iD]

[1] Politeknik Tuanku Syed Sirajuddin, 02600 Arau, Perlis, Malaysia
wanmohdyusoff@ptss.edu.my

[2] Universiti Utara Malaysia, Sintok, 06010 Bukit Kayu Hitam, Kedah, Malaysia

Abstract. Online game addiction refers to the excessive and compulsive use of online games, leading to negative consequences in various aspects of people's life. One concerning aspect is that compulsive players may compromise their security and safety while engaging in gaming activities. Despite the growing concern about this issue, there is still much to understand about providing effective protections and interventions, particularly among adolescents. Thus, this paper aims to investigate the relationship between protection motivation and the severity of online game addiction, with a particular focus on secure intention behavior among adolescents affected by online game addiction. A survey was conducted involving 660 late adolescents (aged 17–19 years) from various Higher Learning Institutions (HLIs) in Peninsular Malaysia. The findings revealed that 35% of the participants were addicted to online games, as assessed by the Online Cognition Scale (OCS) and Online Game Addiction Scale (OGAS). The severity of online game addiction significantly impacted secure intention behavior within the online gaming environment. Additionally, protection motivation emerged as a significant predictor of positive security behavior. These results offer new insights and support the existing hypotheses, emphasizing the importance of investigating the impact of online game addiction severity on secure intention behavior. Understanding the relationship between protection motivation and the severity of online game addiction concerning security intention behavior is crucial to prevent adverse outcomes, such as insecure cyber behavior and vulnerability to cyber threats. The findings from this study can contribute to the development of effective interventions and prevention strategies against cyber threats in the context of online gaming.

Keywords: Protection Motivation · Addiction Severity · Online Game Addiction and Secure Intention Behavior

© The Author(s), under exclusive license to Springer Nature Singapore Pte Ltd. 2024
N. H. Zakaria et al. (Eds.): ICOCI 2023, CCIS 2002, pp. 30–42, 2024.
https://doi.org/10.1007/978-981-99-9592-9_3

1 Introduction

Online gaming has become an extremely popular and immersive form of entertainment in the digital age, particularly among adolescents. While online games can be a fun and engaging way to pass the time, it can also lead to addiction in some individuals. This addiction can have negative effects on various aspects of their lives, including academic performance, social relationships and mental health. Given the increasing prevalence of online game addiction, it is essential to understand the contributing factors and how they can be prevented and treated. The relationship between protection motivation, the severity of online game addiction and secure intention behavior is an important area of study because it can offer insights into how online game-addicted individuals can protect themselves from potential risks while performing other online activities. In addition, this knowledge can aid the development of interventions and prevention programs for online game addiction.

This paper aims to investigate the relationship between protection motivation and the severity of online game addiction in relation to secure intention behavior among online game-addicted adolescents using standardized measures and statistical analysis. The paper is organized as follows; Sect. 1 is the introduction, Sect. 2 reviews the related studies, Sect. 3 elaborates on methodology, Sect. 4 presents the results and findings, and Sect. 5 discusses the importance of secure intention behavior. Finally, Sect. 6 concludes the paper and makes some recommendations for future work.

Xu et al. [1] defined online game addiction as a type of gaming disorder characterized by problematic, repetitive and obsessive use of online gaming platforms that results in a significant impairment over an extended period in various domains of life. The characterization of this behavioral addiction is currently being scrutinized and discussed by members of the scientific, medical and gaming community all of which are experts in their respective disciplines [2–5]. For instance, Balakrishnan et al. [6] and Griffiths [7, 8] mentioned that this addiction might be induced by an individual's engagement in online gaming activities with the intention of achieving a higher responsibility or other wants regardless of the detrimental impacts.

The research conducted by Spil Games [9] found that approximately 1.2 billion people worldwide had played games, with 700 million playing online games. This amounts to roughly 17% of the world population and includes players of all categories. The research also revealed that the age group with the highest number of players was 15–24 years, with late adolescents (17–19 years) accounting for about 45% of the total. The integration of online gaming into daily life and routine has contributed to online game addiction among adolescents [10]. Bekir and Çelik [11] also drew attention to this problem when they discover that adolescents constitute the greatest group of people in a community who have been reported to online game addicts on a daily basis. The addictive nature of online games can be attributed to various special features and elements such as flow experience, competition, versatility, unique simulations and captivating plotlines [12].

Intention reflects a person's determination or willingness to attempt and plan for a behavior that may eventually become a habit [13]. According to Ajzen [14], intention is the key determinant of behavior change. As for Shropshire et al. [15], intention is described as a mental state that represents a commitment to carrying out secure behavior and related actions by individuals in an online gaming environment. Meanwhile, secure intention behavior refers to self-directed instructions to perform actions aimed at attaining secure behavior in the online game environment [16]. As described by prominent scholars [17–20], secure intention behavior is closely related to the concept of information security behavior, which aims to protect individuals or organizations from potential risks and threats. Behavioral intention is the likelihood of translating intentions into actions and it captures both the behavior and commitment levels. Although most behaviors are habitual or triggered by situational cues, forming intentions can be crucial for securing long-term cybersecurity [19]. The evaluation of the intention behavior model is the most debated issue in the IS research field. Previous researchers had revealed inconsistencies in the secure intention behavior related to multiple variables, making it challenging to compare outcomes [21]. In light of this, Briggs et al. [18] also stressed the urgency of finding a comprehensive solution to address these issues.

2 Related Studies

2.1 Secure Intention Behavior in Information Security

Numerous correlational studies have examined the relationship between intention and security factors in information security, suggesting that intention is a predictor of security behavior. One example is the study by Jansen et al. [22], which looked into the impact of fear appeal on user cognition and behavioral intention as a means to minimize the risk of phishing attacks, particularly in the context of cyber threats. Butavicius et al. [17] also investigated the development of trust in technical controls scale to combat phishing attacks, adding to a growing body of literature. Shakela and Jazri [23] determined the spear phishing in financial industries based on experience and awareness. In addition, Goel and Jain [19] suggested new approaches to securing against phishing attacks in the mobile environment, with innovative defense mechanisms integrated into mobile cloud computing. Several researchers have also attempted to develop new models or perspectives on secure intention behavior, while others have conducted systematic literature reviews on intentional behavior related to phishing threat avoidance behavior and mobile phishing attack mitigation [24].

A few correlational studies based on various theories also highlighted that intention is related to security factors that can predict behavior. For example, Lebek et al. [25] conducted a comprehensive synthesis of security results and empirically tested related research models to identify several theories concerning secure intention behavior. They discovered that Protection Motivation Theory (PMT) was influenced by cognitive evaluation. However, the results of the study were only applicable to the employees and co-workers, indicating an improved adherence to information security policies within organizations. The Theory of Planned Behavior (TPB) offers another valuable perspective for exploring the factors that influence information security behavior, which is vulnerable to security breaches [26]. Crossler et al. [27] supported this claim, highlighting the importance of behavioral information security research in protecting and mitigating threats to information assets and computer-based systems. An analysis of the cybersecurity perspective pertaining to mobile usage and digital addiction indicated a positive influence on intention and security behaviors [28]. In addition, the Security Behavior Intention Scale (SeBIS) based on the Serge Egelman Model has gained recognition in the media and popular press as a tool for measuring young people's intentions to engage in secure behavior related to cloud services [29]. Furthermore, an empirical investigation was conducted to explore the factors influencing employee information security behavior and analyze the relationship between attitude, subjective norm, and perceived behavioral control using related theories and models [26].

2.2 Factors Contributing to Online Game Addiction

Figure 1 depicts the factors that contribute to online game addiction as suggested by Yaacob et al. [2], which include Salience, Tolerance, Mood Modification, Problems, Conflict, Withdrawal and Relapse. Such factors categorize individuals with a strong inclination towards online game addiction, who are often driven by escapism and the desire to escape their real-life circumstances. It also indicates a strong propensity to develop addictive behaviors while engaging in online gaming, which may lead to negative habits, such as stress, anxiety and other distractions.

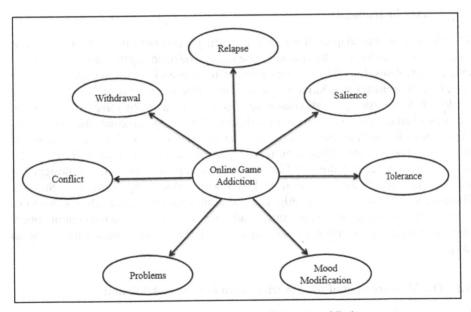

Fig. 1. Factors contributing to online game addiction.

3 Methodology

This study employed a quantitative research approach, utilizing an online survey with the online game addiction scale as its main instrument [5]. This research begins with the development of the scale, which was then distributed via Google Form during scheduled session. The data collection took place over approximately one and a half months, during which adolescents were invited to participate through email and poster announcements. The collected responses were carefully reviewed and compiled until all the necessary details were obtained. The online survey was performed successfully in April 2022 involving 660 late adolescents (17–19 years) from various HLIs including universities, polytechnics and community colleges located in four regions in West Malaysia (Northern, Eastern, Center and Southern). The participants were randomly selected among late adolescents, as recommended by Bekir and Çelik [11] who observed that this particular age range recorded the highest inclination towards online game addiction. The stratified sampling and probability sampling approaches were utilized as the data collection method in order to enrich the results. The sample was split into multiple categories and subsamples were randomly collected from each stratum. This approach enhances the survey's accuracy since it ensures representation of subgroups in the study. The participants were also explicitly informed that their statements would be treated confidentially and solely utilized by researchers for research purposes. This measure was implemented to improve the privacy aspects concerning the responses provided by the participants.

3.1 Survey Instrument

The instrument was adapted from several existing measurements found in literature. These measurements were thoroughly reviewed and deemed highly relevant to the specific context of this study. The two most relevant instruments for assessing security factors (i.e., Cybercognition) are Online Cognition Scale (OCS) and Online Game Addiction Scale (OGAS). A survey questionnaire that meets the research objectives was developed by incorporating two scales and aligning them with the proposed conceptual model and hypotheses. To validate the questionnaire, an expert review session was carried out, involving experts selected based on their experience in the Information Systems (IS) and Information Security domain. Each construct's measurement scale was designed as a five-point Likert Scale, ranging from 1 to 5, with options ranging from '1' Strongly Disagree to '5' Strongly Agree [30]. The five-point Likert Scale was chosen due to its extensive range and ability to discourage participants from choosing the neutral option. Most importantly, using this scale can help reduce the likelihood of bias in the responses [31].

3.2 The Measurement of the Severity of Online Game Addiction

The severity of online gaming addiction is measured with a related algorithm to assess the answers provided, calculate an addiction index and divide the participants into addicted and non-addicted groups [2]. Previous researchers have performed the process of developing the algorithm, which also involved reliability testing. This algorithm started by calculating the addiction index, which was used to compare the recorded score from the participants in the online survey that contributes to the severity of online game addiction. At the end of this stage, two distinct types of clusters were identified: addicted and non-addicted users. Other data on online gaming activity as well as the seven components outlined in the scale, which were thought to strengthen the efficiency and correlate between the levels of online game addiction, were also evaluated.

3.3 Hypotheses

Protection Motivation and Secure Intention Behavior. As highlighted in related studies, secure intention behavior is closely linked to human cognition. For example, Hadlington [32] proposed a hypothesis based on protection motivation emphasizing cognition's role in cyber security. Similarly, Durak [33] found that human cognition, particularly in cybersecurity, is crucial for developing secure intention behavior among adolescents addicted to online games and who share personal information online. However, Blackwell et al. [34] argued that further empirical evidence is needed to support this assumption, as their study on the predictors of addiction in the context of fear of missing out did not find a significant relationship with extraversion and neuroticism. Despite this, Briggs et al. [18] supported the notion that human cognition positively affects behavior change interventions for cybersecurity. Hadlington [35] also drew inspiration from the study by Sparrow et al. [36] on the cognitive consequences of possessing information on addictive behavior. These findings align with the fundamental importance of cognitive and behavioral concepts in cybersecurity activities, as highlighted by Hadlington in 2013 [32]. Given these arguments and the consistent findings, this study believes that further exploration of the relationship between human factors in cybersecurity and online game addiction in relation to cybersecurity behaviors is urgently needed. By building on the previous arguments and the consistent findings, the current study believes that further exploration of the relationship between human factors in cybersecurity and online game addiction in relation to cybersecurity behaviors is urgently needed [37]. Therefore, the current study proposed the following hypothesis:

H1. The protection motivation of respondents positively influences secure intention behavior towards phishing attacks in online game environments.

Addiction Severity and Secure Intention Behavior. For the second hypothesis, the assumption was grounded based on what has been discovered by Briggs et al. [18] regarding behavior change intervention for cybersecurity that related to the severity of online game addiction and secure intention behavior. While research on game addiction has been conducted in various multidisciplinary fields such as sociology, psychology and health care over the past decade [38] studies on game addiction in the context of cybersecurity context are still limited. The studies on addiction in biopsychosocial framework and the game addiction scale for adolescents by prominent scholars like Griffiths [39] and Lemmens et al. [40] have been referred as important fundamentals that support the current study. Regarding to human behavior and online game addiction in the cybersecurity perspective, this notion is also supported by Hadlington [37] and Durak [33]. The current study hypothesizes that the factors related to online game addiction would influence secure intention behavior among adolescents. Previous research has shown a significant correlation between online game addiction and secure intention behavior that support this hypothesis [18, 39, 40]. Therefore, the second hypothesis is proposed as follows:

H2. The severity of online game addiction positively influences secure intention behavior towards phishing attacks in online game environments.

4   Results and Findings

4.1   Demographic Details

The questionnaires were distributed to the selected HLI via online and walk-ins. Out of 850 distributed questionnaires, 713 were returned, accounting for an approximate response rate of 82.0%. The rate of questionnaire completion is impressively high with 87.0% of respondents using the online platform, while 13.0% preferred to answer on paper. The collected responses went through data preparation to eliminate any outliers or missing values as part of the data screening procedure. Of the 660 respondents, 355 were males (53.8%) and 305 were females (46.2%), with an average age of 19 years. The proportion is deemed acceptable since Malaysian gamers typically consist of a larger proportion of males in the adolescent age group. The ratio is considered valid for any statistical analysis as there are no sample size assumptions for comparing the two groups [41]. The respondents were distributed across various levels of education, with university students accounting for 16.2%, polytechnic students comprising 68.0% and community college students making up 15.6% of the sample. The participants were selected based on data from the Ministry of Higher Education Malaysia's website, encompassing urban (60.6% of the sample) and rural settings (39.4% of the sample). Regarding ethnicity, more than 79.1% of the respondents were Malay, while the remaining 20.9% represented ethnic backgrounds. The most common level of education was a diploma (68.2%), followed by a bachelor's degree (16.2%) and a certificate (15.6%). Table 1 presents a detailed breakdown of the demographic characteristics of the respondents.

Table 1. The demographic characteristic of respondents

Demographics	Category	Frequency	Percentages
Gender	Male	355	53.8
	Female	305	46.2
Age	17	105	15.9
	18	135	20.9
	19	420	63.2
Race	Malay	522	79.1
	Chinese	43	7.0
	India	36	5.0
	Others	59	9.0
Education Level	Bachelor	62	9.0
	Diploma	495	75.0
	Certificate	103	16.0

(*continued*)

Table 1. (*continued*)

Demographics	Category	Frequency	Percentages
HLI	University	107	16.2
	Polytechnic	450	68.2
	Community College	103	15.6
Institution Location	Urban	400	60.6
	Rural	260	39.4

4.2 The Severity of Online Game Addiction

Table 2 displays the scores and corresponding categories of online game addiction, utilizing the algorithm described by Yaacob et al. [2]. The data in the table shows that 35.0% of the sample, comprising 251 out of 660 individuals, were classified as addicted users. In contrast, 409 individuals obtained a score of 3 or below, indicating a non-addicted category. This finding strongly supports the notion that a significant portion of individuals in the sample exhibit a pronounced inclination towards online game addiction.

Table 2. Online game addiction level

Score	Amount of user	Category
1	32	Non-Addicted
2	191	Non-Addicted
3	186	Non-Addicted
4	150	Addicted
5	76	Addicted
6	19	Addicted
7	6	Addicted

4.3 Hypotheses Testing

The outcomes from the hypotheses testing in this study indicated a positive significant effect between all the constructs. The first hypothesis H1 investigated in this study hypothesized that protection motivation should positively influence the secure intention behavior. From the PLS path analysis, it was found that these constructs are positively related at 0.01 of the significance level ($\beta = 0.757$, t = 31.683, p < 0.01) (See Table 3).

For the second hypothesis H2, the interaction of the severity of online game addiction has a significant effect ($\beta = 0.106$, t = 4.149, p < 0.05) on the secure intention behavior.

This suggests that the degree of an individual's addiction to online games positively influences their behavior regarding phishing attacks in the context of online games. (See Table 3). Therefore, H2 is supported.

Table 3. Hypotheses testing

Hypothesis		β	T Values	p Values	95% CI	Result
H1	PM -> SIB	0.757	31.683	0.00***	0.709, 0.800	*Supported*
H2	SOGA -> SIB	0.106	4.149	0.00***	0.160, 0.059	*Supported*

Note. PM = Protection Motivation, SOGA = Severity of Online Game Addiction, SIB = Secure Intention Behavior

5 Discussion

Hypothesis H1 proposed in this study postulates that protection motivation would positively influence secure intention behavior. The analysis of the relationship between protection motivation and secure intention behavior is found to be supported and significant at the level of 0.01 ($\beta = 0.757, t = 31.683, p < 0.01$). Most importantly, it indicates that the participants are inclined to avoid sharing personal information in online games to protect themselves from phishing attacks. Furthermore, adolescents are encouraged to follow the practice of not sharing personal information and to act in line with the intention of safeguarding their personal data in online games t to protect themselves from phishing attacks. As a result, they are less likely to click on any message popups that appear while playing online games. The student also should verify any messages and emails that prompt them to provide financial and personal information in the context of online games. Furthermore, they should refrain from responding to messages from unknown sources that request username and password updates, always verifying information before updating online games. Adopting such secure intention behaviors reduces the risk of becoming the falling victim to phishing attacks. This finding justifies that higher protection motivation leads to a greater inclination towards secure intention behavior within the online gaming environment among adolescents. The results obtained from this analysis add to the growing body of research that supports the positive relationship between protection motivation and secure intention behavior from a security perspective [18, 22, 32, 33, 42].

In reviewing the literature, no empirical evidence was found regarding the association between the severity of online game addiction and secure intention behavior (H2) towards phishing attacks in the online gaming environments. Nevertheless, several prior studies [2, 4, 33] have suggested that the severity of online game addiction could significantly influence intentional behavior implementation, leading to the formulation of hypothesis H2. The analysis of the relationship between the severity of online game addiction and secure intention behavior is found to be significant at the level of 0.01 ($\beta = 0.106, t = 4.149, p < 0.05$). This aligns with expectations from the literature, which proposed that the severity of online game addiction would indeed impact the relationship with secure intention behavior [46, 56]. Considering these findings, it can be concluded that the seven factors of online game addiction (salience, tolerance, mood modification, withdrawal, relapse, conflict and problems) positively influence secure intention behavior. For example, the salience factor indicates that gaming activities become adolescents' primary focus to escape from their daily problems. The tolerance factor highlights the increasing time consumption in playing games over time. The mood modification factor suggests that adolescents experience "high" and "buzz" while playing online games all day. The withdrawal factor leads to an unpleasant and depressed feeling when unable to play online games. The relapse factor results in difficulties reducing the time spent on playing online games. The aspect of conflict within online game addiction pertains to adolescents encountering interpersonal disputes arising from their gaming activities. Finally, these adolescents experience problems such as ignoring other activities, assignments and homework due to excessive engagement in online gaming.

6 Conclusion and Future Work

The study sheds light on the importance of considering protection motivation and the severity of online game addiction in fostering secure intention behavior among adolescents. The findings suggest that protection motivation can positively influence secure intention behavior, while the severity of online game addiction may have a detrimental impact on it. Therefore, interventions addressing both these factors could be essential in promoting safe and responsible online behavior. The findings also highlight the importance of education programs aimed at raising awareness about the risks associated with cybercognition and secure intention behavior. Such programs can play a crucial role in enhancing online safety practices among adolescents. Additionally, counseling and therapy programs may be necessary for individuals exhibiting high levels of online game addiction severity. These programs can address the root causes of addiction and encourage the development of healthy coping mechanisms to ensure better overall well-being.

Overall, the study provides valuable insights into the relationship between protection motivation, the severity of online game addiction and secure intention behavior. The findings hold potential to guide the development of interventions that promote safe and responsible online behavior while addressing the negative consequences of online game addiction. Nonetheless, there is still ample room for further research in this field. Future work can build upon these findings and further explore the complex relationships between these variables. Conducting longitudinal studies that track changes in protection motivation, the severity of online game addiction and secure intention behavior over time can provide a more nuanced understanding of these relationships. This can help to identify the specific factors that contribute to changes in these variables over time, leading to the development of targeted interventions. Cross-cultural studies should also be considered to expand the scope of this research. While this study focused on a specific population of late adolescent students in Malaysia, exploring these relationships in different cultural contexts can uncover cultural factors that might influence them. This can lead to the development of culturally appropriate interventions since such studies are essential in this domain. Developing and testing interventions to promote protective behavior and reduce the severity of online game addiction among adolescents can yield valuable insights. Such interventions may include educational programs to raise awareness about the risks associated with cybercognition and therapy programs tailored for individuals with high levels of online game addiction severity. Through these future endeavors, a more comprehensive understanding of the complex relationships between protection motivation, the severity of online game addiction and secure intention behavior in online game addiction among adolescents in the context of online gaming can be achieved. This will contribute significantly to promoting healthier and safer online behaviors among young individuals.

Acknowledgement. This research was supported by Ministry of Higher Education (MoHE) through Fundamental Research Grant Scheme (Ref: FRGS/1/2020/ICT03/UUM/02/1). The content of this article is solely the responsibility of the authors and does not necessarily represent the official views of the MoHE, Malaysia.

References

1. Xu, Z., Turel, O., Yuan, Y.: Online game addiction among adolescents: motivation and prevention factors. Eur. J. Inf. Syst. **21**, 321–340 (2012). https://doi.org/10.1057/ejis.2011.56
2. Yaacob, W.M.Y.W., Zakaria, N.H., Aji, Z.M.: Identification of factors contributing to online game addiction among adolescents. Inf. J. Technol. Commun. **4**, 565–597 (2021)
3. Van Rooij, A.J., Schoenmakers, T.M., Vermulst, A.A., Van Den Eijnden, R.J.J.M., Van De Mheen, D.: Online video game addiction: identification of addicted adolescent gamers. Addiction **106**, 205–212 (2011). https://doi.org/10.1111/j.1360-0443.2010.03104.x
4. Kuss, D.J., Louws, J., Wiers, R.W.: Online gaming addiction? Motives predict addictive play behavior in massively multiplayer online role-playing games. Cyberpsychol. Behav. Soc. Netw. **15**, 480–485 (2012). https://doi.org/10.1089/cyber.2012.0034
5. Başol, G., Kaya, A.B.: Motives and consequences of online game addiction: a scale development study. Noropsikiyatri Arsivi. **55**, 225–232 (2018). https://doi.org/10.5152/npa.2017.17017
6. Balakrishnan, J., Griffiths, M.D.: Loyalty towards online games, gaming addiction, and purchase intention towards online mobile in-game features. Comput. Hum. Behav. **87**, 238–246 (2018). https://doi.org/10.1016/j.chb.2018.06.002
7. Kuss, D.J., Griffiths, M.D.: Online social networking and addiction-a review of the psychological literature. Int. J. Environ. Res. Public Health **8**, 3528–3552 (2011). https://doi.org/10.3390/ijerph8093528
8. Kuss, D.J., Griffiths, M.D.: Internet gaming addiction: a systematic review of empirical research. Mental Health Addict. **10**, 278–296 (2012). https://doi.org/10.1007/s11469-011-9318-5
9. Mojika, E.: Spil Games (2019)
10. Kuss, D.J., Griffiths, M.D.: Internet and gaming addiction: a systematic literature review of neuro imaging studies. Brain Sci. **2**, 347–374 (2012). https://doi.org/10.3390/brainsci2030347
11. Bekir, S., Çelik, E.: Examining the factors contributing to adolescents' online game addiction. Anales de Psicologia. **35**, 444–452 (2019). https://doi.org/10.6018/analesps.35.3.323681

12. Meschtscherjakov, A., De Ruyte, B., Fuchsberger, V., Murer, M., Tscheligi, M.: Persuasive technology. In: 11th International Conference, Persuasive 2016 Salzburg, Austria, 5–7 April 2016 Proceedings. LNCS (including subseries Lecture Notes in Artificial Intelligence and Lecture Notes in Bioinformatics), vol. 9638, pp. 288–300. Springer, Cham (2016). https:// doi.org/10.1007/978-3-319-31510-2

13. Ajzen, I.: From intentions to actions: a theory of planned behavior. In: Kuhl, J., Beckmann, J. (eds.) Action control. SSSSP, pp. 11–39. Springer, Heidelberg (1985). https://doi.org/10. 1007/978-3-642-69746-3_2

14. Ajzen, I.: The theory of planned behaviour: reactions and reflections. Psychol. Health **26**, 1113–1127 (2011). https://doi.org/10.1080/08870446.2011.613995

15. Shropshire, J., Warkentin, M., Sharma, S.: Personality, attitudes, and intentions: predicting initial adoption of information security behavior. Comput. Secur. **49**, 177–191 (2015). https:// doi.org/10.1016/j.cose.2015.01.002

16. Sheeran, P., Webb, T.L.: The intention-behavior gap. Soc. Personal Psychol. Compass. **10**, 503–518 (2016). https://doi.org/10.1111/spc3.12265

17. Alohali, M., Clarke, N., Furnell, S., Albakri, S.: Information security behavior: recognizing the influencers. In: Proceedings of Computing Conference 2017, 2018 January, pp. 844–853 (2018). https://doi.org/10.1109/SAI.2017.8252194

18. Briggs, P., Jeske, D., Coventry, L.: Behavior Change Interventions for Cybersecurity. Elsevier Inc., New York (2017)

19. Jenkins, J.L., Durcikova, A., Nunamaker, J.F.: Mitigating the security intention-behavior gap: the moderating role of required effort on the intention-behavior relationship. J. Assoc. Inf. Syst. **22**, 246–272 (2021). https://doi.org/10.17705/1jais.00660

20. Gratian, M., Bandi, S., Cukier, M., Dykstra, J., Ginther, A.: Correlating human traits and cyber security behavior intentions. Comput. Secur. **73**, 345–358 (2018). https://doi.org/10. 1016/j.cose.2017.11.015

21. Yoon, C., Kim, H.: Understanding computer security behavioral intention in the workplace: an empirical study of Korean firms. Inf. Technol. People **26**, 401–419 (2013). https://doi.org/ 10.1108/ITP-12-2012-0147

22. Jansen, J., van Schaik, P.: Persuading end users to act cautiously online: a fear appeals study on phishing. Inf. Comput. Secur. **26**, 264–276 (2018). https://doi.org/10.1108/ICS-03-2018-0038

23. Shakela, V., Jazri, H.: Assessment of spear phishing user experience and awareness: an evaluation framework model of spear phishing exposure level (SPEL) in the Namibian Financial Industry. In: 2019 - 2nd International Conference on Advances in Big Data, Computing and Data Communication Systems, pp. 1–5 (2019). https://doi.org/10.1109/ICABCD.2019.885 1058

24. Arachchilage, N.A.G., Love, S., Beznosov, K.: Phishing threat avoidance behaviour: an empirical investigation. Comput. Hum. Behav. **60**, 185–197 (2016). https://doi.org/10.1016/j.chb. 2016.02.065

25. Lebek, B., Uffen, J., Neumann, M., Hohler, B., Breitner, M.H.: Information security awareness and behavior: a theory-based literature review. Manag. Res. Rev. **37**, 1049–1092 (2014). https://doi.org/10.1108/MRR-04-2013-0085

26. Hazari, S., Hargrave, W., Clenney, B.: An Empirical investigation of factors influencing information security behavior. J. Inf. Privacy Secur. **4**, 3–20 (2008). https://doi.org/10.1080/ 2333696x.2008.10855849

27. Crossler, R.E., Johnston, A.C., Lowry, P.B., Hu, Q., Warkentin, M., Baskerville, R.: Future directions for behavioral information security research. Comput. Secur. **32**, 90–101 (2013). https://doi.org/10.1016/j.cose.2012.09.010

28. Ö₁ütçü, G., Testik, Ö.M., Chouseinoglou, O.: Analysis of personal information security behavior and awareness. Comput. Secur. **56**, 83–93 (2016). https://doi.org/10.1016/j.cose.2015. 10.002
29. Suarez, L.Y.T.: Young People's Security Behavior Intentions regarding Cloud Service Use: Suggestions for Better Cloud Services, pp. 1–27 (2015)
30. Comrey, A.L.: Factor-analytic methods of scale development in personality and clinical psychology. J. Consult. Clin. Psychol. **56**, 754–761 (1988). https://doi.org/10.1037/0022-006X. 56.5.754
31. Dwivedi, Y.K., Papazafeiropoulou, A., Brinkman, W.P., Lal, B.: Examining the influence of service quality and secondary influence on the behavioural intention to change Internet service provider. Inf. Syst. Front. **12**, 207–217 (2010). https://doi.org/10.1007/s10796-008-9074-7
32. Hadlington, L.: Cybercognition: Brain, Behaviour and the Digital World. SAGE Publications, London (2017)
33. Yildiz Durak, H.: Human factors and cybersecurity in online game addiction: an analysis of the relationship between high school students' online game addiction and the state of providing personal cybersecurity and representing cyber human values in online games. Soc. Sci. Q. **100**, 1984–1998 (2019). https://doi.org/10.1111/ssqu.12693
34. Blackwell, D., Leaman, C., Tramposch, R., Osborne, C., Liss, M.: Extraversion, neuroticism, attachment style and fear of missing out as predictors of social media use and addiction. Personality Individ. Differ. **116**, 69–72 (2017). https://doi.org/10.1016/j.paid.2017.04.039
35. Hadlington, L.: Cybercognition: brain, behaviour, and the digital world. Psychol. Learn. Teach. **17**, 323–325 (2018). https://doi.org/10.1177/1475725718787921
36. Sparrow, B., Liu, J., Wegner, D.M.: Google effects on memory: cognitive consequences of having information at our fingertips. Science **1979**(333), 776–778 (2011). https://doi.org/10. 1126/science.1207745
37. Hadlington, L.: Human factors in cybersecurity; examining the link between internet addiction, impulsivity, attitudes towards cybersecurity, and risky cybersecurity behaviours. Heliyon **3**, e00346 (2017). https://doi.org/10.1016/j.heliyon.2017.e00346
38. You, S., Kim, E., Lee, D.: Virtually real: exploring avatar identification in game addiction among massively multiplayer online role-playing games (MMORPG) Players Sukkyung. Games Cult. **12**, 56–71 (2017). https://doi.org/10.1177/1555412015581087
39. Griffiths, M.: A "components" model of addiction within a biopsychosocial framework. J. Subst. Use **10**, 191–197 (2005). https://doi.org/10.1080/14659890500114359
40. Lemmens, J.S., Valkenburg, P.M., Peter, J.: Development and validation of a game addiction scale for adolescents. Media Psychol. **12**, 77–95 (2009). https://doi.org/10.1080/152132608 02669458
41. Karen: When Unequal Sample Sizes Are and Are Not a Problem in ANOVA - The Analysis Factor (2017)
42. Hadlington, L.: The "Human Factor" in cybersecurity. IGI Global **3**, 46–63 (2018). https:// doi.org/10.4018/978-1-5225-4053-3.ch003

Designing and Developing M-Thyroid Care for Mobile Virtual Consultation

Ahmad Hanis Mohd Shabli[1]([✉]) [iD], Noorulsadiqin Azbiya Yaacob[2] [iD],
and Noor Rafhati Adyani Abdullah[3]

[1] School of Computing, Universiti Utara Malaysia, 06010 Sintok, Kedah, Malaysia
ahmadhanis@uum.edu.my
[2] School of Technology Management and Logistics, Universiti Utara Malaysia, 06010 Sintok,
Kedah, Malaysia
[3] Hospital Sultanah Bahiyah, 05460 Alor Setar, Kedah, Malaysia

Abstract. This research paper presents the design and development process of the M-Thyroid Care app, a mobile application prototype aimed at facilitating virtual video call-based consultations for thyroid clinics using design-based research. The app offers a convenient and accessible platform for remote consultations, enabling patients and healthcare providers, especially doctors, to engage through video calls. Additional features like chat functionality and file-sharing capabilities are incorporated to facilitate seamless communication and information exchange between patients and healthcare providers. The motivation behind developing M-Thyroid Care stems from the need to address the challenges associated with unurgent illness physical visits, specifically focusing on follow-up appointments for thyroid disorder patients. It is important to note that the app is not intended to replace physical visits but to assist clinics and healthcare providers in managing their time more effectively, allowing for more in-clinic consultations, particularly for new thyroid disorder patients. By eliminating the need for physical visits, M-Thyroid Care offers several benefits. Patients can save on travel, parking, childcare, and other related expenses, resulting in enhanced convenience and cost-effectiveness. Moreover, reducing physical visits can reduce traffic congestion and emissions, aligning with sustainable environmental practices. In summary, M-Thyroid Care represents a significant step towards leveraging mobile technology to improve thyroid healthcare consultations. The insights gained from the design and development process of M-Thyroid Care contribute to the broader understanding of designing mobile healthcare apps for remote consultations, serving as a valuable resource for future app development in telemedicine and mobile healthcare.

Keywords: M-Thyroid Care · Mobile Healthcare App · Virtual Consultations

1 Introduction

In recent decades, healthcare innovation improvements in product technology, treatments, and care delivery have successfully increased patient life expectancy and quality of life and made access to care, treatments, and diagnostic path options easier. Healthcare innovation is also generating efficiency, reducing costs and human errors. Mobile

N. H. Zakaria et al. (Eds.): ICOCI 2023, CCIS 2002, pp. 43–55, 2024.
https://doi.org/10.1007/978-981-99-9592-9_4

devices and apps have provided many benefits for health service providers, allowing them to make more rapid decisions with a lower error rate, increasing the quality of data management and accessibility, and improving practice efficiency and knowledge [1–3]. With the advancements in technology and the widespread availability of smartphones and tablets, virtual consultations have become increasingly accessible and convenient for doctors and patients. These mobile devices provide a portable platform for patients to connect with their doctors from their homes, eliminating physical visits to a healthcare facility. Patients can engage in real-time discussions with their doctors, receive medical advice, attend virtual presentations, and collaborate on their treatment plans through mobile apps and web conferencing platforms. The convenience and accessibility of teleconsultations have been widely highlighted in numerous studies [4, 5]. These studies indicate that patients [6–8] and healthcare providers [8–10] generally express high levels of satisfaction with this form of healthcare delivery. The flexibility offered by mobile devices allows doctors to provide personalized care and patients to receive timely medical guidance, even when they cannot visit the doctor's office in person.

In line with this trend, M-Thyroid Care, a functional prototype of a mobile application, has been designed and developed to address the specific needs of thyroid clinics. The primary objective of this app is to implement virtual video call-based consultations, thereby reducing the number of non-critical physical consultation visits among thyroid patients. By leveraging the app's capabilities, patients and doctors can engage in virtual consultations, chat interactions and seamlessly share files, videos, and images. By leveraging virtual consultations, healthcare providers can enhance patient satisfaction by providing convenient and efficient care delivery. This convenience not only saves patients time but also eliminates the need to endure long queues or traffic jams, contributing to reduced emissions. Additionally, the burden of travel expenses, parking fees, and childcare can be minimized, offering cost savings to patients [11–13]. Moreover, virtual consultations allow clinics to optimize their time management, enabling them to accommodate more in-clinic consultations [14, 15], particularly for specialists who need to see new thyroid disorder patients. Adopting virtual consultations in thyroid clinics holds great potential for improving overall patient experience and optimizing healthcare resources.

2 Related Work

Developed countries have made remarkable strides in implementing virtual consultation apps, experiencing widespread adoption and seamless integration into their healthcare systems. Countries such as the United States, Canada, the United Kingdom, Australia, and several European nations have emerged as leaders in embracing virtual consultation apps, recognizing their immense potential in transforming healthcare delivery. The integration of virtual consultation apps into Malaysia's healthcare infrastructure is steadily gaining momentum as the healthcare system recognizes the potential benefits of telemedicine. With ongoing efforts to improve regulations, infrastructure, and reimbursement policies, Malaysia is actively working towards incorporating telemedicine and virtual consultations as integral components of its healthcare delivery model. Several telemedicine apps specific to Malaysia have been developed to facilitate virtual consultations, including DoctorOnCall, BookDoc, MyDoc, HealthMetrics, Teleme, MySejahtera, Naluri, and PingDoc. These apps offer a range of features such as video consultations, chat functionality, e-prescriptions, and access to medical records, providing convenient healthcare services for patients. However, among these apps, MyDoc, developed by MyDoc Pte Ltd, a Singapore-based digital healthcare company, stands out due to its comprehensive platform that can be accessed through iOS, Android, and web-based platforms. In addition to virtual consultations and medical record access, MyDoc includes appointment booking services, health monitoring, medication reminders, and health tips, offering a holistic approach to healthcare management.

While other appointment apps in Malaysia provide convenient ways to find and book appointments with healthcare providers, the specific scenario of thyroid clinics presents unique challenges. In thyroid clinics, doctors determine the appointment dates and times, and any available doctors may see patients. Therefore, there is a need to design and develop a dedicated app like M-Thyroid Care with a specialized appointment booking feature to streamline the process and ensure efficient scheduling and management of appointments, addressing the specific needs of thyroid clinics. By incorporating tailored features and functionalities, M-Thyroid Care can enhance the overall patient experience and optimize healthcare delivery in thyroid care.

3 Methodology

Numerous researchers have explored the application of design-based research as a robust research methodology in various studies [16–18]. The findings from these studies consistently revealed that design-based research was predominantly utilized for technological interventions and applications. For instance, [18] reported that a significant majority of interventions (68%) involved the integration of online and mobile technologies. In this study, the researchers adopted the framework proposed by [19] to define design-based research as a systematic four-step process. The first phase involved the "analysis of practical problems," wherein a specific problem was identified, and relevant literature related to the issue was thoroughly reviewed. The following research questions were formulated after analyzing the practical problem:

RQ1: What are the key components and features required to design an effective functional prototype system for follow-up consultation?

RQ2: How can mobile technology be utilized to develop a functional prototype system for follow-up consultation?

The "development of solutions" for the identified problem was the focus of the second phase that followed. Researchers conceived alternative answers, determined the research topic and development strategy, and then built a prototype to address the issue. The third step of the process was the "evaluation and testing of solutions in practice". Researchers thoroughly studied and tested the offered solutions in real-world settings to gauge their efficacy and viability. Finally, the fourth phase, termed "documentation and reflection," involved generating and documenting design principles derived from the research process. By adopting the framework proposed by [19], the researchers aimed to create an innovative and practical solution to address the specific needs of thyroid clinics, with the ultimate goal of improving patient care and optimizing healthcare resources.

4   Results

This paper focuses primarily on the second phase of the design-based research process, which involves the creation of a solution for the M-Thyroid Care application. During this crucial phase, a mobile application called "M-Thyroid Care" was designed and developed specifically for Android mobile devices. This application's main goal is to improve the entire experience for both doctors and patients by efficiently addressing the practical issues that thyroid clinics face.

4.1   M-Thyroid Care Application Design

M-Thyroid Care has been meticulously designed using a user flow process to establish a clear and structured sequence of steps and interactions for both doctors and patients when utilizing the mobile application. This user flow process serves to illustrate the different paths and decision points that users encounter while pursuing specific goals within the app. Each step in the user flow corresponds to a distinct screen or action that users can engage with during their interaction with the application. The user flow process of M-Thyroid Care encompasses three key stages: login and registration, new appointments, and appointment management.

Login and Registration. For the login and registration, the user flow process is illustrated in Fig. 1. The login process is started by the user by launching the M-Thyroid Care app. The user must input their registered information, including their email address and password, in the appropriate boxes on the login screen in order to log in. The user then taps the "Log-in" button after entering the required information. The app then compares the entered credentials with the user data stored in the system to validate them and gives the user access to their main screen if the credentials are legitimate and match the records. This main screen is especially suited to the user's function within the app, whether they are a patient or a doctor. Users who do not already have an account can register by choosing the appropriate registration option. The user is prompted during the registration process to enter the necessary information, including their name, email address, and preferred password. Once the user submits the registration form, the app starts a phase for email validation.

A user can start the password reset procedure in the M-Thyroid Care app by clicking the "Reset Password" link. The software asks the user to input their registered email address when they click the "Reset Password" option. The app validates the email address after receiving it before starting the password reset process. The user's registered email address is then sent an email with a link to reset their password. The user can access the password reset page on the designated web page by clicking the provided reset link in the email after getting it. The user can then type in and confirm a new password. The app validates the password reset and enables users to log in using their updated credentials once the new password has been successfully set.

New Appointment. For the new appointment, the user flow process is illustrated in Fig. 2. In the M-Thyroid Care app, doctors can set up new appointments with their patients by navigating to the current appointment screen. They can perform a patient search, select a time and date, and enter any relevant information. The patient receives an email

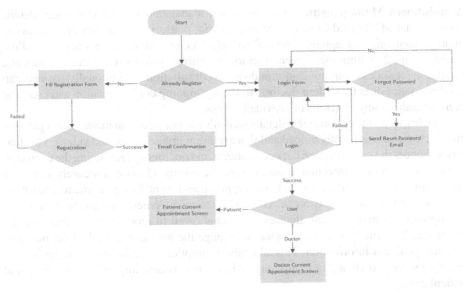

Fig. 1. User Flow Process for Login and Registration

notification with the appointment information after it has been scheduled. On the app's current screen, the patient can also see the appointment details. This procedure guarantees effective communication and makes it simple for doctors to arrange virtual consultations with their patients while keeping patients updated on their upcoming appointments.

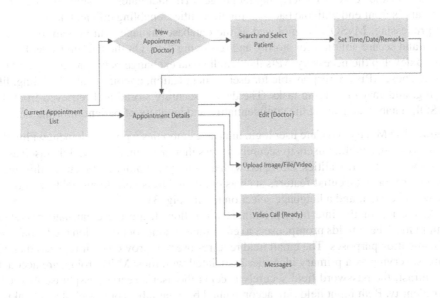

Fig. 2. User Flow Process for User Appointment and Appointment Details

Appointment Management. For appointment management, the appointment details screen in the M-Thyroid Care app serves as a vital platform for patients and doctors to manage their ongoing appointments effectively. The user flow process is further illustrated in Fig. 2. Within this screen, doctors can initiate video calls with their patients, facilitating seamless communication and virtual consultations. Additionally, patients can send messages directly to their doctors, fostering ongoing communication and enabling them to address any concerns or provide updates.

Furthermore, the appointment details screen's file management menu allows patients and doctors to conveniently upload and share relevant images, files, and videos. This feature enhances the collaboration between patients and doctors by facilitating the exchange of necessary medical information and diagnostic results. Users can securely store and access important documents related to the appointment by utilizing this menu, contributing to a comprehensive and organized healthcare management system. In the context of appointment management, doctors are also allowed to modify appointment details if needed. This function allows doctors to change the appointment schedule, purpose, or other pertinent information. This adaptability implies that appointments can be efficiently tailored to changing conditions or individual needs, improving efficiency and patient care.

4.2 M-Thyroid Care Application Development

The development of the M-Thyroid Care application involves leveraging the Flutter Software Development Kit (SDK) to ensure cross-platform compatibility for iOS and Android devices. Flutter's rich set of widgets creates a visually appealing and responsive user interface, providing a seamless user experience. The backend of the app is built using PHP, a versatile server-side scripting language. PHP facilitates the smooth integration of the app's front end with the backend functionalities, enabling efficient data exchange and processing. MySQL is employed as the database management system, offering a robust and secure solution for storing and retrieving data. On the backend side, PHP is used to develop the necessary APIs that handle data exchange between the app and the server. These APIs are responsible for user authentication, appointment scheduling, file sharing, and chat messaging tasks. The data is securely stored and retrieved from the MySQL database, ensuring the confidentiality and integrity of patient information.

Login. The M-Thyroid Care user login interface embodies a pivotal element within the digital system, enabling users to securely access their accounts and avail themselves of the associated functionalities. Designed with a focus on usability and security, this interface incorporates essential features such as email and password input fields, a "Forgot Password" option, and a language selection menu (Fig. 3).

At the top of the interface, prominently positioned, are the email and password input fields. These fields prompt users to enter their unique identification credentials for authentication purposes. The email field requires users to provide their registered email address, serving as a primary identifier associated with their M-Thyroid Care account. In contrast, the password field securely accepts the user's secret passphrase to verify their identity. Both input fields are accompanied by clear labels or placeholders, making it easier to enter the necessary information.

In addition to the email and password fields, the interface includes a "Forgot Password" tool to aid users with password recovery. This option is usually given as a distinct button or a clickable hyperlink. Upon selection, users are redirected to a password recovery page where they can initiate the process of resetting their password. This process commonly involves sending an email notification to the registered email address containing instructions for resetting the password and regaining access to the account.

Fig. 3. M-Thyroid Care Login Interface

Furthermore, the M-Thyroid Care login interface provides a language selection menu, allowing users to choose between English and Malay. Located at the top of the interface, this menu offers a dropdown or a list of language options, enabling users to switch between the desired language preferences. The interface adjusts its textual content and labels upon selection to reflect the chosen language, enhancing user engagement and convenience. The overall design and layout of the M-Thyroid Care login interface prioritize user experience and security. Error handling mechanisms are implemented to display meaningful and descriptive error messages should users encounter issues during login attempts. Such error messages aid in identifying and resolving login failures caused by invalid credentials or other security-related concerns.

Registration. The M-Thyroid Care user registration interface plays a crucial role within the digital system, facilitating the creation of new user accounts for individuals seeking to engage with the platform's healthcare services. This interface incorporates various elements, including user type selection, email, password, name, phone input fields, and a confirmation email feature.

The first step in the user registration procedure is to choose a user type. The interface offers a simple and straightforward way for users to select "Patient" or "Doctor" as their respective roles within the M-Thyroid Care system. This option sets the user's privileges, functions, and access levels after successful registration.

Following the user type option, the interface allows users to provide their email address, which serves as a unique identifier for their M-Thyroid Care account. The email input field facilitates reliable data entry and may include validation techniques to verify the format and authenticity of the provided email address. Aside from the email address, the interface includes a password input field, which allows users to create a secure and confidential password to protect their accounts. The password field typically incorporates security requirements, such as a minimum length or complexity, to enhance data protection.

Furthermore, the user registration interface features a name input field, enabling users to enter their full names. This field personalizes the user's account and facilitates future communication between the user and the healthcare professionals within the M-Thyroid Care system. The interface includes a phone number input field to enhance user registration further. Users are prompted to enter their valid contact number, facilitating potential communication regarding appointments, notifications, or other relevant updates. Similar to other input fields, the phone number input field may incorporate validation measures to ensure accurate data entry.

Upon successfully completing the registration process, users receive a confirmation email from the M-Thyroid Care system. This email serves as a verification mechanism confirming the successful registration of the user's account. It typically contains relevant account details and may include instructions or links for further account setup or activation.

Application Main Screen. The M-Thyroid Care main screen serves as a central hub within the digital system, presenting users with essential information and navigation options. This screen prominently features the current appointments section, menu access to appointment-related functionalities, user profiles, and the logout feature. However, it differentiates between patient and doctor perspectives, offering additional capabilities for doctors, such as creating new appointments using a floating button.

When users enter the main screen, they are greeted by an overview of their current appointments. This section gives a fast overview of upcoming or ongoing appointments, including important details such as appointment time, date, and essential patient or doctor information. The appointments are often structured in a well-ordered and easily scannable format, allowing users to grasp their schedule at a glance quickly.

The main screen has a menu for easy navigation and access to relevant features. This menu provides users with quick access to appointment-specific functionality, such as examining appointment history and accessing the user profile. Users may obtain a comprehensive record of their past appointments by selecting the "Appointment History" option, providing a handy reference for medical history or billing purposes. Similarly, the "Profile" option takes users to their personal profiles, where they can look into and edit their account information, preferences, and other pertinent information.

For improved user control and system engagement, the main screen contains a logout feature. This option allows users to log out of their M-Thyroid Care account securely, protecting critical information and assuring privacy. In terms of available features, the M-Thyroid Care main screen distinguishes between doctors and patients. In the case of doctors, an additional feature in the shape of a floating button created exclusively for creating new appointments is supplied. This floating button enables doctors to quickly start the appointment creation process, streamlining the workflow and allowing for more effective scheduling. Because doctors normally oversee appointment creation, this floating button on the patient main screen is absent.

Patient New Appointment. The New Appointment screen in the M-Thyroid Care system provides doctors with the capability to establish appointments with patients, facilitating efficient scheduling and effective healthcare management (Fig. 4). Within this screen, doctors are empowered to search for patients using various identifiers such as names, IDs, phone numbers, and email addresses. These search options allow doctors to swiftly locate the desired patient swiftly, ensuring accurate selection for appointment creation.

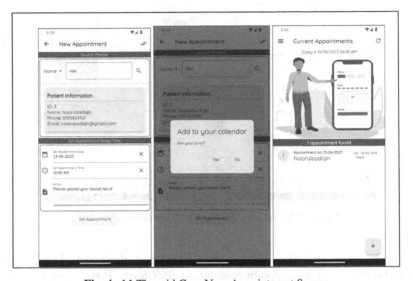

Fig. 4. M-Thyroid Care New Appointment Screen

Once the patient is identified, the New Appointment screen offers doctors the flexibility to specify the date and time of the appointment. Doctors can easily navigate calendar options and input the desired appointment date through an intuitive user interface while time slots are available for selection. This feature allows doctors to effectively manage their schedules and allocate appropriate time slots for patient consultations.

The Add to Calendar dialog in the M-Thyroid Care system offers seamless integration with the device calendar, facilitating the easy setup of appointment reminders. This dialog provides a user-friendly interface allowing users to incorporate appointment details into their device's calendar system effortlessly. Additionally, the New Appointment screen incorporates a remarks section, enabling doctors to include relevant information for the patient. This feature allows doctors to communicate specific instructions, guidance, or additional details related to the appointment. By leveraging this functionality, doctors can enhance patient communication, ensure preparedness, and promote a personalized healthcare experience.

Appointment Details. The Appointment Details screen within the M-Thyroid Care system serves as an essential interface for patients and doctors to access comprehensive information regarding their respective appointments (Fig. 5). Once a new appointment is created, users can navigate to the main screen list and select the desired appointment to view its details. The Appointment Details screen provides patients with crucial information such as the appointment's time and date and any accompanying remarks. However, specific functionalities within this screen are restricted to doctors only.

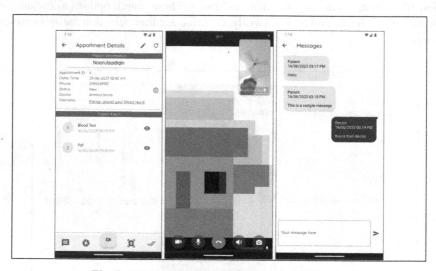

Fig. 5. M-Thyroid Care Appointment Details Screen

The screen design emphasizes user-friendliness and clarity, enabling patients to access and comprehend their appointment details effortlessly. Patients can readily view the scheduled time and date, ensuring they are well-informed about their upcoming medical consultations. Additionally, any remarks or additional information the doctor provides are displayed, offering patients important instructions or details about their appointments. Distinct from patients, doctors possess additional privileges within the Appointment Details screen. They can modify the appointment status to "Ready" to signal their availability and readiness for the appointment. This status change serves as an indication for patients that their doctor is prepared to engage in a video call or consultation.

The M-Thyroid Care application utilizes the WebRTC (Web Real-Time Communication) protocol to facilitate video calls between patients and doctors. WebRTC is a technology framework that enables real-time communication over web browsers without the need for external plugins or software installations. M-Thyroid Care's integration of WebRTC provides users with a seamless and secure video call experience. WebRTC makes use of a number of standardized communication protocols, including the Real-Time Transport Protocol (RTP), the Session Description Protocol (SDP), and the Interactive Connectivity Establishment (ICE). These protocols collaborate to build and maintain a direct peer-to-peer connection between the patient's and doctor's devices, enabling real-time audio and video transmission. There are various stages to integrating video calls utilizing WebRTC within the M-Thyroid Care application. To begin, the application initiates the connection procedure when a doctor sets the appointment status to "Ready" on the Appointment Details screen, indicating their availability for a video call. The SDP protocol is used by the patient's and doctor's devices to exchange session descriptions, which include information on media capabilities, network addresses, and encryption settings.

Following that, the ICE protocol is used to connect the devices, even in the presence of Network Address Translators (NATs) or firewalls. ICE employs several strategies, such as STUN (Session Traversal Utilities for NAT) and TURN (Traversal Using Relays around NAT), to select the best potential communication network path and solve network traversal challenges. Once the connection is established, the WebRTC framework allows for the real-time transmission of audio and video streams. The RTP protocol is used to packetize and transfer media data between the patient and the doctor, assuring timely delivery. WebRTC also enables advanced features such as adaptive bitrate control and echo cancellation, which improve the quality and performance of the video conversation. From a security standpoint, WebRTC's built-in encryption techniques ensure the privacy and integrity of the video call from a security aspect. Secure transport protocols, such as Datagram Transport Layer Security (DTLS), are used to encrypt media streams, preventing eavesdropping and unwanted access to the communication.

Moreover, patients and doctors can also use a menu button at the bottom of the screen. This menu button provides a variety of functions to improve the user experience. Users can attach photos, files, and videos to appointments, allowing for the effective sharing of medical reports, test results, and other associated materials. This feature encourages patients and doctors to communicate and collaborate effectively, allowing for a thorough grasp of the patient's situation.

In addition, the Appointment Details screen has a chat button, which allows patients and doctors to communicate in real time. This chat functionality promotes effective and convenient communication by allowing users to clear up any doubts, ask questions, or provide extra information about the visit or the patient's condition.

Following the conclusion of a video call session between a patient and a doctor within the M-Thyroid Care application, the doctor is prompted to set the appointment status to "Completed", indicating the end of the appointment. This action is an important step in the workflow to ensure proper record-keeping and maintenance of the patient's medical history. Following the completion of the appointment, the session details are made available in the Appointment History screen, allowing for comprehensive and organized documentation. By setting the appointment as "Completed", the doctor confirms that the session has ended satisfactorily and that all necessary medical interactions have happened. This is an important step in the appointment lifecycle since it marks the change from an ongoing consultation to a closed session. It allows both the doctor and the patient to clearly realize that the appointment's objectives have been reached.

The Appointment History screen is a repository for past appointment details, ensuring a complete record of the patient's medical history. This screen gives users, including doctors and patients, access to a list of completed appointments in chronological order. Each appointment entry in the history comprises pertinent information such as the date and time of the appointment, as well as any accompanying remarks and any extra notes provided by the doctor.

Profile. The Profile screen of the M-Thyroid Care application allows users to edit their user profile information, such as name, phone number, and password. This page is critical for keeping user profiles correct and up to date, facilitating effective communication, and assuring secure access to the platform's features. Users are presented with a user-friendly interface on the Profile screen that allows them to alter their personal information. The screen has input forms tailored to each profile attribute, such as the user's name and phone number. Users may quickly modify current information and submit updated details. It is crucial to keep the user's name up to date so that the app displays the user's accurate identity. Users can update this data to preserve accurate records inside the M-Thyroid Care system and promote easy communication with doctors.

5 Discussion and Conclusion

The prototype of the M-Thyroid Care application demonstrates a range of promising features that have the potential to benefit doctors and patients at thyroid clinics greatly. By providing alternative options for doctors, such as remote consultations and flexible appointment scheduling, the application reduces the dependence on physical visits and offers enhanced patient convenience. Specifically, patients with thyroid disorders can benefit from the app's ability to connect them with specialized medical expertise, resulting in improved quality of care. The inclusion of asynchronous communication further facilitates efficient information exchange between patients and healthcare providers, leading to increased patient satisfaction and active participation in self-managing their healthcare. Additionally, the app prioritizes secure data management, safeguarding patient records, and promoting seamless information sharing among healthcare providers. With its expected appeal to a diverse range of patients, including those in remote areas and individuals with chronic diseases, the M-Thyroid Care application holds significant promise. However, it is crucial to acknowledge and address potential technical issues or connectivity problems that may arise during video consultations to ensure a smooth user experience.

Acknowledgment. The authors express gratitude to the Universiti Utara Malaysia for funding this study under Research Generation University Grant S/O Code 21433 and Research and Innovation Management Center, Universiti Utara Malaysia, Kedah.

References

1. Wallace, S., Clark, M., White J.: 'It's on my iPhone': attitudes to the use of mobile computing devices in medical education, a mixed-methods study. BMJ Open **2**(4), e001099 (2012). https://doi.org/10.1136/bmjopen-2012-001099
2. Ozdalga, E., Ozdalga, A., Ahuja, N.: The smartphone in medicine: a review of current and potential use among physicians and students. J. Med. Internet Res. **14**(5), e128 (2012). https://doi.org/10.2196/jmir.1994

3. Mickan, S., Tilson, J.K., Atherton, H., Robert, N.W., Henegan, C.: Evidence of effectiveness of health care professionals using handheld computers; a scoping review of systematic reviews. J. Med. Internet Res. **15**(10), e212 (2013). https://doi.org/10.2196/jmir.2530

4. Gomez, T., Anaya, Y.B., Shih, K.J., Tarn, D.M.: A qualitative study of primary care physicians' experiences with telemedicine during Covid-19. J. Am. Board Fam. Med. **34**(Supplement), S61-70 (2021). https://doi.org/10.3122/jabfm.2021.S1.200517

5. Harrison, R., Macfarlane, A., Murray, E., Wallace, P.: Patients' perceptions of joint teleconsultations: a qualitative evaluation. Health Expect. **9**(1), 81–90 (2006). https://doi.org/10.1111/j.1369-7625.2006.00368.x

6. Agha, Z., Roter, D.L., Schapira, R.M.: An evaluation of patient-physician communication style during telemedicine consultations. J. Med. Internet Res. **11**(3), e36 (2009). https://doi.org/10.2196/jmir.1193

7. Nakornchai, T., Conci, E., Hensiek, A., Brown, J.W.L.: Clinician and patient experience of neurology telephone consultations during the COVID-19 pandemic. Postgrad. Med. J. **98**(1161), 533–538 (2021). https://doi.org/10.1136/postgradmedj-2021-141234

8. Nguyen, M., Waller, M., Pandya, A., Portnoy, J.: A review of patient and provider satisfaction with telemedicine. Curr. Allergy Asthma Rep. **20**(11), 72 (2020). https://doi.org/10.1007/s11882-020-00969-7

9. Bulik, R.J.: Human factors in primary care telemedicine encounters. J. Telemed. Telecare **14**(4), 169–172 (2007). https://doi.org/10.1258/jtt.2007.007041

10. Courtney, E., Blackburn, D., Reuber, M.: Neurologists' perceptions of utilising tele-neurology to practice remotely during the COVID-19 pandemic. Patient Educ. Counsel. **104**(3), 452–459 (2021). https://doi.org/10.1016/j.pec.2020.12.027

11. Moffatt, J.J., Eley, D.S.: Barriers to the up-take of telemedicine in Australia–a view from providers. Rural Remote Health **11**, 1581 (2011)

12. Albert, S.M., Shevchik, G.J., Paone, S., Matich, G.D.: Internet-based medical visit and diagnosis for common medical problems: experience of first user cohort. Telemed. e-Health **17**, 304–308 (2011)

13. Moffatt, J.J., Eley, D.S.: The reported benefits of telehealth for rural Australians. Australian Health Rev. **34**, 276 (2010)

14. Bhowmik, D., Duraivel, S., Singh, R.K., Sampath Kumar, K.P.: Telemedicine - an innovating healthcare system in India. Pharma. Innov. **2**, 1–20 (2013)

15. Cascardo, D.: Telemedicine: advancing from Idea to Implementation. J. Med. Pract. Manag. **31**, 82–84 (2015)

16. Krull, G., Duart, J.M.: Research trends in mobile learning in higher education: a systematic review of articles (2011–2015). Int. Rev. Res. Open Distrib. Learn. **18**(7), 1–23 (2017)

17. Zheng, L.: A systematic literature review of design-based research from 2004 to 2013. J. Comput. Educ. **2**(4), 399–420 (2015). https://doi.org/10.1007/s40692-015-0036-z

18. Anderson, T., Shattuk, J.: Design-based research: a decade of progress in education research? Educ. Res. **41**(1), 16–25 (2012)

19. Reeves, T.C.: Design research from the technology perspective. In: Akker, J.V., Gravemeijer, McKenney, K.S., Nieveen, N. (Eds.). Educational Design Research, pp. 86–109. Routledge, London (2006)

CNN-Based Covid-19 Detection from Two Distinct Chest X-Ray Datasets: Leveraging TensorFlow and Keras for Novel Results

Yaser Mohammed Al-Hamzi[✉] 🄳 and Shamsul Bin Sahibuddin🄳

Razak Faculty of Technology and Informatics, University of Technology Malaysia,
54100 Kuala Lumpur, Malaysia
mayaser1975@graduate.utm.my

Abstract. The Covid-19 pandemic has profoundly influenced global health and daily life across numerous countries, necessitating the urgent implementation of effective diagnostic strategies. This underscores the importance of advancing accurate, efficient, and rapid early detection techniques. In this context, convolutional neural networks (CNNs) have demonstrated remarkable proficiency in image recognition and classification tasks, particularly when applied to large annotated datasets. However, the domain of medical image classification presents significant challenges primarily stemming from the scarcity of annotated medical images such as chest X-rays images. Therefore, this study presents a new deep learning model for Covid-19 diagnosis from chest X-rays. Two distinct chest X-ray datasets from different sources are utilized for model training and testing. The proposed CNN-based model accurately calculates chest X-rays into positive and negative categories, providing an automated and efficient approach to diagnosing viral disease. This work holds significant importance for pandemic control and a safer future.

Keywords: Covid-19 Detection · Chest X-Ray · Convolutional Neural Networks (CNNs)

1 Introduction

The COVID-19 pandemic has had a profound global health and societal impact across numerous countries [1]. In this context, chest X-rays have emerged as crucial tools for testing and diagnosing COVID-19 cases during the recent outbreak [1]. Deep learning has emerged as a powerful disease detection and classification technology, enabling accurate predictions and timely interventions, especially for viral diseases using chest X-rays that are vital in diagnosing Covid-19 [2, 3]. Several studies have generally utilized deep learning techniques for various medical applications. For instance, skin lesion classification [4], cancer diagnosis [5, 6], liver tumour detection [7], early detection of diabetic retinopathy [8], and Alzheimer's progression prediction [9]. In Covid-19, chest radiography plays a crucial role in assessing lung involvement [10, 11]. For example,

© The Author(s), under exclusive license to Springer Nature Singapore Pte Ltd. 2024
N. H. Zakaria et al. (Eds.): ICOCI 2023, CCIS 2002, pp. 56–68, 2024.
https://doi.org/10.1007/978-981-99-9592-9_5

[12, 13] have applied deep learning models to analyze Covid-19 X-ray images. In particular, TensorFlow and Keras offer a high potential for Covid-19 prediction, diagnosis, and treatment planning [12, 14]. In addition, [15, 16] have employed a model based on TensorFlow achieved reasonable accuracy in predicting disease severity using CT scans. Moreover, a study conducted by [17] has developed a Keras-based model that accurately predicted patient mortality using electronic health records. On the other hand, convolutional neural networks (CNNs) have shown promise in medical image classification [11, 18]. However, the limited availability of annotated medical images poses significant challenges to accurate diagnosis [19]. As a result, various related works have explored the effectiveness of deep learning models in predicting Covid-19 progression, patient outcomes, and mortality rates. These advancements have significantly contributed to Covid-19 prediction, diagnosis, and treatment. However, the main limitation of the existing works lies in the relatively small size of the dataset used for model training and evaluation, which may affect the generalizability and robustness of the proposed method [1, 20]. To ensure broader applicability, further research is needed to validate these results on larger and more diverse datasets would be beneficial to assess the effectiveness of these models in real-world scenarios. This ongoing investigation ensures a safer future and effectively combat the pandemic.

1.1 Motivation

Despite some relief from the contagious virus, healthcare institutions worldwide still face many positive cases. Gaining insights from complex biomedical data remains challenging in healthcare transformation [3]. Deep learning models, implemented with frameworks like TensorFlow and Keras, have shown promise in predicting and analyzing viral diseases, including Covid-19 [2, 12, 14]. These models offer the potential for accurate and efficient Covid-19 diagnosis, patient monitoring, and treatment planning [12, 15, 16]. Chest X-rays have proven useful in detecting Covid-19. Therefore, this paper aims to propose a novel approach for Covid-19 prediction using deep learning techniques. The study uses two distinct datasets to develop a convolutional neural network (CNN) model that classifies chest X-rays into Covid-19 positive and negative categories.

1.2 Related Work

Several studies have applied deep learning to predict Covid-19 from chest X-ray images. A study implemented by [21], employed transfer learning achieved 86% accuracy on a small dataset. In addition, CNN and inception-v3-based models showed reasonable results, but more data was needed for better performance [12–14, 22]. Moreover, studies conducted by [1, 20] showcased the potential of deep learning in diagnosing viral diseases and provided valuable insights into the visualization of disease progression in Covid-19. However, the limitation lies in the relatively small final dataset images, potentially impacting the model's performance. Our research addresses limitations in previous studies, proposing a novel approach for accurate automated Covid-19 diagnosis. We utilize larger and diverse datasets, comprehensive data pre-processing, and employ techniques like data augmentation, dropouts, early stopping, and 200 training epochs. Our robust model validation methodology incorporates multiple performance metrics.

2 Problem Statement

The Covid-19 pandemic has significantly impacted global public health, necessitating effective diagnosis [11]. However, despite some relief from the contagious virus, healthcare institutions worldwide still face a significant number of positive cases. In addition, interpreting chest X-rays for Covid-19 detection presents challenges, with previous studies relying on limited data and radiologists' expertise [8, 12, 13, 17]. Therefore, there is a critical need for more accurate, efficient, and automated methods utilizing diverse and sufficient data. This paper addresses this issue by employing two distinct chest X-ray datasets for Covid-19 detection, classifying the data into COVID (+) and COVID (−), and creating separate train and test sets. The model is trained using TensorFlow, Keras, and a deep learning convolutional neural network (CNN) to enhance diagnostic capabilities.

3 Contribution

This study presents a new deep-learning model for Covid-19 prediction and detection using convolutional neural networks (CNNs). Two different datasets of chest X-rays are utilized to train and test the model. Employing multiple datasets from diverse sources enhances the robustness and reliability of the diagnostic and detection models. The research contributes a comprehensive methodology for data pre-processing, augmentation, feature extraction, and model performance evaluation for Covid-19 diagnosis. The study demonstrates the effectiveness of deep learning, TensorFlow, Keras, and related models in accurately predicting Covid-19. The model is trained for 200 epochs using techniques such as early stopping, resulting in high accuracy and low loss. This methodology can be extended to detect other viral diseases, facilitating early detection and timely treatment.

4 Methodology

This study presents a deep learning approach utilizing a CNN algorithm for feature extraction and classification of chest X-ray images into Covid-19 cases. The proposed methodology includes data pre-processing, augmentation, dropout, and early stopping techniques to address overfitting. The CNN architecture consists of multiple convolutional and pooling layers with appropriate activation functions. A dataset of 5,856 chest X-ray images from Kaggle and 930 images (Pneumonia/Normal) from GitHub, totaling 529 MB, was split into 70:30 ratios for training and testing. Bias removal was performed during data pre-processing. A binary classification model was developed using TensorFlow and Keras, employing a CNN with four convolutional layers, max-pooling layers, and dropout regularization. The model's performance was evaluated using metrics such as accuracy, precision, recall, F1 score, receiver operating characteristic (ROC) curve, and area under the curve (AUC). Figure 1 shows samples of selected PA (Posterior-Anterior) images.

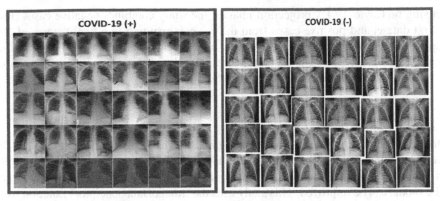

Fig. 1. The (COVID-19) PA (Posterior-Anterior) chest X-ray data images. On the left, we have 30 positive (abnormal cases) X-ray images; on the right, we have 30 negative samples (normal cases).

4.1 Dataset and Justification

This academic study employs two distinct chest X-ray (CXR) image datasets for training and evaluating a deep-learning model for Covid-19 detection Fig. 2. Using two datasets is crucial to ensure diverse representation, enhance model generalization, and validate its performance.

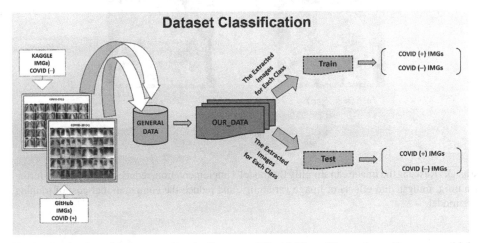

Fig. 2. Final selected dataset consisted of images of Covid-19 positive and negative cases, which were used to train and test the model.

Dataset selection prioritizes quality, relevance, and ethical considerations, omitting datasets containing issues or biases for scientific rigor. The first dataset, from Kaggle, consists of 5,842 expert-graded images, encompassing normal, pneumonia, and various viral cases. The second dataset from GitHub includes 930 images from diverse sources.

Focusing on Covid-19 PA projection images, the study combines negative cases from the first dataset and positive cases from the second, resulting in a final dataset of 392 images. The research highlights the potential of deep learning frameworks in diagnosing viral diseases using CXR images and incorporates data pre-processing, augmentation, and model performance evaluation using various metrics.

4.2 Data Pre-processing

Data pre-processing is crucial in constructing machine learning models as it prepares the data and eliminates noise and inconsistencies that may impact model performance. By performing data normalization, augmentation, and resizing, the accuracy and efficiency of the model can be improved. This study uses the 'ImageDataGenerator' function from the 'tensorflow.keras.pre-processing.image' module was employed for pre-processing. This function applies various transformations to the images, normalizes pixel values between 0 and 1, and resizes the images to dimensions of (224, 224) as shown in Fig. 3. Generators for the train and test datasets were created using the 'flow_from_directory' method of 'ImageDataGenerator', producing batches of augmented images for training and testing. The images were converted to appropriate arrays using the 'img_to_array()' function from the Keras package and then pre-processed using the 'preprocess_input()' method to meet the model's requirements. The processed images and their labels were appended to empty lists and converted to NumPy arrays using the' np.array()' function.

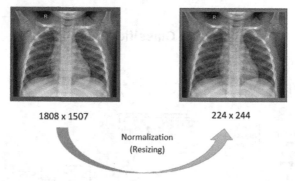

1808 x 1507   224 x 244

Normalization
(Resizing)

Fig. 3. Resizing the image can simplify the model's implementation, reduce memory usage during training, mitigate the effects of image variability, and reduce the computational cost of training the model.

5 Methods and Materials

We conducted experiments in Jupyter Notebook and Google Colaboratory [Colab], using Spyder Notebook to segment the data. TensorFlow, Keras, and CNNs were our main tools. The subsequent subsections elaborate on their roles. The following sections detail the software and hardware components used.

5.1 Software Components

In our experiments, we employed Python as the primary programming language and a 64-bit x64-based processor operating system for the personal PC device. The deep learning model was built and trained using the TensorFlow and Keras frameworks. The model architecture consisted of various layers: input, Conv2D, Max-Pool2D, Flatten, Dense, and Dropouts. ReLU activation function was used for convolutional and dense layers, while Padding, Strides, and Sigmoid were applied to the output layer. Libraries such as numpy, tensorflow.keras, matplotlib.pyplot, sklearn.metrics, and more were utilized for data processing, model building, evaluation, and visualization. Jupyter Notebook, Spyder Anaconda, and Google Colab were platforms for data classification, train-test splitting, and GPU-enabled model training, respectively. The model was optimized using Adam, an adaptive learning rate algorithm, and its performance was evaluated using accuracy, precision, recall, F1 score, ROC curve, and AUC metrics to assess classification and discrimination capabilities.

5.2 Hardware Components

We performed most of the experiments using GPU resources on personal computer devices or online platforms such as Google Colab. The specifications of the PC device we used are AMD Ryzen 73700X8-Core Processor with 3.6 GHz and 32.0 GB RAM and NVIDIA GeForce GTX 1050Ti GPU.

6 Implementation of Experiments

This section describes the practical experiments conducted for this study. The main steps include classifying the selected data into two classes: Covid-19 positive and Covid-19 negative, splitting the data into training and test sets, and training a convolutional neural network (CNN) model using TensorFlow and Keras to detect Covid-19 from the training data. As well as evaluate the model's performance on the test data and report the results.

6.1 Classify the Datasets into Two Classes

The paper proposes a method for classifying medical images as either Covid-19 positive or negative. We utilized the Pandas library to analyze the metadata file and extract technical information. The next step was to store Covid-19 positive and negative cases in a separate folder, managing file paths using the OS library and copying files with the shuttle library. Covid-19 positive cases were selected by iterating through each row of the metadata CSV file, identifying the target value in the "finding" column ("Pneumonia/Viral/Covid-19"), and selecting images with the "PA" view type. Covid-19 negative cases were randomly extracted from the Kaggle platform, choosing only PA images. The resulting dataset comprised 392 images for training and testing the model. This method efficiently and effectively organizes radiographic images for medical data analysis. We finally, partitioned the dataset into a 70/30 train-test split.

6.2   CNN Algorithm for Covid-19-Detection

The proposed training algorithm includes the model's structure, procedures, and details, serving as a concise guide for reproducing and improving the model's performance. The deep neural network architecture illustrated in Fig. 4 consists of convolutional, pooling, dropout, dense layers, and various applied techniques, as described in sextion 5.1. The primary deep learning algorithm employed and its associated inputs and outputs are illustrated as follows:

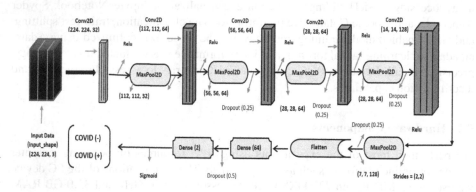

Fig. 4. The General Architecture of our CNN Model used in this Study

Algorithm: Training the Covid-19 detection algorithm and a convolutional neural network (CNN) was implemented in Tenso Flow and Keras to train the data and make predictions on the test dataset.

Input: There are two datasets employed in this study: First, a dataset of 5,842 X-Ray images (JPEG) of Covid-19 patient chest X-ray images (Pneumonia) which included various viruses, including Covid-19 with the size of 2.31 GB. Second, a dataset of 930 X-Ray images (JPEG) of Covid-19 patient chest X-ray images (Pneumonia) which included various viruses, including Covid-19 with a size of 529 MB.

Output: The output of the experiment is a robust automatic model capable of early screening and accurately predicting Covid-19 negative and positive cases.

7   Results

The results demonstrate the effectiveness of the proposed Covid-19 detection model, indicating its potential for clinical application in disease diagnosis and management. The model architecture includes an input layer with dimensions (224, 224, 3) and a Dense output layer with 2 units and sigmoid activation. It consists of a total of 568,706 trainable parameters distributed across various layers.

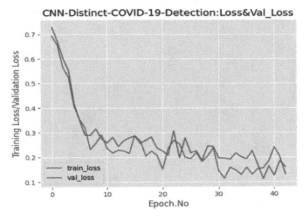

Fig. 5. The CNN model exhibits low loss on both training and validation data, indicating successful avoidance of overfitting.

7.1 Training Loss and Validation Loss

The training history plot of the deep learning CNN model Fig. 5 demonstrates low loss levels for both training and validation data.

The results indicate effective generalization and avoidance of overfitting, as evidenced by the convergence of training and validation loss curves, suggesting minimal error and successful generalization to new data.

7.2 Training Accuracy and Validation Accuracy

The training history plot of our deep learning CNN model indicates high accuracy and validation accuracy, suggesting effective avoidance of overfitting. The proximity of the accuracy and validation accuracy curves demonstrates successful feature learning and generalization. Refer to Fig. 6.

As a summary, the key findings from the results are as follows:

Low Loss: The loss consistently decreased over the initial epochs, indicating effective learning and progress.

Consistent Validation Loss: The validation loss remained consistently low, further supporting the model's ability to generalize well.

Early Stopping: The model did not require training for the full 200 epochs, suggesting convergence and limited additional improvement potential.

Overall, the results demonstrate the model's strong performance, accurate predictions on the validation set, avoidance of overfitting, and generalizability to unseen data.

High Accuracy: The model achieved an impressive accuracy of 97% on the validation set, indicating its ability to make accurate predictions.

Consistent Improvement: Accuracy consistently improved over the first 10 epochs, suggesting ongoing learning and progress.

Validation Accuracy: The validation accuracy remained consistently high, indicating the model's ability to generalize well and avoid overfitting.

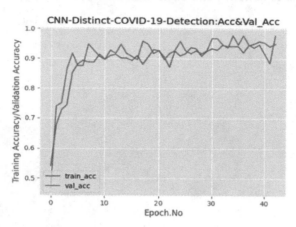

Fig. 6. The CNN model's training history plot demonstrates high accuracy on both training and validation data, indicating successful avoidance of overfitting. Early stopping confirms model convergence and limited scope for improvements.

8 Evaluation

We employed multiple metrics to evaluate our model throughout different phases. We monitored training and validation accuracy and loss in the initial phase, adjusting data augmentation and early stopping parameters accordingly. In the subsequent phase, we utilized Confusion Matrix, Sklearn precision, recall, F-score, and support to compute each class's precision, recall, and F1 score. These metrics assess the model's ability to identify positive and negative cases accurately. The Confusion Matrix, typically presented as a 2×2 matrix [A] in binary classification, summarizes the model's performance by categorizing predictions into true positive (TP), true negative (TN), false positive (FP), and false negative (FN) as illustrated in Table 1. The confusion matrix can be represented as follows:

Table 1. The confusion matric representation based on the actual positive and actual Negative for Covid-19 evaluation

	Actual Positive (P)	Actual Negative (N)
COVID (+) (P)	True Positive (TP)	False Positive (FP)
COVID (−) (N)	False Negative (FN)	True Negative (TN)

In our model the confusion matrix was generated as follows:

$$A_{2 \times 2} = \begin{bmatrix} 97 & 3 \\ 4 & 118 \end{bmatrix}$$

The following equations show how we calculate the accuracy mathematically in this study:

$$Accuracy = (TP + TN)/(TP + TN + FP + FN).$$

where TP is the number of true positives, TN is the number of true negatives, FP is the number of false positives, and FN is the number of false negatives.

$$Accuracy = (97 + 118)/(97 + 118 + 3 + 4) = 0.9685 \approx 0.97.$$

In evaluation stage the we compute the confusion matrix, the classification report, and the evaluation metrics. Thus, we generated the following results illustrating in Table 2.

Table 2. Classification report, precision, recall, F1 Score, and Support with up to 97% high accuracy

Classification Report	Precision	Recall	F1 Score	Support
COVID+	0.97	96	0.97	59
COVID−	1.00	1.00	0.97	59
Accuracy	—	—	0.97	118
Macro Avg	0.97	0.97	0.97	118
Weighted Avg	0.97	0.97	0.97	118

The model consistently achieved 97% accuracy in classifying Covid-19 cases from X-ray images, demonstrating high accuracy and consistency through manual and automatic calculations. The evaluation included using a ROC curve, which displayed excellent discriminative power with an AUC value of 0.93, indicating the model's ability to accurately differentiate between positive and negative samples Fig. 7. Based on the

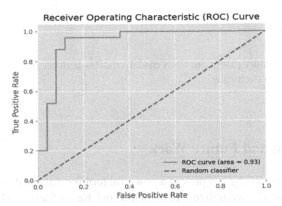

Fig. 7. The area under the ROC curve (AUC) is a measure of how well the model is able to distinguish between positive and negative samples of Covid-19.

results discussed in the evaluation section, the model exhibited exceptional performance in accurately classifying test cases as COVID-positive or COVID-negative. It showcased high accuracy and a minimal error rate, with no mistakes observed within this specific test set.

9   Discussion

This study aimed to explore the potential of deep learning with CNNs using TensorFlow and Keras frameworks for automatic detection and feature extraction in X-ray images related to Covid-19 diagnosis. We trained and evaluated a CNN model, achieving a high accuracy of 97% on training and validation data, as depicted in Fig. 8. The proposed automatic Covid-19 detector attained an accuracy of 0.9504 and validation accuracy of 0.9792, with respective losses of 0.1598 and 0.1312, on a dataset consisting solely of X-ray images. These promising results suggest the CNN model effectively learns relevant features. Nonetheless, this study contributes to the low-cost, rapid, and automatic Covid-19 diagnosis based on X-ray images, potentially reducing staff exposure to outbreaks. Future investigations should ascertain the reliability of features extracted by the CNN model as biomarkers for Covid-19 detection.

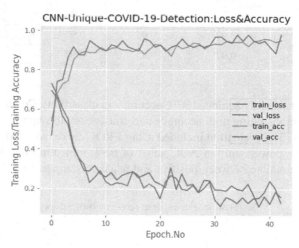

Fig. 8. The training history plot of our CNN model indicates high accuracy on both training and validation data, without overfitting.

10   Conclusion and Future Work

In healthcare, deep learning has proven a powerful tool for disease detection, including Covid-19. In this study, we utilized TensorFlow and Keras frameworks to construct a Convolutional Neural Network (CNN) model for Covid-19 detection using Chest X-ray images. The model achieved a high accuracy of 97% on training and validation data, displaying robust generalization and avoiding overfitting. Precision, recall, and F1 score metrics were high, and ROC and AUC curves demonstrated effective class discrimination. This indicates that the model successfully learned data features and can serve as a reliable tool for Covid-19 detection. However, it is crucial to emphasize that these models should complement clinical judgment rather than substitute it. Further evaluation of additional test data is recommended to ensure generalizability. Deep learning frameworks like TensorFlow and Keras hold significant potential for disease detection, aiding healthcare professionals in accurate diagnoses and improved patient outcomes. Future work should include larger and more diverse datasets, particularly for emerging and evolving viruses, and address the challenge of distinguishing mild symptom cases from pneumonia symptoms in X-ray images.

Acknowledgment. We sincerely thank all contributors for their valuable insights and suggestions, which significantly enhanced the quality of this article. We acknowledge that no funding source was involved, and the authors declare no conflicts of interest.

References

1. Zebin, T., Rezvy, S.: COVID-19 detection and disease progression visualization: deep learing on chest X-rays for classification and coarse localization. Appl. Intell. **51**(2), 1010–1021 (2021). https://doi.org/10.1007/s10489-020-01867-1
2. Lavecchia, A.: Deep learning in drug discovery: opportunities, challenges and future prospects. Drug Discov. Today J. **24**(10), 16 (2019). https://doi.org/10.1016/j.drudis.2019.07.006
3. Han, S.S., Kim, M.S., Lim, W., Park, G.H., Park, I., Chang, S.E.: Classification of the clinical images for benign and malignant cutaneous tumors using a deep learning algorithm. J. Investig. Dermatol. **138**(7), 1529–1538 (2018). https://doi.org/10.1016/j.jid.2018.01.028
4. Daneshjou, R., He, B., Ouyang, D., Zou, J.Y.: How to evaluate deep learning for cancer diagnostics – factors and recommendations. Biochim. Biophys. Acta Rev. Cancer **1875**(2), 188515 (2021). https://doi.org/10.1016/j.bbcan.2021.188515
5. Jiang, W., Zeng, G., Wang, S., Wu, X., Xu, C.: Application of deep learning in lung cancer imaging diagnosis. J. Healthc. Eng. **2022**, 1–12 (2022). https://doi.org/10.1155/2022/6107940
6. Zhang, H., Luo, K., Deng, R., Li, S., Duan, S.: Deep learning-based CT imaging for the diagnosis of liver tumor. Comput. Intell. Neurosci. **2022**, 1–7 (2022). https://doi.org/10.1155/2022/3045370
7. Mayya, V., Kamath, S., Kulkarni, U.: Automated microaneurysms detection for early diagnosis of diabetic retinopathy: a comprehensive review. Comput. Methods Prog. Biomed. Update **1**, 100013 (2021). https://doi.org/10.1016/j.cmpbup.2021.100013
8. Rahim, N., El-Sappagh, S., Ali, S., Muhammad, K., Del Ser, J., Abuhmed, T.: Prediction of Alzheimer's progression based on multimodal deep-learning-based fusion and visual explainability of time-series data. Information Fusion **92**, 363–388 (2023). https://doi.org/10.1016/j.inffus.2022.11.028
9. Yang, J., et al.: Prevalence of comorbidities and its effects in coronavirus disease 2019 patients: a systematic review and meta-analysis. Int. J. Infect. Dis. **94**, 91–95 (2020). https://doi.org/10.1016/j.ijid.2020.03.017
10. Abbas, A., Abdelsamea, M.M., Gaber, M.M.: Classification of COVID-19 in chest X-ray images using DeTraC deep convolutional neural network. Appl. Intell. **51**(2), 854–864 (2021). https://doi.org/10.1007/s10489-020-01829-7

11. Wang, S., et al.: Imaging informatics and artificial intelligence a deep learning algorithm using CT images to screen for Corona virus disease (COVID-19), pp. 6096–6104 (2021)
12. Apostolopoulos, I.D., Mpesiana, T.A.: Covid-19: automatic detection from X-ray images utilizing transfer learning with convolutional neural networks. Phys. Eng. Sci. Med. **43**(2), 635–640 (2020). https://doi.org/10.1007/s13246-020-00865-4
13. Kumar, S., Kiran, S., Mishra, N.: Face mask detection using OpenCV. Int. J. Health Sci. (Qassim) **2022**, 5282–5288. https://doi.org/10.53730/ijhs.v6ns2.6331
14. Song, Y., et al.: Deep learning enables accurate diagnosis of novel coronavirus (COVID-19) with CT images. IEEE/ACM Trans. Comput. Biol. Bioinform. **18**(6), 2775–2780 (2021). https://doi.org/10.1109/TCBB.2021.3065361
15. Zhang, J., et al.: Viral pneumonia screening on chest X-rays using confidence-aware anomaly detection. IEEE Trans. Med. Imaging **40**(3), 879–890 (2021). https://doi.org/10.1109/TMI.2020.3040950
16. Wang, L., Lin, Z.Q., Wong, A.: COVID-net: a tailored deep convolutional neural network design for detection of COVID-19 cases from chest X-ray images. Sci. Rep. **10**(1) (2020). https://doi.org/10.1038/s41598-020-76550-z
17. Tartaglione, E., Barbano, C.A., Berzovini, C., Calandri, M., Grangetto, M.: Unveiling COVID-19 from chest x-ray with deep learning: a hurdles race with small data. Int. J. Environ. Res. Public Health **17**(18), 1–17 (2020). https://doi.org/10.3390/ijerph17186933
18. Shi, F., et al.: Review of artificial intelligence techniques in imaging data acquisition, segmentation, and diagnosis for COVID-19. IEEE Rev. Biomed. Eng. **14**, 4–15 (2021). https://doi.org/10.1109/RBME.2020.2987975
19. Osman, A.H., Aljahdali, H.M., Altarrazi, S.M., Ahmed, A.: SOM-LWL method for identification of COVID-19 on chest X-rays. PLoS One **16**(2) (2021). https://doi.org/10.1371/journal.pone.0247176
20. Wang, Y.X., Balle, B., Kasiviswanathan, S.P.: Subsampled Rényi differential privacy and analytical moments accountant. In: Proceedings of the 22nd International Conference on Artificial Intelligence and Statistics (AISTATS 2019), no. 1, pp. 1–29 (2020). https://doi.org/10.29012/jpc.723
21. Hemdan, E.E.: COVIDX-Net : A Framework of Deep Learning Classifiers to Diagnose COVID-19 in X-Ray Images (2021)
22. Al-Hamzi, Y.M.: Neural network-based framework for understanding machine deep learning systems' open issues and future trends: a systematic literature review. Turkish J. Comput. Math. Educ. (TURCOMAT) **12**(12), 1567–1625 (2021)

Eye-Tracking Usability Data of BacaDisleksia for an Informed Dyslexia-Friendly Design Decision

Husniza Husni[1]([⊠]) [iD], Nurul Ida Syaheera Mohd Nasri[2] [iD], and Mohamed Ali Saip[1] [iD]

[1] Universiti Utara Malaysia, 06010 Sintok, Kedah, Malaysia
husniza@uum.edu.my
[2] SMT Technologies, 08000 Sungai Petani, Kedah, Malaysia
nurul.is@esmtt.com

Abstract. BacaDisleksia is an application specifically designed for children with dyslexia learning to read. The application aims to facilitate dyslexic children and ease their reading by carefully considering the Human-Computer Interaction and Interaction Design fundamentals that could facilitate them to read better. However, the design of BacaDisleksia is yet to be empirically confirmed. Therefore, a usability testing was conducted using Tobii eye-tracker to further examine its design. Six dyslexic children as participants were involved in the testing revealing design issues related to BacaDisleksia that can be improved based on eye-tracking data such as heat maps and gaze plots. As a results, this paper presents the eye-tracking usability findings that could inform dyslexia-friendlier design decisions for any application with a similar aim as BacaDisleksia. Such design decisions are crucial in digital innovation to provide better digital solutions for dyslexia and other learners with reading difficulties, in line with one of UNESCO's aims for having the technology to support inclusivity for children with disabilities, including learning disabilities such as dyslexia.

Keywords: Eye-tracking usability · human-computer interaction · interaction design · dyslexia

1 Introduction

Eye tracking data can be very useful and informative in facilitating the right design decision for certain specific aims, such as in education, as it provides insights into studying processes, revealing mental representation, and assessing subconscious aspects [1]. Especially when designing for specific users, in this case children with dyslexia that often push for non-standard design decisions, eye-tracking data can reveal significant details to inform further the design of such digital applications to facilitate and possible reduce cognitive load while learning to read. Hence, that is why it is important to obtain as much data as possible to gain insights into eye-tracking data from the children, such as gaze plots and heat maps. These two data could lead to improvement in the design.

N. H. Zakaria et al. (Eds.): ICOCI 2023, CCIS 2002, pp. 69–80, 2024.
https://doi.org/10.1007/978-981-99-9592-9_6

BacaDisleksia is an application designed and developed with the aim to ease the reading process by offering the children an interactive, self-assessed intervention for a stress-free reading session. Its fundamentals are based on three Interaction Design (IxD) dimensions [2] – text (1D), visual representation (2D), and behavior (5D) – leaving the other two dimensions untouched, i.e., space (3D) and time (4D). The three dimensions are selected based on the needs of children with dyslexia when it comes to an application for reading, as most of the interaction covers text, visual representation, and the application's behavior. The other two dimensions are not considered, as each child requires a different time and reads at an individual pace (4D). The interaction with BacaDisleksia is mainly using a mouse and very minimal use of keyboards. Since 3D is concerned with tangible means of control, it is not included, as any changes or improved aspects concern this dimension. Besides IxD, the Human-Computer Interaction (HCI) interaction model also serves as its base for the design, following the classic [3] interaction model. This application aims to provide an interactive reading tool that can facilitate children's reading better by introducing features that could ease learning to read, such as Irlen color theory [4] for the reading background.

In this paper, we explore the potential of using an eye tracker in a usability study with dyslexic children to uncover design decisions we could have missed when designing and developing the application. Such intricate eye-tracking data could potentially be considered to improve further the design aspects, not only on the user interface but also the interaction that comes with it. What are the usability issues that can be uncovered from BacaDisleksia? How does the eye-tracking help in conducting usability testing with children with dyslexia? What design suggestions can be made to improve the interaction and user experience for the children?

2   Eye-Tracking for Dyslexia

2.1   Dyslexia

Dyslexia is a neurological learning disability that particularly hinders a child's reading abilities [5, 6]. Despite having normal intelligence, these children frequently read at substantially lower levels than expected. People with dyslexia often struggle with spelling, reading comprehension, and the ability to learn a second language. Nonetheless, these issues are independent of their overall IQ level, as dyslexia is an unforeseen reading challenge for a child who is intelligent enough to be a far better reader. However, children with dyslexia who happen to be slow readers often, paradoxically, are very fast and creative thinkers with strong reasoning [6]. Dyslexia can be inherited in some families, and recent studies have identified a number of genes that may predispose an individual to develop dyslexia.

The main focus of remediation for dyslexia should be on the specific learning problems of affected individuals. The usual course is to modify teaching methods, tools, and the educational environment to meet the specific needs of the individual with dyslexia. That said, a good interactive tool should be designed and developed to suit dyslexics to assist their learning. A study by Lebeničnik [7] spells out that the key problems experienced by dyslexic users are confusing page layout, unclear navigation, poor color selections, graphics and text too small, and complicated language. Designers must consider these problems in creating learning material for a better course or program for a dyslexic child. This is where HCI and IxD pave the potential to assist in designing for specific users, using eye-tracking as a tool to dig deeper and understand better what is going on when users, especially children, use interactive digital solutions to learn to read.

2.2   Eye Tracking and Usability

Aside from traditional usability studies, particularly among usability professionals, usability experts have begun to use psychophysiological approaches to gain a deeper understanding of the user's attentional and cognitive processes [8]. One of the approaches is eye tracking. Eye tracking is a psychophysiological technique that has recently become very popular. Eye tracking has been employed to study visual attention distribution in various visual tasks, from visual search to reading advertisements to watching online videos. Eye tracking has also been applied in multiple usability studies to provide insights regarding the design of websites, digital TV menus, and games, to name a few [9].

The most popular method of visualizing data from eye-tracking studies is heat mapping. Heat maps are based on how many views each area receives. The term "heat map" refers to a visual representation of hot and cold spots on a page using various colors [10]. Users' focus will be presented in a color-coded section based on most paid to least paid attention areas. Figure 1 is an example of the heat map. The red area represents the most paid attention area, and the blue is the least paid attention area. Heat maps can also represent either the number of fixations or the duration of fixations.

Fig. 1.   An example of the heatmap by one of the participants captured while using BacaDisleksia to read the target word displayed.

Another data collected through eye-tracking is gaze plot. Gaze plots show a single user's visit to a page or software. Fixation will be presented by a dot. The bigger the dot, the longer the fixation of the users. Figure 2 is an example of gaze plotting. Blue dots represent the fixation, and the lines between dots represent saccades. A saccade is a rapid eye movement between two fixations, and saccades range in amplitude from small movements to large ones. Wu et al. [11] discovered, for example, that eye movement info, such as fixation duration and fixation point number, had been useful in showing what users search for target information on a smartwatch interface, revealing usability issues of specific features on the smartwatch. However, this view quickly becomes cluttered for long recordings, and the dynamic gaze replay or the hotspot visualization described below becomes more suitable [12].

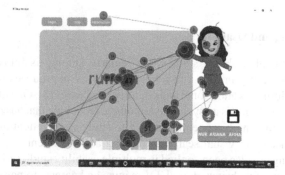

Fig. 2. An example of the gazeplot by one of the participants captured while using BacaDisleksia to read the target word displayed.

Although eye-tracking technology has been around for some time, studies on utilizing eye-trackers to observe design issues are very limited when it concerns dyslexic children. Most eye-tracking studies performed with dyslexia in mind are performed with adult dyslexics or focus on other aspects pertinent to reading, such as cognitive or neurological origin vs. eye movement for adults with dyslexia [13], cognitive impairment among children with dyslexia [14], and screening [15, 16].

3   Methods

3.1   Participants

Six children formally screened with dyslexia by Persatuan Disleksia Malaysia, Sungai Petani, participated in this study. The participants are children between 10 and 12 years old, sharing various demographics. They are purposively selected as they are bigger and have prior knowledge and skills in using the computer. Bigger and taller children are needed for a better eye-tracker calibration process. One limitation of using an eye tracker is its poor or limited detection when it comes to small children. Various reasons contributed to the poor calibration process with children, including sitting position, constant movement as children tend to move around, and difficulty sitting still at times, heights, and focusing on the screen. Nonetheless, we recommend the children from 10 to 12 years old, as they gave good calibration and smooth running eye tracking sessions.

3.2   Tools and Settings

The usability testing is conducted at Persatuan Disleksia Malaysia in Sungai Petani, Kedah. BacaDisleksia application is displayed using a computer attached to Tobii eye-tracker. The children were briefed and given a short tutorial on how to use the software before the start of the test. At the beginning of the test, the eye gaze of each participant is calibrated.

The calibration process may take quite some time to complete. Participants were advised to follow the following regulation to ensure successful calibration and avoid further issues during eye tracking. The regulations are no glasses, no hat, no physical objects that could potentially get between the eye and the eye-tracker, sitting relatively straight in the chair, does not fidget or move too much, and remains at about 20 to 23 inches from the monitor at all times, and remain positioned in the middle of the monitor at all times.

3.3 The Tasks

Five tasks have been identified based on the main functions and purpose of BacaDisleksia as listed in Table 1. With the five tasks, the participants were asked to express their thoughts during the test, following the Thinking Out Loud method. The premise is that users keep up a running commentary to say what they think as they attempt their tasks. This can help to better understand usability issues and suggest solutions to the problems faced. However, the tester has to facilitate the process by asking probing questions, considering that the participants are children with limited expression of thoughts and actions.

Table 1. The tasks specified for the usability test using an eye tracker.

No.	Tasks
1	Log in to the application
2	Change the colour of the syllables (avatar's clothing)
3	Change the colour of the background
4	Find the word 'bapa' and spell it aloud
5	Find and record the pronunciation of the word 'sayang'

While the participants carried out these tasks, the data on the achievement of each task, the duration taken to complete each task, and the difficulties encountered in performing the tasks were observed and recorded.

4 Results and Discussion

This section presents the results from the eye-tracking usability test conducted with the children and discusses the findings. Table 2 tabulates the performance of each participant in seconds. T1 to T5 denote Task 1 to Task 5, with 1 referring to successful attempt and 0 unsuccessful attempt. As can be seen, all five participants successfully completed all five tasks but with different duration spent to attempt each task.

Table 2. Performance tasks data recorded by eye-tracker.

Participant	T1	Time	T2	Time	T3	Time	T4	Time	T5	Time	Total time taken
P1	1	13	1	27	1	9	1	13	1	26	88
P2	1	55	1	19	1	22	1	18	1	38	152
P3	1	25	1	19	1	8	1	24	1	37	113
P4	1	23	1	12	1	5	1	12	1	35	87
P5	1	56	1	20	1	6	1	12	1	173	267
P6	1	49	1	40	1	15	1	21	1	27	152
Mean		37		23		11		17		56	

Referring to Table 2, Task 1, i.e., login into the application, has a fairly high average time as two participants, i.e., P2 and P5 spending over 50% than the average time. While Task 2 (change the avatar's appearance) has one participant that almost doubled the average time of all the participants. In addition, all participants' performances for Task 4 is almost around the average time suggesting that all participants did not have much problem completing the task. For task 3 "Change the colour of the board's background", the mean time taken to complete is the lowest. However, there is an outlier for this task as participant P2 took the longest time taken to complete at 22 s which is double the average time.

As for task 5 "Find and record the pronunciation" of the word 'sayang', the mean duration is the highest at 56 s. This task requires participants to find the word 'sayang' and record their pronunciation. Although all participants managed to complete the task, participant P5 however took the longest time of 173 s. Participant P5 also had the longest time recorded for Task 1 (56 s) which is "Log in to the application". Participant 5 also had the longest total time taken to complete all of the tasks, where the participant spent almost half of the time completing Task 5. The eye-tracking data was examined to understand usability issues in detail related to the task as only participant P5 had difficulty accomplishing the task.

Looking at the heat map in Fig. 3(a) and (b), the participant focused on the wording and the left and right arrows to find the word 'sayang', which is the critical area in searching for the word. This can be seen in the heat map zone that is represented in colour, for which area the participant focuses heavily on. The red color presents the most focused area followed by yellow and green. The heat zones at the arrow area to find next words and also the time spend on the wording at center also proved that the participant had difficulty in searching the words 'sayang' as compared to participant P1 which has a lesser density of colour in the two area.

In addition, from the gaze plot in Fig. 4(a) for participant P5 as compared to participant P1 in Fig. 4(b), the eye gaze of the participant P5 started to wander to another part of the interphase when the participant failed to find the word 'sayang'. Participant P1, which has the lowest completion time, shows much less fixation count. This shows that the focus and attention of the children started to lessen when they faced difficulty finding the word. Hence, choosing the right font, size, and design of how the word is

Fig. 3. a) Heat map for P5 Task 5, and b) Heat map for P1 Task 5.

presented is essential in aiding dyslexic children in finding the correct word. According to this data, the participant took a lot of time to complete the task.

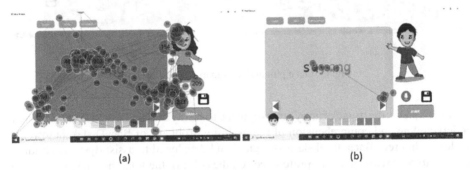

Fig. 4. a) Gaze plot for P5 Task 5, and b) Gaze plot for P1 Task 5.

For Task 1, participants P2 and P5 both have a high completion time to complete the login task. Participant P2 took high time to complete because instead of a nickname, the participant keyed in the full name. While participant P5 took some time to complete the task because participant P5 made a lot of typing errors and had difficulty differentiating the alphabet on the laptop's keyboard. According to the gaze plot in Fig. 5(a), Fig. 5(b) and Fig. 5(c), two participants spent quite some time typing their names, which showed that they had issues with either spelling their names or finding the letters on the keyboard, or both. Only one participant, i.e. P1 in Fig. 5(c) seems to not having much problem with the task the gaze plots are rather focused on the targeted area. All participants are computer literate but not frequent users except for P1.

Another notable finding is on Task 3 (Change the color of the board's background). The heat map and gaze plot data, as depicted in Fig. 6, participant P2 shows the gaze is not focused on the color-board palette at the bottom side of the interface, which is the area of interest for the task. The red colored shade is located in many areas – the character's area, level of difficulty area, and even at the word displayed. Hence, the placement of the color palette menu is also essential to avoid confusion to dyslexic children. The placement should be more visible and easier to reach.

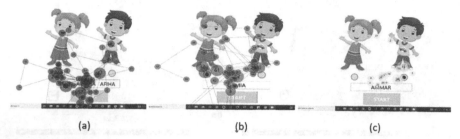

(a)   (b)   (c)

Fig. 5. a) Gaze plot for P2 Task 1, b) Gaze plot for P5 Task 1, and c) Gaze plot for P1 Task 1.

(a)   (b)

Fig. 6. Gaze plot and heat map for P2 Task 3.

In this study, the usage of an eye tracker in the usability of BacaDisleksia gives a better understanding and comprehension of the usability problems of BacaDisleksia towards dyslexic children. BacaDisleksia is designed and developed to assist dyslexic children to learn to read with their own preferences on the color of the font, the background, and the levels of difficulties, presumably reducing their cognitive load while attempting to read. To determine its usability issues, the evaluation was made to understand problems encountered during the children's learning session thus improving the design.

In addition to the traditional usability study such as the study of effectiveness, efficiency, and satisfaction, the usage of eye-tracker provides data visualization in the form of heatmaps and gaze plots. These two visualization data indicate the amount of time and the focus of the eye gaze spent and its movement. The significant intensity of the heatmap accumulated can be observed from participant P5 upon completing Task 5. The participant spent a lot of time at the word, causing the color intensity to darken thus showing the area of eye focus.

The significant gaze plot that shows a lot of eye movement can be found in participant P2 task 5. The eye movement of the participant shows that she encountered problems when trying to find the color palette to change the reading background colour. The color palette's position is located at the bottom side of the interface and besides the word level difficulties (denoted by three facial expressions). Participant P2 eye movement went all over the user interface rather than going straight to the designated palette to complete the task given. The user interface design may need to be reconsidered; for example, moving the color palette to the side of the user interface as the focus of the children may be distracted by the facial expressions (level of difficulties icons) at the bottom. Besides, the left side of the interface is not as crowded as the bottom side.

Although the children successfully completed all tasks, they were having difficulty operating the software because most dyslexic children are not good at using computers or have less experience using a computer. Most of them are novice users and rarely use computers. This can be shown when some of the children had difficulty typing their names, perhaps due to them having dyslexia and thus making it harder for them to find the alphabet. The arrangement of the alphabet on the keyboard is one of the reasons for the delay in completing the task. The children are used to the sequence of 'ABCs' that they need to find the alphabet one at a time. They often encounter typing errors and confusion to differentiate the alphabet, such as 'D' and 'O'. One of the children took almost one minute just to log in to the application even though her name only contains five alphabets. She obviously had difficulty differentiating the alphabet. She confused 'D' with 'O', 'A' with 'R', and 'M with 'N'.

However, most children only encountered difficulty operating the computer while logging in. After logging in, they did not have much difficulty. They can operate the software fairly well. This was proven for participant P5. Even though she had difficulty during login which is the first task, she managed to perform well for the subsequent tasks. She understood the task well and knew how to operate BacaDisleksia application with minimal error.

This can also be observed in "Find the word 'bapa' and spell it outloud" task (Task 4). All the children managed to complete the task on average at the same time. The dyslexic children find the word 'bapa', which only has four alphabets in a two-syllable word. Compared to Task 5, which is to find the words 'sayang', although it is a two-syllable word, the second syllable 'yang' imposed some difficulty to some of the children comes with the diphthong ('ng'), making it more challenging to spell and read correctly. Thus, more time is needed to find, identify, and read the word. Therefore, the design of how the word should be presented could be considered to assist dyslexic children in reading longer, more difficult words.

5 Design Decisions and Recommendation

The eye tracking data, provides valuable and insightful design suggestions for the improvement of BacaDisleksia. Of course, the fundamentals remain, but the user interface could be improved further for better interaction, providing enhanced reading experience. Firstly, the namespace in the login interface. As the blank space to fill in their name use a feature that can fill in unlimited alphabet, by limiting the alphabet, children can only enter their nickname in the space which can prevent them from entering their full name thus reducing the error and can improve their emotional distress. There is obviously the pros and cons to it – on the positive note, it is easier for them to spell out short names rather the long ones; on the other hand, it could also be a platform for them to learn to spell their full name. Anyway, it is a matter of choice and what objective we are aiming for. Technically, both can be easily accomplished.

Secondly, the representation of the word. Having different levels of difficulty with the word is a great idea, but how the word is represented is also an important element to assist dyslexic children. In addition to different syllables having different colors, adding a hyphen in between two or more syllables can also help children who are suffering from severe dyslexia, as suggested by [17, 18]. This would assist in terms of its visual representation, which further enhanced the separation of the syllables in a word and between alphabets. Dyslexic children find crowded words jumpy, making reading difficult and stressful [19]. Eliminating or reducing stress and cognitive load is important for their successful design.

Thirdly, the placement of the color palette for choosing the background color. This feature is considered one of the important factors leading to correct spelling and reading. Based on the eye-tracking data, the current position at the bottom of the user interface has caused some distractions to the children. This is probably due to the somewhat crowded space at the bottom of the user interface with many icons and features. Instead of putting it at the bottom of the page, the background color could be place near the font color (or syllable color) selection located at the right side of the user interface. Re-positioning this color palette would satisfy one of the Gestalt Principles as it groups similar, related features, thus reducing cognitive load in terms of interaction.

Such design suggestions could be mapped and summarized into suitable Interaction Design (IxD) dimensions for design recommendation. The IxD dimensions considered include text (1D), visual representation (2D), and behavior (5D). There are also potential considerations of careful design of time (3D) and space (4D) to enhance the learning experience for the children using BacaDisleksia. However, based on the findings and new insights obtained from the eye-tracking usability conducted, much of the design decisions and recommendations fall under 2D and 5D, leaving 1D not so much affected. This suggests improving the representation of the words and the layout of the user interface following Gestalt Principle and mapping it back to what children with dyslexia really need to read better and more accurately using an application. The login user interface suggests considering the third IxD dimension, i.e., time (3D), towards improving the interaction. The time recorded to accomplish each task, as depicted in Table 2, could also point out areas of the interaction that can be further improved. By providing the mapping of IxD dimensions and existing principles in HCI, having the characteristics of children with dyslexia and their specific needs serving as the foundation of such inclusive design, a reading application such as BacaDisleksia could be leveraged as an assistive technology for facilitating reading to these struggling readers. This could lead to positive development in inclusive design for children with learning disabilities, as careful consideration is crucial, and adaptation to such specific needs requires careful design, understanding, and empathy.

6 Conclusion

Eye-tracking usability could uncover unnoticed issues that potentially lead to insightful design improvement. The eye movement, eye gaze, and the children's focus can be evaluated with the tasks prepared for them. The study results are presented in the form of heat maps and gaze plots. From the testing, all of the children completed all the tasks given even though a few children took longer to complete the task. The heat map and gaze plot of these participants were analyzed and compared to children with little difficulty completing the tasks given. With the aid of an eye tracker in usability testing, the data received can be portrayed visually, making the analysis process much easier. From the analyzed data, issues regarding the application can be identified. Based on the result, a few suggestions have been made to discuss the application's design to enhance the user experience of children learning to read using BacaDisleksia, mapped to the IxD dimensions, including text, visual representation, behavior, and time. By considering more dimensions in the design decision for dyslexia, it is hoped that the application or solution could lead towards providing inclusivity for the children, whose struggles are real and therefore demand more effort in assisting them to learn.

References

1. Strohmaier, A.R., MacKay, K.J., Obersteiner, A., Reiss, K.M.: Eye tracking methodology in mathematics education research: a systematic literature review. Educ. Stud. Math. **104**, 147–200 (2020)
2. Interaction Design Foundation. The five languages or dimensions of interaction design. https://www.interaction-design.org/literature/article/the-five-languages-or-dimensions-of-interaction-design
3. Abowd, G.D., Beale, R.: Users, systems and interfaces: a unifying framework for interaction. In: People and Computers (HCI 1991), vol. 4, pp. 73–87. Elsevier, Stuttgart (1991)
4. Irlen, H.: Reading by the Colors: Overcoming Dyslexia and Other Reading Disabilities Through the Irlen Method. Perigree Book, New York (2005)
5. U.S. Department of Health and Human Services. Dyslexia. National Institute of Neurological Disorders and Stroke. https://www.ninds.nih.gov/health-information/disorders/dyslexia
6. Shaywitz, S.: Overcoming Dyslexia, 2nd edn. Knopf Doubleday Publishing Group, New York (2020)
7. Maja, L., Pitt, I., Andreja, I.S.: Optimal multimedia combination for students with dyslexia. Adv. Methodol. Statist. **17**(2) (2020)
8. Wang, J., Antonenko, P., Celepkolu, M., Jimenez, Y., Fieldman, E., Fieldman, A.: Exploring relationships between eye tracking and traditional usability testing data. Int. J. Hum. Comput. Interact. **35**(6), 483–494 (2018)
9. Cowen, L., Ball, L.J., Delin, J.: An eye movement analysis of web page usability. In: People and Computers XVI-Memorable Yet Invisible, pp. 317–335. Springer, London (2002)
10. Nielsen, J., Pernice, K.: Eyetracking Web Usability. Pearson (2011)
11. Wu, Y., Cheng, J., Kang, X.: Study of smart watch interface usability evaluation based on eye-tracking. In: International Conference of Design, User Experience, and Usability, pp. 98–109. Springer, Cham (2016)
12. Manhartsberger, M., Zellhofer, N.: Eye tracking in usability research: what users really see. Empowering software quality: how can usability engineering reach these goals? Usab. Symp. **198**, 141–152 (2005)
13. Franzen, L., Stark, Z., Johnson, A.P.: Individuals with dyslexia use a different visual sampling strategy to read text. Sci. Rep. **11**, 6449 (2021). https://doi.org/10.1038/s41598-021-84945-9
14. Nerušil, B., Polec, J., Škunda, J., et al.: Eye tracking based dyslexia detection using a holistic approach. Sci. Rep. **11**, 15687 (2021). https://doi.org/10.1038/s41598-021-95275-1
15. Benfatto, N.M., Seimyr, Ö.G., Ygge, J., Pansell, T., Rydberg, A., Jacobson, C.: Screening for dyslexia using eye tracking during reading. PLoS One **11**(12) (2016)
16. Gran Ekstrand, A.C., Benfatto, N.M., Seimyr, Ö.G.: Screening for reading difficulties: comparing eye tracking outcomes to neuropsychological assessments. Front. Educ. **6**, 643232 (2021)

17. Harley, T.A., O'Mara, D.A.: Hyphenation can improve reading in acquired phonological dyslexia. Aphasiology **20**(8), 744–761 (2006)
18. Häikiö, T., Luotojärvi, T.: The effect of syllable-level hyphenation on novel word reading in early finnish readers: evidence from eye movements. Sci. Stud. Read. **26**(1), 38–46 (2021)
19. Ismail, R., Jaafar, A.: Important features in text presentation for children with dyslexia. J. Theor. Appl. Inf. Technol. **63**(3), 694–700 (2014)

Hexa-Net Framework: A Fresh ADHD-Specific Model for Identifying ADHD Based on Integrating Brain Atlases

Dalia A. Al-Ubaidi[1]([envelope]) [iD], Azurah A. Samah[1] [iD], and Mahdi Jasim[2] [iD]

[1] Faculty of Computing, Universiti Teknologi Malaysia, 81310 Skudai, Johor, Malaysia
dalial_ubaidi@uoitc.edu.iq
[2] University of Information Technology and Communications, Baghdad, Iraq

Abstract. Attention Deficit Hyperactivity Disorder (ADHD) is a frequent neurodevelopmental disorder affecting children and adults, which is routinely diagnosed based on subjective observations and behavioural assessments. Recent advancements in neuroimaging, particularly in resting-state functional magnetic resonance imaging (rs-fMRI), have provided a better understanding of the functional brain network impairments linked to ADHD. The human brain naturally consists of resting-state networks (RSNs) that are spatially distinct and functionally homogenous. Therefore, identifying ADHD biomarkers using the human brain's RSNs is a promising approach. In order to make accurate statistical inferences in brain science, it is necessary to utilize brain atlases for localizing network-of-interest (NoIs). However, locating the spatial components of these RSNs using human brain functional atlases poses challenges due to a lack of disease-specific atlases and atlases concordance issues. This research (1) conducts a study and addresses six RSNs that are frequently referenced in ADHD literature: (Auditory-, Cognitive Control-, Dorsal Attention-, Default Mode-, Sensorimotor-, and Ventral Attention-) Networks (2) Introduces a framework that attempts to enhance the generation of ADHD-specific brain reference, named "Hexa-Net"; This comprehensive approach may improve the reliability and applicability of ADHD studies to a fresh level via segregating and integrating the brain into (NoIs) by evaluating predetermined brain atlases. We hypothesize that the Hexa-Net Model can offer a more precise and unbiased method for identifying ADHD-related impairments. As a result, this framework serves as a practical guide for analyzing biomarkers from rs-fMRI scans to aid in diagnosing ADHD.

Keywords: ADHD identification Framework · Brain Networks Analysis · Functional Brain atlases · Resting-state networks · Hexa-Net Model

1 Introduction

Attention Deficit Hyperactivity Disorder (ADHD) is a neurodevelopmental disorder that primarily affects children and continues to adulthood [1, 2]. Diagnosing ADHD is difficult due to various factors, such as the absence of gold standards or single tests

© The Author(s), under exclusive license to Springer Nature Singapore Pte Ltd. 2024
N. H. Zakaria et al. (Eds.): ICOCI 2023, CCIS 2002, pp. 81–94, 2024.
https://doi.org/10.1007/978-981-99-9592-9_7

that can precisely identify the condition [3]. Clinicians frequently diagnose ADHD by utilising the criteria outlined by "the Diagnostic and Statistical Manual of Mental Disorders, 5th edition (DSM-V)" [4, 5], as stated in Fig. 1.

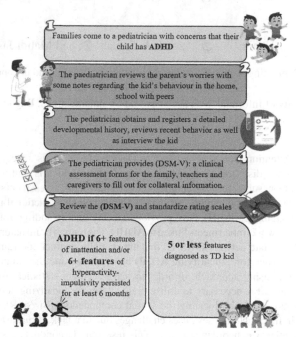

Fig. 1. Conventional Strategy for Classifying and Diagnosing ADHD (based on DSM-V)

ADHD symptoms are believed to originate from an atypical organisation of brain networks along with impaired connectivity [6]. Therefore, neuroimaging has become another technique for studying brain syndromes and disorders such as ADHD [7, 8], among them, resting-state fMRI (rs-fMRI) is commonly used to study the primary brain networks [9]. The organisation of the human brain is achieved through the interconnection of a system of neurons. Recent techniques in decomposition and clustering have been used to study whole-brain rs-fMRI data, exposing various cortical regions that are physically separated but functionally connected. This phenomenon is referred to as "Resting-State Networks (RSNs)" or "intrinsic connectivity networks" [10]. This approach enables examining the brain and how it works from a novel standpoint that considers the intricacy of its internal organisation.

Studies have indeed indicated that individuals with ADHD experience extensive oddities in the brain network rather than specific in certain regions [11]. The incorporation of network theory into the brain connectivity analysis has demonstrated considerable promise in understanding the organisational principles of the brain and how they pertain to cognitive processes along with neurological pathologies [12].

However, defining network nodes is crucial in constructing brain connectivity networks [13]. Utilizing a vertex- or voxel-based depiction could give rise to a network exhibiting abundant noise and exceedingly high dimensionality. Consequently, the task of analysing brain networks might frequently pose a challenge [14]. An alternate approach for defining the brain's nodes involves segregating the brain into discrete regions, also known as brain parcellation. Each parcel is then assigned as a node within the connectivity network [15]. Research indicates network-level brain segregation might be the best practice for analyzing cognitive function to identify reliable biomarkers for neuropsychiatric disorders [16].

In brain science, connectivity-based parcellation involves grouping voxels in brain areas that share similar connectivity patterns. However, to ensure precise statistical inferences, it is important to use brain atlases to locate regions of interest as an initial stage. Brain atlases are crucial to the reliability of brain network research that tries to solve the issue of brain segregation, reveal network features and assist in identifying diseases by utilizing neuroimaging data; proper atlases allow the integration of structural and functional brain network analysis [16]. Although there are numerous deployed structural and functional brain atlases, but there is no uniformity in the parcellations created by those atlases [17], which poses "Brain Atlases Concordance Problem" as clarified in Fig. 2 [18, 19]. This is because each atlas represents a brain label based on the knowledge available at the time of its creation. There is no ground truth parcellation of the cerebral cortex especially for a particular syndrome or disorder, which makes it hard to evaluate the effectiveness and the accuracy of parcellation algorithms [20].

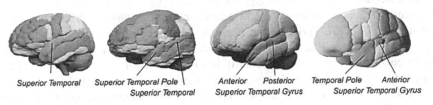

Superior Temporal   Superior Temporal Pole \   Anterior   Posterior   Temporal Pole   Anterior
                              Superior Temporal   Superior Temporal Gyrus   Superior Temporal Gyrus

Fig. 2. This image clarify that the parcellations defined by different atlases lack consistency and is adopted from [18] to visualize the **"Brain Atlases Concordance Problem"**: The Superior Temporal gyrus defined at different ways by four different atlases (from left to right AAL1, CerebrA, Hammersmith and Harvard Oxford (HO)).

Insufficient attention has been given to standardizing brain atlases [21]. As far as researchers know, no ADHD-specific brain functional atlas or reference is obtained from rs-fMRI data; thus, neuroimaging studies targeted at comprehending the functional connectivity and cognitive performance of the ADHD brain may be restricted without a frame of reference. One challenge arises when different catalogues/atlases assign the same label to RSNs despite their distinct spatial composition.

To overcome these challenges with the target of creating an ADHD-specific brain reference, this work suggested an approach in the context of unifying and integrating multiple brain networks from predefined brain atlases into one model, this work proposes a systematic framework for conducting a methodical evaluation of several functional brain parcellations regardless of their generating approaches and the number of delineated networks to identify and label multi-source RSNs into single brain reference accurately.

An introduction to ADHD, its diagnostic criteria, and the contribution of neuroimaging of the disorder diagnosis was provided above; then, the rest of the paper is organized as follows: Sect. 2. Dives into the state of arts on methods identified ADHD-based (RSNs) and the commonly used pre-computed brain atlases. Then Sect. 2 offers a schematic framework for selecting a parcellation tailored to ADHD brain investigations. Additionally, in Sect. 3, the researcher discusses how to use the suggested framework could standardize brain RSNs identification in ADHD research. Furthermore, Sect. 4 concludes the work.

2 Related Works

2.1 The Role of RSNs in Identifying ADHD

Functional and structural connectivity alterations have been documented in various neuropsychiatric conditions [22]. Evidence revealed that individuals with ADHD experience dysregulation of neural networks (i.e., across multiple brain regions) as DAN, DMN, and AUN, not just specific ones, as proofed by extensive research in this field [23, 24]. This section explores the question of how many networks are thought to have dysfunctional behaviour in ADHD.

The exact delineation of brain regions and networks is an essential concept in neuroscience; function, connectivity, architecture, and topography are crucial in defining these regions [22, 25]. Variability in network nomenclature across studies limits the integration of findings. Recent research indicates that ADHD may arise from alterations in brain connectivity patterns, particularly in functional connectivity networks (RSNs) among different brain regions that coordinate cognition and activity [24].

Acknowledging that various atlases may utilize different terminology when describing identical anatomical regions and (RSNs) is essential. In depth, the Cognitive Control Network (CCN) simultaneously known as Fronto-Parietal Control Network (FPCN) or Executive Control Network (ECN) as stated in [26, 27], while Yeo, Krienen [28] used the term Ventral Attention Network (VAN) which is referred to Salience Network (SN) in [29] and Cingulo-Opercular Network in [17]. Furthermore, "Affective or Motivational Network" is sometimes referred to as "Limbic Network"; Sect. 4 provides more information about this challenge. Another issue is that RSNs are frequently categorized by authors who often exhibit biases that arise from their subjective understanding of the network's spatial or functional configurations.

Finally, some atlases offer individual maps for subdivisions within the same RSN, and they require integration to represent the complete RSN; For instance, some scholars have employed the Sensorimotor Network (SMN) to signify the incorporated Sensorimotor and Auditory Networks (AUN). Conversely, others have deemed it appropriate to split it into two discrete (RSNs): the primary SMN and the Auditory Network (AUN) [17].

Three theories have been introduced here, from the perspective of RSNs, to advance the study of ADHD Brain Connectivity. These theories are based on previous studies and aim to build upon existing knowledge:

Default Mode Network Hypothesis. In this hypothesis, the (DMN) is considered the major Network-of-Interest (NoI) to examining ADHD brains [14, 30]; DMN is a RSN that is mostly active during rest that made it optimal to study on resting-state experiments.

Tri-Network Hypothesis. Also known as Menon's Tri-Network model originated by Vinod Menon who proposed theoretical framework on the justification that "different forms of psychopathology or symptom profiles are caused by disturbances in the interactions between different brain networks"; those three distinct brain networks that are associated with different symptom patterns are: DMN, Central Executive Network (CEN) and Silence Network [31]. However, examining the functional connectivity and interactions among these three networks can yield valuable insights into the fundamental mechanisms associated with (ADHD).

Hypothesis Established on RSNs Connectivity Trends in ADHD Studies. Our hypothesis depends on exploring emerging ADHD studies to conclude RSNs connectivity trends. Authors observed that individuals with ADHD exhibit decreased anticorrelations between the DMN and task-based networks (i.e., CEN) during rest [6]. However, another study has found that individuals with ADHD tend to have reduced FC within DMN-DAN and increased FC between DMN-DAN [32]. Furthermore, Sutcubasi, Metin [27] noted that no impacts related to ADHD were detected on (Affective/Motivational Network or limbic network); so based on that this study excludes exploring it.

It is essential to acknowledge that the lack of studies deals with alterations in AUN and SMN, and the limited number of voxels detected at these regions on previous studies, could have various reasons beyond sample size differences. Prior studies revealed that ADHD individuals were more sensitive to noise, potentially linked to an increased FC in the auditory network [33]. Kids with ADHD exhibit poor Auditory Processing [39], so this network would be included in the suggested model. Table 1 states the frequently discovered RSNs in ADHD.

Table 1. Resting-State Network discoveries in ADHD studies

Ref.	RSNs discoveries
[34]	hyperconnectivity between DAN-VAN and within DMN and VAN;
[35]	focus on measuring rs-FC at all RSNs; and draw a valuable conclusion for brain network dysregulation hypothesis of ADHD
[27]	interconnectivity within: (DMN), (CCN), (VAN), and Affective/Motivational Network (AMN);
[33]	assumed that ADHD related to the (AUN), (DAN), (VAN), and (SMN);
[23]	investigated (DAN), (DMN), and (VAN) in ADHD children, and they reported that there is hyperconnectivity in (DMN-DAN), (DMN-SMN), (DMN-AUN); No alterations among VAN regions compared to Typical Development (TD);
[36]	ADHD subjects were shown to have decreased FC between their Visual and VAN networks;

Based on the mentioned findings, the root cause of ADHD-related brain dysfunction seems to be an imbalance in brain network organization.

According to the previously stated hypotheses plus the outlined findings, this study sought to name six (RSNs) with uniform labels to be integrated into one consensual model to be a disease-specific or particularly an ADHD-specific brain reference, which are: Auditory Network (AUN), Cognitive Control Network (CCN), Dorsal Attention Network (DAN), Default Mode Network (DMN), Sensorimotor Network (SMN), and Ventral Attention Network (VAN) and integrated into a "Hexa-Net Model"; this model could serve as the basis for future ADHD identification studies.

2.2 Pre-Defined Human Brain Atlases in ADHD Studies

The more adaptable method in rs-fMRI data analysis is starting with an atlas to define brain seeds/nodes which perform a controlled clustering to dive into the available data. The idea of a brain template was established to get a standard brain parcellation that spatially constrained with functionally homogenous clusters. Several brain atlases are available in the neuroscience literature. Brain parcellations are time templates that extract the functional brain regions utilized based on data mining approaches [37].

Many common brain atlases were used in ADHD identification studies. Table 2, an overview of the commonly adopted structural and functional brain atlases that have proven valuable for ADHD researchers.

Table 2. An overview to the commonly utilized Brain atlases in ADHD studies

	#ROI	Analytical Approach	Ref.
Structural Brain Atlases			
AAL	115	anatomically/ structurally defined digital human brain in software package;	[38]
EZ	115	generated using the max-propagation atlas that was provided with the SPM Anatomy Toolbox. The atlas was divided into functional space using nearest-neighbor interpolation and then translated into template space using the Colin-27 template	[18]
TT	93–110	subsequently divided into functional space using nearest neighbors' interpolation after being co-registered, warped, and shifted into template space	[18]
HO	110	consists of probabilistic atlases for the cortical and subcortical regions	[18]
Functional Brain Atlases			
	# Parcel	**Analytical Approach**	Ref
Yeo	7–17	Spectral clustering algorithms; the number of final parcels depends on the stability of clustering algorithm;	[28]

(continued)

Table 2. (*continued*)

	#ROI	Analytical Approach	Ref.
Power	10–13	Global similarity approach based on a graph-based community detection algorithm (Infomap);	[39]
CC200	190–200	spatially constrained spectral clustering using 200 ROIs with homogeneous functional connectivity;	[40]
CC400	351–400	CC400 is a reproduction of the CC200 but it to spanning 400 regions;	[40]
Schaefer	100–1000	The integrated gradient-weighted Markov Random Field (gwMRF) model; starts from 100 to 1000 parcels and is incremented by 100	[41]

2.3 ADHD-200 Dataset

The NeuroBureau ADHD-200 dataset is the primary foundation for the ongoing rs-fMRI research on ADHD [42]. ADHD-200 a large-scale fMRI neuroimaging dataset. In ADHD-200, each subject's data usually contain structural images (T1-weighted) and functional images (fMRI). Furthermore, phenotypic information (e.g., demographic attributes, and clinical evaluation data) was made publicly available [43]. Applying sophisticated methods for diagnosing ADHD was accomplished by the availability of the ADHD-200 dataset [14]. The ADHD-200 dataset is the primary data source used in the ongoing rs-fMRI studies on ADHD [44]. Detailed information related to ADHD-200 dataset (scan parameters, experiment details, handedness, IQ, and other PCD) and the pre-processing pipelines can be found on the (https://fcon_1000.projects.nitrc.org/indi/adhd200/) and [45] provide extra information about ADHD-200. It's worth noting that, Cortese, Aoki [46] conducted a meta-analysis study and reported that ADHD-200 project provided the proof of concept.

3 Proposed Framework

3.1 Hexa-Net Framework: A New Modeling Framework to Conceptualize ADHD Brain Parcellation

Concordance across multiple anatomical and functional atlases continues to be a subject of ongoing study in neuroimaging [18]. Choosing a suitable brain atlas for a study is affected by factors as: (1) delineating identical labels to RSNs, despite their spatial composition and (2) drawing a meaningful comparison across brain parcellations that have been produced independently by different research labs, using different datasets, and/or in different coordinate systems [20, 41].

From the aforementioned and based on studies conducted by [17, 20, 25], this study suggested a Hexa-Net framework, that aims to be a researcher's guide for analyzing biomarkers from rs-fMRI scans using muti-source brain atlases in terms of ADHD identification, refer to Fig. 3 for detailed information.

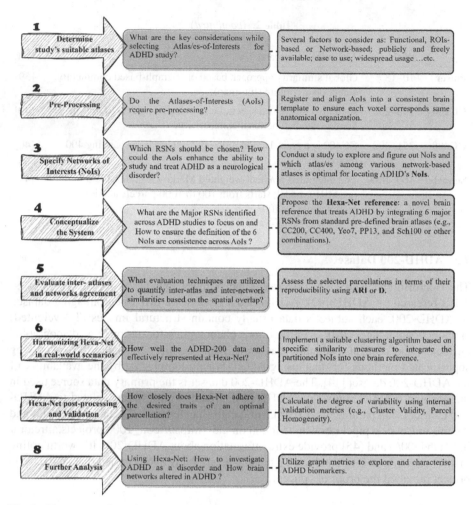

Fig. 3. The proposed roadmap to standardize ADHD brain navigation and analysis: A Novel Schematic Approach to Generate Hexa-Net as an ADHD-specific Brain reference as an ADHD lesion map based on six NoIs; likewise, the paradigm above could be integrating any functional brain atlases instead of stated ones as well as studying other brain disorders.

3.2 Methods for Founding Hexa-Net Brain Reference

Parcellating the brain into distinct regions is a practice that varies across atlases, with various standards and regional definitions. To evaluate results across studies that hire distinct atlases, concordance between the atlases must be established. Nonetheless, determining agreement between brain seeds (i.e., regions or networks) of disparate atlases is complex. The following steps state the process of creating a consensus brain reference by integrating multiple brain atlases:

Selecting an Atlas-of-Interest for ADHD Study. This step is about naming study's specific brain atlases to ensure their compatibility for further analysis. Brain atlases are significant maps that facilitate the segregation of the cerebral cortex based on structural or functional features [16]. To build an ADHD-related lesion brain map, researchers should list more than three atlases based on research considerations and questions. More details about precomputed brain atlases that are extensively used in ADHD studies stated in Sect. 2.2.

Network-of-Interests (NoIs). According to the investigation conducted in Sect. 2.1, this study identifies six major networks (i.e., Network-of-Interests (NoIs)) named (AUN, CCN, DAN, DMN, SMN, and VAN), as it has attracted significant attention in recent ADHD studies. Subsequently, the researcher is required to partition (AoIs) and analyze the spatial configuration of those (NoIs) utilizing the methodologies outlined in Table 2.

Evaluating Interatlas Spatial Overlap. Assessing the effectiveness of parcellation models can be difficult as there is no definitive segmentation of the cerebral cortex to serve as a benchmark [20, 47]. This stage aims to clarify the differences between Atlases-of-Interests and their respective representations while also serving as a comparative tool for brain parcels across atlases. Several factors should be considered while analyzing multiple source brain atlases at once.

To provide a detailed explanation of how to measure interatlas similarities which could be measured using measures stated in Table 3, each has its pros and cons. A systematic comparison should be performed across the selected atlases (1) to compare the entire spatial overlap among functional brain atlases that are chosen in the study by applying one of the reproducibility metrics (2) to measure the spatial configuration among the NoIs, the similarity among the six NoIs could be evaluated using accuracy metrics (3) to validate the resultant brain reference many researchers suggest evaluating homogeneity by measuring it within and between parcels.

Table 3. A list of the proposed measurements for evaluating the agreements of the pre-defined brain parcellations similarities and how to quantify the resultant brain reference.

Validation Measures	Technique	Specification
Dice Coefficient, Rand Index, Adjusted Rand Index, Adjusted Mutual Information	**Reproducibility**	evaluates the similarity of two distinct sets of parcellations acquired from separate groups or different numbers of clusters (e.g., ROIs or NoIs)
Silhouette coefficient, Dice Coefficient, Clustering Homogeneity measures (e.g., Kendall's coefficient of concordance or variance percentage)	**Accuracy**	(1) evaluating voxels fidelity to the underlying network; (2) measuring the clustering separation quality of the new parcellation

3.3   Generating the Hexa-Net Reference Based on Multi-source RSNs Fusion

The Hexa-Net brain reference is an ADHD-specific brain template that relies on the original parcellations. The modelling phases intended to be implemented by adhering to the Hexa-Net framework guidance are depicted in Fig. 4. After conducting a comparative analysis of the atlases-of-interests (AoIs) agreement and evaluating how accurately they identified the (NoIs), it is necessary to extract the BOLD signals from rs-fMRI that reflects the spatial composition of the determined (NoIs) as defined by the AoIs for ADHD-200 subjects. Moreover, a clustering analysis is performed to successfully detect clusters of highly interconnected voxels based on their functional connectivity (FC) strengths.

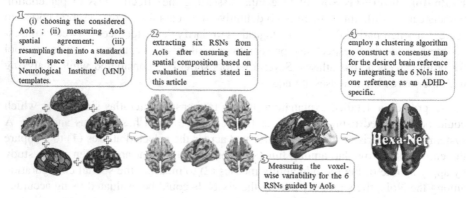

(i) choosing the considered AoIs ; (ii) measuring AoIs spatial agreement; (iii) resampling them into a standard brain space as Montreal Neurological Institute (MNI) templates.

extracting six RSNs from AoIs after ensuring their spatial composition based on evaluation metrics stated in this article

employ a clustering algorithm to construct a consensus map for the desired brain reference by integrating the 6 NoIs into one reference as an ADHD-specific.

Measuring the voxel-wise variability for the 6 RSNs guided by AoIs

Fig. 4. The suggested pipeline of Hexa-Net Model as ADHD-specific brain reference

4   Discussion

Selecting appropriate research methods is a crucial, albeit challenging, aspect of analyzing brain functional connectivity. ADHD identification lies in understanding the exact etiology of ADHD. Atlases-of-Interests and parcellation evaluation measures could be regarded as a study benchmark in neuroimaging data analysis. Despite the availability of diverse atlases being valuable for researchers, the utilization of distinct parcellations across studies poses a challenge in evaluating the reproducibility of brain studies [21]. Brain parcellations may be established through (a) anatomical criteria, (b) functional criteria, or (3) a combination of both. The present study, conducted an in-depth exploration of the ADHD RSNs studies and the brain atlases that have extensively been published in the domain of neuroscience and ADHD in specific. Based on this exploration a Hexa-Net framework for replicating RSN findings in ADHD studies. The AUN, CCN, DAN, DMN, SMN, and VAN networks have been identified as RSNs that consistently correlate with ADHD across the literature [27, 30, 48]. Yet, there is considerable variance in these networks' spatial layout across studies, which translates to the established functional atlases. The approach employed for RSN extraction and the size of the parcellation did not appear to affect the inter-atlas similarity when examined five popular atlases. The approach employed for RSN extraction and the size of the parcellation did not appear to affect the inter-atlas similarity when examining five elected atlases.

Table 3 listed a collection of evaluation techniques and metrics commonly used in literature to assess parcellations models, refer to [17, 20, 49] for extra details. These techniques have been divided into various categories.

Hexa-Net framework offers a guide to the problem of RSN standardization and tries to overcome the drawbacks of the Atlases Concordance Problem. Drawing to a conclusion, Hexa-Net has been constructed as a lens for identifying ADHD, and it offers some key benefits over current approaches.

The Hexa-Net approach seeks to simplify the process of standardizing new atlases and observing meta-data. Hexa-Net aims to reduce the search space of each RSNs by limiting it to the expected average cluster size, then leads to improved computational loads. Moreover, Hexa-Net might provide a replicable template of the six cognitive RSNs for other disease detection. However, creating ADHD-specific identification atlases using this framework could lead to the loss of certain brain regions due to sampling and registration reduction challenges.

5 Conclusion

To our knowledge, there is a lack of ADHD studies that addressed the issue of consistencies across brain atlases in the context of standardizing RSNs. This work proposes a framework for creating an ADHD-specific brain reference guided by predefined brain atlases, which can help us better understand disrupted functional connectivity in ADHD brains. The proposed framework presents an obvious strategy for utilizing the integration/segregation regulations to identify variations in brain integration and segregation to specific Networks-of-Interest. By modelling six brain functional networks extensively stated in literature (AUN, CCN, DAN, DMN, SMN, and VAN) based on integrating multi-source brain atlases. This approach aims to balance network integration and segregation to achieve the best possible outcomes. Through this framework, researchers can assess the suitability of a group of brain atlases for blending the six RSNs. As a result, a "Hexa-Net framework" is suggested based on these considerations. All crucial details regarding the Hexa-Net model have been documented with a focus on addressing ADHD-specific brain references. This ensures that it can be easily utilized in future research with minimal effort. This methodology can be employed to assess the reliability of an atlas utilized in a disorder investigation.

References

1. Markovska-Simoska, S., Pop-Jordanova, N.: Quantitative EEG spectrum-weighted frequency (brain rate) distribution in adults with ADHD CNS Spectr. **16**(5) 111–119 (2011)
2. Silk, T.J., et al.: A network analysis approach to ADHD symptoms: More than the sum of its parts. PLoS ONE **14**(1), e0211053 (2019)
3. Miranda, L., et al.: Systematic review of functional MRI applications for psychiatric disease subtyping. Front. Psych. **12** (2021)

4. Substance Abuse and Mental Health Services Administration: DSM-5 Changes: Implications for Child Serious Emotional Disturbance. Substance Abuse and Mental Health Services Administration (US) (2016)
5. American Psychiatric Association: Diagnostic and statistical manual of mental disorders (DSM-5®). American Psychiatric Pub. (2013)
6. Henry, T.R., Cohen, J.R.: Chapter 5 - Dysfunctional brain network organization in neurodevelopmental disorders. In: Munsell, B.C. et al. (ed.) Connectomics, pp. 83–100. Academic Press (2019)
7. Smith, S.M., et al.: A positive-negative mode of population covariation links brain connectivity, demographics and behavior. Nat. Neurosci. **18**(11), 1565–1567 (2015)
8. Xue, G., et al.: Brain imaging techniques and their applications in decision-making research. Xin Li Xue Bao **42**(1), 120–137 (2010)
9. Valsasina, P., et al.: Characterizing rapid fluctuations of resting state functional connectivity in demyelinating, neurodegenerative, and psychiatric conditions: from static to time-varying analysis. Front. Neurosci. **13** (2019)
10. Sporns, O.: Network attributes for segregation and integration in the human brain. Curr. Opin. Neurobiol. **23**(2), 162–171 (2013)
11. Samea, F., et al.: Brain alterations in children/adolescents with ADHD revisited: A neuroimaging meta-analysis of 96 structural and functional studies. Neurosci. Biobehav. Rev. **100**, 1–8 (2019)
12. Sporns, O.: Connectome networks: from cells to systems. In: Micro-. m, pp. 107-127. Springer, Cham (2016). https://doi.org/10.1007/978-3-319-27777-6_8
13. Eickhoff, S.B., Constable, R.T., Yeo, B.T.: Topographic organization of the cerebral cortex and brain cartography. Neuroimage **170**, 332–347 (2018)
14. Castellanos, F.X., Aoki, Y.: Intrinsic functional connectivity in attention-deficit/hyperactivity disorder: a science in development. Biolo. Psychiat: Cognitive Neurosc. Neuroimaging **1**(3), 253–261 (2016)
15. Sporns, O.: Graph theory methods: applications in brain networks. Dialogues in clinical neuroscience (2022)
16. Yao, Z., et al.: A review of structural and functional brain networks: small world and atlas. Brain Inform. **2**(1), 45–52 (2015)
17. Doucet, G.E., Lee, W.H.,Frangou, S.: Evaluation of the spatial variability in the major resting-state networks across human brain functional atlases. Human Brain Mapping **40**(15), 4577–4587 (2019)
18. Revell, A.Y., et al.: A framework For brain atlases: lessons from seizure dynamics. Neuroimage **254**, 118986 (2022)
19. Bohland, J.W., et al.: The brain atlas concordance problem: quantitative comparison of anatomical parcellations. PLoS ONE **4**(9), e7200(2009)
20. Arslan, S., et al.: Human brain mapping: a systematic comparison of parcellation methods for the human cerebral cortex. Neuroimage **170**, 5–30 (2018)
21. Lawrence, R.M., et al.: Standardizing human brain parcellations. Scientific Data **8**(1), 78 (2021)
22. Eickhoff, S.B., et al.: Connectivity-based parcellation: critique and implications. Hum. Brain Mapp. **36**(12), 4771–4792 (2015)
23. Lin, H., et al.: Functional connectivity of attention-related networks in drug-naïve children with ADHD. J. Atten. Disord. **25**(3), 377–388 (2021)
24. Tang, Y., Zheng, S., Tian, Y.: Resting-state fMRI whole brain network function plasticity analysis in attention deficit hyperactivity disorder. Neural Plast. **2022**, 4714763 (2022)
25. Uddin, L.Q., Yeo, B., Spreng, R.N.: Towards a universal taxonomy of macro-scale functional human brain networks. Brain Topogr. **32**(6), 926–942 (2019)

26. Kaboodvand, N., Iravani, B., Fransson, P. Dynamic synergetic configurations of resting-state networks in ADHD. NeuroImage, **207** (2020)
27. Sutcubasi, B., et al.: Resting-state network dysconnectivity in ADHD: a system-neuroscience-based meta-analysis. The World Journal of Biological Psychiatry 21(9), 662–672 (2020)
28. Yeo, B.T., et al.: The organization of the human cerebral cortex estimated by intrinsic functional connectivity. J. Neurophysiol. **106**(3), 1125–1165 (2011)
29. Gao, Y., et al.: Impairments of large-scale functional networks in attention-deficit/hyperactivity disorder: A meta-analysis of resting-state functional connectivity. Psychol. Med. **49**(15), 2475–2485 (2019)
30. Hong, S.-B., Hwang, S.: Resting-state brain variability in youth with attention-deficit/hyperactivity disorder. Front. Psych. **13** (2022)
31. Menon, V.: Large-scale brain networks and psychopathology: a unifying triple network model. Trends Cogn. Sci. **15**(10), 483–506 (2011)
32. Cole, M.W., Schneider, W.: The cognitive control network: Integrated cortical regions with dissociable functions. Neuroimage 37(1), 343–360 (2007)
33. Zhang, H., et al.: Aberrant functional connectivity in resting state networks of ADHD patients revealed by independent component analysis. BMC Neurosci. **21**(1), 39 (2020)
34. Sidlauskaite, J., et al.: Altered intrinsic organisation of brain networks implicated in attentional processes in adult attention-deficit/hyperactivity disorder: a resting-state study of attention, default mode and salience network connectivity. Eur. Arch. Psychiatry Clin. Neurosci. **266**, 349–357 (2016)
35. Icer, S., Gengec Benli, S., Ozmen, S.: Differences in brain networks of children with ADHD: Whole-brain analysis of resting-state fMRI. In: International Journal of Imaging Systems and Technology 29(4), pp. 645–662 (2019)
36. Thomson, P., et al.: Longitudinal maturation of resting state networks: Relevance to sustained attention and attention deficit/hyperactivity disorder. Cogn. Affect. Behav. Neurosci. **22**(6), 1432–1446 (2022)
37. Ashourvan, A., et al.: Pairwise maximum entropy model explains the role of white matter structure in shaping emergent co-activation states. Communications Biology **4**(1), 1–15 (2021)
38. Tzourio-Mazoyer, N., et al.: Automated anatomical labeling of activations in SPM using a macroscopic anatomical parcellation of the MNI MRI single-subject brain. Neuroimage **15**(1), 273–289 (2002)
39. Power, J.D., et al.: Functional network organization of the human brain. Neuron **72**(4), 665–678 (2011)
40. Craddock, R.C., et al.: A whole brain fMRI atlas generated via spatially constrained spectral clustering. Hum. Brain Mapp. **33**(8), 1914–1928 (2012)
41. Schaefer, A., et al.: Local-global parcellation of the human cerebral cortex from intrinsic functional connectivity MRI. Cereb. Cortex. Cortex **28**(9), 3095–3114 (2018)
42. Wang, Z., et al.: Multiple measurement analysis of resting-state fMRI for ADHD classification in adolescent brain from the ABCD study. Transl. Psychiatry **13**(1), 45 (2023)
43. Brown, M.R., et al.: ADHD-200 Global Competition: diagnosing ADHD using personal characteristic data can outperform resting state fMRI measurements. Front. Syst. Neurosci. **6**, 69 (2012)
44. Lu, H., et al.: Multiple measurement analysis of resting-state fMRI for ADHD classification in adolescent brain from the ABCD Study. Transl. Psychiatry **13**, 45 (2022)
45. Bellec, P., et al.: The Neuro Bureau ADHD-200 Preprocessed repository. Neuroimage **144**(Pt B), 275–286 (2017)
46. Cortese, S., et al.: Systematic review and meta-analysis: resting-state functional magnetic resonance imaging studies of attention-deficit/hyperactivity disorder. J. Am. Acad. Child Adolesc. Psychiatry **60**(1), 61–75 (2021)

47. Moghimi, P., et al.: Evaluation of functional MRI-based human brain parcellation: a review. J. Neurophysiol. **128**(1), 197–217 (2022)
48. Lanzetta-Valdo, B.P., et al.: Auditory processing assessment in children with attention deficit hyperactivity disorder: an open study examining methylphenidate effects. Int Arch Otorhinolaryngol **21**(1), 72–78 (2017)
49. Thirion, B., et al.: Which fMRI clustering gives good brain parcellations? Front. Neurosci. **8**, 167 (2014)

An Automated Enhancement System of Diabetic Retinopathy Fundus Image for Eye Care Facilities

Nurul Atikah Mohd Sharif[1] (iD), Nor Hazlyna Harun[1,2](✉) (iD),
Nur Azmielia Muhammad Sharimi[1], Juhaida Abu Bakar[1] (iD), Hapini Awang[2] (iD),
and Zunaina Embong[3] (iD)

[1] Data Science Research Lab, School of Computing, University Utara Malaysia, 06010 Sintok, Kedah, Malaysia
hazlyna@uum.edu.my

[2] Institute for Advanced and Smart Digital Opportunities, School of Computing, University Utara Malaysia, 06010 Sintok, Kedah, Malaysia

[3] Ophthalmologist, Department of Ophthalmology, School of Medical Sciences, Health Campus, Universiti Sains Malaysia, 16150 Kubang Kerian, Kelantan, Malaysia

Abstract. Examining retinal fundus images is compulsory for ophthalmologists to spot features of eye diseases. Some problems, including low contrast and blurred retinal fundus image, may seriously affect the diagnostic procedure, leading to misdiagnosis. Low quality of retinal fundus image makes recognition of features for Diabetic Retinopathy (DR) to be harder for the ophthalmologist. Moreover, there is a lack of eye care facilities infrastructure with ophthalmologists to serve multimorbid DR patients in rural areas, specifically Malaysia. Hence, this research proposed the development of an automated enhancement system based on computer vision and the Artificial Intelligence (AI) field to improve the quality of fundus images captured. The DR Enhancement System (DRES) helps ophthalmologists in the screening aspect by improving the detection of aberrant fundus images. Several methods for improving the fundus image are utilized: Retinex, Contrast Limited Adaptive Histogram Equalization (CLAHE), and Low-light enhancement. Results show that all methods performed better when improving low-contrast and blurred images. This study contributes to the screening process of DR by improving the quality of the retinal fundus image. The developed AI-based system can also help to solve healthcare logistics problems of reaching DR patients in rural areas.

Keywords: Contrast Enhancement · Retinal Fundus Image · Diabetic Retinopathy · CLAHE · Low-light enhancement

1 Introduction

Nowadays, the study of Artificial Intelligent (AI) applications in healthcare institutions is crucial for innovation that can increase productivity, reduce costs, and increase the profit of the institution [1]. In addition, computer vision is one of the fields under AI that could interpret the visual world, and retinal fundus image is one of the implemented AI imaging subjects [2]. Retinal fundus image captured to define staging of diabetic retinopathy (DR), which is one of the chronic diseases. DR is a complication related to long-term diabetic diseases. It is pathologically affected by prolonged high blood sugar level that causes damage to the blood vessels in the retina. Damaged blood vessels can be seen as enlargement and leakage of the blood vessel. There are two types of DR: non-proliferative (NPDR) and proliferative (PDR). NPDR is a type of DR that is less severe and does not cause symptoms. PDR is a well-known type of DR that creates new fragile blood vessels in the retina [3]. There are a lot of people that have lost their eyesight because of DR. Earlier diagnosis and treatment, DR can be prevented from progressing to blindness. In order to diagnose DR, an ophthalmologist will look for abnormal signs such as haemorrhages, microaneurysms, and hard exudates that appeared on the retinal fundus image [4]. The examination of retinal fundus images is frequently employed in the current day to assist ophthalmologists in gathering essential information about a patient's retina to detect DR [5].

In Malaysia nowadays, we are facing a shortage of ophthalmologists [6]. With the increasing trend of DR, it burdens ophthalmologists with more workload and fewer staff. Consequently, it contributes to long appointment waiting times and worsened DR staging prognoses. Furthermore, the procedure for treating the DR is usually made through an appointment with an ophthalmologist. Most patients only meet the ophthalmologist when the eye vision has blurring and or even blindness has set in. Problems also appeared as most of the retinal fundus images captured always faced low image quality, such as low contrast, low illumination, and colour inconsistency. Hence, due to aging populations, a shortage of ophthalmologists, and medical sustainability challenges, an efficient and accurate system is needed to make the procedure and the results accurate [7]. Therefore, this system's existence can help the ophthalmologist make an early diagnosis and prognosis for the patient as the image can be automatically enhanced. This motivational approach may directly increase efficiency and creativity for eye care facilities infrastructure, specifically in rural areas.

The research aims to design and construct an AI-based system for eyecare facilities that can improve retinal fundus images for detecting DR patients in rural areas. One of the most significant aspects of screening DR is detecting abnormal fundus images. Some problems, like low contrast and blur image, may seriously affect the diagnostic stages. The authors used three methods for improving the fundus image: Retinex, Contrast Limited Adaptive Histogram Equalization (CLAHE), and Low-Light Enhancement. These methods perform better in handling low-contrast images and blurred images [8]. So, based on this system, ophthalmologists can precisely identify a patient with a DR problem. Hopefully, it will improve systematic DR screening program, human resources, and infrastructure distribution that align with the population's needs especially in rural areas. This study consists of six topics: introduction, related work, methodology, result and evaluation, and conclusion.

2 Related Work

This section explains the related study of image enhancement for diabetic retinopathy (DR). Dorothy et al. [9] developed a way to create colour retinal image enhancement depending on their understanding of retina architecture and imaging parameters. Researchers had presented a new improved method using a non-uniform sampling-based forecast of the degradation components and reviewed the findings of implementing it to a single colour plane; a colour image enhancement solution combining a linear colour remapping technique. The chromatic information of the original image is used in the remapping of colour procedure for retinal colour enhancement images. The RGB was converted to HSV (hue saturation value). An image with RGB colour space is created by integrating the increased intensity and saturation components with the original hue component. Enhancement's influence on dark and bright lesions in a retinal image was investigated [10]. While in another study, RGB is transformed to Uniform Color Space. The Discrete Shearlet Transform (DST) divides the brightness components into many coefficients. It also has a non-linear mapping function that improves contrast and performs gamma correction—modified coefficient inverse DST. Finally, updated colour planes are combined to improve the image [11].

A study had modified Contourlet coefficients to improve image contrast. The results of the experiments demonstrate that this strategy is an effective and promising method for improving retinal images. Contrast Stretching relies on a number of features [4]. The strategy used in this study was to enhance brown regions by applying gamma correction to each red, green, and blue-bit picture. The histograms of each red, blue, and blue-bit picture were then stretched. After that, the studies utilized density analysis, and the bleeding candidates were identified. Finally, false positives were eliminated using the rule-based strategy. The researchers tested on 125 fundus images, 35 of which had haemorrhages and 90 of which were normal, to see how well the novel method for detecting haemorrhage worked [12]. While Feng et al. [5] used independent component analysis to improve low contrast retinal vasculature in the ocular fundus image by estimating the retinal pigment makeup, namely haemoglobin, melanin, and macular pigments.

Several studies have used Retinex method for image enhancement. To investigate the influence of brightness variations in labelling and to demonstrate the accuracy of the suggested procedure, Vázquez et. al. Used two alternative ways [13]. The study concentrated on estimating illumination so that the Retinex on an image could be accurately performed. The image is filtered with the help of a Gauss Mask with various settings and scale [14]. The suggested method, which is based on an enhanced image formation model, effectively raises global and local contrasts concurrently, avoids colour change by boosting only the component picture, and practically eliminates halo artefact due to the use of JND-based non-linear LPF [15].

Zhang et al. [11] used RGB colour retinal image and break the colour image channel into three separate images: R, G, and B. Contrast Limited Adaptive Histogram Equalization (CLAHE) method is used in the G channel since it has more blood vessel structural information than the others. The image of the G channel is improved. The following step combines the three image channels (R, enhanced G, and R). The researchers were able to obtain an improved colour retinal image at the end of the procedure [11]. Furthermore, another study implemented a low-light method to enhance the image. The test photos were collected from several data sets, and the improved photographs' quality was assessed using subjective and objective evaluation. Clearly, the proposed method produces clear photographs with natural colour, regardless of whether the scene is close or far away, demonstrating the method's effectiveness and usefulness [8]. By replicating the mechanisms involved at the particular level of retina, the suggested model improves foggy images. The suggested approach particularly contains physiologically inspired processing [9]. Other researchers used histogram equalization to assess image quality. This technique is frequently used to increase global contrast of a large number of photos, especially when close contrast values represent the images' usable data. The levels on the histogram can have higher impact with this change. This enables locations with generally low contrast to obtain an increase in contrast [16]. This study has identified the best strategy for enhancing contrast in medical photos. It examines four strategies for equalizing a histogram of medical images: Histogram equalization (HE), Cumulative Histogram equalization (CHE), CLAHE, and Quadrant Dynamic Histogram Equalization (QDHE). It assesses each technique's reaction using three criteria based on five medical images parameters: PSNR, MSE, and SD are acronyms for Peak Signal to Noise Ratio (PSNR), Mean Square Error (MSE), and Standard Deviation (SD) [17]. CLAHE was used to improve the image's green channel contrast [18]. A new improved technique based on fuzzy set theory has been devised for grayscale non-uniform illumination images. The results showed that the proposed method improved image quality and outperformed other methods in terms of image contrast and fuzziness measurement without adding to existing noise in the image [19].

3   Methodology

This study was conducted based on Agile Software Development approach. In system analysis, agile methodology emphasizes flexibility, continuous improvement, reducing complexity, and timeliness. Figure 1 illustrates the five phases of this methodology: requirements, design, development, testing, and deployment.

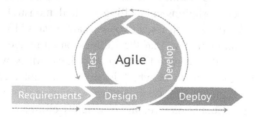

Fig. 1. Agile Methodology.

The interface for the system was designed, sketched, and all the necessary data for the system, such as the information needed in the report, was prepared in the first phase. The retinal fundus image dataset and details images information were obtained from the Hospital Univeristi Sains Malaysia (HUSM) Kubang Kerian Kelantan. The ophthalmologist determines data obtained such as retinal fundus image interpretation and

DR classification. The system's function has been designed and implemented, as well as the system's interface. The image processing approach is built using MATLAB software. The system has been tested to ensure that there is no bug. HUSM ophthalmologists test the system by employing the system in the last step.

3.1 Image Processing

A flow chart of image processing is shown in Fig. 2. First, the fundus camera captured retinal fundus image and converts RGB to Hue Saturation Value (HSV). Retinex, CLAHE, and Low-light enhancement are three types of enhancement methods applied on the converted HSV image. Finally, the visual quality of the enhanced retinal fundus image is measured using the Mean Squared Error (MSE), Peak-Signal Noise Ratio (PSNR) and Structural Similarity Index Measure (SSIM).

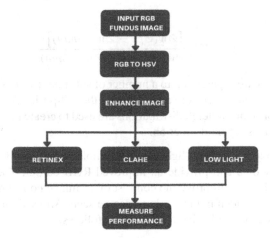

Fig. 2. Flow chart of Image Processing.

3.2 Retinal Fundus Image Dataset

The image size is 3008 x 2000 pixels. The retinal fundus image has been classified into three categories by ophthalmologists: normal, NPDR, and PDR.

3.3 Image Method Enhancement

In this section, each enhancement method is explained. There are three enhancement method types: Retinex, CLAHE and Low-light enhancement.

Retinex Enhancement. To achieve colour consistency, the retinex approach attempts to build a model of the human visual system. The brightness is estimated in this technique, and the output image is created by eliminating the estimated illumination from the original image. To attain colour consistency and improve the retinal fundus image, this study has utilized Multi-Scale Retinex techniques. The formula of Multi-Scale Retinex is as follows:

$$R_{MSR} = \sum_{n=1}^{N} w_n R_n \tag{1}$$

N represents the number of scales, R_n is the n-th scale's component from Eq. (1). The MSR raises several obvious concerns, including the actual number of scales, scale values, and associated weights (w_n).

CLAHE Enhancement.   The technique of Contrast Limited Adaptive Histogram Equalization (CLAHE) is also used in this study to improve the colour retinal fundus image. The contrast of an image is created by combining the intensity value range and separating the upper and lower limits pixel values. Equalization of the histogram spreads the frequency content and modifies the original image's contrast. The CLAHE is defined by Eq. (2).

$$g = 255 \frac{\left[\varnothing w(\varnothing f) - \varnothing w(\varnothing fmin)\right]}{[\varnothing w(\varnothing fmax) - \varnothing w(\varnothing fmin)} \tag{2}$$

The input images are separated into a number of sub-images (tiles), and the contrast transform function is calculated for each tile using the 'Clip Limit' contrast factor. The Exponential, Uniform, or Rayleigh distributions are used to create the contrast transform function. Where $\varnothing w$ is sigmoid function.

Low-Light Enhancement.   Low-light imaging employs the use of a camera to analyse the preliminary data and provide an improved RGB output. The low-light image enhancement is utilized to improve the contrast of an image concentration and performance so that details hidden in the shadows can be seen. A low-light enhancement has been used, and this equation is given in Eq. (3) as follows:

$$I = R * T + a(1 - T) \tag{3}$$

R is the scene radiance, the global atmospheric light is a, and the medium transmission is T which describes the part of the light that isn't scattered. The comparison of the original and enhanced retinal fundus image using retinex enhancement, CLAHE enhancement, and low-light enhancement are shown in Fig. 3, 4, and 5 respectively.

3.4   Performance Evaluation

There are three performances in this study which are Mean Squared Error (MSE), Peak-Signal Noise Ratio (PSNR) and Structural Similarity Index Measure (SSIM). The equation of MSE, PSNR and SSIM has shown in Eq. (4), (5) and (6).

$$MSE = \frac{\sum_{M,N} [I_1(m, n) - I_2(m, n)]^2}{M * N} \tag{4}$$

where, $I_1(x, y)$ is the original image

ORIGINAL   **RETINEX**

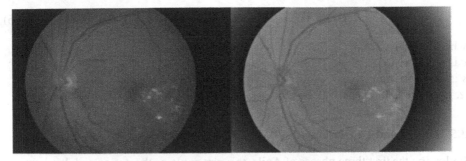

Fig. 3. Image of Retinex Enhancement.

ORIGINAL   **CLAHE**

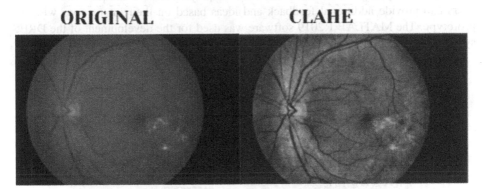

Fig. 4. Image of CLAHE Enhancement.

ORIGINAL   **LOW LIGHT**

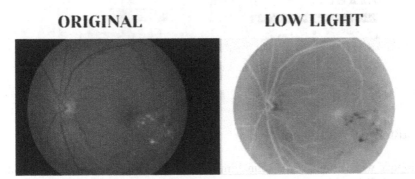

Fig. 5. Image of Low-Light Enhancement.

$I_2(x, y)$ is the enhanced image

$$PSNR = 10log_{10}\left(\frac{R^2}{MSE}\right) \tag{5}$$

where, R is the maximum pixel value

$$SSIM(xy) = [l(x, y)]^{\alpha} . [c(x, y)]^{\beta} . [s(x, y)]^{y} \qquad (6)$$

where, I is luminance
c is the contrast.
s is the structure.
α, β and γ are the positive constants.

3.5 Design and Development

Following the first three phases of Agile, this part explains the design and development of the system. DR Enhancement System (DRES) is developed as a standalone system. Software prototyping is a common method of displaying software requirements so that users can provide additional feedback and ideas based on their interactions with the prototype. The MATLAB R2019 software was used for the development of the DRES system. Figure 6, 7 and 8 show the interfaces of the system.

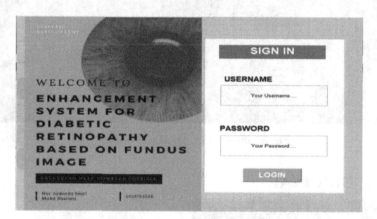

Fig. 6. Login Page.

4   Result and Evaluation

The technique was verified on 45 retinal images provided by Hospital Universiti Sains Malaysia (HUSM) with three stages: Normal, NPDR, and PDR. The metrics (MSE, PSNR, and SSIM) are used in this research to get the best quality metrics. The obtained image quality has been applied to the above metrics. The retinal images contrast was improved. The processed image has higher contrast than the original. Furthermore, the Retinex, CLAHE, and Low-Light enhancements standardized the image's color. Tables 1, 2 and 3 display the average value outcomes of the performance for resultant images.

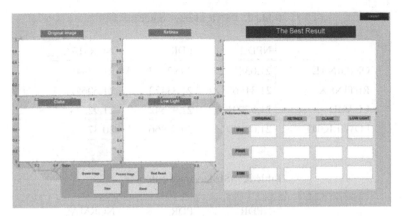

Fig. 7. Image Processing Page.

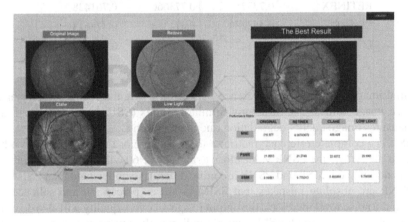

Fig. 8. Result of Image Processing Page.

Table 1. MSE average outcome

	NPDR	PDR	NORMAL
ORIGINAL	512.1768	526.2727	512.0213
RETINEX	0.007385	0.00736	0.006915
CLAHE	412.4731	414.5039	417.3661
LOW LIGHT	515.4757	530.1767	531.0909

The peak signal-to-noise ratio (PSNR) is an expression of a signal's maximum possible value (power) ratio to the strength of distorting noise that influences the quality. The mean squared error (MSE) compares the original image's "true" pixel values to our degraded image. MSE is the squared average of the "errors" between our normal and

Table 2. PSNR average outcome

	NPDR	PDR	NORMAL
ORIGINAL	21.03817	20.92193	21.03946
RETINEX	21.31665	21.33473	21.60657
CLAHE	21.97791	21.95642	21.92573
LOW LIGHT	21.00849	20.88866	20.87951

Table 3. SSIM average outcome

	NPDR	PDR	NORMAL
ORIGINAL	0.998395	0.997382	0.995934
RETINEX	0.77325	0.773666	0.761428
CLAHE	0.468239	0.474384	0.473613
LOW LIGHT	0.751273	0.716465	0.665399

abnormal images. Error is the difference between the original image's values and the degraded image values. The Structural Similarity Index (SSIM) is a perceptual metric that measures image quality degradation due to processing.

MSE is a complete reference metric; a lower value close to zero indicates a better image output. While the PSNR value close to and above 60 will indicate a better image. SSIM is normalized. MSE and PSNR are more difficult to understand than SSIM. MSE and PSNR are absolute mistakes, but SSIM produces perception and salience-based errors. If the noise level increases, the output image recovery quality will also deteriorate [20]. A value close to one for SSIM metric indicates the image does not change much on the structure.

Therefore, based on MSE metric evaluation in Table 1, comparing between three enhancement method, Retinex enhancement method produce the best average output with value of 0.007385, 0.00736, and 0.006915 for the NPDR, PDR and normal retinal image respectively. While based on PSNR evaluation in Table 2, the result between the three methods does not have much difference where CLAHE enhancement method have slightly higher value close to 60 compares to others method. The value is 21.97791 (NPDR), 21.95642 (PDR), and 21.92573 (Normal), respectively. Hence, of the three methods, Retinex enhancement became the most outstanding method based on the metric evaluation.

For expert evaluation, a questionnaire is designed using Google Forms to determine system performance feedback from the end-user. 14 ophthalmologists from HUSM are evaluating the system. Usability specialists analyzed this system interface and compared it to acknowledged usability criteria in a heuristic evaluation. The investigation had listed the possible usability issues. The user manual for system installation, is emailed to the ophthalmologists. Follow-up of the questionnaire is also done over the phone.

Table 4 shows the list of statements included in the questionnaires. Figure 9, 10, and 11 summarize the output from the expert evaluation.

Table 4. List of statements for expert evaluation.

No	Statement
1.	This system can provide the statistical performance of the output image enhancement
2.	The fundus image abnormalities can be seen clearly and result in good brightness
3.	This technique gives a better image output than the original image
4.	This technique/method is suitable to be used for fundus images
5.	The technique/method applied to the image synchronized with the theory of the techniques/methods

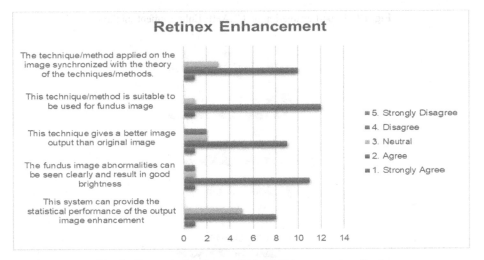

Fig. 9. Expert evaluation on Retinex Enhancement method.

Based on chart presented in Fig. 9, the expert evaluation on the Retinex enhancement method show 57%, 79%, 64%, 86% and 71% had agree with the statements from Table 4 respectively. While expert evaluation on the CLAHE enhancement method (Fig. 10), the percentage of agreed statement lesser than Retinex enhancement evaluation which are 43% (Statement 1), 64% (Statement 2), 50% (Statement 3), 43% (Statement 4), and 64% (Statement 5). Each statement for CLAHE enhancement method has a small percentage of experts who disagree with the statement. There are strongly disagree by expert on the statement for Low-light enhancement method. Even though strongly disagree only 7% for each statement, it gives the feedback that the method lacked performance from the expert view.

Figure 12 shows 64%, 64%, 50%, and 50% agree with statement 1, 2, 4, and 6 listed in Table 5 respectively, which are higher among the other agreement. While on

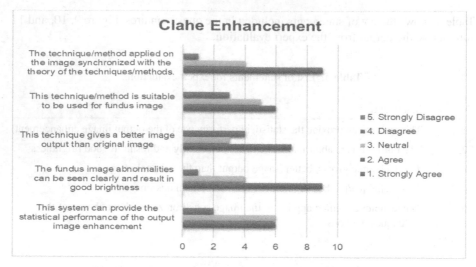

Fig. 10. Expert evaluation on CLAHE Enhancement method.

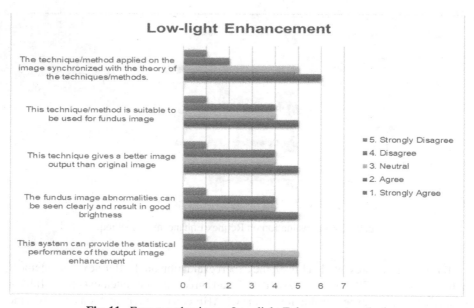

Fig. 11. Expert evaluation on Low-light Enhancement method.

statement 3 and statement 5 obtained 50% and 64%, a neutral statement and 7% of the expert disagree with the statement. The expert evaluation output indicates that there is an area that need to be improved from the system's performance.

Table 5. List of statement for overall system performance evaluation.

No.	Statement
1.	The organization of information on the system screens was clear
2.	The interface of this system was pleasant
3.	The information is well organized and functions are easy to find
4.	The speed of this system is fast
5.	This system has all the functions and capabilities I expect it to have
6.	Overall, I am satisfied with this system

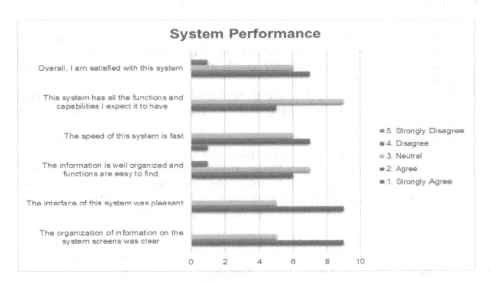

Fig. 12. An overall system performance evaluated by the expert.

5 Conclusion and Future Work

In this paper, image enhancement methods including Retinex, CLAHE and Low-light were applied to automate enhancing low quality retinal fundus image to support the diagnosis of DR. The results of the experiments demonstrated that DRES (AI-based system) can improve retinal fundus images significantly, using Retinex enhancement method. The results tested in the DRES system showed that Retinex enhancement was the best method. Retinex had the highest performance value compared to CLAHE and Low-light enhancement. The features using Retinex enhancement such as hard exudates and haemorrhage was clear enhanced rather than original retina image. This study explored different image enhancement techniques for the same dataset to determine the variation of the output image.

Although DRES helps overcome issues of related to the lack of ophthalmologists visiting rural areas for elderly and multi-morbid DR patients, the biggest challenge for healthcare institutions is sustainability development to create a safe and secure workplace that will guarantee the health and well-being of patients in rural areas. Future work should be considered more blurred image tested in developing sustainable healthcare logistics, especially in rural areas.

Acknowledgement. This research was supported by Ministry of Higher Education (MoHE) of Malaysia through Fundamental Research Grant Scheme (FRGS/1/2019/ICT02/UUM/02/1). The substance of this finding is exclusively the responsibility of the authors and does not inevitably signify the official opinions of the MoHE, Malaysia.

References

1. Bazel M. A., Mohammed F., Ahmed M.: Blockchain technology in healthcare big data management: Benefits, applications and challenges. In: 1st International Conference on Emerging Smart Technologies and Applications. eSmarTA 2021 (2021). https://doi.org/10.1109/eSm arTA52612.2021.9515747
2. Kemper, A.R., Wallace, D.K., Quinn, G.E.: Systematic review of digital imaging screening strategies for retinopathy of prematurity. Pediatrics **122**(4), 825–830 (2008). https://doi.org/ 10.1542/peds.2007-3667
3. Ministry of Health Malaysia: Diabetic retinopathy screening: Training module for healthcare providers, 88 (2017). https://doi.org/10.1038/eye.2001.40
4. Hatanaka Y., Nakagawa T., Hayashi Y., Hara T., Fujita H.: Improvement of automated detection method of hemorrhages in fundus images. In: Proceedings 30th Annual International Conference of the IEEE Engineering in Medicine and Biology Society, EMBS 2008 - "Personalized Healthcare Through Technology, pp. 5429–5432 (2008). https://doi.org/10.1109/ iembs.2008.4650442
5. Feng, P., Pan, Y., Wei, B., Jin, W., Mi, D.: Enhancing retinal image by the Contourlet transform. Pattern Recognit. Lett. **28**(4), 516–522 (2007). https://doi.org/10.1016/j.patrec.2006.09.007
6. Yahaya, N.A., Musa, A., Azemin, M.Z.C., Rahman, N.A.A.: Implementing primary eye care in private practises in Malaysia: the challenges faced by optometrists. Med. J. Malaysia **78**(3), 357–363 (2023)
7. Martins J., Cardoso J.S., Soares F.: Offline computer-aided diagnosis for Glaucoma detection using fundus images targeted at mobile devices. Comput. Methods Programs Biomed. (192) (2020). https://doi.org/10.1016/j.cmpb.2020.105341
8. Feng, X., Li, J., Hua, Z.: Low-light image enhancement algorithm based on an atmospheric physical model. Multimed. Tools Appl. **79**(43–44), 32973–32997 (2020). https://doi.org/10. 1007/s11042-020-09562-6
9. Dorothy R., Rajendran S., Joany R.M., Rathish R.J., Santhana Prabha S., Rajendran S.: Image enhancement by Histogram equalization Image enhancement by Histogram equalization Image enhancement by Histogram equalization. Int. J. Nano. Corr. Sci. Engg **2**(4), 21–30 (2015). https://www.researchgate.net/publication/283727396
10. Abbas, Q., Farooq, A., Abbas, T., Celebi, E., Garcia, I.F., Carmona, J.: Features preserving contrast improvement for retinal vascular images. Int. J. Innov. Comput. Inf. Control **9**(9), 3731–3739 (2013)
11. Zhang X.S., Gao S.B., Li C.Y., Li Y.J.: A retina inspired model for enhancing visibility of hazy images. Front. Comput. Neurosci. **9**, 1–13 (2015). https://doi.org/10.3389/fncom.2015. 00151

12. Fadzil, A., Hani, M., Adi, N.H.: Retinal vasculature enhancement using independent component analysis. J. Biomed. Sci. Eng. **02**(07), 543–549 (2009). https://doi.org/10.4236/jbise. 2009.27079
13. Vázquez, S.G., Barreira, N., Penedo, M.G., Saez, M., Pose-Reino, A.: Using retinex image enhancement to improve the artery/vein classification in retinal images. In: Campilho, A., Kamel, M. (eds.) ICIAR 2010. LNCS, vol. 6112, pp. 50–59. Springer, Heidelberg (2010). https://doi.org/10.1007/978-3-642-13775-4_6
14. Parihar A.S., Singh K.: A study on Retinex based method for image enhancement. In: Proceedings of 2nd International Conference Inventory Management System, pp. 619–624 (2018). https://doi.org/10.1109/ICISC.2018.8398874
15. Choi D.H., Jang I.H., Kim M.H., Kim N.C.: Color image enhancement using single-scale retinex based on an improved image formation model. In: Eur. Signal Process Conference (2008)
16. Comput, P.: Salem N., Malik H., Shams A., Medical image enhancement based on histogram algorithms. In. Sci. **163**, 300–311 (2019). https://doi.org/10.1016/j.procs.2019.12.112
17. Umapathy A., Sreenivasan A., Nairy D. S., Natarajan S., Rao B.N.: Image processing, textural feature extraction and transfer learning based detection of diabetic retinopathy. In: ACM International Conference Proceeding Series, pp. 17–21 (2019). https://doi.org/10.1145/331 4367.3314376
18. Hasikin K., Isa N.A.M.: Enhancement of the low contrast image using fuzzy set theory. In: Proceedings 2012 14th International Conference on Computer Modeling and Simulation, pp. 371–376 (2012) https://doi.org/10.1109/UKSim.2012.60
19. Setiawan A.W., Mengko T.R., Santoso O.S., Suksmono A.B.: Color Retinal Image Enhancement using CLAHE. In: International Conference on ICT for Smart Society, Jakarta, Indonesia, pp. 2–4 (2013). https://doi.org/10.1109/ICTSS.2013.6588092
20. Sara, U., Akter, M., Uddin, M.S.: Image quality assessment through FSIM, SSIM, MSE and PSNR—A comparative study. J. Comput. Commun. **07**(03), 8–18 (2019). https://doi.org/10. 4236/jcc.2019.73002

Persuading People to Fight Dengue and Sustaining It via Mobile Application

Masitah Ghazali[1(✉)], Nur Zuraifah Syazrah Othman[2], Zatul Alwani Shaffiei[1], Suriati Sadimon[2], Zuraini Ali Shah[2], and Zuriahati Mohd Yunos[2]

[1] Malaysia-Japan International Institute of Technology, Universiti Teknologi Malaysia, Kuala Lumpur, Malaysia
masitah@utm.my
[2] Faculty of Computing, Universiti Teknologi Malaysia, Johor Bahru, Malaysia

Abstract. The challenge to dengue prevention lies in sustaining the preventive activity among the community, which commonly occurs periodically, i.e., when there are dengue outbreaks, with health officers under the Communication for Behavioural Impact (COMBI) campaign. In this paper, a mobile application is specifically developed based on the COMBI Behavioural Change model, which focuses on persuading users to adopt and sustain new habits. The application was carefully designed to reflect the stages of behavioural change. Combining both quantitative and qualitative approaches, an experiment was performed over a four-week study with eight participants, and based on the empirical findings, it is found that with careful design, users can be persuaded to take up the new habit. Two traits that are deemed important are understanding the 'why', and the trait of being responsible citizens. In addition, at the end of the study, users felt comfortable continuing with the cleaning activities without the application. Thus, more thoughts should be considered for the application to remain relevant in the sustainable phase.

Keywords: Dengue Prevention · Persuasive Technology · Behavioural Change

1 Introduction

Technology that supports and promotes behavioural change is commonly known as persuasive technology and is mostly employed in areas such as healthcare [1], education [2], and productivity [3]. Getting the right information displayed on the devices is crucial as it could lead to an impactful result, i.e., change behavior could become a habit. Developing motivational technology to support long-term behaviour change is challenging [4], especially sustaining behavioural change [5]. To design effective persuasive technologies, many designs draw upon theories of behaviour change to understand what factors influence people's behaviour change decisions [6–9]. In the context of dengue, some examples that already utilize mobile devices for dengue prevention include [10–12]. But none of these adopts the behaviour change theory. In addition, there is no well-established method to translate theoretical constructs and insight into persuasive or motivational interaction designs for practice [4] for dengue prevention.

N. H. Zakaria et al. (Eds.): ICOCI 2023, CCIS 2002, pp. 110–122, 2024.
https://doi.org/10.1007/978-981-99-9592-9_9

Many case studies in tropical and subtropical countries around the world succeed in preventing and controlling dengue through community participation [13–17]. The key to success is the sustainability shown by the community in the activity, and for sustainability to happen, behavioural change must occur, or it would become a periodic event. But behaviour change is not easy to achieve. In Malaysia, many awareness activities have been carried out by the *Pejabat Kesihatan Daerah* (District Health Office) of every state through COMBI [18, 19]. However, the impact is still very small and unsustainable [20, 21]. Sustainable community participation is paramount to the surveillance system that is a part of the national health information system. By doing so, a harmonized effort across national dengue surveillance systems can inform the critical data of the disease's burden, which is necessary to assess progress in reaching mortality and morbidity reduction goals [19].

In this study, we designed an experiment to investigate the effect of usage of a mobile application that is designed based on the COMBI Behavioural Change model [22]. In particular, the created features of the application were intended to translate each of the phases we identified for the behavioural change to be initiated, progressed, and sustained. We deployed the application for a four-week user study with 8 participants. Our study explores, in the specific domain of behavioural change, how persuasive applications can create change in user attitudes and sustain it. Both qualitatively and quantitatively, we examine how the features of the application affect the users' perceptions and awareness of their activities, creating the potential for behaviour change.

2   Experiment Design

We developed a working prototype mobile application based on the found model derived from self-previous work [22] with 8 users for 4 weeks. In this section, we describe the design of the application and the methods of the experiment.

2.1   System Description

2.1.1   Data

In Malaysia, the dengue prevention initiative recommended by COMBI and the Ministry of Health is to spend at least 10 min per week cleaning. Based on this guideline, we collected data on the types of activities performed by each user and the time spent to conduct the activity. We also recorded the images of places involved in the cleaning activity. In addition, to support the eco-system of COMBI at the community level, data on the COMBI team that one joins with its leader are also considered.

All recorded data are presented to users, where they can see their performance, either weekly or monthly, i.e., the accumulated time spent on cleaning and the activities performed. If the user is the COMBI leader, he/she can also monitor the accumulated time of his/her members. The ability to review past activities is an important feature as part of a persuasive design strategy [23].

2.1.2 Design

There are five stages in the COMBI Behavioural Change model [22]. The following sub-sections illustrate how each phase is translated into the application's design.

Pre-contemplation. This phase is the beginning where no prevention activity is engaged, and there is yet an intention to do so. The intervention strategies identified in this phase are education, advice, and self-monitoring, while the trigger is spark. The splash screens in Fig. 1 are the screens as the user successfully installed and ran the application on his/her phone. The strategies can be observed in the wordings and images used, where the user will begin to understand dengue's importance and fatality. The arrows and the *Get Started* button to the next screen act as the spark.

Fig. 1. Pre-Contemplation phase (first, second) and Contemplation phase (third) splash screens

Contemplation. In this phase, no prevention activity is engaged, but there is already an intention to do so. This phase's intervention strategies are education, advice, and comparison. The trigger element is the spark. As soon as the *Get Started* button is clicked, it brings a user to the login screen, where there are options to either sign up with their Google account or proceed with the registration process (Fig. 2 first and second images). Figure 2, the third image, where the user is ready to start, can first explore what he/she does as part of the prevention activity. One can learn more from News, FAQ, and Community pages to set goals and compare how others are doing.

Fig. 2. Sign up and register as part of the Contemplation phase (first and second images), and the home screen as the Preparation phase (third image)

Preparation. User in this phase has started to be involved in the prevention activity, where the intervention strategies are setting goals and comparison. Facilitator is the trigger for this phase. In the set of images in Fig. 3, they show the flow of screens when recording their cleaning activity, by first taking a picture, starting the cleaning time, stopping the cleaning time, and choosing the type of cleaning activity they have performed. Every step of the sequence facilitates the user to accomplish the activity.

Competence. In this phase, the user has been consistently involved in prevention activity for a certain amount of time, where the intervention strategies are engagement, communication, and reward. Signal is used as the trigger. Figure 4 shows the community screens where one could connect and engage with other users.

Maintenance. The final phase refers to when the user has been consistently involved in prevention activity for a longer period that has broken the old habit. Communication and reward are the intervention strategies applied, and the signal is the trigger. Consistent users can view their past activities (Fig. 5).

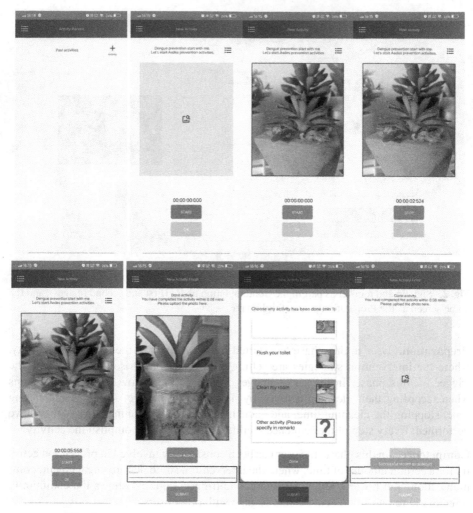

Fig. 3. Recording the cleaning activity as part of the Preparation phase

2.2 Participants

We recruited participants who are familiar with Android through social media sites, emails, and word of mouth. A total of 6 participants completed the 4-week study in November 2022, with 2 participants abandoning the study after 2 weeks. Participants ranged from 22 to 40 years old and occupations including graduate student, web developer, and customer service representative. All participants were never involved in any activities similar to this before.

Fig. 4. Engaging with the community

Fig. 5. Checking the past activities

2.3 Methods and Procedure

We combined quantitative and qualitative methods, ranging from online surveys (one before the 4-week experiment and the other at the end) to analysis of 4-week usage logs. The surveys and log data from each participant are used to derive descriptive system usage statistics.

Pre-experiment Survey. All participants interested in joining were first asked to complete a survey provided online before they proceeded to install the application. We aimed to know their knowledge, and exposure towards the dengue cleaning activity.

4-week Field Experiment. At the beginning of the 4-week study, we created a Telegram group as a platform to touch base with participants. We held an introductory session with the participants via Google Meet to share the aim of the study and provided them with brief information about the application. We informed the participants that we wanted to understand how they would use the application to help fight dengue through cleaning activities. A short survey was distributed at the end of the second week as an interim to gauge the participants' motivation level. The chronological recorded time and activities for the four weeks may provide evidence of the possible behaviour change on the individual level in a semi-longitudinal manner. We hypothesized the frequent logged time and activity would reflect the participant's attempt to change his or her habit of dengue prevention.

Post-completion Survey. At the end of the 4-week use period, we posted the URL link to the final survey via Telegram. Through the survey, our goal is to evaluate these concerns; (i) user experience with the application and (ii) the transition one had throughout the 5 phases, although we did not explicitly mention the phase to them. In addition, we asked about their current awareness of dengue prevention and whether they will resume this habit.

3 Results

We obtained the results of the participants at the end of the experiment. Our analysis showed each individual's persuasion toward behaviour change is varied and gradual. We also present the results of the detailed findings of every phase.

3.1 General Performances

Before the study, none of the participants knew much about COMBI cleaning initiatives as part of dengue prevention by the Ministry of Health (MoH) Malaysia. The participants were briefed about the common activities recommended during the introductory session, but they were free to add other cleaning-related activities. Over four weeks, turning over water containers is the most frequent activity. While the least frequent are the bottom four as in Fig. 6, where the participants add these activities to the cleaning activities.

Over the course of four weeks, the pattern of the weekly participation is only consistent for three participants: P2, P3, and P6. In addition, what is noticeable from the data (see Fig. 7), all weekly participants did not spend close to 10 min per week as recommended by MoH. Nonetheless, as newcomers who just started, and even more so for the three consistent participants, this can be considered an accomplishment.

3.2 Behavioural Change Phases

We are also interested in understanding the experiences the participants went through as they used the application. Without disclosing the phases to the participants, we inquired about their experiences in the final survey as they were at specific stages and the respective application screens.

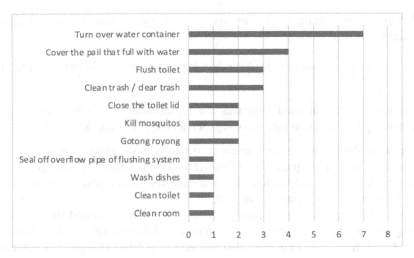

Fig. 6. The frequency of the recorded cleaning activities

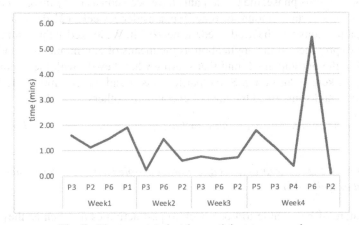

Fig. 7. Time spent (mins) by participants per week

Pre-contemplation. Participants have yet to have intention in the prevention activity, so when asked whether they hesitated to be involved in the very beginning, the majority (75%) did not hesitate, and the remaining were not quite sure but stayed on, nonetheless.

Contemplation. This phase is closely related to the previous phase, as now they decided to proceed and have intention in the prevention activity. Some participants had a strong drive due to her personal experience (P4). While some others being as responsible citizens, feeling called to proceed (P3 and P5).

"To reduce the dengue cases in my community as I was infected with dengue fever before. (P4)"

"I hope to help mitigate dengue and protect myself from my surroundings mosquitoes. (P3)"

"To educate myself and take action on how to improve the environment and prevent dengue. (P5)"

The trigger element used here was the registration page, where 87.5% of the participants found it easy to sign up or register, and 12.5% found it neutral.

Preparation. Participants were now about to start with the prevention activity. When inquired about the landing page, 75% of them found the landing page manageable where with the features they were facilitated to learn and start to set goals. The remaining (2 users), found it overwhelming and neutral.

As they learned about the cleaning activity, 87% of them found the examples of cleaning activities provided were self-explanatory, and the remaining didn't. And as they started, 62.5% felt it was easy and relatively easy, 1 (12.5%) thought it was relatively difficult, and 2 (25%) felt neutral about this.

Competence. In this phase, the participants have been consistently involved in prevention activity for a certain amount of time. We consider 3 weeks (21 days) as the phase where the participants may have adopted the new habit. We looked at the community and team features provided in the application as the means of communication and engagement. Half of the participants found that sharing what they do with the community by making a post kept them going. Some participants found the community feature kept them in check, and some liked the idea of encouraging others.

"Yes, especially after we were able to look at our previous recorded activities. (P4)"

"... It is good to know our actions affect other people as it encourages them to get involved as well. (P5)"

The feature of being able to trace back to past activities as often as they like also kept them going, and useful, with 62.5% checking their historical data regularly. For one participant in particular, this had in some ways impacted the way she thinks (P3).

"I was constantly thinking about what to do with my surroundings to help. (P3)"

There are however times when the participants struggled with the application and cleaning just slipped their minds.

"I have an issue during recording the activity at first as the application takes time to update the records on our device. Besides that, the application also does not provide many option buttons for the user, such as a delete button to delete any activities that we accidentally recorded twice. (P4)"

"...but some days I would forget about it. (P7)"

Maintenance. Going into the final week, most participants have shown positive changes in their behaviour. There were incidents where they forgot to use the application but continued with the prevention activity. This is a sign of the activity adopted to be sustainable.

"...without the app also I will have habits already now as I was doing for 4 weeks. (P3)"

"(I) Always want (to) carry out with the apps, but since I just do it straight away, I forget (about) it and just realize after finishing the cleaning. (P8)"

To keep it more engaging, another participant wishes the community to be taking a more active role in sharing what they do on the platform.

"It was cool to me, and I was eager to see what people posted in the community, I think it would be more fun if we could see people posting their activities to know what they do every week. (P2)"

In sustaining the new habit, the participants had mixed reactions to doing the cleaning activities with the application or without. Some who are already comfortable with the cleaning activities do not feel the urge to keep using the application unless more features are added to enhance the experience and make it more impactful.

"Yes because my living area had many dengue cases, without the app, it was attractive to me at first since I wanted to learn more about the info to avoid dengue. If there are more updates, news, games, and people involved in the app, I might consider to continue using the app." (P2)

"Yes, I would continue even without the applications as cleanliness is essential to build a safe and healthy environment. However, with the application that is able to record and share the cleaning activities, it is able to spread awareness of dengue diseases in our community, besides motivating them to perform cleaning more. (P4)"

4 Discussion

The results of our study answered our research question on the role played by an application if properly designed can persuade people and sustain a new habit. We also have discovered other pertinent findings from the study. Here we articulate three remarks derived from the analysis of the result.

4.1 Adopting New Habit Through Persuasion

We learned that providing the Why is very essential in the persuasion of behaviour change. This is supported in psychology [24] to get everyone on the same page. Cleaning activities are trivial, but understanding how it impacts dengue prevention gives users a new perspective. We also noticed that self-responsibility is another trait that we found contributed to behaviour change. Seeing how others do and how others can see one's contribution also play roles in persuading oneself to continue doing the activity.

4.2 Making Application Still Relevant for Sustainability

We were quite surprised as we learned that once the users were already comfortable with the habit, they tended to see the application as no longer relevant. While we are glad and somewhat feel convinced that they will continue doing this, design enhancement must be made to the application for it to stay relevant to users. Some design features surrounding gamifications and tangible rewards are seen to be most suitable. Another suggestion is to make the impact made by the users visible. For example, showing how today's activity has helped reduce the number of outbreaks, to make them feel valuable and appreciated.

4.3 Translating Conceptual Model to Tangible Design

The mobile application used in this study is developed based on a model from fundamental research. The identification of phases or stages, strategies, and triggers elements facilitated in the translation to user interface design. While the model guided the flow and the transitions, detailed usability should not be missed. We plan to further enhance the model by incorporating suitable UI features to best translate each element.

5 Conclusion

We developed a mobile application for dengue prevention and we performed a study with 8 participants. The results supported our argument that the mobile application is suitable for persuasion to take up the new activity but may yet be eligible for sustaining the new habit. Our research contributes to the persuasive design and behavioural change in HCI research.

Acknowledgement. The authors would like to acknowledge the financial support from the Universiti Teknologi Malaysia for the funding under UTM Encouragement Research (UTMER) vote no. Q.K130000.3843.31J17. This study is also supported by the Universiti Teknologi Malaysia Prototyping Grant (UTMPR) vote no Q.J130000.2851.00L48, and the Ministry of Higher Education Malaysia (MOHE), in collaboration with COMBI unit, PKU, UTM.

References

1. Orji, R., Moffatt, K.: Persuasive technology for health and wellness: state-of-the-art and emerging trends. Health Inform. J. **24**, 66–91 (2018). https://doi.org/10.1177/146045821665 0979
2. Mintz, J., Aagaard, M.: The application of persuasive technology to educational settings. Educ. Technol. Res. Dev. **60**, 483–499 (2012). https://doi.org/10.1007/s11423-012-9232-y
3. Harris, A., ul Islam, S., Qadir, J., Khan, U.A.: Persuasive technology for human development: review and case study. EAI Endorsed Trans. Game-Based Learn. **4**, 153401 (2017). https://doi.org/10.4108/eai.8-12-2017.153401
4. De Vries, R.A.J., Truong, K.P., Kwint, S., Drossaert, C.H.C., Evers, V.: Crowd-designed motivation: motivational messages for exercise adherence based on behavior change theory. Conf. Hum. Factors Comput. Syst. Proc. 297–308 (2016). https://doi.org/10.1145/2858036.2858229

5. Adaji, I., Adisa, M.: A review of the use of persuasive technologies to influence sustainable behaviour. In: UMAP2022 - Adjunct Proceedings of 30th ACM Conference on User Modeling, Adaptation and Personalization, pp. 317–325 (2022). https://doi.org/10.1145/3511047.3537653

6. Fishbein, M., Triandis, H.C., Kanfer, F.H., Becker, M., Middlestadt, S.E., Eichler, A.: Factors influencing behavior and behavior change. Handb. Heal. Psychol. **3**, 3–17 (2001)

7. Lee, Y.H., Hsieh, G.: Does slacktivism hurt activism?: The effects of moral balancing and consistency in online activism. Conf. Hum. Factors Comput. Syst. Proc. 811–820 (2013). https://doi.org/10.1145/2470654.2470770

8. Musingafi, M.C.C., Mapuranga, B., Chiwanza, K., Zebron, S.: Challenges for open and distance learning (ODL) students: experiences from students of the Zimbabwe Open University. J. Educ. Pract. **6**, 59–66 (2015)

9. Pintar, A., Erjave, J.: A framework for designing behavioural change with the use of persuasive technology. Int. J. Manag. Knowl. Learn. **10** (2021)

10. Carrillo, M.A., Kroeger, A., Cardenas Sanchez, R., Diaz Monsalve, S., Runge-Ranzinger, S.: The use of mobile phones for the prevention and control of arboviral diseases: a scoping review. BMC Publ. Health **21**, 1–16 (2021). https://doi.org/10.1186/s12889-020-10126-4

11. Dammert, A.C., Galdo, J.C., Galdo, V.: Preventing dengue through mobile phones: evidence from a field experiment in Peru. J. Health Econ. **35**, 147–161 (2014). https://doi.org/10.1016/j.jhealeco.2014.02.002

12. Delmelle, E.M., Zhu, H., Tang, W., Casas, I.: A web-based geospatial toolkit for the monitoring of dengue fever. Appl. Geogr. **52**, 144–152 (2014)

13. Gubler, D.J., Clark., G.G.: Community involvement in the control of Aedes aegypti. Acta Trop. **61**, 169–179 (1996)

14. Patra, M.: Community participation in dengue prevention and control in a government housing complex, Kolkata, India. Int. J. Sci. Res. **64**, 75–76 (2022). https://doi.org/10.36106/ijsr/4726932

15. Romani, M.E.T., et al.: Achieving sustainability of community-based dengue control in Santiago de Cuba. Soc. Sci. Med. **64**, 976–988 (2007)

16. Suwanbamrung, C., Nukan, N., Sripon, S., Somrongthong, R., Singchagchai, P.: Community capacity for sustainable community-based dengue prevention and control: study of a sub-district in Southern Thailand. Asian Pac. . Trop. Med. **3**, 215–219 (2010). https://doi.org/10.1016/S1995-7645(10)60012-0

17. Tapia-Conyer, R., Méndez-Galván, J., Burciaga-Zúñiga, P.: Community participation in the prevention and control of dengue: the patio limpio strategy in Mexico. Paediatr. Int. Child Health. **32**, 10–13 (2012). https://doi.org/10.1179/2046904712Z.00000000047

18. Suhaili, M.R., Hosein, E., Mokhtar, Z., Ali, N., Palmer, K., Isa, M.M.: Applying communication-for-behavioural-impact (COMBI) in the prevention and control of dengue in Johur Bahru, Johore, Malaysia. Dengue Bull. **28**, 39–43 (2004)

19. World Health Organization: Communication for Behavioural Impact: Field Workbook. Field Workbook for COMBI Planning Steps in Outbreak Response, https://apps.who.int/iris/handle/10665/75170. Accessed 14 July 2023

20. Mashudi, D.N., Ahmad, N., Said, S.M.: Level of dengue preventive practices and associated factors in a Malaysian residential area during the COVID-19 pandemic: a cross-sectional study. PLoS ONE **17**, 1–15 (2022). https://doi.org/10.1371/journal.pone.0267899

21. Nani Mudin, R.: dengue incidence and the prevention and control program in Malaysia. Int. Med. J. Malaysia **14**, 5–9 (2015). https://doi.org/10.31436/imjm.v14i1.447

22. Ghazali, M., Rosli, A., Ibrahim, N., Hisham, H.: A conceptual design for COMBI dengue prevention based on an integrated psychology and persuasive technology models. Int. J. Innov. Comput. **12**, 99–106 (2022). https://doi.org/10.11113/ijic.v12n1.340

23. Consolvo, S., McDonald, D.W., Landay, J.A.: Theory-driven design strategies for technologies that support behavior change in everyday life. Conf. Hum. Factors Comput. Syst. Proc. 405–414 (2009). https://doi.org/10.1145/1518701.1518766
24. Sinek, S.: Start with Why: How Great Leaders Inspire Everyone to Take Action. Penguin, London (2011)

Usability Study of UUM Student Portal Using Eye Tracker

Nur Farah Amalina Azmi[1,2]([✉]) [iD], Mohamed Ali Saip[1] [iD], and Husniza Husni[1] [iD]

[1] Universiti Utara Malaysia, 06010 Sintok, Kedah, Malaysia
nurfarah_amalina@dxn2u.com, husniza@uum.edu.my
[2] DXN Holdings Berhad, Alor Setar, Kedah, Malaysia

Abstract. Universiti Utara Malaysia (UUM) Student Portal is a comprehensive platform dedicated to UUM students. This one-stop portal facilitates our community's access to learning, academic, and administration information. This study evaluates the portal's usability using an eye-tracker involving 15 participants (9 males and 6 females) who were third-year students from the School of Computing (SOC). During the Usability Test session at UUM Computer Lab, participants were given six specific tasks to perform. The study analysed heat maps and gaze plots to identify the correlation between eye movement and potential usability issues. Overall, most participants were able to perform the tasks successfully. However, the study identified usability problems such as unclear terminologies, leading to user confusion. Additionally, some recommendations were put forward to enhance the usability and user experience of the UUM Student Portal.

Keywords: Eye-tracking usability · human-computer interaction · student portal

1 Introduction

User experience has become an increasingly important topic for any digital product, especially for websites. Almost all people of different ages, educational and geographical backgrounds have easy access to the Internet nowadays. A functional, attractive website design and a pleasant user experience are essential to stand out, boost website credibility, and sustain among a countless number of websites available. Furthermore, the quality of a website is crucial for most users who seek specific information or services [1]. When the users cannot use the system due to a bad or poor interface design, they will search for an alternative service provider or product [2]. To evaluate the usability of certain websites, usability testing must be done during the website development and after the website has been launched. The purpose of conducting usability testing for a website or any digital product is to evaluate the effectiveness, efficiency, and user satisfaction, as well as to identify any issues related to the usability of the websites.

Usability testing can be described as the activity that focuses on observing users performing the tasks given. The traditional usability tests that are widely used initially do not include eye-tracking analysis to collect additional data from the eye movement of the participants. The common web usability techniques include Thinking-Out-Loud,

N. H. Zakaria et al. (Eds.): ICOCI 2023, CCIS 2002, pp. 123–135, 2024.
https://doi.org/10.1007/978-981-99-9592-9_10

Heuristic Evaluation, and Remote Usability Testing. Usability testing aims to evaluate digital products' effectiveness, efficiency, and user satisfaction. All the above methods do not involve eye-tracking to analyse eye fixation to explain human behaviour while using a website.

Eye-tracking in a web-usability test is a technique where the eye movement is recorded while the participant performs the tasks given during the test. The eye will not be fixed in one position for too long but normally moves several times per second. The eye-tracking software usually captures the fixation and saccades. The data from the eye tracker are analysed through several methods: gaze replay, gaze plots, and heat maps [3]. The eye-tracking patterns analysed from the data collected will be correlated to the usability problems. Data from eye-tracking can be used to assist in a better understanding of user reactions.

The motivation to study the usability of the UUM Student portal is that the students will use it frequently throughout their study period. Problems related to the interface or system identified during the test will help improve the website's usability. Suggestions can be made to improve and elevate the user experience. This study aims to identify the usability problems of the UUM Student Web Portal through usability testing using eye-tracking data. The second objective is to provide suggestions for improvement to enhance the user experience while using UUM Student Web Portal. This paper discusses the related work in which eye-tracking is used to gain insight into a webpage's usability. Then, the method, results, and suggestions to improve the usability of the UUM Student Portal are also discussed in this paper.

2 Related Works

Eye-tracking might not be a popular technique or tool to collect additional data for the traditional usability test because fewer journals report usability with eye-tracking metrics than the traditional usability method. However, the growing demand for eye-tracking analysis in usability research is sparked by the Just and Carpenter concept [4], which holds that what a person is looking at corresponds to what they are thinking about right now. Other than that, the advancement of technologies also plays a significant role in the growing demand for eye-tracking research.

In the recent work [5], eye-tracking is used alongside with authentic task-based usability testing to evaluate Massive Open Online Courses (MOOCs), which is Coursera. MOOCs offer online courses and become an alternative for most of students during the lockdown due to the Corona Virus Disease (COVID-19) outbreak. The research is divided into two phases. In the first phase, usability analysis based on ISO 9241-11 involves 12 participants. Nine tasks and a questionnaire with three open-ended questions were given to each participant during the test. Effectiveness, efficiency, and satisfaction were evaluated in the first phase of the study. The effectiveness of Coursera was analysed based on the successful completion of tasks. Overall, the Coursera's effectiveness was measured at 70.3% denoting that the Coursera's usability is acceptable. Meanwhile, the efficiency was analysed based on the time taken on the tasks. Coursera offers users acceptable efficiency with some limitations in certain situations. It can be concluded that participants with a higher level of computer and Internet literacy perform the least time taken to complete a task. The participants spend too much time using the site's search option to find and register for courses. Thus, the search options must be re-designed to increase Coursera's efficiency.

The participants' opinions examined the satisfaction of Coursera. Most participants state it was difficult to use, while a group of participants are satisfied with Coursera's usability. Some factors that reduce user satisfaction are no language support provided and only a part of the website is translated into Turkish. Language support and translation are also essential to improve the usability of the website. In the second part of the study, the eye-tracking study was carried out to support the Coursera usability study. The test took place at the eye-tracking laboratory with three participants who were not involved in the study's first phase. The participants are also given nine tasks, similar to the first phase tasks. The data from the eye tracker is visualized as heat maps and gaze plots. The data from heat maps and gaze plots shows that the participant did not focus on the search bar, which is the most important function of the task. The statement is made based on the evidence from the heat zones on the heat maps which shows the participants focus more on the menu and content part. These findings suggest that the search bar may need to be re-designed and to be placed in a more visible area.

Zardari et al. [6] also use eye tracking and other usability tests to evaluate e-learning portals. Three usability experts were involved in this study for heuristic evaluation using the 10 usability heuristics by Nielsen. From the heuristic evaluation, problems that are related to navigation are detected. For example, when the user browses to any other page, the current page in the navigation bar becomes highlighted to show the current position of the user. But in the portal, the highlighted navigation bar was different from the page that was visible. Nielsen [7] advises that one should create a system that is similar to the real world. For the eye-tracking component of this study, twenty students are involved. The data collected from the eye-tracking session are dynamic gaze maps, gaze fixations and heat maps. The data collected from the eye tracker provides additional information regarding the portal's user interface (UI) elements. Heat maps showing the higher heat around the menu suggest that the user faced some difficulty to find the desired feature or button. This situation can be associated with the complexity of the interface.

It can be concluded as the eye-tracking evaluation can help to locate usability problems regarding its UI. For example, the higher fixations showed signs of confusion and may lead to the discovery of the usability problems of the webpage. Additionally, Goldbergs and Kotval [8] investigate the correlations between eye-tracking metrics and usability problems. Table 1 shows the summary of the eye movement metrics and their related cognitive process or usability problems.

Integrating eye trackers in a usability test could enhance the findings. The data visualization from the eye tracking can provide extra information that will lead to the discovery of trends or patterns in eye movement that can suggest the possible usability problems of a website.

Table 1. Summary of eye movement metrics and related cognitive process or usability problems [8].

Eye movement metrics	Cognitive process or usability problems
Fixation-related	
Fixations on target are divided by the total number of fixations	Low search efficiency
Number of fixations overall	Less efficient search due to sub-optimal layout
Repeated fixations	Lack of meaningfulness or visibility
Saccades-related	
More saccades	More Searching
Regressive saccades (backtrack/regression)	No meaningful visual clues are mismatched between the user's expectation and the observed interface layout
Scanpath-related	
Longer scanpath duration	Less efficient scanning
Scanpath regularity	Search problems due to lack of training or interface layout problems
Transition matrix (back and forth between areas)	Uncertainty in search

3   Methodology

There are four stages involved in this study. Firstly, participants are selected according to the following criteria: an active UUM student with access to UUM Student Portal, not wearing spectacles that have thick rims and voluntarily agreeing to participate in this Usability Test. Secondly, the venue for the usability test was set up before the usability test. The third stage involves the usability test where participants must perform six dedicated tasks. The data collected from the Usability Test will be analysed in the fourth stage of the study to evaluate the usability problem of the UUM Student Portal.

The participants' responsibilities were to complete a set of 6 representative task scenarios presented to them as efficiently and timely as possible. An eye tracker will be used to track the eye movement of the participants. Fifteen participants aged between 20 to 25 years old were selected to participate in the usability test of the Web UUM Student Portal. All the participants are students from Universiti Utara Malaysia that has access to the student portal. All participants had experience in the use of the UUM Student Portal. All the participants are 3rd-year students, so the participants have the same familiarity with using the portal. To minimize the error of the eye-tracker, the participants should not be wearing hats or caps that could get between the eye and the eye-tracker, which can impair the calibration and eye-tracking [9].

This study was conducted at the Network Computer Lab, School of Computing, Universiti Utara Malaysia. A consent form was given to each participant to obtain the participants' consent for the study. The participants' sitting positions and postures were adjusted before the tasks started. The study was performed using a Tobii Pro X3-120 eye tracker, a non-invasive device which was set up underneath the monitor. The eye tracker was calibrated for each user before the test starts.

The task scenario is created for the participants to perform while using UUM Student Web Portal. Only the web version of the UUM Student Portal is considered in this usability testing, while the mobile application is not considered as the eye-tracking device is more suitable to be put underneath the computer monitor. Each participant needed to complete 6 main tasks, including 3 simple (Task 1, 2 and 3) and 3 complex tasks (Task 4, 5 and 6). Each participant was handed a card consisting of the following tasks to perform during the test. The facilitator explained the task prior to the test.

Task 1. Log in to the UUM Student Portal using your username and password.
Task 2. Check the timetable for the current semester.
Task 3. Change the background of the portal to the "Ocean Blue" background.
Task 4. Check the list of courses taken to date.
Task 5. Access Student Portal FIMS via UUM Student Portal.
Task 6. Access e-resources from UUM student portal.

There are no post-usability test questionnaires for this usability test session because we use the data from eye tracking to evaluate the usability problems. The metrics for analysis are heat maps and gaze plots. Heat maps and gaze plots are used to visualise the data obtained from the Tobii eye tracker. The participants' eye gazes are compiled on a single page in gaze plots. Gaze plots display a variety of key data points, such as the location of the user's fixations, numbers in the dots representing the sequence in which the user glanced at the things, and the size of the dot representing how long the user gazed at the item. Each gaze plot is analysed, and the pattern of the gaze plot is identified. The pattern is then compared with the literature findings to associate or correlate with the possible usability problems. Heat maps show the parts of a website where users focused most of their attention. The heat map location indicates the user's focus on the interface. We can identify the usability problem by analysing the heat maps. Each data set will be analysed to determine the usability issues encountered by participants. The eye-tracking patterns of the participants will be recognised, studied, and correlated to the usability issues.

4 Findings

In total, 15 participants participated in this usability testing, and six tasks were performed with eye-tracking tools. Table 2 shows the data for task completion and the time taken to complete the task for each participant, P (1 is complete; 0 is incomplete). The data was extracted from the eye-tracking records.

Most of the participants managed to perform almost all of the tasks. However, for Task 4 (T4) "Check the list of courses taken to date", there are three failures. Task 1 (T1) "Logging into the UUM Student Portal using your username and password," Task 2 (T2) "Checking the timetable for the current semester," Task 3 (T3) "Changing the background of the portal to the 'Ocean Blue' background," Task 5 (T5) "Accessing Student Portal FIMS via UUM Student Portal," and Task 6 (T6) "Accessing e-resources from the UUM student portal" all achieved a 100% completion rate.

Table 2. Data for Completion of Task and Time Taken for Each Participant.

P	T1	Time (s)	T2	Time (s)	T3	Time (s)	T4	Time (s)	T5	Time (s)	T6	Time (s)
P1	1	117.34	1	7.69	1	16.22	0	19.47	1	4.88	1	37.91
P2	1	18.42	1	4.41	1	42.78	1	14.25	1	11.66	1	6.19
P3	1	35.14	1	12.84	1	7.33	1	25.69	1	11.87	1	3.76
P4	1	30.70	1	15.43	1	8.94	1	14.98	1	15.14	1	9.72
P5	1	16.09	1	5.60	1	12.99	1	17.19	1	23.31	1	6.68
P6	1	15.34	1	8.43	1	4.62	0	48.03	1	9.20	1	5.70
P7	1	22.19	1	2.89	1	12.48	0	17.38	1	8.40	1	80.41
P8	1	32.20	1	4.04	1	9.21	0	25.79	1	5.36	1	6.39
P9	1	42.38	1	5.81	1	8.69	1	25.14	1	3.60	1	27.20
P10	1	60.92	1	4.20	1	7.04	1	14.89	1	21.04	1	11.69
P11	1	13.38	1	17.10	1	6.59	1	11.92	1	11.07	1	4.47
P12	1	25.87	1	6.90	1	5.80	1	10.44	1	16.74	1	9.09
P13	1	19.35	1	8.44	1	9.13	1	79.60	1	10.39	1	6.11
P14	1	29.83	1	21.25	1	5.52	1	45.19	1	6.72	1	8.08
P15	1	60.01	1	12.45	1	5.15	1	12.38	1	12.80	1	10.30

(P = participant, T = Task, 1 = completed task, 0 = incomplete task)

The average time taken for Task 1 is 35.94 s, while Participants P1, P10 and P15 took 117.34 s, 60.92 s and 60.01 s respectively. From the observation, the reason for the longer time to complete the task is unrelated to the interface. Participants P1, P10 and P15 are able to perform the given tasks, but the Internet connection and/or longer time taken to connect to the UUM Student Portal Server are identified as the main problem when performing this task.

Figure 1(a) and 1(b) show the visualization of the eye-tracking data for Participant 1 for Task 1. The data is represented in the form of heat maps and gaze plots. Analysis from the heat maps and gaze plot shows that the participant had more focus on the login area. It is apparent that the participant concentrates extensively on darker or red-coloured heat zones within the login area. This suggests that there is no problem with the interaction between the participant and the interface of the portal itself. The gaze plot also shows the participant's gaze is concentrated in the Login area.

For Task 2, the average time taken is 9.17 s. 10 out of 15 participants completed the task under 10 s. This is a straightforward task where the participants only need to scroll down the main page of the UUM Student Portal to check the timetable. Five participants that take longer time, check the timetable at the "Lecture" tab, which is also acceptable.

Figure 2 shows the heat map for Task 2 performed by Participant P7, who recorded the shortest completion time. In contrast, Fig. 3 shows the heat map for Task 2, Participant P14, who takes the longest time to complete the task. Figure 2 shows that the participant

Fig. 1. (a). Heat Maps for Participant 1, Task 1. (b). Gaze Plot for Participant 1, Task 1.

only focuses on the class timetable. In Fig. 3, the heat map shows that the focus is more concentrated on the "Lecture" tab area. This participant takes an extra step to perform the task. This is acceptable and can be considered as the task is completed with extra time.

Task 3 has achieved a 100% completion rate, with an average time of 10.83 s taken to complete the task. The majority of participants perform the task proficiently, with only Participant P2 taking the longest time at 42.78 s. Additionally, this task is considered straightforward.

Figure 4(a) and 4(b) show the heat maps and gaze plot for Participant P2, Task 3. The participant has more focus on the left side of the portal. He tries to search for the

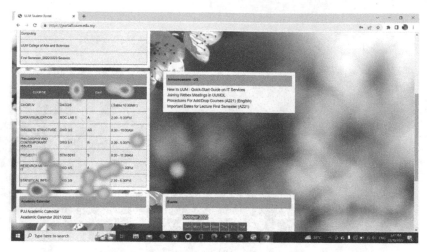

Fig. 2. Heat Maps for Participant P7, Task 2.

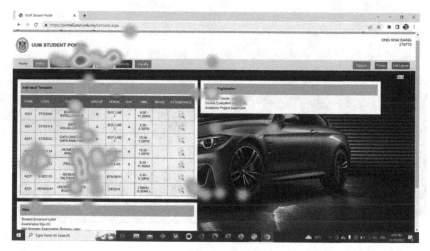

Fig. 3. Heat Maps for Participant P14, Task 2.

button to change the background on the left side of the portal. Less focus is given to the right side of the portal. The gaze plot also observes the same pattern as the heat maps. From the gaze plot, it can be concluded that the participant tried to look for the button to change the background on the left side for a longer time than in the end he just discovered the button is on the top right of the portal.

Task 4 has the lowest completion rate with the average time taken to complete the task is 25.49 s. 11 out of 15 participants are able to perform this task. Participants P1, P6, P7, and P8 record four failures. Participant P6 just gives up after trying to complete the task a few times. This task is quite complicated and requires participants to select one of many menus in the Academic tab in the UUM Student Portal. The failure recorded for

Fig. 4. (a). Heat Maps for Participant P2, Task 3. (b). Gaze Plot for Participant P2, Task 3.

this task is because the participant checks the course structure that lists all the subjects that need to be completed to be able to graduate. However, the task asks for a list of the courses taken as up to date.

Participant P6 is one of the participants who failed the task and took the longest time which is 48.03 s. Figure 5(a) and 5(b) show the heat map and gaze plot for Participant P6 performing Task 4. The heat map and gaze plot show that the participant is struggling to perform the task as the eye movement is captured scattered throughout the screen. The participant is trying to figure out how to complete the task by trying out every single function on the interface. The participant also surfed different pages and by doing trial-and-error methods to try to complete the task.

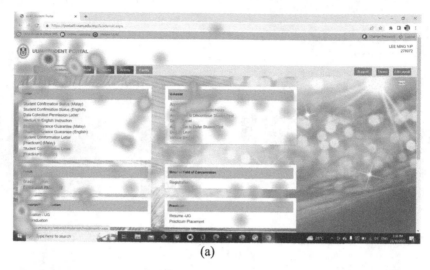

(a)

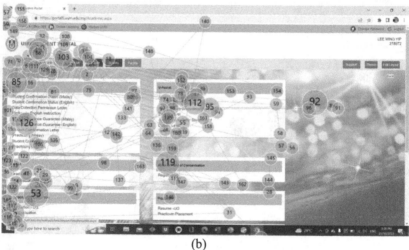

(b)

Fig. 5. (a). Heat Maps for Participant P6, Task 4. (b). Gaze Plot for Participant P6, Task 4.

The average time recorded for Task 5 is 11.48 s. All the participants were able to complete this task efficiently. Only two participants complete this task with time taken to complete the task more than 20 s. This is also because of the bad gateway to access the FIMS Portal via UUM Student Portal. Because there is no failure and all the participants are doing well on this task, there will be no further analysis of the heat map and gaze plot.

Task 6 has been successfully completed by all participants, with an average completion time of 15.58 s. However, there are three participants who significantly take more time than the average. Participants P1, P7 and P9 take 37.91 s, 80.41 s and 27.20 s respectively. A longer time taken observed for participants P1 and P9 because of the poor gateway to access the E-Resources Portal via UUM Student Portal. While for Participant P7, a combination of the longer time taken to search the e-Resources link at the UUM Student Portal and a poor gateway to connect to the E-Resources server.

Figure 6(a) and 6(b) show where Participant P7 focuses when completing the task. The heat map shows the darker colour that denotes more attention given to the Main Menu. The pattern of eye movement recorded throughout the page also indicates that this participant also used trial-and-error to perform Task 6.

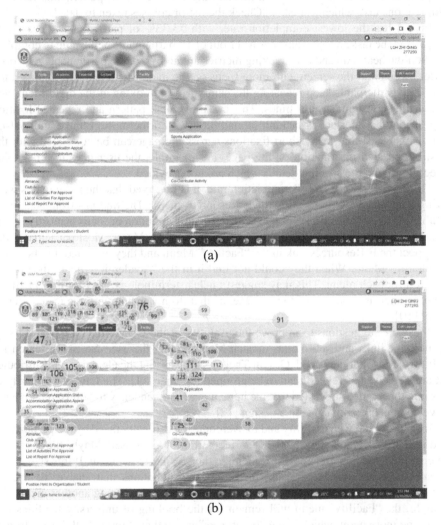

(a)

(b)

Fig. 6. (a). Heat Maps for Participant P7, Task 6. (b). Gaze Plot for Participant P7, Task 6.

5 Discussion and Suggestion

In this study, the usability of the UUM Student Portal was investigated using eye-tracking devices to gain insight into the usability problems of the portal. The portal is essential to all active students in UUM. By looking at the completion of the task, it is sufficient to say that the usability of the portal is generally acceptable. In general, 11 out of 15 participants are able to complete the tasks while the other four participants are able to complete five out of six tasks. That means only four out of 15 participants failed to complete one task which is Task 4 "Check the list of courses taken to date".

Task 4 has the lowest completion rate, with 73.33% of participants successfully completing the task, which translates to 11 out of 15 participants being able to complete it. When the heat map and eye-tracking metrics are analysed, the participants' eye does scatter throughout the screen with more focus on the main Menu and sub-Menu on the page. The participants keep repeating the same pattern, looking at the main Menu and then at the sub-Menu several times. This eye movement pattern and repeated fixation suggest that the interface is lacking in visibility [8]. Furthermore, Ehmke and Wilson [10] also suggest that many short fixations across the page can be correlated with the missing expected information on the page. For example, the user goes to a page site expecting to find the specific details which are not provided.

Although Task 5 has a full completion rate, it is observed that the participants were having some difficulty in locating the E-Resources menu. The findings from heat maps are able to support the observation. The participant's attention or focus is mostly on the main Menu. The link to E-Resources is in the "Facility" Menu. Most participants did not expect the E-Resources link in the "Facility" Menu and they expected it to be in the "Academic" Menu. When they could not find it in the "Academic" Menu, they began to search for each menu. This may suggest unclear terminology used for the "Facility" Menu or unclear grouping of the sub-Menus that do not match with the user's mental model [10].

These are suggestions to improve the usability of the UUM Student Portal. Firstly, organize the links and sub-menus in each Menu so that the user can easily search for the information that they need. Gestalt Theory suggests that the elements with attributes that are perceived as related tend to be grouped together [11]. The Law of Similarity in the same theory also suggested that the human eye has a tendency to build a relationship between similar components in a design [12].

To improve the web usability and to overcome the difficulty faced by the participants to complete Task 6, it is suggested that correct terminology is used. Maybe the developer can consider changing the "Facility" menu to the "E-Services" menu. If this suggestion appears to be not suitable because there are some functions that enable the user to book any university's facility in this menu, we can suggest creating another menu. For example, the "Facility" menu will remain for the booking of university facilities and create one more menu which is the "E-services" menu that compiled all the electronic-based services links under one menu, including the E-Resources link.

6   Conclusion

This study aims to investigate the usability of the UUM Student Portal using an eye-tracker. Based on the study's findings, the usability of the UUM Student Portal appears to be satisfactory for use by UUM students, particularly those who are predominantly computer literate. A few suggestions were made to improve the web usability and user experience. The developer needs to consider organizing the menus and submenus for better accessibility. Furthermore, some recommendations and alternative terminologies were proposed. In conclusion, UUM Student Portal is usable in general but needs to be improved to elevate the user experience among the students.

References

1. Al-Sakran, H.O., Alsudairi, M.A.: Usability and accessibility assessment of Saudi Arabia mobile e-government websites. IEEE Access **9**, 48254–48275 (2021). https://doi.org/10.1109/ACCESS.2021.3068917
2. Hussain, A., Mkpojiogu, E.O.C., Abduljabbar, A.M., Almadhagi, A.H.G.: A usability evaluation of UUM mobile for student app on IOS and Android platforms. 020052 (2018). https://doi.org/10.1063/1.5055454
3. Nielsen, J., Pernice, K.: Eyetracking Web Usability. New Riders, Indianapolis (2010)
4. Just, M.A., Carpenter, P.A.: A capacity theory of comprehension: individual differences in working memory. Psychol. Rev. **99**(1), 122–149 (1992). http://www.ccbi.cmu.edu/reprints/Just_Carpenter_PsychRev-1992_capacity-theory.pdf
5. Tanış, H., Akçay, A., Yilmaz, N., Yiğit, M.F., Tüzün, H.: How usable is Coursera? A usability analysis through eye-tracking and authentic tasks. Participatory Educ. Res. **9**(4), 379–395 (2022). https://doi.org/10.17275/per.22.96.9.4
6. Zardari, B.A., Hussain, Z., Arain, A.A., Rizvi, W.H., Vighio, M.S.: QUEST e-learning portal: applying heuristic evaluation, usability testing and eye tracking. Univ. Access Inf. Soc. **20**(3), 531–543 (2020). https://doi.org/10.1007/s10209-020-00774-z
7. Nielsen, J.: 10 Usability Heuristics for User Interface Design. Nielsen Norman Group, Fremont (1994). https://www.nngroup.com/articles/ten-usability-heuristics/
8. Goldberg, J.H., Kotval, X.P.: Computer interface evaluation using eye movements: methods and constructs. Int. J. Ind. Ergon. **24**(6), 631–645 (1999). https://doi.org/10.1016/S0169-8141(98)00068-7
9. Nielsen, J., Pernice, K.: How to Conduct Eye-Tracking Studies. Nielsen Norman Group, Fremont (2009). https://www.nngroup.com/reports/how-to-conduct-eyetracking-studies/
10. Ehmke, C., Wilson, S. G.: Identifying web usability problems from eye-tracking data. In: Proceedings of HCI 2007 The 21st British HCI Group Annual Conference University of Lancaster, UK (2007). https://doi.org/10.14236/ewic/HCI2007.12
11. Wertheimer, M.: Gestalt Theory. A Source Book of Gestalt Psychology, pp. 1–11. Kegan Paul, Trench, Trubner & Company (1938). https://doi.org/10.1037/11496-001
12. Soegaard, M.: The law of similarity—Gestalt principles (Part 1). The Interaction Design Foundation (2022). https://www.interaction-design.org/literature/article/the-law-of-similarity-gestalt-principles-1

Education Transformation Through Technology

University Student Dashboard: Enhancing Student Trend Analysis and Decision-Making Processes

Teh Soon Li[1] , Mohamad Sabri bin Sinal[1]([✉]) , Mazni Omar[1] ,
and Muhammad Nur Adilin bin Mohamad Anuardi[2]

[1] Universiti Utara Malaysia, 06010 Sintok, Kedah, Malaysia
msabri@uum.edu.my
[2] Hiroshima University, 1-7-1 Kagamiyama, Higashi-Hiroshima, Hiroshima 739-8521, Japan

Abstract. In today's data-driven era, organizations are constantly seeking ways to improve their decision-making processes, and dashboards have emerged as an effective solution for this purpose. Dashboards provide a real-time visual representation of an organization's critical data, metrics, and performance indicators, allowing decision-makers to quickly comprehend key insights and make informed decisions. Universities are increasingly adopting dashboards to facilitate data-driven decision-making, allowing administrators to identify areas of strength and weakness in various academic and administrative functions. The objective of this study is to propose a holistic dashboard model for universities that includes critical aspects of student data on campus implemented in a higher education institution in Malaysia. The model will provide extensive student data segments that can be monitored and supported regularly, providing the top management with a broader perspective on the student's condition on campus. To assess the efficacy of the proposed dashboard model, the Datus model, a comprehensive framework that aids organizations in designing and implementing efficient dashboards in terms of accessibility, appropriate recognizability, effectiveness, efficiency, learnability, operability, satisfaction, and user interface aesthetic, will be utilized. The results indicate that the user interface design received a favorable response, while the usability evaluation revealed that operability, appropriate recognizability, and accessibility were areas that require improvement.

Keywords: University Dashboard · Business Intelligence · Usability Evaluation

1 Introduction

In the present era of data-driven businesses, organizations are continually seeking ways to enhance their decision-making processes. Dashboards have emerged as an effective approach to achieving this goal by providing a real-time visual representation of an organization's critical data, metrics, and performance indicators. This enables decision-makers to quickly comprehend key insights and make informed decisions. Due to their ability to provide real-time data visualization and facilitate informed decision-making, dashboards have gained widespread popularity across various sectors, including healthcare,

N. H. Zakaria et al. (Eds.): ICOCI 2023, CCIS 2002, pp. 139–153, 2024.
https://doi.org/10.1007/978-981-99-9592-9_11

education, finance, and retail [1–5]. Moreover, dashboards have become an indispensable tool for organizations seeking to improve their operational efficiency and elevate their decision-making processes.

There has been a growing trend in the adoption of dashboards in the field of education, with universities increasingly utilizing dashboards to facilitate data-driven decision-making. Dashboards offer a visual representation of key performance metrics and data, enabling university administrators to identify areas of strength and weakness in various academic and administrative functions. This facilitates effective resource allocation, strategic planning, and decision-making. Furthermore, dashboards can be customized to cater to the specific needs of different stakeholders, such as students, faculty, and administrators. With the increasing availability of data in universities, the trend towards dashboard utilization is expected to continue, with future research focusing on developing more sophisticated dashboard models that incorporate advanced analytics techniques and machine learning algorithms [6–8] to enhance the accuracy and efficiency of data-driven decision-making.

The primary objective of higher education institutions such as universities is to provide quality education and produce graduates who are well-rounded. In Malaysia, universities aspire to become centers of excellence for education, leading referral centers for all aspects of education scholarship, and premier resource centers for various studies. However, the current economic situation presents significant challenges for these institutions in terms of achieving their objectives. Despite the challenges, universities in Malaysia are determined to become the world's top university. To achieve this goal, it is essential to address issues such as the development of a comprehensive decision-making process for students. Students are critical to universities, as they are the fundamental basis of these institutions. Thus, it is vital for universities to prioritize the well-being of their students, considering their function as the primary revenue source, reputation enhancers, key players in the research and innovation framework, future alumni, and deserving beneficiaries of a safe and supportive educational environment, aligned with the social obligations of universities. The top management of universities plays a crucial role in developing appropriate policies and making informed decisions that benefit the students. To address this challenge, higher institutions like universities recognize the need for a platform that can provide the university's top management with a well-organized and systematic presentation of the university and student data. An innovative approach such as the business intelligence approach is necessary to provide the required perspective to solve the problem at hand. The business intelligence approach encompasses the processes, technologies, and tools that organizations use to collect, analyze, and present data that enables the analysis of information to optimize decisions and performance [9, 10].

The aim of this research paper is to present a new university dashboard model that integrates all essential components of student data on campus, implemented in a higher education institution in Malaysia. This model will provide extensive and regular monitoring of various student data segments, enabling top management to gain a more comprehensive perspective on the students' condition on campus. To ensure the usability of the dashboard model while balancing the target audience's needs with technicality and information, we will evaluate it using the Datus model. The Datus model is a comprehensive framework that supports organizations in designing and implementing effective dashboards, considering multiple factors such as data sources, data quality, visualization techniques, user requirements, and performance indicators.

The remaining sections of this paper are organized as follows: Sect. 2 presents related works to address the issues of existing methods in designing a university dashboard model. Section 3 outlines the proposed dashboard model and its methodology for developing the dashboards. Section 4 presents and discusses the procedure of evaluation and the evaluation results of the proposed models in detail. Finally, Sect. 5 provides concluding remarks, including a discussion of potential future research areas.

2 Related Work

Mihaela et al. [11] presented a performance dashboard model designed to enhance the efficiency of measuring, monitoring, and managing organizational performance for executives. Their work included a SWOT analysis to implement a performance management system and dashboard for Romanian universities, currently undergoing significant changes to remain competitive in the market. The study focused on the critical components of a performance dashboard that can provide accurate and timely information to university management. Although the proposed dashboard model covered six dimensions of university focus, including research, finance, business processes, staff and workplace satisfaction, student teaching and learning, and faculty, the authors did not provide detailed explanations for refining each component. The student segment, for example, only covers a few parameters such as enrollment, retention rate, student outcomes, and students living on campus, which does not offer a comprehensive view of student life on campus. The dashboard's requirement was considered weak due to the absence of a user acceptance test model to confirm its relevance. This study proposes a well-constructed requirement for the university's performance dashboard, including all necessary and accurate information related to students on campus. The proposed dashboard model evaluates and refines each focus of the student through a series of processes with top management, leading to high user acceptance.

Erna et al. [12] introduced a tactical dashboard model designed to present program study information at a university in Indonesia. The primary objective of this research was to develop a dashboard model that emphasized accurate presentation of pertinent information based on the university's requirements. While the proposed dashboard model describes a well-refined process for identifying the appropriate parameters, the refinement process was based on assumptions and not on any specific dashboard development model or collection requirements obtained from targeted audience feedback. As a result, the proposed model is considered inadequate, as it did not receive proper evaluation to ensure it met the needs of the intended audience. Therefore, in this proposed study, the authors aim to incorporate targeted audience feedback to create a stronger foundation for developing a suitable dashboard for top management. Additionally, the study aims to balance the needs of top management with the technicality of the dashboard and the information displayed on it.

Mohd Tuah et.al [13] introduced a smart system that uses data analytics and a dashboard to facilitate university students' self-monitoring, progress tracking, and management of important information related to their final year project. The system was developed using a Rapid Application Development methodology to create the prototype. To ensure that the dashboard meets user requirements, the author utilized Technology Acceptance Model (TAM) to measure system acceptance and user behavior intention in using the proposed system. Although TAM has shown significant impacts, it does not fully account for social and contextual factors that may influence technology adoption. TAM primarily focuses on individual users' perceptions of the technology's usefulness and ease of use, ignoring how social context and relationships between users and their peers may affect their adoption behavior. Therefore, an alternative model, Datus, was utilized in this paper, which recognizes social influence and trust as critical factors that may influence technology adoption. Datus considers the influence of interpersonal and social network relationships, providing a more comprehensive view of user behavior and representing user feedback towards the dashboard's quality and usability more accurately.

3   Methodology

This section outlines the proposed dashboard model development process, which employs Agile methodology to achieve research objectives. The Agile methodology was chosen for this research project due to its suitability in addressing the challenges of changing requirements from stakeholders. The ability for universities to adapt quickly to the uncertainties and fast-paced changes in business is crucial for improving efficiency and meeting stakeholder expectations [14].

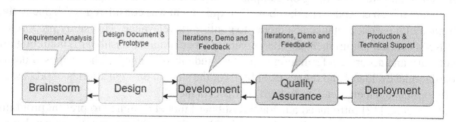

Fig. 1. Agile software development methodology

The Agile methodology employed in this research involved five stages: brainstorming, design, development, quality assurance, and deployment. These stages are illustrated in Fig. 1, and their particulars are as follows:

Brainstorm: In the requirement gathering phase, the university's top management was involved in three iterations of the process. Meetings were held with various stakeholders to identify the necessary information for the dashboard. The framework draft was subjected to an initial iteration, followed by gathering feedback from the strategic and corporate planning division staff member from a higher education institution, and then underwent subsequent revisions. Further feedback was obtained to create the final framework, which formed the basis for the storyboard design.

Design: In the design phase, a low-fidelity prototype for the dashboard was created. The team conducted several iterations to enhance the dashboard's effectiveness in displaying relevant information. The dashboard's elements and content were scrutinized and justified based on feedback from the target audience.

Development: During this phase, the development of the dashboard has been done using the MicroStrategy platform. The process will include multiple iterations of development and revision, incorporating feedback from the target audience to ensure an optimal user experience. The previously created storyboard will guide the development process, with work continuing the MicroStrategy dossier until its completion. The placement of each visualization in the dashboard will be carefully designed based on the storyboard.

Quality Assurance: In the testing phase, numerous iterations and demos have been conducted to ensure optimal user experience. Extensive testing will be performed to validate each layer of the dashboard, verifying that it is error-free and displays the required information accurately. Users have been provided with a questionnaire and task list to evaluate the dashboard's usability. Any feedback or findings provided by the users will be analyzed, and feasible enhancements will be implemented. Suggestions that are difficult to implement will be noted as future work.

Deployment: In this phase, after the dashboard has undergone thorough stress testing, it will be uploaded to the online library and prepared for deployment. Regular maintenance will be carried out to ensure the dashboard operates seamlessly and remains free of errors.

3.1 The Proposed University Student Dashboard Model

This section provides a detailed explanation of the components of the proposed university student dashboard model. The dashboard comprises eight components, including enrollment, intake, achievement, entrepreneurship, demographics, graduate employability, mobility program, and alumni, as shown in Fig. 2. The dashboard model is structured into three levels, namely level 0, level 1, and level 2. An illustration of the proposed dashboard prototype is presented in Fig. 3 and Fig. 4. The content presented in the dashboard is solely for illustrative purposes, as it is based on dummy data that does not reflect actual real-world conditions.

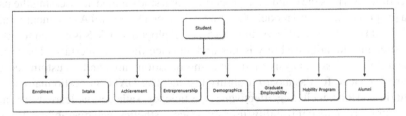

Fig. 2. University Student Dashboard Framework

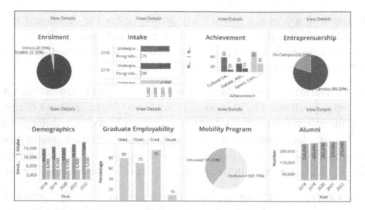

Fig. 3. University student dashboard level 0 for main page

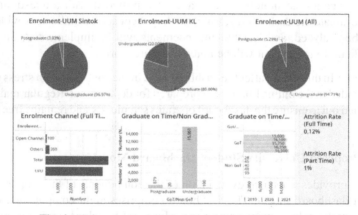

Fig. 4. University student dashboard level 1 for enrollment

4   Evaluation and Results

4.1   Evaluation Strategy

This section describes the evaluation procedure for a study aimed at assessing the usability of a proposed dashboard model. To achieve this, the Dashboard Assessment Usability Model (DATUS), developed by Antunes [15], is employed. DATUS is chosen for its ability to efficiently identify usability issues and enhance the user interface. The model is formulated through an analysis of six existing questionnaires and a customized questionnaire is created for dashboard usability testing. The DATUS questionnaire consists of eight dimensions, including effectiveness, efficiency, satisfaction, learnability, accessibility, appropriate recognizability, user interface aesthetics, and operability. The study applies DATUS, and the results of the mapping and analysis of DATUS questions based on the eight dimensions are presented in Tables 1, and 2, respectively.

To ensure an accurate representation of the broader outcomes and requirements of the university dashboard in the study, the participation of 11 staff members from

Table 1. DATUS Questionnaires

No	Questions	Strongly Disagree				Strongly Agree
		1	2	3	4	5
1	Overall, I am satisfied with how easy it is to use this dashboard					
2	It was simple to use this dashboard					
3	I can effectively complete my work using this dashboard					
4	I am able to complete my goals (tasks) quickly using this dashboard					
5	I am able to efficiently complete my goals (tasks) using this dashboard					
6	I feel comfortable using this dashboard					
7	It was easy to learn to use this dashboard					
8	I believe I became productive quickly using this dashboard					
9	Whenever I make a mistake using the dashboard, I recover easily and quickly					
10	The information (on-screen messages) provided with this dashboard is clear					
11	It was easy to find the information I needed					
12	The information displayed in the dashboard is easy to understand					
13	The information displayed in the dashboard is effective in helping me complete the tasks and scenarios					
14	The organization of the information on the dashboard is clear					

(*continued*)

Table 1. (*continued*)

No	Questions	Strongly Disagree				Strongly Agree
		1	2	3	4	5
15	The interface of this dashboard is pleasant					
16	I like using the interface of this dashboard					
17	This dashboard has all the functions and capabilities I expect it to have					
18	Overall, I am satisfied with this dashboard					
19	Data on the dashboard is easy to read					
20	Visual encoding of data is consistent throughout the dashboard					

Table 2. Mapping of DATUS questionnaires with the dimension

Dimensions	Questions
Satisfaction	Items 1, 6, 16 and 18
Effectiveness	Items 3 and 13
Efficiency	Items 4 and 5
Operability	Items 2, 9, 11, 14 and 20
Learnability	Items 7, 8, 10, 12
User interface aesthetics	Item 15
Appropriate recognizability	Item 17
Accessibility	Item 19

the Strategic and Corporate Planning Division of a higher education institution was selected. This department plays a crucial role in the university's decision-making process as they manage and analyze essential university data, which informs the formulation, modification, or removal of policies aimed at enhancing stakeholder satisfaction and is presented to top management for consideration.

Each participant will be given a questionnaire and a set of tasks to perform based on the information presented in the dashboard. Participants will be encouraged to explore the dashboard to complete the tasks listed in Table 3 and Table 4. The testing session for each participant will be recorded and evaluated based on three factors: (1) the number of goals accurately achieved, (2) the number of errors, and (3) the time taken to complete a task. The first evaluation establishes the importance of achieving accurate outcomes for each task by determining the correct goal attainment based on the number of accurately answered goals or tasks. The second evaluation quantifies errors by computing the average number of incorrect outcomes executed by the participants during task or goal completion. Lastly, the third evaluation measures task completion time.

Table 3. List of tasks

Task Id	Task Description
1	The total number of students enrolled in UUM Sintok
2	The number of students with the enrollment channel of open channel
3	The number of students that graduate on time in 2019
4	The number of students that dropout in 2021
5	The number of postgraduate intake in 2020
6	The number of students in the b40 category in 2018
7	The number of undergraduates in SEFB
8	The number of students won in sport competition
9	The number of students won in debate, advocacy, and oratory competition at the international level
10	The number of students with university job in semester 1
11	The number of students with diploma as their entry qualification
12	The number of students with B40 status in Pahang
13	The number of rooms available in "*Inasis* TM"
14	The percentage of graduate employability in STHEM
15	The percentage of graduate employability in less than 12 months in SBM
16	The number of students that went for outbound mobility in the b40 category
17	The number of students that have mobility programs in Europe
18	The number of alumni in 2019
19	The number of female alumni in 2021
20	The number of alumni that has the position of senior executive in the non-government sector

4.1.1 The Calculation of the List of Task

In this section, a detailed breakdown of the assessment approach, including the presentation of relevant evaluation formulas, is discussed and shown in Table 5.

Once the tasks listed in Table 3 are completed, the participants will be asked to fill out the DATUS questionnaire, as shown in Table 1. The questionnaire will use a Likert

Table 4. Open-ended questions

No	Questions
1	Is there any information you would like to see that has not been considered on the dashboard?
2	Do you have any other comments or suggestions you want to share with us?

Table 5. Calculation of The List of Task

Items	Calculation
Number of goals answered correctly	$x = \frac{Total number of correct outcomes}{Number of Tasks}$
Number of errors	$y = \frac{Total number of incorrect outcomes}{Number of Tasks}$
Time taken to complete a task	Seconds

scale ranging from 1 (strongly disagree) to 5 (strongly agree) to assess the dashboard's quantitative usability aspects. Additionally, two open-ended questions will be provided to obtain feedback and suggestions for enhancing the dashboard, as described in Table 4. The qualitative aspect of the evaluation will involve analyzing the feedback provided. The usability testing session will be conducted on-site with the respondents.

4.2 Results

This section presents a comprehensive discussion of the study's findings. The first test's results, measuring the number of correctly answered goals, will be discussed, followed by the second test's findings, measuring the number of errors. The third test's evaluation of the time taken to complete each task will also be presented. Additionally, the DATUS Satisfaction Questionnaire Analysis will be conducted to validate whether the findings align with the anticipated outcome. Further details of the discussion are provided in the following subsection.

4.2.1 The Number of Goals Answered Correctly

This section provides an evaluation of the first test, which analyzed data collected from 11 participants. The results showed that 82% (9/11) of the participants successfully completed all goals with the correct outcome. One participant (6%) completed 95% (19/20) of the goals correctly, while another participant (6%) completed 90% (18/20) of the goals correctly. These findings suggest that the majority of participants understood the tasks and were able to navigate the dashboard effectively to find the correct answers.

4.2.2 The Number of Errors

This section focuses on the assessment of the second evaluation test. The results showed that majority of the participants, accounting for 82% (9/11), did not make any errors during the evaluation. However, 18% (2/11) of participants made one or two mistakes, with each category accounting for 6% (1/11) of the total number of participants. It is possible that this could be attributed to the Corporate Planning Division members' familiarity with working with data.

Table 6. Number of wrong outcomes per task

Task Id	1	2	3	4	5	6	7	8	9	10	11	12	13	14	15	16	17	18	19	20
Wrong answers	0	0	1	0	0	0	0	0	1	0	0	0	0	0	1	0	0	0	0	0

According to the data presented in Table 6, each task is identified by a unique task ID, while the number of wrong answers indicates the total count of incorrect responses provided by the participants. In total, the 11 participants answered 220 questions, which comprised a list of 20 tasks. Based on the analysis, the current study achieved a significantly lower error rate (1.36%) than the previous study conducted by Antunes, which reported an error rate of 5.2% [15]. This suggests that the proposed dashboard model developed in this study is more effective in conveying information to users compared to the dashboard model used in Antunes' study. Additionally, it is important to note that the error rate of 1.36% is well within an acceptable range for this type of study, indicating that the proposed dashboard model is both accurate and effective in meeting the needs of its intended audience. The specific tasks that had a single incorrect response each were tasks 3, 9, and 15. To determine the root cause of the inaccuracies observed, a more comprehensive inquiry is imperative. This could involve a detailed examination of the test recordings of the participants, in addition to providing additional explanations to support the findings.

4.2.3 Time Taken to Complete a Task

This section presents the findings of the third test evaluation, which assesses the time taken by participants to complete each task. Figure 5 displays the relationship between task ID and time taken, with task ID on the x-axis and time taken in seconds on the y-axis. Task 14 had the longest average completion time of 38 s, followed by tasks 3 and 7 with an average time of 37 s each. These tasks required participants to navigate to a deeper level to access relevant information. Tasks 1 to 14 exhibited a fluctuating trend, with the average completion time increasing until it peaked at Task 14, indicating participants were trying to familiarize themselves with the dashboard's layout. However, Tasks 15 to 20 had an average completion time of no more than 30 s, suggesting participants had become more familiar with the dashboard's layout and placement. Task 1 had the shortest average completion time of 20 s. The proposed study can be considered better than Antunes' study in terms of completion time, as it achieved an average time of 28 s per task, which is only one second longer than Antunes' study. However, it should be noted that the proposed study has additional features and functionalities that were not present in Antunes' study, such as the incorporation of user feedback to improve the dashboard's usability. Therefore, despite the slightly longer completion time, the proposed study provides more comprehensive and user-centric insights, making it a more robust and effective approach to dashboard development.

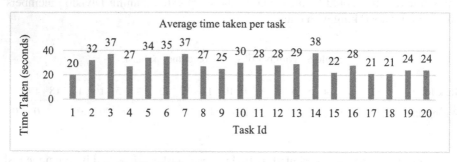

Fig. 5. The average time taken per task

4.2.4 DATUS Satisfaction Questionnaire Analysis

The Dashboard Assessment Usability Model (DATUS) Satisfaction Questionnaire is utilized to evaluate participants' satisfaction with the usability of the dashboard. Table 7 presents the mean, median, and standard deviation of each task ID mapped to the dashboard's usability dimensions, including accessibility, appropriate recognizability, effectiveness, efficiency, learnability, operability, satisfaction, and user interface aesthetics. Based on the results of the DATUS Satisfaction Questionnaire, the current study achieved a slightly lower mean score (90.38) and median score (92) compared to the scores achieved in Antunes' study, which reported a mean score of 92.73 and a median score of 99 [15]. However, it is important to note that the scores achieved in the current study are still well within an acceptable range and indicate a high level of user satisfaction with the proposed dashboard model. Furthermore, it is worth noting that the proposed dashboard model developed in this study encompasses all crucial aspects of student data on campus in a single dashboard, which may provide users with a more efficient and effective means of accessing information compared to the dashboard model used in Antunes' study. Overall, the findings of this study suggest that the proposed dashboard model is effective in meeting the needs of its intended audience and can potentially improve user satisfaction with the dashboard interface. Table 8 provides a summary of the analysis conducted in Table 7, which presents the analysis results based on the usability dimensions.

Based on the results presented in Table 8, user interface aesthetics emerged as the usability dimension with the highest average score of 4.82, followed by effectiveness and satisfaction, with scores of 4.59 and 4.57, respectively. Meanwhile, efficiency was ranked fourth highest, with a score of 4.5. On the other hand, four usability dimensions, namely learnability, operability, appropriate recognizability, and accessibility, had an average score lower than 4.5, specifically 4.48, 4.47, 4.45, and 4.3, respectively. These

Table 7. DATUS satisfaction questionnaire analysis based on task id

Dimension	Task id	Mean	Median	Standard Deviation
Accessibility	19	4.36	4	0.505
Appropriate recognizability	7	4.45	5	0.522
Effectiveness	3	4.55	5	0.522
	13	4.64	5	0.505
Efficiency	4	4.55	5	0.522
	5	4.45	4	0.522
Learnability	7	4.45	4	0.522
	8	4.73	5	0.467
	10	4.27	4	0.467
	12	4.46	4	0.522
Operability	2	4.27	4	0.467
	9	4.64	5	0.505
	11	4.36	4	0.505
	14	4.55	5	0.522
	20	4.55	5	0.522
Satisfaction	1	4.27	4	0.467
	6	4.55	5	0.522
	16	4.82	5	0.405
	18	4.64	5	0.505
User Interface Aesthetic	15	4.82	5	0.405
	Score	**90.38**	**92**	-

Table 8. DATUS satisfaction questionnaire analysis summary based on usability dimension

Dimensions	Mean	Median	Standard Deviation
Accessibility	4.36	4	0.505
Appropriate recognizability	4.45	5	0.522
Effectiveness	4.59	5	0.503
Efficiency	4.5	5	0.502
Learnability	4.48	5	0.5
Operability	4.47	5	0.499
Satisfaction	4.57	5	0.478
User Interface Aesthetic	4.82	5	0.405

lower scores suggest that these dimensions have potential for improvement. The lower average score for accessibility could be attributed to the presence of elements such as tabs and sliders, which made it difficult for some participants to locate and access certain information. To enhance accessibility, careful attention is required during the dashboard design process.

There are two open-ended questions that are optional for the participants of this usability evaluation which are "Is there any information you would like to see that has not been considered on the dashboard?" and "Do you have any other comments or suggestions you want to share with us?". All the participants do not have a comment for the question "Is there any information you would like to see that has not been considered on the dashboard?". The suggestions gained from the participants are shown in Table 9. These suggestions will be analyzed and considered in future work.

Table 9. Suggestions from participants for the open-ended questions

Suggestions
Bigger font for the items in the dashboard
Placing the view details button below the visualization

5   Conclusion and Future Work

In conclusion, the University Student Dashboard model has the potential to greatly benefit the university's top management by providing a reliable platform for monitoring key performance indicators and making data-driven decisions. The careful design of the information visualization enables the dashboard to serve as a great enabler for top management to have an overview of the university's operations. While the user interface design was well received, the usability evaluation identified operability, appropriate recognizability, and accessibility as areas needing improvement.

Future works could include the introduction of a machine learning algorithm for predictive capabilities and anomaly detection to identify rare occurrences in the university, ultimately saving resources. These enhancements would further increase the dashboard's value for top management in long-term planning. Overall, the University Student Dashboard model presents an effective tool for improving the university's decision-making processes and optimizing its operations.

References

1. Pedretti, A.S., et al.: Evaluation of telehealth service for COVID-19 outpatients: a dashboard to measure healthcare quality and safety. Stud. Health Technol. Inform. **290**, 369–372 (2022)
2. Victor, S., Farooq, A.: Dashboard visualisation for healthcare performance management: Balanced scorecard metrics. Asia Pac. J. Health Manag. **16**(2), 28–38 (2021)

3. Susnjak, T., Ramaswami, G., Mathrani, A.: Learning analytics dashboard: a tool for providing actionable insights to learners. Int. J. Educ. Technol. High. Educ. **19** (2022)
4. Birogul, S., Gültekin, H.: Reviewing the effect of business intelligence on decision support process: an application on the finance sector. Bilişim Teknolojileri Dergisi **13**(2), 197–206 (2020)
5. D'Hauwers, R., Borghys, K., Vannieuwenhuyze, J.T.A., Walravens, N., Lievens, B.: Challenges in data-driven policymaking: using smart city data to support local retail policies. ISPRS Ann. Photogram. Remote Sens. Spat. Inf. Sci. **6**, 55–61 (2020)
6. Raj, S., Paliwal, M.: Higher education dashboard implementation using data mining and Data Warehouse: a review paper. Int. J. Innov. Res. Comput. Sci. Technol. 107–111 (2022)
7. Sushma Rao, H.S., Suresh, A., Hegde, V.: Academic dashboard—descriptive analytical approach to analyze student admission using education data mining. In: Mishra, D., Nayak, M., Joshi, A. (eds.) Information and Communication Technology for Sustainable Development. LNNS, vol. 2, pp. 423–432. Springer, Singapore (2018). https://doi.org/10.1007/978-981-10-3920-1_43
8. Oqaidi, K., Aouhassi, S., Mansouri, K.: Towards a students' dropout prediction model in higher education institutions using machine learning algorithms. Int. J. Emerg. Technol. Learn. (Online) **17**(18), 103 (2022)
9. Gartner.   https://www.gartner.com/en/information-technology/glossary/business-intelligence-bi. Accessed 03 Apr 2023
10. Investopedia. https://www.investopedia.com/terms/b/business-intelligence-bi.asp. Accessed 03 Apr 2023
11. Muntean, M., Sabau, G., Bologa, A.-R., Surcel, T., Florea, A.: Performance dashboards for universities. In: Proceedings of the 2nd International Conference on Manufacturing Engineering, Quality and Production Systems, pp. 206–211 (2010)
12. Piantari, E., Megasari, R., Hidayat, K.: Tactical dashboard design for study program in university. In: Proceedings of the 7th Mathematics, Science, and Computer Science Education International Seminar, MSCEIS 2019, Bandung, West Java, Indonesia (2020)
13. MohdTuah, N., Yoag, A., Mohd Nizam, D.N., Wan Chin, C.: A dashboard-based system to manage and monitor the progression of undergraduate IT degree final year projects. Pertanika J. Sci. Technol. **29**(4), 235–256 (2021)
14. Prejean, E.A., Kilcoyne, M.S., Liao, W., Parker, C.: Is higher education talking and walking agile management: a review of the literature. Am. Int. J. Bus. Manag. **2**(7), 8–18 (2019)
15. Antunes, R.S.D.S.: DATUS: dashboard assessment usability model: a case study with student dashboards. Doctoral dissertation (2020)

Fostering Cyber-Resilience in Higher Education: A Pilot Evaluation of a Malware Awareness Program for College Students

Norliza Katuk[1]([⊠]) [ID], Nur A.' fyfah Zaimy[1], Suren Krishnan[1,2],
Raj Kumar Kunhiraman[3], Hwee-Hsiung Lee[4], and Derar Eleyan[5]

[1] Institute for Advanced and Smart Digital Opportunities, Universiti Utara Malaysia, 06010
Sintok, Kedah, Malaysia
k.norliza@uum.edu.my
[2] Intel Microelectronics, 11900 Bayan Lepas, Penang, Malaysia
[3] Cyber Intelligence, 63000 Cyberjaya, Selangor, Malaysia
[4] CyberSecurity Malaysia, 63000 Cyberjaya, Selangor, Malaysia
[5] Applied Computing Department, Palestine Technical University, Kadoorie, Palestine

Abstract. This study evaluated the effectiveness of a malware awareness program designed to enhance college students' knowledge of malware prevention strategies and promote responsible online behavior. The program group discussions and presentations are designed to address misconceptions and improve students' understanding of malware prevention, including identifying security attacks, understanding malware spreading mechanisms, and avoiding risky online behavior. A study was conducted following the pre-test and post-test assessments to measure the program's impact on students' knowledge levels. The results revealed significant improvements in post-test scores indicating the program's success in achieving its objectives. The observed enhancements in students' knowledge can be attributed to the program's focus on delivery techniques, which have been proven effective in enhancing knowledge retention and promoting learning. The implications of this study underscore the value of providing targeted and engaging cybersecurity education to college students. By incorporating malware awareness programs into the educational system, institutions can foster a more secure digital environment and promote a culture of cyber-resilience among future professionals. Furthermore, the program's success suggests that similar interventions may be beneficial in other areas of cybersecurity, encouraging ongoing research and development of educational initiatives that address the diverse range of threats in today's interconnected world.

Keywords: Security · cybersecurity awareness · malware attacks · prevention · Higher education

1 Introduction

The human element is often considered the weakest link in cybersecurity, making it crucial to prioritize cybersecurity awareness (CSA) in higher education to protect students from cyberattacks [1]. With technology playing an increasingly significant role

© The Author(s), under exclusive license to Springer Nature Singapore Pte Ltd. 2024
N. H. Zakaria et al. (Eds.): ICOCI 2023, CCIS 2002, pp. 154–167, 2024.
https://doi.org/10.1007/978-981-99-9592-9_12

in our lives, it is essential to educate Internet users from a young age about Internet safety issues [2]. By fostering a solid cybersecurity knowledge and practices foundation, young people can better navigate the digital world and reduce their vulnerability to potential threats. In addition, Information Technology (IT)-related organizations particularly need robust cybersecurity awareness [3]. Employees in these organizations should be equipped with the necessary skills and knowledge to identify, prevent, and respond to cyber threats effectively. By implementing comprehensive CSA programs in educational institutions and IT-related organizations, it can foster a culture of security and vigilance that empowers individuals to protect their digital assets actively. Investing in cybersecurity education and awareness benefits individuals and strengthens the overall security posture of organizations and the broader digital ecosystem.

Malware awareness is paramount among higher education students, as cybercriminals often target them due to their limited experience and knowledge in dealing with digital threats [4]. In addition, the prevalence of malware attacks on college and university networks has been steadily increasing, with institutions reporting numerous incidents involving ransomware, phishing, and other forms of malicious software [5]. Given the vast amount of sensitive information stored in educational institutions, students must be well-informed about the risks and types of malware and how to protect themselves [2]. Therefore, educational institutions are critical in equipping students with the necessary skills to identify and avoid malware threats [6]. By incorporating malware awareness into their cybersecurity curriculum, higher education institutions can ensure that students develop a solid understanding of the primary attack vectors and the proactive steps they can take to secure their devices and data [4]. Furthermore, regular training sessions and workshops can help students stay up-to-date with the latest malware trends and defense strategies [7].

The lack of malware awareness among students can have severe consequences for individuals and higher learning institutions [8]. On a personal level, students unaware of malware prevention strategies risk exposing sensitive data, such as academic records and financial information, to cyber criminals [6]. Malware attacks can lead to identity theft, financial loss, and damaged reputations, affecting students' prospects and well-being. Higher learning institutions also suffer from the consequences of inadequate malware awareness [9]. Generally, cyberattacks can compromise institutional data, disrupt academic activities, and erode the institution's credibility.

Furthermore, the financial costs of recovering from a cyberattack can be immense, diverting resources from essential academic programs [7]. Given these potential consequences, this study aims to investigate and develop suitable and relevant malware awareness programs for higher-education students. Although organizations conducted awareness programs, limited studies were conducted on the effectiveness of the materials and the methods of conducting these programs. While the importance of malware awareness is recognized, there is a need for more comprehensive research that evaluates the specific materials, resources, and instructional approaches employed in these programs.

On the other hand, equipping the students with the knowledge to recognize and prevent cyber threats can foster a more secure digital environment, safeguard personal and institutional data, and promote academic success [10]. Investing in the research and implementation of robust malware awareness initiatives will ultimately benefit students and higher learning institutions in the long run. Specifically, this study is significant as it assesses the effectiveness of a specific intervention, namely the malware awareness program, through a pilot evaluation. This evaluation helps determine the program's impact on students' knowledge, attitudes, and behaviors related to malware threats, providing valuable insights for improving similar initiatives.

2   Related Studies

2.1 Malware

Malware, short for malicious software, is a term that encompasses a wide range of software programs intentionally designed to cause harm to computer systems, networks, and users. A clear definition of malware remains an open challenge in computer virology, as various studies have comprehensively attempted to understand the concept [8, 9]. For example, Saeed, Selamat, and Abuagoub [11] defined malware as software created to harm a computer in some way, be it by slowing it down, monitoring its activities, stealing personal information, or gaining unauthorized access to secure areas. These threats pose significant risks to computer systems and the sensitive data they contain. Cisco [12] also defined malware as any malicious program created by cybercriminals, or hackers, intending to steal information from, disrupt, or even destroy computers and computer networks. According to Cisco, there are seven common distinct categories of malware:

1. Virus: A type of malware that attaches itself to legitimate programs and files, spreading from one file to another, often causing damage to system files and data.
2. Worms: Self-replicating malware that spreads through networks can consume system resources, potentially causing system crashes.
3. Trojan virus: Malware disguised as a legitimate program, gaining access to a user's system to steal information or create a backdoor for further attacks.
4. Spyware: Software designed to monitor and collect information about a user's activities, often without the user's knowledge or consent.
5. Adware: Malware that delivers unwanted advertisements or redirects user searches to advertising websites, potentially exposing users to additional threats.
6. Ransomware: A type of malware that encrypts a user's data or restricts access to their system, demanding payment in exchange for the decryption key or restored access.
7. Fileless malware: A sophisticated form of malware that resides in a computer's memory or other temporary storage, making it difficult to detect and remove.

Each category represents a unique threat to computer users and networks, requiring a multifaceted approach to prevention and mitigation [13]. As the tools and techniques employed by cybercriminals continue to evolve, individuals and organizations must remain vigilant in protecting their systems and data from the ever-growing threat of malware. To counter these threats, a combination of user education, robust security protocols, and up-to-date antivirus and anti-malware software can help minimize the risk of infection and mitigate the damage caused by malware attacks. In addition, by understanding the various types of malware and their potential impact, users can make informed decisions about their online activities and the security measures they employ to protect their digital assets.

2.2 Malware Prevention

In recent eras, victims who have been infected with malware or have never been infected have sought further preventative measures. The majority of malware attack reports in 2017 were ransomware. According to statistics collected by researchers, the victims may have been infected with ransomware when they used the website's services [14]. A few solutions are available to prevent malware attacks, including installing and updating antivirus. Installing antivirus software and keeping it up-to-date helps protect a computer from viruses and other malware (malicious software). For example, Microsoft Defender is free antivirus software that comes with Windows and is kept up to date automatically through Windows Update. Students can also choose to install antivirus products made by other companies on their computer devices.

Using a complex password and constantly using the most up-to-date browser and operating system (OS) versions is essential to protect oneself from malware attacks. Students should immediately use complex passwords on whatever device or application they use. These passwords should have a mix of uppercase and lowercase letters, numbers, and symbols and be at least eight characters. It is not enough for students to maintain their antivirus software up to date; they must also guarantee that their OS and browser are always up to current. The research carried out by Jones [15] claimed that clicking on spam messages or suspicious links could expose users to malware attacks. Once the user has clicked on a phishing link [16], the attacker will instantly acquire some basic data, such as users' device statistics, approximate location, and whatever other information they may have voluntarily provided. Thus, all students must avoid opening spam emails and not click on suspicious links sent by the unknown sender to avoid experiencing malware attacks.

Students also must be cautious of suspicious files and abstain from downloading them, especially from dubious sources [15]. It is a good practice for the student to check the SSL certificate of the website, such as 'HTTPS' and scan the file before downloading it. Another prevention to the malware attack that can be done is to set a proper firewall in the system and never execute untrustworthy programs on the device [17]. A firewall is an additional layer of protection that delivers more robust security to the devices and network. A firewall works as a barrier between the internet and the computer system, blocking unauthorized access or harmful content from entering the network. Furthermore, users should avoid running untrustworthy programs on their devices, as these may contain hidden malware that can compromise system security [17]. Instead, students should only download and run software from reputable sources and pay attention to warning signs, such as substantial file sizes or unexpected permissions requests. Regularly backing up essential data is another crucial step in protecting oneself against malware attacks. In a ransomware attack, having a recent backup of essential files can significantly reduce the attack's impact and help users recover their data without paying the ransom. It is recommended that students use a combination of local and cloud-based backup solutions to ensure multiple copies of their data are always available.

An awareness program targeting higher education students is crucial in equipping them with the knowledge to protect themselves from malware attacks. Students often use various digital platforms and devices for research, collaboration, and communication, making them vulnerable to cyber threats. By implementing an awareness program, institutions can educate students on the latest malware strains, phishing techniques, and other cyber risks, empowering them to recognize and avoid potential dangers. Additionally, such programs can provide practical guidance on essential security measures, like using complex passwords, updating antivirus software, and enabling two-factor authentication. This education benefits the individual and promotes a culture of cybersecurity within the academic community, ultimately reducing the potential for large-scale attacks. Cybersecurity awareness programs equip higher education students with the knowledge and skills to thwart malware attacks, safeguard their data, and contribute to a more secure digital environment.

3 Methodology

3.1 Study Design

The study design for the malware awareness program aimed at higher learning institution students involved a comprehensive, step-by-step approach to ensure its effectiveness. First, the target group of users within higher learning institutions was identified, focusing primarily on students as they frequently use digital platforms for academic purposes. Next, relevant content for the malware awareness program was identified, addressing the most pressing cyber threats and best practices to mitigate them. The program's material was then designed to cater to the student's needs and keep them engaged throughout the process. Finally, pre-test and post-test questions were prepared based on the material to evaluate the participants' knowledge before and after attending the program. Subsequently, content validation was conducted for the pre-test and post-test questions and the materials, ensuring their accuracy and relevance.

Planning for the schedule and protocol of the awareness program was the next step, considering the student's availability and the optimal duration for effective learning. Next, a rehearsal was conducted to identify potential issues or improvement areas before the program. Participants were invited and recruited, ensuring a diverse and representative student population sample. Finally, the awareness program was conducted, engaging students in awareness activities, including a poster demonstration and discussions to increase their understanding of malware threats and prevention strategies. Following the program, the pre-test and post-test results were analyzed, along with the respondents' open-ended feedback, to measure the program's effectiveness and identify areas for improvement. A comprehensive report was prepared, summarizing the program's outcomes and highlighting key findings from the analysis. Finally, a post-mortem was conducted on the awareness program, discussing the successes, challenges, and lessons learned to inform and enhance future iterations of the program. This study design ensures a robust and effective malware awareness program that equips higher education students with the essential knowledge and skills to protect themselves from cyber threats.

3.2 Materials

The materials for the awareness program were carefully designed to effectively deliver crucial cybersecurity information to students, empowering them to protect themselves from malware attacks. The primary educational material used was a visually engaging and easily digestible poster that captured students' attention and concisely conveyed the essential information. The poster outlined ten key measures that students can implement to safeguard their devices and personal information from malware attacks as a valuable reference for students to consult and apply daily. In addition, digital tools such as Google Meet and Google Forms were employed to ensure the seamless delivery of the awareness program and facilitate student interaction. Google Meet provided a user-friendly platform for conducting the pilot test with students, enabling real-time collaboration and discussion on the material. Meanwhile, Google Forms offered a convenient method for collecting students' feedback and evaluating their understanding of the malware protection measures outlined in the poster. Leveraging these digital tools not only enhanced the accessibility and interactivity of the awareness program but also allowed for greater flexibility in reaching students across different locations and schedules. Figure 1 demonstrates the poster.

Fig. 1. The poster as the main material used for the awareness program

The awareness program incorporated pre-test questions focusing on malware, consisting of ten multiple-choice items and four demographic queries. This pre-test evaluated respondents' prior knowledge and understanding of malware-related topics while capturing essential demographic information. The same pre-test questionnaire was later repurposed as a post-test assessment following the educational session. This approach allowed for a direct comparison of respondents' knowledge and understanding before and after exposure to the awareness program, effectively highlighting the impact and effectiveness of the educational content provided Table 1 lists the questions.

Table 1. The pre-test and post-test questions

Num	Questions	Answers
1)	Security attacks include	a) Malware b) Antivirus c) Computer system d) Firewall
2)	A/An _____ is a computer program that spreads by inserting copies of itself into other executable codes or documents	a) Computer Virus b) Antivirus c) Computer system d) Firewall
3)	How is malware distributed?	a) Through spam email attachment that contains a suspicious link b) Download files or documents from unreliable resources c) Running source codes that cannot be trusted d) Installing licensed Adobe and Microsoft Office software on a personal computer
4)	One of the ways to avoid malware attacks is not to visit sites with a lot of clickbait	a) Yes b) No c) May be
5)	Installing and keep updating software on the computer helps to avoid malware attacks	a) Yes b) No c) May be
6)	Which of the following is not the prevention of malware attacks?	a) Clicking on links to suspicious websites in emails, messaging apps, or social network posts b) Install and update antivirus c) Avoid using open Wi-Fi network d) Avoid downloading files from unreliable resources
7)	What is an antivirus?	a) Computer software used to prevent, detect and remove malicious software b) Software used to duplicate viruses c) A bigger and more dangerous virus
8)	Worms can spread and harm independently	a) True b) False

(continued)

Table 1. (*continued*)

Num	Questions	Answers
9)	Malware is used to describe all types of bad software. Malware is a combination of what two words?	a) Malicious and software b) Magnificient and software c) Normal and adware
10)	Downloading files from unreliable sources can be exposed to malware attacks	a) Yes b) No c) May be

3.3 Respondents

The awareness program was done on thirteen respondents, all of whom were students from Kedah Matriculation College in Malaysia with a background in accounting. These participants provided valuable insights into the effectiveness of the malware awareness program for a specific demographic of young learners. The age distribution among participants was relatively homogenous, with approximately 100 per cent of respondents falling within the 17 to 18 age range, which is typical for matriculation college students. Regarding gender representation, the group of respondents was relatively balanced. Female participants comprised 50 per cent of the respondent pool, while 40 per cent identified as male. The remaining respondents chose not to disclose their gender, respecting their individual preferences and maintaining an inclusive environment for all participants. This diverse representation of gender identities within the respondent group contributed to a richer understanding of the malware awareness program's impact across different student perspectives. In addition, the participants' composition has allowed for a comprehensive evaluation of the awareness program's effectiveness in educating and empowering students to protect themselves against malware attacks. The findings from this diverse group of respondents will inform future iterations of the program, ensuring that it remains relevant, engaging, and accessible to all students within higher learning institutions.

3.4 Procedure

The security awareness program, which emphasized the prevention of malware attacks, was thoughtfully designed and delivered to students utilizing the Google Meet platform. Its primary objective was to educate students on effective strategies to safeguard themselves against malware attacks, equipping them with the knowledge and tools to navigate the digital world securely. A facilitator led the session and was assisted by a technical support person. Before presenting the visually engaging poster as the core awareness material, students were asked to complete a pre-test questionnaire of ten questions—this preliminary assessment aimed to gauge their baseline understanding of malware attacks and prevention techniques. The pilot test questionnaires were distributed using the Google Form platform, with students allotted three to five minutes for completion. After finishing the pre-test questionnaire, the program distributed the informative poster outlining ten actionable measures to ward off malware attacks. The presentation took approximately ten to twelve minutes, ensuring a concise and focused material delivery. Subsequently, a 'Question and Answer' (Q&A) session was conducted, fostering open dialogue and addressing students' concerns or queries. Finally, post-test questionnaires containing identical questions to the pre-test were administered to the students after the Q&A session. The post-test evaluated the student's knowledge and understanding of malware prevention strategies due to exposing them to the malware awareness material. They were also encouraged to provide open-ended comments on the awareness program. This valuable feedback would inform the program's continual refinement and improvement for future iterations. Figure 2 illustrates the procedure for the malware awareness program.

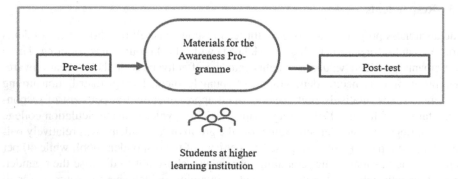

Fig. 2. The procedure of the awareness program

4   Results and Discussions

4.1   Demographic Information

An advertisement was distributed through Whatsapp for selected classes of the college. As a result, 20 students voluntarily joined the Whatsapp group. They answered the pre-test questions, but only thirteen answered the post-test questions. The respondents are between the ages of 17 and 1. While for the gender of respondents, half of the respondents were female, 40%of respondents identified were male, and the rest preferred not to reveal their gender. Most respondents used the Android OS as their mobile OS, and only 40% used the iOS operating system. In addition, 70% of the respondents utilized Windows on their personal computers, and the rest used Linux OS, MacOS OS, and others.

4.2   The Effectiveness of the Malware Awareness Program

The pre-test and post-test assessments of the malware awareness program demonstrated significant improvements in students' knowledge of malware prevention strategies, as shown in Table 2. For example, a 13.6% improvement was observed with the 65% pre-test score and 78.6% post-test score related to the student's knowledge of the types of security attacks. The result indicates that students better understood security attacks after participating in the program. In addition, a substantial improvement of 22.1% was observed, highlighting the increased awareness of how malware spreads among students. Regarding malware distribution methods, individual improvements for each answer choice were A: 8.6%, B: -1.4%, and C: 11.4%. The negative improvement for option B suggests that some misconceptions might persist. Finally, a 10.7% improvement was observed in avoiding risky online behavior, with the pre-test score at 75% and the post-test score at 85.7%. The result showcases the program's effectiveness in teaching students how to evade malware attacks.

When addressing the importance of software updates, a modest 4.3% improvement was observed, with the pre-test score at 60% and the post-test score at 64.3%. It indicates that students gained some further understanding of the role of software updates in preventing malware attacks. Further, a significant 45.7% improvement was observed in clarifying misconceptions around malware prevention techniques, with the pre-test score at 40% and the post-test score at 85.7%. Regarding antivirus software and its role in malware prevention, the program demonstrated a 7.9% improvement, with the pre-test score at 85% and the post-test score at 92.9%. A slight 1.4% improvement was observed in how worms operate, with the pre-test score at 70% and the post-test score at 71.4%. The result suggests that students already had a basic understanding of this aspect. A 5.7% improvement was also observed in the student knowledge about the term "malware", with 80% pre-test and 85.7% post-test scores. It indicates that students gained a clearer understanding of the term. Lastly, in teaching students about the risks associated with downloading files from untrustworthy sources, a significant 25.7% improvement was observed, with the pre-test score at 60% and the post-test score at 85.7%.

Table 2. The overall score for each of the pre-test and post-test questions

Num	Questions	Pre-test (%)	Post-test (%)	% of improvement
1)	Security attacks include	65	78.6	13.6
2)	A/An _____ is a computer program that spreads by inserting copies of itself into other executable codes or documents	35	57.1	22.1
3)	How is malware distributed?	A - 70 B - 80 C - 60	A - 78.6 B - 78.6 C - 71.4	A-8.6 B-(1.4) C-11.4
4)	One of the ways to avoid malware attacks is not to visit sites that have a lot of clickbait	75	85.7	10.7

(continued)

Table 2. (*continued*)

Num	Questions	Pre-test (%)	Post-test (%)	% of improvement
5)	Installing and keep updating software on the computer helps to avoid malware attacks	60	64.3	4.3
6)	Which of the following is not the prevention of malware attacks?	40	85.7	45.7
7)	What is an antivirus?	85	92.9	7.9
8)	Worms can spread and harm independently	70	71.4	1.4
9)	Malware is used to describe all types of bad software. Malware is a combination of what two words?	80	85.7	5.7
10)	Downloading files from unreliable sources can be exposed to malware attacks	60	85.7	25.7

The malware awareness program demonstrated remarkable improvements in college students' understanding of malware prevention strategies, as evidenced by the results of the pre-test and post-test assessments. A comparative analysis of the means and standard deviations revealed a significant increase in knowledge acquisition among the respondents. On average, the pre-test scores were 65%, with a standard deviation of 16.83, indicating a relatively diverse range of understanding among students before the program. In contrast, the post-test scores witnessed a substantial increase, with a mean of 78.57% and a standard deviation of 11.18, pointing towards a more uniform level of comprehension among participants. This improvement of 13.57% in the mean scores highlights the effectiveness of the malware awareness program in enhancing students' knowledge and skills in malware prevention. Furthermore, the reduction in standard deviation by 5.65 further suggests that the program successfully narrowed the knowledge gap among respondents, fostering a more consistent understanding across the board. Table 3 lists the statistics.

Table 3. The means and standard deviation of the pre-test and post-test questions

Statistics	Pre-test (%)	Post-test (%)	Improvement
Means	65	78.57	13.57
Standard deviation	16.83	11.18	5.65

The results of the pre-test and post-test assessments of the malware awareness program provide valuable insights into the program's effectiveness in enhancing knowledge of malware prevention strategies among higher learning institution students. The results show that the program has successfully improved students' knowledge of various aspects of malware prevention. In addition, the improvements in the scores across the ten questions indicate that the program has effectively addressed misconceptions and enhanced knowledge in areas such as identifying security attacks, understanding malware-spreading mechanisms, and avoiding risky online behavior. The effectiveness of the malware awareness program can be measured by the significant improvements in the post-test scores compared to the pre-test scores. The results highlight the program's success in achieving its objectives and providing students with the necessary knowledge and skills to protect themselves from malware attacks. The program's success can also be attributed to its focus on delivery techniques, such as group discussions and presentations. These techniques have been proven effective in enhancing knowledge retention and promoting active learning [18]. Overall, the results of the pre-test and post-test assessments demonstrate the effectiveness of the malware awareness program in improving college students' knowledge of malware prevention strategies. Again, the program's success can be attributed to its engaging delivery techniques, which have enhanced knowledge retention and promoted active learning. In conclusion, the malware awareness program has enriched college students' ability to recognize and combat malware threats. Furthermore, by addressing the students' diverse levels of understanding, the program has successfully cultivated a more secure and informed digital environment for its participants.

5 Conclusion

In conclusion, the malware awareness program has successfully improved college students' understanding of malware prevention strategies. The significant improvements in the post-test scores compared to the pre-test scores highlight the program's efficacy in addressing misconceptions and enhancing knowledge in various aspects of malware prevention. The results also emphasize the importance of engaging delivery techniques, such as group discussions, case studies, and interactive presentations, which have been proven effective in enhancing knowledge retention and promoting active learning. However, while the malware awareness program has achieved notable success, there is room for future improvements to ensure that students are well-equipped to protect themselves from the ever-evolving landscape of cyber threats. One area of potential future work could be the development of more advanced and adaptive learning modules that consider the students' existing knowledge and tailor the content accordingly. It would provide a more personalized learning experience and could help improve students' understanding of malware prevention strategies.

Additionally, hands-on activities, such as simulated malware attacks or practical exercises in identifying and mitigating security vulnerabilities [19], could further enhance students' skills and reinforce the knowledge gained from the program. It may also be beneficial to explore integrating the malware awareness program into the core curriculum of college courses, ensuring that all students have access to this essential knowledge as part of their education. Lastly, continuous evaluation and updating of the program's content are crucial to ensure that it remains relevant and effective in addressing the latest trends and developments in the field of cybersecurity [20]. By building upon the successes of the current malware awareness program and implementing these suggested improvements, future iterations of the program can continue to educate and empower college students to protect themselves against malware threats effectively. It, in turn, will contribute to a more secure digital environment and a greater understanding of the importance of cybersecurity in today's interconnected world.

Acknowledgements. The authors thank the School of Computing, Universiti Utara Malaysia, for funding this study.

References

1. Matyokurehwa, K., Rudhumbu, N., Gombiro, C., Mlambo, C.: Cybersecurity awareness in Zimbabwean universities: perspectives from the students. Secur. Privacy **4**(2), e141 (2021)
2. Raju, R., Abd Rahman, N.H., Ahmad, A.: Cyber security awareness in using digital platforms among students in a higher learning institution. Asian J. Univ. Educ. **18**(3), 756–766 (2022)
3. Omar, N.S., Foozy, C.F.M., Hamid, I.R.A., Hafit, H., Arbain, A.F., Shamala, P.: Malware awareness tool for internet safety using gamification techniques. Journal of Physics: Conference Series, p. 012023. IOP Publishing (2021)
4. Hunt, T.: Cyber Security Awareness in Higher Education. Central Washington University (2016)
5. Ulven, J.B., Wangen, G.: A systematic review of cybersecurity risks in higher education. Future Internet **13**(2), 39 (2021)
6. Rezgui, Y., Marks, A.: Information security awareness in higher education: an exploratory study. Comput. Secur.. Secur. **27**(7–8), 241–253 (2008)
7. Fouad, N.S.: Securing higher education against cyberthreats: from an institutional risk to a national policy challenge. J. Cyber Policy **6**(2), 137–154 (2021)
8. Khader, M., Karam, M., Fares, H.: Cybersecurity awareness framework for academia. Information **12**(10), 417 (2021)
9. Sadaghiani-Tabrizi, A.: Revisiting cybersecurity awareness in the midst of disruptions. Int. J. Bus. Educ. **163**(1), 6 (2023)
10. Bhatnagar, N., Pry, M.: Student attitudes, awareness, and perceptions of personal privacy and cybersecurity in the use of social media: an initial study. Inf. Syst. Educ. J. **18**(1), 48–58 (2020)
11. Saeed, I.A., Selamat, A., Abuagoub, A.M.: A survey on malware and malware detection systems. Int. J. Comput. Appl. **67**(16) (2013)
12. Cisco. https://www.cisco.com/site/us/en/products/security/what-is-malware.html
13. Noorbehbahani, F., Taghiyar, A., Rezvani, A.: RSAM: a questionnaire for ransomware security awareness measurement. J. Comput. Secur.Comput. Secur. **10**(1), 1–15 (2023)
14. Tiu, Y.L., Zolkipli, M.F.: Study on prevention and solution of ransomware attack. J. IT Asia **9**(1), 133–139 (2021)
15. Warren Averett CPAs & Advisors. https://warrenaverett.com/insights/what-happens-if-you-click-on-a-phishing-link/
16. Manoharan, S., Katuk, N., Hassan, S., Ahmad, R.: To click or not to click the link: the factors influencing internet banking users' intention in responding to phishing emails. Inf. Comput. Secur. **30**(1), 37–62 (2022)

17. MakeUseOf. https://www.makeuseof.com/safely-run-suspicious-programs-applications-win dows/
18. Wang, R., Ryu, H., Katuk, N.: Assessment of students' cognitive-affective states in learning within a computer-based environment: effects on performance. J. Inf. Commun. Technol. **14**(1), 153–176 (2015)
19. Angafor, G.N., Yevseyeva, I., Maglaras, L.: Scenario-based incident response training: lessons learnt from conducting an experiential learning virtual incident response tabletop exercise. Information & Computer Security, (Inprint) (2023)
20. Afenyo, M., Caesar, L.D.: Maritime cybersecurity threats: gaps and directions for future research. Ocean Coast. Manag.Manag. **236**(April), 106493 (2023)

Analysis of the Effectiveness of Feedback Provision in Intelligent Tutoring Systems

Nur Hafiza Jamaludin[1] and Rohaida Romli[2]($\boxtimes$)

[1] School of Computing, Universiti Utara Malaysia, UUM Sintok, 06010 Kedah, Malaysia
[2] Data Management & Software Solution, Research Laboratory, School of Computing, Universiti Utara Malaysia, UUM Sintok, 06010 Kedah, Malaysia
za5828@gmail.com

Abstract. The effectiveness of feedback provision in an Intelligent Tutoring System (ITS) is a crucial aspect to be considered when developing a tutoring system. The system is proven beneficial if it can act like a one-to-one human tutor, which provides feedback based on student learning aptitude and performance. Many researchers have developed ITSs with the intention of assisting students in teaching programming concepts, algorithms, and writing computer programs. However, there have been very few studies that have focused on reviewing these works. The studies are merely concerned with reviewing the characteristic, application, evaluation, and supplementary features of ITSs across different educational fields from 2007 until 2017. As a result, a comparative evaluation was conducted with the goal of analyzing the feedback provided by existing works in ITSs as well as the techniques used to develop a student model. The results of this study have indicated that Constraint-Based modeling, Model Tracing, Natural Language processing, and Deep Learning with delayed feedback are the most appropriate feedback for students learning to code. Bayesian Network is the most commonly used technique by researchers with immediate and delayed feedback to help students learn programming concepts and algorithms better.

Keywords: Intelligent Tutoring System (ITS) · Feedback and Hints provision · Modeling Technique

1 Background

Computer programming is not easy to learn or master [6, 30]. This circumstance resulted in low student achievement in computer programming courses, and many beginners struggled to learn programming and develop the necessary problem-solving skills near the end of the learning process [25]. Therefore, many educators pay great attention to cultivating students' programming abilities by creating beneficial tools to support learning programming, setting up many courses related to programming [49], and also researching effective strategies for learning and teaching programming. Many researchers have verified Intelligent Tutoring System (ITS) effectiveness for sustainable students and teachers in teaching and learning programming [44, 51]. It could complement conventional classroom teaching, efficiently supporting the learning process, making the learning practice

N. H. Zakaria et al. (Eds.): ICOCI 2023, CCIS 2002, pp. 168–179, 2024.
https://doi.org/10.1007/978-981-99-9592-9_13

very pleasing, cultivating distance learning, and prolonging the learning process, and allowing learners to learn personally at their own pace, anytime and anywhere, based on their own progress [2]. However, learning and teaching without appropriate feedback is insufficient to enhance students' skills in programming.

The effectiveness of feedback provision in ITSs is a crucial aspect to consider when developing a tutoring system. The system's capabilities depend not only heavily on its architecture; however, the timing and style of the system's feedback significantly impact its effectiveness. The feedback is also considered effective if it is error-specific and supports students' needs based on their abilities and knowledge gaps [39]. The system is proven beneficial if it can act like a one-to-one human tutor, which provides feedback based on student learning aptitude and performance [9, 46]. The results indicate that private tutors help 98% of students in the learning process, and average student achievement was higher than two standard deviations from the conventional approach [9]. Although Intelligent Tutoring Systems can support students learning programming with the biggest advantage of teaching students according to their ability, providing personalized guidance for different students, and improving students' independent learning ability and learning efficiency, the system seems appropriate for experienced students [49]. This shows that the requirement to make improvements in providing personalized feedback is still demanding to help novice users learn programming. Also, Perikos et al. [39] have highlighted the importance of modeling techniques to generate effective and efficient feedback generation and hints to support students learning since they are able to model students' metacognitive learning behavior.

Thus far, only two studies [14, 36] have focused on reviewing existing ITS studies. The review in these studies was only concerned with the characteristics, application, evaluation, and supplementary features of ITSs in various educational fields from 2007 to 2017. Thus, to provide a more comprehensive review of recent works, a comparative evaluation was conducted to analyze the feedback provided by existing works in ITS and the techniques used to develop a student model. Its findings will furnish suggestions on the appropriate techniques to be used in developing a student model for an ITS.

The remaining content of this paper is structured as follows: Sect. 2 discusses the related work; Sect. 3 highlights the detailed discussion of the methodology; Sect. 4 portrays the analysis and result of comparative evaluation; and Sect. 5 concludes this paper and provides suggestions for future research direction.

2   Related Work

Abu-Naser [2] demonstrated in his research that tutors outperform teachers in this regard because they can provide students with more immediate feedback than most teachers. Furthermore, Wang et al. [47] stated that ITS is an important tool for developing problem-solving skills as the feedback provided is critical in the problem-solving process. Sullins [42] has proposed AutoTutor LITE with LCC functions that improve the student model with the capability to provide appropriate feedback like an experienced human tutor. In addition, Black and William [8] clarified that feedback can be useful for enhancing student learning when used appropriately.

According to the research carried out by Ivelisse [45], system guidance combined with supportive and appropriate feedback provided during the learning process makes learning tools significantly better than others. Gutierrez and Atkinson [24] demonstrated that negative feedback can be used to correct students' misconceptions about programming so that they do not repeat the same mistake. According to Al-Rekhawi's [4] research, the Andes system could provide immediate hints and comments when students encountered difficulties with the questions. Students can guess and get correct answers even when they do not fully understand the concept. Many researchers, however, agree that improvements are needed to manage more complex dialogues [1].

Graesser et al. [22] have discussed three levels of providing feedback in AutoTutor (to simulate the dialogue patterns of typical human tutors): backchannel feedback, evaluative pedagogical feedback, and corrective feedback. Providing students with informative error feedback rather than telling them their misconceptions is considerably more beneficial [5]. KERMIT, as an ITS database, has discussed six levels of providing personalized feedback, which are "Correct," "Error flag," "Hint," "Detailed Hint," "All errors," and "Solution". Sadler [40] said that researchers are interested in the effect of different feedback characteristics such as immediacy, pertinence, data form, and encouragement on the retention of learned information. This emphasis, which came from behaviorist stimulus-response models of learning, is today seen as being overly limited. The student model is a critical part to consider when designing, especially when providing feedback to students.

Mitrovic et al. [34] said that a student model that adequately assesses a student's knowledge is a challenging part to be created in ITS since it requires the technique of obtaining relevant data to determine a student's knowledge level and requires modifying its actions in accordance with their requirements and skills. Currently, typical online judgement is considered simple with limited function to provide appropriate feedback tailored to the learners' abilities. Wang et al. [49] said that an online judgment would be more educationally beneficial to beginners if it can be more intelligent if it has features such as classifying the answer codes of the problem and visualizing them, providing corresponding hints or repair methods for program errors, and tracking students' mastery of various knowledge points. Hooshyar et al. [26] have developed a novel flowchart-based Intelligent Tutoring system (FITS) that adapted a multi-agent system text-to-flowchart conversion approach and Bayesian Network to justify the level of students' knowledge and provide adaptive guidance to improve problem-solving skills through the interactive menu, prerequisite recommendations, and flowchart development. The most crucial component of the system's assistance is providing the correct answer when the students deal with the exercises. In addition, when students receive appropriate feedback, their knowledge and performance can be significantly improved [50]. According to Bryfczynski [10], the clustering technique can detect potential students who are at risk. He also discussed clearly how to cluster the students into different groups by using colors based on the number and types of mistakes they have made. Wang et al. [49] suggest that deep learning and natural language processing can be used as a future method to improve the function of repairing the error in order to provide personalized feedback to the students. Mohamed et al. [35] have developed an Intelligent Tutoring System with a Reporting Module that plays a specific function, such as providing feedback that assists the instructor in changing or adapting to and fitting different student learning styles. He also used the Bayesian Network to cluster the students' understanding while learning.

Lin et al. [32], in their research exploring the effects of simple feedback and elaborate feedback, discovered that students who were given simple feedback performed lower than those given elaborate feedback. The research by Grivokostopoulou et al. [23] in teaching FOL equivalence has developed feedback based on feedback classification and combination by offering the feedback into five types, which are minimal feedback, error-specific feedback, procedural feedback, bottom-out hints, and knowledge on meta-cognition Abu-Naser [1] has mentioned in his research that the timing and style of the system's feedback significantly impact its effectiveness. Timing describes the moment at which students receive an answer to the solution. What the students should be regulated by is their feedback. The system should postpone input for lower-level concepts and provide rapid feedback for higher-level concepts that the students are striving to acquire. Fwa [19] has developed a system that dispenses hints that explain the bugs or errors that the learner is stuck with if requested by learners and also contains functions like the button 'Submit,' 'Check Answer,' and an output window for the compilation output or errors and is marked as completed if the correct output is obtained. The study by Grawemeyer et al. [21] presents findings from an experiment that compared feedback based solely on performance (non-affect condition) with input that was affect-aware (affect condition). Results indicate that students in the emotional condition learned more than those in the non-affect condition. Black and William [8] said that task selection and the potential types of feedback a task can produce necessitate a cognitive theory that can shed light on how learners' comprehension and interactions with assessment tasks relate to each other and can be envisioned and understood. Assessment and feedback are also important features of mastery learning programs. Shute [41] has discovered three important components of formative feedback: the reason the feedback is required, the chance that the learner can take advantage of the feedback, and the ability and willingness to use the feedback given.

3 Methodology

A comparative evaluation proposed by Vartiainen [47] was chosen as the method for analyzing and comparing previous works in ITS. The comparison focuses primarily on the feedback provided in ITSs and the techniques used to develop a student model. The processes involved in the comparative evaluation are depicted in Fig. 1.

a) A Theoretical Study

A theoretical study helps discover concepts, definitions, and existing theories used for a certain study. The method used for this phase is a literature survey that covers the topics related to ITS, particularly in the Computer Science domain and is focused on the feedback and hints with related modeling techniques. Through the existing work, it discovers the appropriate way of providing feedback and hints, as well as the techniques used for student models. The outcome of this theoretical study is the technique used in designing student model and providing personalized feedback and hints in an ITS.

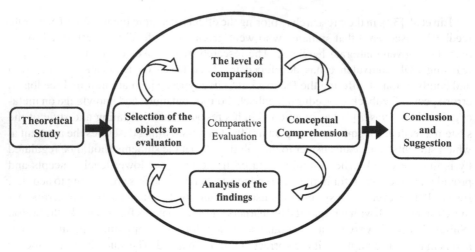

Fig. 1. Comparative evaluation process [47]

b) Comparative Evaluation

Four main activities that comprise the comparative evaluation phases are discussed below:

i. Selection of the object for evaluation: In this process, the selection of the object for evaluation was based on retrieving related articles from Google Scholar and IEEE databases. All articles were obtained using search strings related to feedback and hints, intelligent tutoring systems, and computer science, "feedback" AND "intelligent tutoring system", "feedback" AND "intelligent tutoring system" AND "computer science", "feedback and hints" AND "intelligent tutoring system", "feedback and hints" AND "intelligent tutoring system" AND "computer science". Only the articles that met the inclusion and exclusion criteria were reviewed and underwent the comparative evaluation process. The inclusion criteria involved articles related to ITS that provide feedback and hints, discuss modeling techniques, and being cited more than three times in related articles. The exclusion criteria were based on articles that are not related to ITS and are not in the domain of Computer Science or similar discipline articles.

ii. Determine the level of comparison: In this phase, the level of comparison can be determined based on internal aspects, different systems, and also in terms of similarity and/or dissimilarity. The comparison is done among the components of the comparison. The evaluation involved related studies ranging from the year 1990 to 2022 that covered the name of ITSs with respective domains, year involved, feedback and hints, modeling technique adapted, and learner characteristic deliverables.

iii. Conceptual comprehension: This phase is concerned with analyzing and identifying the most effective methods of providing feedback and hints in ITSs, as well as the most practical techniques for modeling the student model.

iv. Analysis of the findings of an evaluation: Through this phase, the comparative evaluation makes it possible for the analysis and evaluation to determine the most effective way to enhance the function of feedback and hints can be given in the system and the most practical techniques to be adapted in modeling the student model.

c) Conclusion and suggestion

This section involves reporting the findings obtained from the comparative evaluation conducted in this study. The aim of the study is considered achieved after completing all the phases involved in the comparative evaluation.

4   Analysis and Result of Comparative Evaluation

ITSs have been developed widely in all domains. Table 1 shows the comparative analysis of different Intelligent Tutoring Systems that have been developed in chronological order from 1990 until 2022, with the domain, name of related ITS, feedback and hints provided in the system, modeling technique used for the student model, and also advantages delivered by the system.

Table 1. Comparative analysis of different ITSs

Year	Name of ITS	Domain	Feedback and Hints	Modeling Technique	Learner Characteristics
1990	PROUST [29]	Pascal	Delayed feedback	Model-Tracing and Constraint-Based Modelling	NA
1995	The LISP Tutor [5]	Lisp	Immediate feedback	Model-Tracing	NA
1998	J-LATTE [38]	SQL	Delayed feedback	Constraint-Based Modelling	NA
2002	SQL-Tutor [34]	SQL	Immediate and Delayed feedback	Constraint-based Modelling	Learners' performance and knowledge
2005	OOPS [20]	OOP	NA	Constraint-Based Modelling	Learners' knowledge and learning methods
	JITS [43]	Java	Immediate feedback	Model-Tracing	NA
2008	BITS [11]	C/C++	No feedback	Bayesian	Programming topics

(*continued*)

Table 1. (*continued*)

Year	Name of ITS	Domain	Feedback and Hints	Modeling Technique	Learner Characteristics
2009	iList [17]	Linked list	Immediate and Delayed feedback	Procedural Knowledge Model	Learners' knowledge
	DEPTHS [28]	Software Design Patterns	Real-time and on-demand statistical feedback	Condition-action rule-Based reasoning	Learners' performance, knowledge, and cognitive capacity
2010	JavaGuide [27]	Java	Delayed feedback	NA	Programming questions
2012	BeSocratic [9]	CS	Further feedback	Condition-action rule-Based reasoning and data mining techniques	Learners' performance and behaviour
2013	The PHP ITS [53]	PHP	Multi-level hints	Model-Tracing and Constraint-Based Modelling	Exercises
	FOL equivalence system [23]	AI	Delayed feedback	Natural Language Processing	Learners' knowledge level
2014	BEETLE II [16]	Physics	Delayed feedback	Natural Language Processing and Condition-Action Rule-Based Reasoning	Students' responses to lecture questions
2015	FITS [26]	C++	Immediate feedback	Intelligent multi-agent, Bayesian, and Natural Language Processing	Learners' knowledge and feedback
	iTutor [48]	Basic computer skills	Immediate feedback	Intelligent multi-agent	Learners' performance, knowledge, and responses to learning activities

(*continued*)

Table 1. (*continued*)

Year	Name of ITS	Domain	Feedback and Hints	Modeling Technique	Learner Characteristics
	Java Sensei [7]	Java	NA	Neural Networks, Fuzzy Logic	Learners' cognitive and emotional capacity
2016	iTalk2Learn [21]	Math	Immediate and Delayed feedback	Bayesian	Learners' affected states
2017	PLTutor [35]	Java	NA	Rule Base	NA
2018	CNC-Tutor [31]	CNC Programming	Delayed feedback (Hints Button)	CNC interpreter	Learners' learning styles
2020	Novel ITS [49]	C and Phyton	Delayed feedback (Hints and Repair Button)	Improved CLARA engine and KT	Code Classification, error repair, and knowledge tracing
2022	CQACD [52]	Computer Basics	Immediate feedback	Mixed-initiative and Natural Language Processing	Learners' knowledge

Intelligent Tutoring Systems have become very popular in teaching across many domains, including Computer Science subjects. Some related ITS discussed in the table above have been developed in teaching programming domains such as PROUST, The LISP Tutor, J-LATTE, OOPS, JITS, BITS, iList, JavaGuide, BeSocratic, The PHP ITS, FITS, Java Sensei, PL Tutor, and Novel ITS. The researcher critically considered the way feedback is given to the student since it helps the student learn better. There are varieties of techniques adapted in an effort to provide personalized feedback, either through immediate feedback or delayed feedback, provided hints or repair buttons, and one-way or two-way conversation.

The feedback given has a significant relationship with the student model. The technique used is crucial to determining the appropriate feedback given to the student. Mitrovic et al. [33] said that a student model that adequately assesses a student's knowledge is a challenging part to be created in ITS since it requires the technique of obtaining relevant data to determine a student's knowledge level and requires modifying its actions in accordance with their requirements and skills. The previous study shows that clustering techniques in data mining were beneficial in recognizing low-achieving students. Bryfczynski [10] has stated in his thesis that the clustering technique is capable of recognizing potential students who are at risk. He also discussed clearly how to cluster the students into different groups by using colors based on the number and types of mistakes they have made. Some of the most commonly used clustering techniques by researchers include Bayesian Networks, Neural Networks, and Knowledge Tracing techniques such as the hidden Markov method. Those techniques are also proven to be successful in developing the student model and helping the researcher generate appropriate feedback to help students learn better.

Some researchers are concerned with two-way conversation because they believe it can help students participate actively during the learning process. BEETLE II [16], FOL equivalence systems [23], and the CQACD system [52] are examples of Intelligent Tutoring Systems that provide two-way conversation using a dialogue box and take advantage of Natural Language Processing (NLP). FITS [26] has also used the upgraded version of NLP as an agent for providing feedback. Additionally, Java Sensei [6] has successfully implemented Neural Networks and Fuzzy Logic techniques in research on providing feedback based on students' states and emotions.

Johnson [29] has implemented Model Tracing and Constraint-Based modeling in his Intelligent Tutoring System. The PROUST [29] has successfully helped the students write code by helping them repair bugs in the program. Other Intelligent Tutoring systems, such as J-LATTE [38] and iList [17], also take advantage of Constraint-Based modeling since it can help students while coding. Research by Wang et al. [48] suggests that deep learning and natural language processing can be used in future research to improve the function of repairing errors in order to provide personalized feedback to students.

5   Conclusion

In our study, a comparative evaluation was carried out to analyze and compare existing works in ITS, specifically to gauge how feedback was provided to students and the technique used in modeling the student model. Table 1 has depicted the feedback and hints and the techniques used in various ITSs to support various purposes of student learning. ITSs in the programming domain were created with the goal of assisting in the teaching of programming concepts and algorithms, such as using pseudocode and flowcharts, as well as providing proper guidance for students to write code correctly.

The results of the comparative evaluation point to the use of Constraint-Based modeling, Model Tracing, Natural Language Processing, and Deep Learning as student model techniques. While delayed feedback is the most appropriate feedback for helping students learn to code, previous research on The LISP Tutor [5] indicates that instant feedback is also beneficial. However, the feedback message may distract the students, causing them to miss out on the experience of a real programmer.

On the other hand, ITS in Computer Science education are primarily designed to assist students in learning programming concepts and algorithms such as pseudocode and flowcharts. Clustering techniques such as Bayesian networks are frequently recommended for these ITS. Many researchers have used this technique, which has been shown to help students by providing appropriate feedback. In ITS, both immediate and delayed feedback can be used to help students learn more effectively.

In conclusion, it is imperative to provide feedback that is customized to the individual student's abilities. When developing an effective Intelligent Tutoring System (ITS), it is crucial to consider the student model and feedback technique.

Acknowledgment. The authors would like to thank the School of Computing (SOC), Universiti Utara Malaysia (UUM) for funding the publication fee of this article.

References

1. Abu-Naser, S.S.: An agent based intelligent tutoring system for parameter passing in Java programming (2008)
2. Abu-Naser, S.S.: Developing an intelligent tutoring system for students learning to program in C++ (2008)
3. Abu-Naser, S.S.: Predicting learners performance using artificial neural networks in linear programming intelligent tutoring system (2012)
4. Al Rekhawi, H.A.: Android applications development intelligent tutoring system (2020)
5. Anderson, J.R., Corbett, A.T., Koedinger, K.R., Pelletier, R.: Cognitive tutors: lessons learned. J. Learn. Sci. **4**(2), 167–207 (1995)
6. Barrón-Estrada, M.L., Zatarain-Cabada, R., Oramas-Bustillos, R., Alor-Hernández, G.: How an affective learning environment for learning java impacts the student's learning results. In: 2016 IEEE 16th International Conference on Advanced Learning Technologies (ICALT), pp. 363–365. IEEE (2016)
7. Barrón-Estrada, M.L., Zatarain-Cabada, R., Hernández, F.G., Bustillos, R.O., Reyes-García, C.A.: An affective and cognitive tutoring system for learning programming. In: Advances in Artificial Intelligence and Its Applications: 14th Mexican International Conference on Artificial Intelligence, MICAI 2015, Cuernavaca, Morelos, Mexico, October 25–31, 2015, Proceedings, Part II 14, pp. 171–182. Springer, Cham (2015). Doi: https://doi.org/10.1007/978-3-319-27101-9_12
8. Black, P., Wiliam, D.: Assessment and classroom learning. Assessment in Education: Principles, Policy & Practice **5**(1), 7–74 (1998)
9. Bloom, B.S.: The 2 sigma problem: the search for methods of group instruction as effective as one-to-one tutoring. Educ. Res. **13**(6), 4–16 (1984)
10. Bryfczynski, S.P.: BeSocratic: An intelligent tutoring system for the recognition, evaluation, and analysis of free-form student input (Doctoral dissertation, Clemson University) (2012)
11. Butz, C.J., Hua, S., Maguire, R.B.: A web-based bayesian intelligent tutoring system for computer programming. Web Intell. Agent Syst.Int. J. **4**(1), 77–97 (2006)
12. Cooper, S., Nam, Y.J., Si, L.: Initial results of using an intelligent tutoring system with Alice. In: Proceedings of the 17th ACM Annual Conference on Innovation and Technology in Computer Science Education, pp. 138–143 (2012)
13. Costello, R.: Adaptive intelligent personalised learning (aipl) environment (U621351 Ph.D.), University of Hull (United Kingdom), Ann Arbor. https://search.proquest.com/docview/1654740829?accountid=41304 ProQuest Dissertations & Theses A&I; ProQuest Dissertations & Theses Global database (2012)
14. Crow, T., Luxton-Reilly, A., Wuensche, B.: Intelligent tutoring systems for programming education: a systematic review. In: Proceedings of the 20th Australasian Computing Education Conference, pp. 53–62 (2018)
15. Danial, H.: A flowchart-based intelligent tutoring system model to improve students' problem-solving skills/Danial Hooshyar (Doctoral dissertation, University of Malaya) (2016)

16. Dzikovska, M., Steinhauser, N., Farrow, E., Moore, J., Campbell, G.: BEETLE II: deep natural language understanding and automatic feedback generation for intelligent tutoring in basic electricity and electronics. Int. J. Artif. Intell. Educ.Artif. Intell. Educ. **24**, 284–332 (2014)
17. Elmasri, R., Navathe, S.: Foundations of Database Systems (1994)
18. Fossati, D., Di Eugenio, B., Brown, C., Ohlsson, S.: Learning linked lists: experiments with the iList system. In: Intelligent Tutoring Systems: 9th International Conference, ITS 2008, Montreal, Canada, June 23–27, 2008 Proceedings 9, pp. 80–89. Springer, Heidelberg (2008). Doi: https://doi.org/10.1007/978-3-540-69132-7_13
19. Fwa, H.L.: Predicting non-completion of programming exercises using action logs and keystrokes. In: 2019 International Symposium on Educational Technology (ISET), pp. 271–275. IEEE (2019)
20. Gálvez, J., Guzmán, E., Conejo, R.: A blended E-learning experience in a course of object oriented programming fundamentals. Knowl.-Based Syst..-Based Syst. **22**(4), 279–286 (2009). https://doi.org/10.1016/j.knosys.2009.01.004
21. Grawemeyer, B., Mavrikis, M., Holmes, W., Gutierrez-Santos, S., Wiedmann, M., Rummel, N.: Affecting off-task behaviour: how affect-aware feedback can improve student learning. In: Proceedings of the Sixth International Conference on Learning Analytics & Knowledge, pp. 104–113 (2016)
22. Graesser, A.C., VanLehn, K., Rosé, C.P., Jordan, P.W., Harter, D.: Intelligent tutoring systems with conversational dialogue. AI Mag. **22**(4), 39 (2001)
23. Grivokostopoulou, F., Perikos, I., & Hatzilygeroudis, I.: An intelligent tutoring system for teaching FOL equivalence. In: The First Workshop on AI-supported Education for Computer Science (AIEDCS 2013), vol. 20 (2013)
24. Gutierrez, F., Atkinson, J.: Adaptive feedback selection for intelligent tutoring systems. Expert Syst. Appl. **38**(5), 6146–6152 (2011)
25. Fwa, H.L.: Predicting non-completion of programming exercises using action logs and keystrokes. In: 2019 International Symposium on Educational Technology (ISET), Hradec Kralove, Czech Republic, pp. 271–275 (2019). https://doi.org/10.1109/ISET.2019.00064
26. Hooshyar, D., Ahmad, R.B., Yousefi, M., Yusop, F.D., Horng, S.J.: A flowchart-based intelligent tutoring system for improving problem-solving skills of novice programmers. J. Comput. Assist. Learn.Comput. Assist. Learn. **31**(4), 345–361 (2015)
27. Hsiao, I.H., Sosnovsky, S., Brusilovsky, P.: Guiding students to the right questions: adaptive navigation support in an E-Learning system for Java programming. J. Comput. Assist. Learn.Comput. Assist. Learn. **26**(4), 270–283 (2010)
28. Jeremic, Z., Jovanovic, J., Gasevic, D.: Evaluating an intelligent tutoring system for design patterns: the DEPTHS experience. J. Educ. Technol. Soc. **12**(2), 111 (2009)
29. Johnson, W.L.: Understanding and debugging novice programs. Artif. Intell.. Intell. **42**(1), 51–97 (1990)
30. Lopez-Pernas, S., Gordillo, A., Barra, E., Quemada, J.: Examining the use of an educational escape room for teaching programming in a higher education setting. IEEE Access **7**, 31723–31737 (2019)
31. Li, Q., Hsieh, S.J.: An intelligent tutoring system for computer numerical control programming. Int. J. Eng. Educ. **35**, 252–261 (2018)
32. Lin, L., Atkinson, R.K., Christopherson, R.M., Joseph, S.S., Harrison, C.J.: Animated agents and learning: does the type of verbal feedback they provide matter? Comput. Educ.. Educ. **67**, 239–249 (2013)
33. Mitrovic, A., Mayo, M., Suraweera, P., Martin, B.: Constraint-based tutors: a success story. In: Engineering of Intelligent Systems: 14th International Conference on Industrial and Engineering Applications of Artificial Intelligence and Expert Systems, IEA/AIE 2001 Budapest, Hungary, June 4–7, 2001 Proceedings 14, pp. 931–940. Springer, Heidelberg (2001). Doi: https://doi.org/10.1007/3-540-45517-5_103

34. Mitrovic, A., Martin, B., Mayo, M.: Using evaluation to shape ITS design: results and experiences with SQL-Tutor. User Model. User-Adap. Inter.Adap. Inter. **12**, 243–279 (2002)
35. Mohamed, I.N., Aljahdali, S., Idhris, S.M.: Intelligent tutoring systems—an advanced understanding of the programming concepts. In: 2013 IEEE International Conference on Computational Intelligence and Computing Research, pp. 1–4. IEEE (2013)
36. Mousavinasab, E., Zarifsanaiey, N., R. Niakan Kalhori, S., Rakhshan, M., Keikha, L., Ghazi Saeedi, M.: Intelligent tutoring systems: a systematic review of characteristics, applications, and evaluation methods. Interact. Learn. Environ. **29**(1), 142–163 (2021)
37. Nelson, G. L., Xie, B., & Ko, A. J.: Comprehension first: evaluating a novel pedagogy and tutoring system for program tracing in CS1. In: Proceedings of the 2017 ACM Conference on International Computing Education Research, pp. 2–11 (2017)
38. Ohlsson, S.: Constraint-based student modelling. J. Interact. Learn. Res. **3**(4), 429 (1992)
39. Perikos, I., Grivokostopoulou, F., Hatzilygeroudis, I.: Assistance and feedback mechanism in an intelligent tutoring system for teaching conversion of natural language into logic. Int. J. Artif. Intell. Educ.Artif. Intell. Educ. **27**, 475–514 (2017)
40. Sadler, D.R.: Beyond feedback: Developing student capability in complex appraisal. Assess. Eval. High. Educ. **35**(5), 535–550 (2010)
41. Shute, V.J.: Focus on formative feedback. Rev. Educ. Res. **78**(1), 153–189 (2008)
42. Sullins, J., Craig, S.D., Hu, X.: Exploring the effectiveness of a novel feedback mechanism within an intelligent tutoring system. Int. J. Learn. Technol. **10**(3), 220–236 (2015)
43. Sykes, E. R., & Franek, F.: A prototype for an intelligent tutoring system for students learning to program in Java (TM). In: Proceedings of the IASTED International Conference on Computers and Advanced Technology in Education, pp. 78–83 (2003)
44. Thinakaran, R., Chuprat, S.: Students' characteristics of student model in intelligent programming tutor for learning programming: a systematic literature review. Int. J. Adv. Comput. Sci. Appl. **13**(7). https://doi.org/10.14569/IJACSA.2022.0130778 (2022)
45. Torres, I.T.M., Sentí, V.E.: Intelligent tutor system for learning. Object Oriented Programming. Int. Res. J. Eng. Technol. (IRJET) **4**(10), 1 (2017)
46. VanLEHN, K.: The relative effectiveness of human tutoring, intelligent tutoring systems, and other tutoring systems. Educ. Psychologist **46**(4), 197–221 (2011). https://doi.org/10.1080/00461520.2011.611369
47. Vartiainen, P.: On the principles of comparative evaluation. Evaluation **8**(3), 359–371 (2002)
48. Wang, D., Han, H., Zhan, Z., Xu, J., Liu, Q., Ren, G.: A problem solving oriented intelligent tutoring system to improve students' acquisition of basic computer skills. Comput. Educ.. Educ. **81**, 102–112 (2015)
49. Wang, M., Wu, W., & Liang, Y.: A novel intelligent tutoring system for learning programming. In: 2020 International Conference on Development and Application Systems (DAS), pp. 162–168. IEEE (2020)
50. Wang, S.L., Wu, P.Y.: The role of feedback and self-efficacy on web-based learning: the social cognitive perspective. Comput. Educ.. Educ. **51**(4), 1589–1598 (2008)
51. Weber, G., Brusilovsky, P.: ELM-ART: an adaptive versatile system for Web-based instruction. Int. J. Artif. Intell. Educ. (IJAIED) **12**, 351–384 (2001)
52. Wen, Y., Zhu, X., Zhang, L.: CQACD: A concept question-answering system for intelligent tutoring using a domain ontology with rich semantics. IEEE Access **10**, 67247–67261 (2022)
53. Weragama, D., Reye, J.: The PHP intelligent tutoring system. In: Artificial Intelligence in Education: 16th International Conference, AIED 2013, Memphis, TN, USA, July 9–13, 2013. Proceedings 16, pp. 583–586. Springer, Heidelberg (2013)

Unlocking the Potential of Enhancing User Experience in Portal GREaT: Cultivating Great Ideas Through Brainwriting Method

Fauziah Baharom[1]([✉]) [iD], Rohaida Romli[1] [iD], Wan Hussain Wan Ishak[1] [iD],
Haslina Mohd[1] [iD], Yuhanis Yusof[1] [iD], Mohamed Ali Saip[1] [iD], Osman Ghazali[1] [iD],
Rahayu Ahmad[1] [iD], Mohd Hasbullah Omar[1] [iD], Suzilah Ismail[1] [iD],
Juhaida Abu Bakar[1] [iD], and Salwati Badroddin[2]

[1] Data Management & Software Solution Research Lab, School of Computing,
Universiti Utara Malaysia, 06010 Kedah, Malaysia
fauziah@uum.edu.my
[2] Strategic Planning Division, Ministry of Higher Education, 62200 Putrajaya, Malaysia

Abstract. Portal GREaT is a one-stop center developed by the Ministry of Education Malaysia (MoHE) to provide Malaysian graduates with information on career opportunities, advancement, upscaling, and rescaling programs. It consists of various modules designed to cater to the specific needs of different users, including graduates, industries, and MoHE. However, the functionalities of Portal GREaT are continuously expanding based on user requests. These circumstances are deemed improper planning in software development, and the extension of modules has resulted in an unstructured interface design for the application. To address these issues, prioritizing user experience (UX) in the application design is crucial. A well-designed UX can effectively guide users through the application and help them achieve their goals efficiently. One effective approach to enhancing UX design is by utilizing the Brainwriting method. Consequently, we conducted a workshop with 24 participants, consisting of web developers and designers, to improve the UX design of Portal GREaT by using the Brainwriting method. Brainwriting is a group creativity technique that encourages individual ideation and collaborative refinement. This technique allows developers and designers to generate diverse and innovative ideas to enhance the application's UX. Ultimately, this can lead to a more intuitive and user-friendly interface, improving user satisfaction and the application's overall success. The outcomes of the Brainwriting workshops are a list of innovative ideas to improve the portal. One of the innovative ideas is chosen to be applied in the portal. Consequently, the new design of the Portal Great has been launched. In conclusion, any web application that continuously expands in its functionalities must prioritize the UX in the software development plans. The Brainwrit-ing method is an effective tool to cultivate innovative UX ideas and enhance the overall user experience of the application.

Keywords: Web application design · Brainwriting method · User experience · Portal GREaT

© The Author(s), under exclusive license to Springer Nature Singapore Pte Ltd. 2024
N. H. Zakaria et al. (Eds.): ICOCI 2023, CCIS 2002, pp. 180–189, 2024.
https://doi.org/10.1007/978-981-99-9592-9_14

1   Introduction

Web applications have become an integral part of our lives in the digital age, with millions of people using them daily, from social media to e-commerce. Web applications differ from websites in design and user interaction, providing customers with dynamic features and functionalities across various platforms [1]. As businesses and organizations continue to leverage the power of web applications, innovation and creativity are critical factors. Users engage more with applications that are visually appealing, easy to use, and provide quick response times. Enhancements such as improved navigation, faster load times, and responsive design can increase the user experience and make web applications more attractive to users.

Usability and User Experience (UX) are important concepts in product or system design intended for human use [2], making the interface of an application one of the most critical elements when developing applications [3]. Usability is vital, as it is one factor contributing to the software application's success besides functionality [4, 5]. UX design is a method developed to design products with a user focus, creating an enjoyable, intuitive, and engaging experience when interacting with a website or application [6].

Good UX design increases user satisfaction, loyalty and can improve a company's reputation [20]. Several key factors must be considered to unlock the potential of enhancing user experience in web applications, including adopting a user-centered design approach, optimizing navigation and layout, tailoring content, and continuously improving UX design. However, developing a successful web application that enhances user experience is not easy and requires significant time, effort, and resources.

In this paper, we share our experience enhancing the design of our web application, the portal Graduates Reference Hub for Employment and Training (GREaT), using the Brainwriting method. The portal GREaT is a one-stop center for graduates to obtain information on career opportunities, programs, and career advancement. It contains several modules developed to meet the needs of specific target users, and development began in 2020, with a launch in October of the same year.

Since its launch, the Portal GREaT's functionalities have expanded based on users' or product owners' needs. Its user base has grown from graduates to higher education institutions, industries, students, and public users. These circumstances are considered improper software development plan since its functionalities continue to grow, leading to complaints that its goals or purposes are unclear and unintuitive. Additionally, the application's interface design has become unstructured due to the extension of modules.

To improve the portal's goals and interface design, we conducted an e-voting session and a workshop. The e-voting session was an online survey that identified user preferences for colors. We also conducted a workshop introducing our technical staff to User-Centered Design (UCD) and User Experience (UX) concepts. Our technical team was considered novices in UCD and UX, and an expert was invited to conduct the workshop. In this paper, we share how we utilized the Brainwriting method to generate brainstorming ideas for improvement.

2   Literature Review

2.1   A User-Centered Design and User Experience

User-Centered Design (UCD) was first proposed by Don Norman in 1980 as a framework for a design process that increases the usability and acceptance of a system [7]. UCD is a design philosophy that emphasizes a user interface design process and aims for a high level of usability [8]. A high level of usability can be obtained by placing users' needs, wants, and desires at the center of the design process, allowing these needs and desires to drive the development of a product, system, or service[9]. UCD captures the needs of the end-users in the context of use, which leads to an increase in user experience [9] and reduces the risks associated with using a product [10].

User experience (UX) broadly describes all aspects of interactions between a user and a product, and it covers three main elements: effect, user value, and usability [11]. Every product creates an experience for its users. However, creating an experience instead of just a working product is not an easy process; it requires deliberate thinking about design. As mentioned, UX usually refers to the user's feelings, including the effects of usability, usefulness, and emotional impact. On the other hand, usability is the pragmatic component of user experience, including effectiveness, efficiency, productivity, ease of use, learnability, the pragmatic and non-emotional aspects of user satisfaction, and qual-itative data about usability problems [12]. There are three elements when determining the usability of a product: look, feel, and usability or functionality [13]. An excellent usable design will spark joy and ease of use, making it a breeze for users to achieve their goals. On the contrary, when a design has a poor visual, and the functionality is confusing and full of errors, users would associate it with a bad experience.

2.2   Brainwriting and Its Benefits

To sustain the software development industry, it must be innovative and creative in solving problems. Creativity is also critical when producing new ideas, products, or services. Brainstorming is the most commonly used method for generating inventive and creative ideas within organizations. However, this method is not without its drawbacks. For instance, brainstorming can be time-consuming, and a proficient facilitator must ensure its effectiveness [14]. The brainstorming process can also be disrupted if one or more members monopolize the discussion. Another issue is that individuals may choose to keep their ideas to themselves, believing their ideas are not good enough to be shared [15]. Furthermore, participants must expend mental effort trying to remember their ideas until they can share them, listening to others, and adhering to brainstorming rules, detracting from their capacity to generate additional ideas [16].

In contrast to verbal brainstorming, Brainwriting involves a collaborative process where a group of individuals silently write down their ideas on sticky notes and share them with the group [14, 15]. The primary objective of this method is to promote creativity and idea generation by allowing each participant to contribute their ideas without the influence of others. Brainwriting is essentially an adapted version of brainstorming in which team members record their ideas on paper and pass them on to other team members for further refinement or development. Adopting this method can facilitate the exchange of ideas [17] and encourage the creation of innovative and imaginative solutions from diverse perspectives, resulting in a broad and varied range of ideas. Brainwriting potentially reduces the impact of status differentials, interpersonal conflicts, domination by a few members, pressure to conform to group norms and deviations from the main topic [14]. Additionally, it may eliminate production blocking, minimize social loafing, and encourage thoughtful processing of shared ideas [18].

Van Gundy [19] categorized Brainwriting into six types: Nominal Group Technique (NGT), Collective Notebook (NCB), Brainwriting Pool, Pin Cards, Battelle-Bildmappen-Brainwriting (BBB), and the Successive Integration of Problem Elements (SIL) method. According to van Gundy, the first four techniques are pure Brainwriting since they do not involve group discussion of written ideas during the idea-generation process. In contrast, the last two techniques (battelle-bildmappen-Brainwriting and the SIL method) are hybrids as they incorporate oral brainstorming and silent Brainwriting. Brainwriting is a robust approach to promoting idea generation and collaboration, which can result in more innovative and effective solutions.

3 Research Methodology

As discussed earlier, this study aims to improve the design of Portal GREaT. The UX approach was used in this study to generate ideas for improving the web application. Therefore, this study conducted a simple e-voting session and a Brainwriting workshop to achieve the goal.

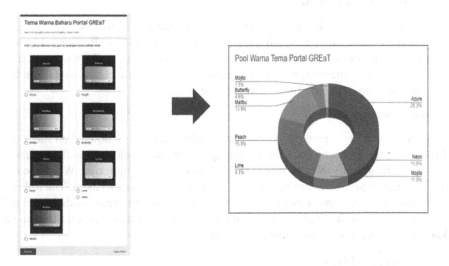

Fig. 1. Simple e-voting session for color selection

During the e-voting session, the users were asked to choose a new color for the portal. There were 555 participants in the session. The participants were given seven colors, as shown in Fig. 1. As a result, the majority of the participants have chosen

Azure. Therefore, the color of the portal will be improved by applying Azure. Apart from that, the study also held a workshop in which participants used the Brainwriting method to generate ideas for improving the web application. A UX research expert led the workshop, and 24 participants from the technical staff are currently working on our project. They had at least three years of experience in web application development. The following section will discuss the findings obtained from the workshop.

4   Discussion

The goal of the workshop was to put the Brainwriting method into practice. As a result, the following procedures were followed:

1. Defining the Theories

The majority of the participants are software developers. They have good programming skills but lack web design. Therefore, the workshop began with the instructor explaining the concept of web design and UX. Then, it continued with an explanation of some characteristics and principles of good design and the importance of UX. The instructor also explained the Brainwriting method and how it can be used for ideas generation.

2. Group Formation

Following an introduction to the concepts and theories, the participants were divided into six (6) groups of four (4).

3. Explanation of Problem

The project leader was asked to explain the problems that needed to be solved. The leader stated that the application needs to be improved. The existing application was created ad-hoc, and the requirements are constantly changing. As a result, the application's goal is unclear, and the design is unstructured. When the group clearly understands the problem, they can begin the Brainwriting process.

4. Idea Generation

Each team was given a piece of digital paper and asked to write down their ideas using Miro.com as a support tool for implementing the Brainwriting method. Each group is assigned a duration (5 min) to record their ideas on digital platforms. When the timer goes off, each team passes their sheet of paper to the group next to them. The following group reads the ideas and adds their own, building on what has been written previously. This process is repeated until each group has had an opportunity to contribute to each idea. Figure 2 depicts the outcome of this step.

5. Reviewing the Ideas

Every group will have a collection of ideas refined and improved by multiple group members by the end of the Brainwriting session. When the Brainwriting session is finished, the group can go over the ideas and try to understand the suggestions made by each group. Table 1 shows the ideas generated by each group.

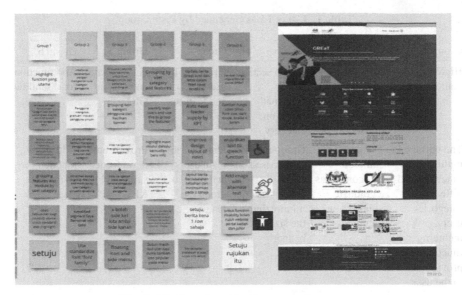

Fig. 2. Findings from the idea generation step

6. Prioritization of the Idea

After everyone has grasped the ideas generated by each group, all participants are asked to evaluate and prioritize the ideas. The ideas are prioritized based on "Most Rational", "Most Delightful", "Darling", and "Long Shot", which reflect their feasibility, impact, and alignment with the problem statement.

"Most Rational" refers to a decision or action based on logical and objective reasoning without being influenced by emotions or biases. It is the most sensible and reasonable option available. While "Most Delightful" refers to something extremely pleasing, enjoyable, or satisfying. It is the most pleasurable and delightful experience one can have. Then, "Darling" is an endearing term to describe someone or something cherished or beloved. It is often used to express affection or fondness towards a person, pet, or object. Finally, "Long shot" refers to a possibility or outcome that is unlikely or has a low probability of success. It is a risky option or an unlikely event worth attempting but may not be expected to succeed. Figure 3 depicts the outcome of the prioritization process.

According to the outcome of this process, most participants agreed that the idea generated by Group 2 is feasible and necessary to implement. Group 2's concept focuses on improving the design by focusing on various user categories. Users are divided into three groups: graduates, industry, and public users, with each group having different module or feature requirements. Furthermore, the banner size must be reduced.

On the other hand, the idea from Group 6 is considered a "Long Shot" where the group proposed additional functions to assist users with disabilities. Adding this functionality is a good idea. However, it may necessitate extra time and budget to implement. In the future, the group can include this functionality, where the features can be identified by

Table 1. List of Ideas Generated by Each Group.

Group 1	Group 2	Group 3	Group 4	Group 5	Group 6
Highlight the main function	Improve the design by considering the category of user	Group section "saya berminat" based on category	Grouping by user category and features	Auto update news about GREaT	Add function for disabilities
The portal has multiple functions and different categories of users, including functions to provide info to the user	The user could be categorized as a graduate, industry, or public user	Grouping icons based on users' categories and minimizing the size of the banner	Identify the main users and used to group the features	Provide auto news feeder supplied by KPT	Add a new function for disabilities
Divide the menu based functionality	Improve the design based on color, organization, and category	Design side navigation based on users' category	Highlight the main modules before providing detailed info	Improve the design layout of the news	Provide text-to-speech function
Grouping features and modules based on user category	Simplify the design by grouping the features and modules based on the user category	Side navigation is not suitable for the multi category of users	Prioritize the importance of modules	Improve the layout of the news	Add an image with alternate text
Reorganize and prioritize the modules, and highlight the most important ones	Simplify the segment "saya berminat"	-	Need to determine which module has been accessed by many users	Agree, news only 1 row	Improve function for disabilities (refer to portal Kedah and Johor)
Agree	Use the standardized font "font-family."	Improve the floating icon and side menu	Organize based on user and use popular icon	Reorganize news	Agree

referring to the Kedah and Johor portals. Based on the findings, the group can start implementing and testing the ideas on the web application.

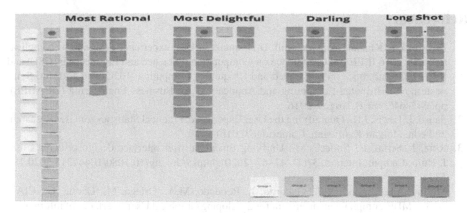

Fig. 3. Prioritization of the idea.

5 Conclusion

A good web application is designed with the user in mind, making it easy to use, navigate, and understand. This enhances the user experience and makes them more likely to return to the site in the future. Developing a good web application is important for creating a positive user experience, building a brand reputation, gaining a competitive advantage, improving efficiency, and ensuring scalability. It conveys a sense of professionalism and trustworthiness, which can lead to increased brand loyalty and customer retention. However, enhancing user experience in web application design is a difficult task. It requires creative skills and collaboration between the developers and users. As a result, Brainwriting is a great way to generate creative ideas.

Brainwriting is particularly useful for idea generation, where some participants are hesitant to speak up or share their thoughts in front of others. Additionally, it can help to prevent groupthink, which occurs when group members may conform to the dominant ideas or opinions in the group, resulting in a lack of diverse ideas. Besides, this method encourages participants to think independently and generate ideas without being influenced by others in the group. By creating a written record of ideas, participants can build upon each other's suggestions and ideas, creating a more robust list of potential solutions or strategies. Based on the workshop findings, Portal GREaT's design has been improved. Because different users have different functionalities, all features or functionalities are reorganized accordingly. The next step is to conduct an expert evaluation of the application.

In conclusion, by following the well-defined steps, the workshop has successfully identified the requirements for improving the Portal GREaT. The Brainwriting method manages to help unlock the potential of enhancing web applications by generating many ideas in a short time.

Acknowledgement. This work has been funded by the Malaysian Ministry of Higher Education (MoHE) through the consultation grant scheme (P-58/614).

References

1. Kiruthika, J., Khaddaj, S., Greenhill, D., Francik, J.: User experience design in web applications. In: 2016 IEEE Intl Conference on Computational Science and Engineering (CSE) and IEEE Intl Conference on Embedded and Ubiquitous Computing (EUC) and 15th Intl Symposium on Distributed Computing and Applications for Business Engineering (DCABES), pp. 642–646. IEEE, August 2016
2. Sauro, J., Lewis, J.R.: Quantifying the User Experience: Practical Statistics for User Research, 2nd edn. Morgan-Kaufmann, Cambridge (2016)
3. Ruiz, J., Serral, E., Snoeck, M.: Unifying functional user interface design principles. Int. J. Hum.-Comput. Interact. 37(1), 47–67 (2020). https://doi.org/10.1080/10447318.2020.180 5876
4. Molina, A.I., Giraldo, W.J., Gallardo, J., Redondo, M.A., Ortega, M., García, G.: CIAT-GUI: a MDE-compliant environment for developing Graphical User Interfaces of information systems. Adv. Eng. Softw.Softw. 52, 10–29 (2012)
5. van Schaik, P., Ling, J.: Modelling user experience with web sites: Usability, hedonic value, beauty and goodness. Interacting Comput. 20(3), 419–432
6. (PDF) Modelling user experience with web sites: Usability, hedonic value, beauty and goodness. https://www.researchgate.net/publication/222530367_Modelling_user_experie nce_with_web_sites_Usability_hedonic_value_beauty_and_goodness#fullTextFileContent. Accessed April 16 2023 (2008)
7. Nilsson, A., Hansen, J.: Creating a Wiki through User Experience design (2021). https://www. diva-portal.org/smash/get/diva2:1612406/FULLTEXT01.pdf
8. Norman, A.D., Draper, W.S.: User centered system design; new perspectives on human-computer interaction. L. Erlbaum Associates Inc. (1986)
9. Dwivedi, M.S.K.D., Upadhyay, M.S., Tripathi, A.: A working framework for the user-centered design approach and a survey of the available methods. Int. J. Sci. Res. Publ. 2(4), 12–19 (2012)
10. Dorrington, P., Wilkinson, C., Tasker, L., Walters, A.: User-centered design method for the design of assistive switch devices to improve user experience, accessibility, and independence. J. Usability Stud. 11(2) (2016)
11. Norman, D.: The design of everyday things. Doubleday, New York, NY (1988)
12. Park, J., Han, S.H., Kim, H.K., Cho, Y., Park, W.: Developing elements of user experience for mobile phones and services: survey, interview, and observation approaches. Human Factors and Ergonomics in Manufacturing & Service Industries 23(4), 279–293 (2011). https://doi. org/10.1002/hfm.20316
13. Hartson, R., Pyla, P.S.: The UX Book: Process and Guidelines for Ensuring a Quality UX. Morgan Kaufmann Publisher, San Francisco (2012)
14. Soegaard, M. Usability: A part of the User Experience, [online] The Interaction Design Foundation (2019). https://www.interaction-design.org/literature/article/usability-a-part-of-the-user-experience
15. van Gundy, A.B.: Brainwriting for new product ideas: an alternative to brainstorming. J. Consum. Mark.Consum. Mark. 1, 67–74 (1983)
16. Heslin, P.A.: Better than brainstorming? Potential contextual boundary conditions to Brainwriting for idea generation in organizations. J. Occup. Organ. Psychol.Occup. Organ. Psychol. 82(1), 129–145 (2009). https://doi.org/10.1348/096317908x285642
17. Nijstad, B.A., Stroebe, W.: How the group affects the mind: a cognitive model of idea generation in groups. Pers. Soc. Psychol. Rev. 10, 186–213 (2006)
18. Brown, V.R., Paulus, P.B.: Making group brainstorming more effective: recommendations from an associative memory perspective. Curr. Dir. Psychol. Sci.. Dir. Psychol. Sci. 11(6), 208–212 (2002). https://doi.org/10.1111/1467-8721.00202

19. Paulus, P.B., Yang, H.: Idea generation in groups: A basis for creativity in organizations. Organ. Behav. Hum. Decis. Process.Behav. Hum. Decis. Process. **82**, 76–87 (2000)
20. Van Gundy, A.B.: Brain writing for new product ideas: an alternative to brainstorming. Journal of Consumer Marketing (1984)
21. Rane, N.L., Achari, A., Choudhary, S.P.: Enhancing customer loyalty through quality of service: effective strategies to improve customer satisfaction, experience, relationship, and engagement. Int. Res. J. Modernization Eng. Technol. Sci. **5**(5), 427–452 (2023)

The Effectiveness of Conducting STEM Projects Using Design Thinking Approach in Rural Schools in Kedah, Malaysia: A Smart Farming Project

Suwannit Chareen Chit(✉) ⓘ, Ahmad Hanis Mohd Shabli ⓘ,
and Massudi Mahmuddin ⓘ

Universiti Utara Malaysia, Sintok, 06010 Kedah, Malaysia
chareen@uum.edu.my

Abstract. STEM education is vital in today's learning curriculum. Incorporating Design Thinking into STEM projects such as smart farming, particularly in rural schools in Malaysia where access to technology and resources are scarce, allow teachers and students to experience an enriching teaching and learning experience. In this paper, we employ the Design Thinking approach to gauge the effectiveness of implementing STEM projects such as smart farming to the teachers and students in rural schools. A survey is carried out to measure the effectiveness of the approach and it is shown that the Design Thinking approach helped both teachers and students to develop innovative solutions to benefit the society. Students and teachers also demonstrate increased creativity, problem-solving skills, empathy, and collaborative learning when they solve STEM problems using the Design Thinking approach.

Keywords: STEM Education · Internet of Things · Smart Farming

1 Introduction

The Malaysian Education Blueprint 2013–2025 [1] has identified Science, Technology, Engineering and Mathematics (STEM) education to be a critical component and important agenda in transforming students to meet the challenges of the 21st century. This blueprint places great emphasis on key areas namely problem-solving and critical thinking skills, creativity and innovation, and global competitiveness among Malaysian schoolchildren. Three thrusts have been identified to propel the implementation of STEM education effectively. These thrusts include curriculum reform, infrastructure development, and human capacity development particularly among teachers. These reforms, however, are impeded by social and geographical boundaries. Many schools in rural Malaysia are lacking technical competencies among teachers and face financial constraints to access to hardware and software resources which allow them to develop and build their technical competencies in STEM education.

© The Author(s), under exclusive license to Springer Nature Singapore Pte Ltd. 2024
N. H. Zakaria et al. (Eds.): ICOCI 2023, CCIS 2002, pp. 190–203, 2024.
https://doi.org/10.1007/978-981-99-9592-9_15

To address this shortcoming, the MCMC-UUM MakerSpace Laboratory in Universiti Utara Malaysia (UUM) have designed STEM-related projects to inculcate interests among teachers and students alike. Two schools namely Sekolah Kebangsaan Telaga Mas (Telaga Mas National Primary School) and Sekolah Kebangsaan Sungai Batu (Sungai Batu National Primary School) were chosen to be the pioneer in this project. A smart farming project was initiated in each school where both students and teachers were given the exposure on developing and implementing smart farming based on the Internet of Things (IoT) technology based on the Design Thinking [2, 3, 10] approach. The teachers and schoolchildren were assisted by student volunteers from UUM.

In this paper, we document the experiences of seven teachers and 20 schoolchildren from both schools, as well as 12 UUM student volunteers who participated in this project. A survey based on the phases in Design Thinking was adapted to gauge the participants understanding on project implementation and reflection from each of them is recorded to gain better insights on the project. The experiences the teachers, schoolchildren and student volunteers undergo would set a pathway and best practices for school and small community development, as well as deliver actionable and sustainable solutions which benefit the community.

The research questions and research objectives related to the STEM smart farming project aim to gauge the following:

Research Questions 1: How effective is the Design Thinking approach in allowing participants to understand societal problems and formulating a smart farming solution? Research Question 2: How effective is the Design Thinking approach in nurturing creativity, innovation and problem solving among participants of smart farming project?

Reflecting on the research questions above, the following research objectives are outlined:

Research Objective 1: To investigate the awareness on Design Thinking approach among teachers and students when implementing the smart farming project. Research Objective 2: To investigate the effectiveness of Design Thinking approach in nurturing creativity, innovation and problem solving among teachers and students (participants) in smart farming project.

This paper is organized as follows. In Sect. 2, this paper provides an overview of the related concepts of STEM education, IoT-based smart farming and the implementation of smart farming in both schools. In Sect. 3, this paper describes the sampling and instrument used in this study. The findings and results are then presented in Sect. 4, while Sect. 5 discusses pertinent observations from this study. Section 6 concludes the paper.

2 Background

The Malaysian Education Blueprint (MEB), launched in 2013, is a holistic plan aimed at transforming the Malaysian education system to be ready for 21st century challenges. In essence, the MEB outlines several thrusts which include ensuring universal access, from preschool to tertiary education, for Malaysian from all walks of life. The MEB also aims to provide equity access and halving achievement gap between the rich and poor in all Malaysian states regardless of socio-geographical settings.

Several strategic and operational shifts were planned to achieve these targets which include curriculum reforms, human capacity building, infra- and infostructure development, student assessment reforms, and strong parent-community synergy. Within these shifts, STEM education is regarded as a vital ingredient to ensure the goals of the MEB are achieved.

2.1 STEM Education

STEM education is a key component in the MEB 2013, and three key areas have been identified as necessary for Malaysian students. The three areas are problem-solving and critical thinking, creativity and innovation, and global competitiveness [2, 3]. Several STEM initiatives have been implemented which include the setting up of STEM Centres of Excellence and STEM School Network in Malaysian public schools. In the recent years, there has been increased funding for STEM infrastructure. The Government of Malaysia and non-Governmental Organisations (NGOs) also organise STEM-related activities [4]. The STEM Education Framework outlined by the Malaysian Ministry of Education (MoE) is illustrated in Fig. 1.

The MCMC-UUM MakerSpace Lab was established in 2018 to promote STEM education in the northern region of Kedah, Malaysia. To date, the laboratory has conducted activities such as IoT-based development and solutions, 3D-printing, drone training and other knowledge-sharing activities. In February 2023, the laboratory developed smart farming projects in two schools in rural Kedah.

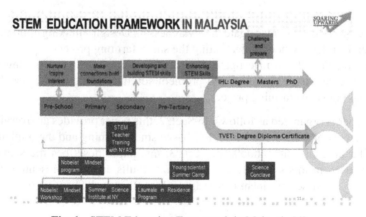

Fig. 1. STEM Education Framework in Malaysia [4].

2.2 Smart Farming

Smart farming uses sensors and other technologies to improve crops, livestock, and the environment. Often, smart farming involves environmental monitoring, data collection and analysis on crop planting, irrigation, fertilisation, and pest-control which results in making informed decisions.

The MCMC-UUM MakerSpace Lab initiated two IoT-based smart farming projects in Kedah, Malaysia. These schools - Sekolah Kebangsaan Telaga Mas (SKTM) and Sekolah Kebangsaan Sungai Batu (SKSB) are rural primary schools located in Pokok Sena and Kulim respectively. Each school has a population of roughly 200 students, whose parents are predominantly farmers and fall under the Bottom-40 (B40) poverty bracket. In our observation, the students have little or no access to Internet technology, low awareness on STEM, and have not used or developed any smart farming applications.

The farm in both schools currently plant crops such as chillies, ladyfingers and brinjal. These crops are mainly sold to the teachers, and the schools' cooperatives derive some income from selling the crops. In this smart farming project, we worked together with the teachers to develop an IoT-based farm watering system. We employed the Design Thinking [2, 6, 8] method which consists of five phases in product development, namely "Empathise", "Define", "Ideate", "Prototype" and "Test" to formulate appropriate solutions for the project, as shown in Fig. 2.

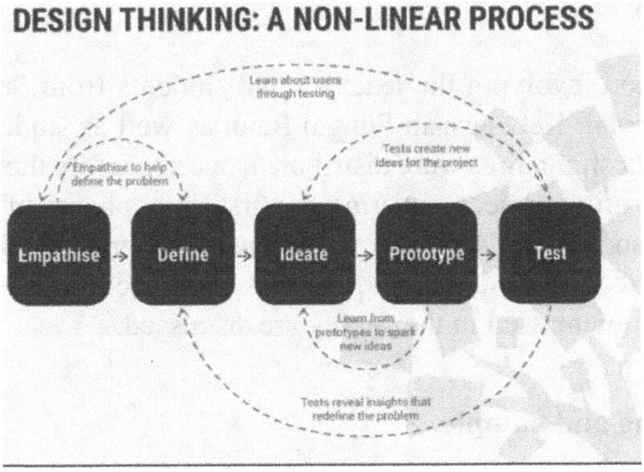

Fig. 2. Design Thinking Process [6, 11]

Environmental sustainability is applied by using recycled items such as water basin and pipes sourced from the school. In this project, rainwater is collected and kept in a basin. The sensor monitors the farm's temperature and soil humidity and will activate the pump to start watering the farm when temperature rises, or humidity reaches a certain threshold. Figure 3 shows the farming activity conducted in Sekolah Kebangsaan Telaga Mas.

During the installation, teachers and students from both schools were given the opportunity to test the system, and questionnaires in relation to the design, development and testing of the smart farming were handed to them.

Fig. 3. Smart farming in Sekolah Kebangsaan Telaga Mas.

3 Methodology

A survey is conducted involving the teachers and students from Sekolah Kebangsaan Telaga Mas and Sekolah Kebangsaan Sungai Batu, as well as student volunteers from UUM. Two sets of questionnaires were distributed; one set before the participants implemented the smart farming project, covering the first three phases of Design Thinking - Empathise, Define, and Ideate. Another questionnaire, covering the Prototype and Testing phase is distributed after the project has been completed. In the following section, the sample and instrument used in the survey are discussed.

3.1 Context Setting and Sample

This study is conducted to investigate the effectiveness of inculcating intrinsic learning among 39 teachers, students, and student volunteers by incorporating Design Thinking in their smart farming. The participants consist of seven teachers and 20 schoolchildren from Sekolah Kebangsaan Telaga Mas and Sekolah Kebangssan Sungai Batu, and 12 student volunteers from Universiti Utara Malaysia. Table 1 below provides a summary of the sample of the participants in this program.

Table 1. Smart Farming Project Participants Sample

Group	Age	Sample (N)
Teacher (T)	34–56	7
Student (S)	11–12	20
Student Volunteer (V)	20–25	12

All teachers, students, and student volunteers were provided with two sets of questionnaires. The first set of questionnaire was distributed before the smart farming project was implemented. The goal of this questionnaire is to measure the sample's understanding on the Design Thinking approach, awareness of project as well as gauging the intrinsic skills of the sample participants. Set 1 of the questionnaire covers the "Empathise", "Define" and "Ideate" phase of Design Thinking.

The next set of questionnaire was intended to gauge the innovative, creativity and problem-solving skills among the participants. Set 2 of the questionnaire measures the effectiveness of the Design Thinking approach in prototyping and implementing the smart farming project. At the end of the project, an interview was conducted to gain the participants' feedback on the experience of conducting a smart farming project using Design Thinking approach.

3.2 Instrument

In order to evaluate the impact of incorporating Design Thinking in the smart farming project, a questionnaire adapted from Tu, Liu and Wu [5] was designed. Participants of smart farming project were asked to answer and rate the questionnaire. The questionnaire measures the degree of Likert scale from 1 to 5 (1—I do not agree at all; 5—I totally agree). The number of participants who participated in the questionnaire is 39. The questionnaire measures the degree of learning effectiveness on the following based on the various phases of Design Thinking. A simple statistical analysis which is straight forward and covers the constructs and items of the questionnaire is conducted. Table 2 summarizes the questionnaire constructs used to measure effectiveness of Design Thinking in the smart farming project.

Table 2. Questionnaire constructs.

Set	Design Thinking Phase	Questionnaire Construct	Item	Number of Items (n)
1	Empathise	To measure effectiveness in Empathise Phase	The Empathize Stage helps me identify key societal problems in the community	2
			The Empathize Stage helps me understand key societal problems in the community	

(*continued*)

Table 2. (*continued*)

Set	Design Thinking Phase	Questionnaire Construct	Item	Number of Items (n)
	Define	To measure effectiveness in Define Phase	The Design Stage helps me understand the difference between "needs" and "insights"	5
			The Design Stage helps me understand community needs	
			The Design Stage deepens my understanding of targeted groups' needs	
			The Design Stage helps me develop design concepts	
			The Design Stage helps me be certain about implementation	
	Ideate	To measure effectiveness in Ideation Stage	The Ideate Stage helps me feel certain about the implementation	4
			The Ideate Stage helps me identify requirements for the implementation	
			The Ideate Stage helps me develop design concepts	
			The Ideate Stage helps me design solutions to solve problems	
2	Prototyping	To measure effectiveness in Prototyping Stage	The Prototyping Stage helps me convey my design concepts	5
			The Prototyping Stage helps turning design concepts into reality	

(*continued*)

Table 2. (*continued*)

Set	Design Thinking Phase	Questionnaire Construct	Item	Number of Items (n)
			The iterative process in Prototyping Stage helps me improve my design	
			The Prototyping Stage helps me understand community/societal problems better	
			The Prototyping Stage makes me to be certain of implementation	
	Testing	To measure effectiveness in Testing Stage	The Testing Stage deepens my understanding of community/societal needs	4
			The Testing Stage makes my design more complete	
			The Testing Stage lets me review my design concepts	
			The Testing Stage makes me to be certain about implementation	

4   Results

In this project, a smart farming application is developed. Two schools namely Sekolah Kebangsaan Telaga Mas, and Sekolah Kebangssan Sungai Batu were chosen. In executing this project, the Design Thinking approach is employed, and this paper discusses the effectiveness on the approach in facilitating learning and project execution.

The first questionnaire aims to gauge the participants' (teachers, students, and student volunteers) understanding on the problem at hand and formulating a solution. This questionnaire is aligned to and focusses on the "Empathise", "Define", and "Ideate" phase in Design Thinking. During this exercise, the teachers and students have identified the need to develop a smart farming application and Table 3 summarises the results.

In the "Empathise" phase, the participants were asked to identify a problem and relate it to their personal experiences and perception. Based on the exercise, the participants were able to identify the problem that they face. 84.6% of the participants strongly agree they were able to identify the problems that needs to be addressed, while 15.4% agree with the statement. None disagreed nor remained neutral with regards to this item. A significant 84.6% of the participants strongly agree that they empathize with the problem while 15.4% agreed that they understood the problem they were facing but have yet to have a complete grasp of the problem that they are facing. Generally, we that this is due to the participants having very initial understanding of the Design Thinking concept and a clear overview the the problem at hand.

It is expected of the participants to think creatively and distinguish between what is necessary and what is an insight in the "Define" phase. This enables them to give the issue they are tackling top priority and prioritise it. Participants now envision the remedies they believe are best suited to deal with the problem. Nearly 90% of participants strongly agree that Design Thinking may help with idea design, and more than 90% of participants acknowledged the necessity for a solution to be developed. It should be mentioned that some groups are unsure about how to identify and create a workable solution to the issue. This pattern is typically observed when participants disagree on a particular issue and seek ways to resolve their differences. Through this exercise, participants can display a greater confidence to develop concepts and ideas when they converge on the ideation phase. The exercise in this phase promotes problem solving, communication and leadership skills as elaborated by Calavia et.al [7] and Cohen et.al [9].

In the third phase, participants are encouraged to think "outside the box" and come up with innovative solutions. This approach led to a significant improvement in the quality of the responses, as participants were able to deconstruct traditional boundaries and devise new ways to solve problems [9]. Generally, they were able to think more holistically about the problem and consider all possible solutions and what are the best approaches to address the problem. The participants were able to identify and overcome potential challenges more effectively. A number of participants, however, need better grasp of the proposed solution as noted in the findings.

The second questionnaire was intended to measure the effectiveness of developing a smart farming solution using the Design Thinking approach. This questionnaire was distributed after the implementation of the smart farming application, and it focusses on the "Prototyping" and "Testing" phase. In this phase, the participants designed a solution they deemed suitable to address the problem, and test if the proposed solution works. The findings from this exercise is tabulated in Table 4.

In the "Prototyping" phase, the participants laid out the plan for the smart watering system. Teachers and student volunteers laid the pipes according to the schema. A ESP8266 microcontroller was designed and installed to a water pump, and power adaptor. More than 90% of the participants felt that the prototyping exercise helped them to helps them to convey their design concepts and turned the prototype into a reality. At this stage, most of the participants, especially students, get to see and understand the implementation of the smart farming project better. This strengthens our belief that through hands-on approach, students will consolidate their understanding which results in effective learning experience [9].

Finally, all participants were given the opportunity to test the smart farming system. Based on the findings, the participants are confident that the solution is able to address the issue and can be scaled and implemented for other applications. We also interviewed the participants and some of the testimonies are as follows:

"I come from a farming family and I know the struggles my father goes through as a farmer. I could imagine what it would be like if I could use smart farming to help my family in our farm. I really truly enjoyed the session" - S14.

"I really think that the MCMC-UUM team was being very helpful with our smart farming ideas. I can now teach my students about farming the smart way." -T8.

"It was fun working with the teachers and students. I realised that learning outside the classroom allows me to practice my knowledge and further strengthens my understanding on IoT" - V3.

Table 3. Effectiveness of Empathise, Define, and Ideate in Design Thinking for Smart Farming Project

Phase	Likert Scale	5 (Strongly Agree)		4 (Agree)		3 (Neutral)		2 (Disagree)		1 (Strongly Disagree)		N	
	Item	f	%	f	%	f	%	f	%	f	%	f	%
Empathise	The Empathize Stage helps me identify key societal problems in the community	33	84.6	6	15.4	0	0	0	0	0	0	39	100.0
	The Empathize Stage helps me understand key societal problems in the community	33	84.6	6	15.4	0	0	0	0	0	0	39	100.0
Define	The Define Stage helps me understand the difference between "needs" and "insights"	37	94.9	2	5.1	0	0	0	0	0	0	39	100.0
	The Define Stage helps me understand community needs	37	94.9	2	5.1	0	0	0	0	0	0	39	100.0
	The Define Stage deepens my understanding of targeted groups' needs	35	89.7	4	10.3	0	0	0	0	0	0	39	100.0

(continued)

Table 3. (*continued*)

Phase	Likert Scale	5 (Strongly Agree)		4 (Agree)		3 (Neutral)		2 (Disagree)		1 (Strongly Disagree)		N	
	Item	f	%	f	%	f	%	f	%	f	%	f	%
	The Define Stage helps me develop design concepts	35	89.7	4	10.3	0	0	0	0	0	0	39	100.0
	The Define Stage helps me be certain about implementation	35	89.7	4	10.3	0	0	0	0	0	0	39	100.0
Ideate	The Ideate Stage helps me feel certain about the implementation	26	66.7	13	33.3	0	0	0	0	0	0	39	100.0
	The Ideate Stage helps me identify requirements for the implementation	26	66.7	13	33.3	0	0	0	0	0	0	39	100.0
	The Ideate Stage helps me develop design concepts	22	56.4	15	38.5	2	5.1	0	0	0	0	39	100.0
	The Ideate Stage helps me design solutions to solve problems	22	56.4	15	38.5	2	5.1	0	0	0	0	39	100.0

Table 4. Effectiveness of Empathise, Define, and Ideate in Design Thinking for Smart Farming Project.

Phase	Likert Scale	5 (Strongly Agree)		4 (Agree)		3 (Neutral)		2 (Disagree)		1 (Strongly Disagree)		N	
	Item	f	%	f	%	f	%	f	%	f	%	f	%
Prototype	The Prototyping Stage helps me convey my design concepts	37	94.8	2	5.2	0	0	0	0	0	0	39	100.0

(*continued*)

Table 4. (*continued*)

Phase	Likert Scale	5 (Strongly Agree)		4 (Agree)		3 (Neutral)		2 (Disagree)		1 (Strongly Disagree)		N	
	Item	f	%	f	%	f	%	f	%	f	%	f	%
	The Prototyping Stage helps turning design concepts into reality	35	89.7	4	10.3	0	0	0	0	0	0	39	100.0
	The iterative process in Prototyping Stage helps me improve my design	37	94.8	2	5.2	0	0	0	0	0	0	39	100.0
	The Prototyping Stage helps me understand community/societal problems better	36	92.3	3	7.7	0	0	0	0	0	0	39	100.0
Testing	The Testing Stage deepens my understanding of community/societal needs	39	100.0	0	0.0	0	0	0	0	0	0	39	100.0
	The Testing Stage makes my design more complete	37	94.8	2	5.2	0	0	0	0	0	0	39	100.0
	The Testing Stage lets me review my design concepts	39	100.0	0	0.0	0	0	0	0	0	0	39	100.0
	The Testing Stage makes me to be certain about implementation	39	100.0	0	0.0	0	0	0	0	0	0	39	100.0

5   Discussion

The implementation of smart farming using the Design Thinking approach has brought new paradigm for teaching and learning experience for the teachers and students in Seko-lah Kebangsaan Telaga Mas, and Sekolah Kebangsaan Sungai Batu. Design Thinking, being a structured problem-solving approach, allows the teachers and students to experience real-life problem-solving method, as well as enriching their learning experience. Our observations from the sessions conducted while implementing the smart farming project show that the teachers, students as well as student volunteers took an active role in devising for a solution, working collaboratively and seeking creative solutions to the problem at hand. Indirectly, these sessions set an avenue for all to share their ideas, communicate and promote openness in both teaching and learning. These traits are necessary for the students and student volunteers as they require the necessary skills in the 21st century curriculum as outlined by the MEB. The smart farming project also exposes students from the rural communities, who are predom-inantly from the B40 family bracket to technology. This will spur the students' interest to embrace STEM. The introduction to STEM also allows the community to be aware of technological advancements that would bring positive changes to the people. On another front, the MCMC-UUMs effort in promoting STEM education to the society paves way for all to have equitable access to technology and technology education, align with its goals to serve an inclusive community.

6 Conclusion

STEM education plays an important role in both teaching and learning. It is vital that STEM education is expanded to not only in smart farming, but to include a diverse sector which will bring positive change to the community. A structured teaching approach such a Design Thinking presents opportunities for all to explore various problem-solving approach that can bring benefits to everyone. In this paper, we seek to measure the effectiveness of the Design Thinking approach in implementing a smart farming project. Our findings show that Design Thinking help improve learning experiences. This project, however, has its limitations such as a small number of participants and the projects conducted is is limited to smart farming projects only. In our future work, we aim to have a larger sample and involve various types of projects to cover the diverse communities that the MCMC-UUM MakerSpace Laboratory serves.

References

1. Malaysia education blueprint 2013–2025 1 Foreword - Portal KPM. https://www.moe.gov.my/menumedia/media-cetak/penerbitan/dasar/1207-malaysia-education-blueprint-2013-2025/file
2. Floor, N.: Learning experience design vs design thinking. learning experience design. https://lxd.org/news/learning-experience-design-vs-design-thinking. Accessed 20 Dec 2021
3. Pande, M., Bharathi, S.V.: Theoretical foundations of design thinking – a constructivism learning approach to design thinking. Thinking Skills Creativity 36, 100637 (2020). https://doi.org/10.1016/j.tsc.2020.100637
4. Halim, L., Ah Nam, L., Mohd Shahali, E.H.: STEM education in Malaysia. STEM Educ. Asia, 33–48 (2021). https://doi.org/10.4324/9781003099888-2
5. Curriculum Development Centre, Ministry of Education Malaysia: Implementation Guide for Science, Technology, Engineering, and Mathematics (STEM) in-Teaching and Learning. MOE, Putrajaya (2016)
6. Tu, J.-C., Liu, L.-X., Wu, K.-Y.: Study on the learning effectiveness of stanford design thinking in integrated design education. Sustainability 10(8), 2649 (2018). https://doi.org/10.3390/su110082649
7. Building Computational Thinking. In: Recruiting, Preparing, and Retaining STEM Teachers for a Global Generation, pp. 163–189 (2019). https://doi.org/10.1163/9789004399990_007
8. Calavia, M.B., Blanco, T., Casas, R., Dieste, B.: Making design thinking for education sustainable: training preservice teachers to address practice challenges. Thinking Skills and Creativity 47, 101199 (2023). https://doi.org/10.1016/j.tsc.2022.101199

9. Cohen, L., Abreu Faro, S., Tate, R.: The effects of effects on constructivism. Electron. Notes Theor. Comput. Sci. **347**, 87–120 (2019). https://doi.org/10.1016/j.entcs.2019.09.006
10. Stickdorn, M., Schneider, J.: This is Service Design Thinking: Basics, Tools, Cases, 1st edn. Wiley (2012)
11. Interaction design foundation. What is interaction design? The interaction design foundation. https://www.interaction-design.org/literature/topics/interaction-design. Accessed 15 June 2021

Enhancing Supervisor Response Time: An Exploration of the Social Representation Theory of Shame in ELISTA

Jefri Marzal[1] (iD), Edi Elisa[2] (iD), Pradita Eko Prasetyo Utomo[1],
and Suwannit Chareen Chit[3(✉)] (iD)

[1] Universitas Jambi, Mendalo Indah 36361, Jambi, Indonesia
jefri.marzal@unja.ac.id
[2] Universitas Pendidikan Ganesha, Bali, Indonesia
[3] Universiti Utara Malaysia, 06010 Sintok, Kedah, Malaysia
chareen@uum.edu.my

Abstract. The Final Project is a student research course guided by a supervisor, involving activities from research proposal to reporting. Slow supervisor response times hinder project completion. This action research applies the social representation theory of shame to improve response times. A response time display feature is introduced in the ELISTA web application, visible to lecturers, colleagues, and leaders. The hypothesis is that this visibility will lead to shame, prompting lecturers to improve their responsiveness. Results show a significant increase in the percentage of lecturers responding within the six-day limit, rising from 9.37% in the pre-action to 36% in the third cycle. Supervisors feel embarrassed by extended response times in the "red zone." The web application with response time display accelerates student final project completion effectively.

Keywords: Final Project · Response Time · Shyness · Social Representation Theory

1 Introduction

The Final Project represents a critical component of student research activities, typically culminating in a comprehensive report known as a thesis. This endeavor involves proposing, implementing, and reporting on a specific research topic, often with the guidance of two or more supervisors. The role of the supervisor is paramount in ensuring the success of the student's final project [1]. As supervisors are tasked with directing and supporting the implementation process, they play a crucial role in providing students with valuable research experience.

Throughout the final project, students engage in various interactions with their supervisors, encompassing topic selection, proposal writing and revisions, research activities, and publishing research outcomes. Just like in a marriage, a successful partnership between students and supervisors relies on mutual agreement and trust, establishing a master plan that encompasses meeting times, deadlines, and objectives [2].

N. H. Zakaria et al. (Eds.): ICOCI 2023, CCIS 2002, pp. 204–216, 2024.
https://doi.org/10.1007/978-981-99-9592-9_16

However, a major challenge encountered during the final project is that many students face project durations longer than initially planned. In an effort to address this issue and enhance project management, information and communication technology (ICT) have been harnessed through the development of a final project information system [3] and mobile applications [4]. By leveraging ICT tools, it is expected that final project completion will become more efficient and focused [5].

The duration of final project completion has a direct impact on the overall time taken for students to complete their studies. Timely graduation is an essential performance criterion for universities. To further improve the final project process and encourage timely graduation, universities have explored creating a list of functional requirements in the thesis management system [6]. Additionally, the implementation of a prototype web-based management system has been proposed to enhance monitoring [7]. Nevertheless, despite the aid of ICT, issues surrounding extended project durations persist, and the COVID-19 pandemic in 2019 has exacerbated the situation [8]. Achieving a smooth and timely completion of the final project with outstanding output remains a challenging task.

One crucial determinant of successful final project completion is the response time of lecturers to students' guidance requests. A prompt response from the lecturer expedites the project's progress, while delayed responses result in longer project durations. Therefore, response time significantly influences the satisfaction of both students and lecturers [9].

To improve response times and ensure consistency, effective evaluation methods are necessary. One potential approach is evaluating lecturers' response times to student guidance requests. Such evaluations can be made accessible to individuals, colleagues within a department, or even throughout an institution. This process might evoke feelings of shyness among lecturers due to its connection to self-efficacy, personal achievement, and attitudes towards their assigned tasks [10]. This sense of shame can motivate individuals to adhere to group norms and improve their response times [11]. Studies have shown that displaying response times can accelerate recipients' follow-up actions [12].

This research endeavors to investigate the impact of displaying response times for both lecturers and students concerning final project management. The study employs the online application ELISTA, tailored specifically for final project activities at the University of Jambi, one of Indonesia's state universities. Additionally, this study aims to comprehend the central core of shyness that emerges during the final project's implementation, drawing upon insights from the social representation theory. Understanding this sense of shame can provide valuable input for enhancing the ELISTA feature, ultimately shortening the completion time of final projects.

In conclusion, addressing the challenges in final project management is crucial to ensure timely graduation and enhance the overall quality of research experiences for students. By focusing on response time evaluation and utilizing the ELISTA application, this research seeks to contribute to the optimization of the final project process and foster more efficient and fruitful collaborations between students and supervisors.

2 Background

2.1 Final Project Management Application

The student final project application is an information system used to manage student final projects. The business process of this application starts from inputting research titles, checking title similarities in the final project database, determining supervisors, mentoring processes, and inputting final project exam scores. The Online Thesis Guidance Application can help the communication process between students and lecturers and make communication easier [13].

Jambi University currently has an application to manage web-based final assignments with the address https://elista.unja.ac.id. One of the features of this application is to record guidance activities carried out online or face to face. This final project application has been completed with a timeline and guidance monitoring. With the timeline, students will be reminded by the system about the stages. Monitoring guidance is essential because the process of guidance activities can be recorded properly and supporting documents. Another benefit of monitoring guidance is the existence of service time data that can display several statistics, for example, the average length of completion of the final project the average response time from lecturers and students.

2.2 Social Representation Theory

In simple terms, social representation is how a concept is understood, believed, and implemented by a group of people [14]. Social representation theory believes that individuals and society influence each other and interact in constructing meaning and reality in society [15]. Individuals are not only considered as passive objects that are influenced by their groups, but also actively participate in building the meaning and views of the group.

Social representation is a collective phenomenon related to the community that is coordinated by individuals in their daily conversations and actions. Social representation is the unity of thoughts and feelings that are expressed in verbal and open behavior of actors who are objects for social groups [16].

In its development, Jodelet stated that there are a number of approaches commonly used in studying social representation, namely genetic, dynamic, and structural [17]. The genetic approach emphasizes the processes and conditions for the formation and transformation of social representations. The dynamic approach emphasizes the dynamics of social representation, including the dialogical character of social representations that can be seen through social communication that occurs daily, especially discourse. Finally, the structural approach describes the content of social representations as attributes consisting of central core and peripheral elements.

The presence of discourse in the formation of social representation becomes a dynamic process that represents individuals to be part of the group or not or the assessment that has been agreed upon by the group. Efforts to present psychological feelings in social attributes are represented through social attributes, for example emojis that present feelings of guilt or satisfaction in carrying out tasks assigned by the group. The response to the degree of importance or rank that is used as a reference in social representations is described through the desire of a lecturer to assess himself through the emoji he sees on the application screen. When a lecturer has the highest degree of importance or rank / often appears in meeting the needs of completing a student's final project, the representation of the central core will be present, and present peripheral elements related to shame [16].

2.3 Shame

Humans are taught to have shame since childhood. Some forms of shame such as shame to be disrespectful, and shame to do not comply with the norms adopted by a community. The meaning of the word shame shows that shame is closely related to ethics and morality. Shame as one of the basic emotions, continues to develop according to age levels and social changes that occur. For example, the meaning of shame in the younger generation is related to self-doubt, events that cause negative judgments, non-ideal physical appearance, violations of moral principles and inappropriate etiquette [18].

Shame triggers a person to modify his behavior so that it is easier to adapt to the environment. Shame arises when group performance is higher than personal performance [19]. Shame is a determining factor of social behavior [20]. In several studies in the field of psychology, it was found that shame arises when someone judges himself to feel unable to do something [21], feelings of helplessness and failure [22].

3 Methodology

This research is action research, which is trying to improve a process to get the desired result. Action research is suitable for introducing treatment changes to practice and observing the effects of these changes. The first objective of this research is to improve the response time of lecturers in following up on a request for guidance. By utilizing spirit to improve the process, this research adopts an iterative process consisting of three iterations (cycles) which aims to improve response time plus a pre-cycle. Pre-cycle activities are intended to prepare algorithms to calculate response times and prepare initial information about response times before actions are given.

The activities in each cycle have stages of diagnosis, planning, action, and evaluation. The diagnosis phase is how the management of the final project by the lecturer is associated with shame. Meanwhile, the planning phase is used to develop a response time presentation feature which will then be broadcast at a certain time period in the action phase. Displays are carried out in stages, and stop at a response time that meets service process standards. The evaluation phase is used to test the changes that occur by measuring the response time. If the ideal response time has not been achieved then return to the diagnosis and corrective action. The success indicator of this action research is a significant increase in the number of supervisors who have a response time of at least 6 × 24 h. This action research has four stages consisting of pre-action and three cycles. Each cycle is illustrated in Fig. 1 below:

Furthermore, a quantitative approach was carried out to obtain attributes in the form of a central core of social representation of shame by using the Hierarchized Evocation method [23]. In this method, 200 participants were asked to write down what came to

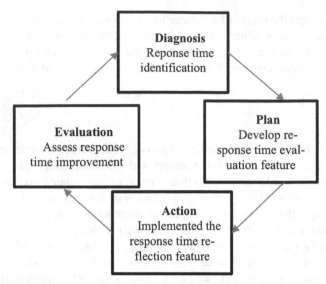

Fig. 1. Four steps of action research

mind when they heard the word'shame in guiding the final project'. The responses are then ranked by the participants according to their degree of importance.

The data obtained by using the hierarchized evocation method can be analyzed in stages, (1) lexical analysis and categorization of the attributes that appear. At this stage, attributes that are semantically the same will be categorized in the same category and then their frequency is calculated, (2) statistical processing by calculating the percentage of the frequency of occurrence of the categorized attributes. The result of calculating the percentage of frequency is accompanied by a sequence of degrees of importance or ranking, which is used as a reference to determine the central core of social representation of "embarrassment in guiding the final project through the ELISTA application". The responses that often appear and get the highest order in the degree of importance are the central core of social representation, while the responses that appear infrequently but get the highest order in the degree of importance and the responses that occur frequently but get low rankings are not counted as the central core of shame.

3.1 Pre-action

There are two activities carried out in the pre-action. The first is to determine the type of response that will be counted as response time. This is important to identify because not all responses from lecturers are counted in response time. The second is to prepare an algorithm for calculating the lecturer's response time. The pseudocode to calculate the average response time has input in the form of requesting guidance from students, response times from lecturers, other response times if there are responses from students. Lecturer responses are classified in the form of text and text accompanied by files. The time that will be calculated as response time is presented in the following table (Table 1).

Table 1. Average response time

Student	Time T_1	Supervisor	Time T_2	Supervisor	Student	Time T_3	Supervisor
Open (file/text	$\checkmark$	Response form (file/text)			Response form (file/text)	$\checkmark$	Close
Open (file/text	$\checkmark$	Response form (text)	$\checkmark$	Response form (file)	Response form (File/text)	$\checkmark$	Close
Open (file/text	$\checkmark$	Response form (file)		Response form (text)	Response form (File/text)	$\checkmark$	Close

Average lecturer response time = $(T_1 + T_2 + \ldots + T_n)/n$

The total-counted-action function is the total lecturer response that is calculated, including the lecturer's first response to the request for supervising and the lecturer's response in the form of a text accompanied by a file for students. This describes the actual state of supervision, where students submit files for correction, and lecturers return corrected files to students. The Read-counted-response-time() function is used to get the lecturer's response time to the student's request for guidance. The average response time of a lecturer, average-time, is the division of total-time by total-counted-action. The detail of the pseudocode is as follows (Fig. 2).

```
Function calculateAverageResponseTime():
    Declare totalResponseTime = 0
    Declare totalCountedActions = 0

    Call readCountedResponseTime()

    While not EndOfFile:
        totalResponseTime = totalResponseTime + responseTime
        totalCountedActions = totalCountedActions + 1
        Call getNextRead()

    averageTime = totalResponseTime / totalCountedActions
    Return averageTime
End Function
```

Fig. 2. Pseudocode response time

Meanwhile, the calculated baseline component includes the number of applications for supervising, the number of lecturers who have used the Elista application for supervising, the number of lecturers with a small response time of or equal to 2 days, between 2 days to 4 days, between 4 days to 6 days, between 6 to 8 days, and large from 8 days.

3.2 First Cycle

This research aims to address the issue of extended response times among lecturers. To achieve this, the researchers first categorize the lecturer response times based on their speed of response, relying on past experience to determine the classification. Typically, the supervising lecturer provides guidance once a week. After processing the data on lecturer response times, specific actions were undertaken to tackle the problem.:

1. Create a feature to display the response time with the information submitted are:

   - If the average response time is small equal to 2 days, then the message that appears is Very Good in the green box,
   - If the average response time is more than 2 days and up to 4 days, the message that appears is Good in the blue box,
   - If the average response time is more than 4 days and up to 6 days then the message that appears is Normal in the yellow box,
   - If the average response time is more than 6 days and up to 8 days, the message that appears is the response time is Poor in the orange box,
   - If the average response time is more than 8 days then the message that appears is the response time is Very Poor in the red box,
   - And if you don't have a response time, the message that appears is "you don't have a response time" in the black box.

2. To strengthen the message about the response time zone, the service zone is equipped with text and emoji. Emojis can express emotions [24], and feelings easily [25].
3. Disseminate the feature to all lecturers through various WhatsApp groups of lecturers and leaders.

After the socialization is carried out, the response time reflection feature is applied within one month. The subjects in this study were all lecturers. At the end of cycle one, the researcher re-measured the response time and the number of lecturers who used Elista as a guidance tool. Figure 3 is an example of the response time display on a supervisor's user account.

3.3 Second Cycle

Based on the evaluation of the first cycle, the thing that will be done to increase response time is to display personal response times and peer response times on a supervisor's account. It is hoped that with friends in one work unit seeing the response time, everyone will try to increase their respective response times. The information displayed is the name of the lecturer, the number of responses, the time, and the response zone. With this display, people may try to manipulate their behavior to avoid embarrassment by speeding up response times.

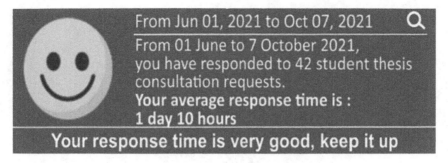

Fig. 3. User response time

3.4 Third Cycle

The third cycle was conducted to increase response time by touching the shame of the work unit. The response time of a study program is defined as the number of lecturers' average response divided by the number of lecturers in the study program. Meanwhile, faculty response time is defined as the number of lecturers' average response divided by the number of lecturers in that faculty. Likewise, the university response time is the number of lecturers' average response time divided by the number of lecturers at the university divided by the number of lecturers in that faculty. The hypothesis used is that each work unit has pride, and they will be embarrassed if there is a negative identity attached to their work unit. Thus, members in the work unit will try to display positive behavior.

The implementation is to add a work unit response time display on the account of each lecturer. Furthermore, the study program leader's account also displays the response time of the study program and the response time of the study program under a faculty. The Dean can see the response time of the study program and the response time of other faculties. Study program response time is the average number of lecturers in a study program divided by the number of lecturers, and faculty response time is the average number of lecturers in a faculty.

4 Results and Analysis

The main finding from displaying the response time of personal, peer, and work units is the increasing number of lecturers who have response times and lecturers who have at least normal response times (very good, good, and normal). As a summary, the percentage of lecturers who have response times and groups of response times in each cycle is shown in Fig. 4.

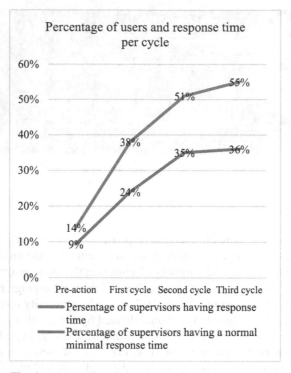

Fig. 4. Percentage of users and response time per cycle.

From Fig. 4 above, it can be seen that there is an increase in the percentage of lecturers who have a response time and the percentage of supervisors who have a response time of a minimum normal category. Based on this graph, it can be temporarily concluded that displaying personal response times on a supervisor's personal account that can be seen by the lecturer or colleagues in a study program can increase the response time. Supervisors will try to increase their response time so they do not feel embarrassed if they are labeled as slow lecturers in responding to the needs of student assignments. Meanwhile, the display of group response times will also encourage supervisors to increase their response times. This is based on group shame where the lecturer jointly avoids group shame.

As a triangulation of the conclusions obtained above, an open questionnaire was distributed to the supervisors. This activity aims to find out the central core of shame in managing the final project. The response percentage is called high if it is greater than 10%, and the response ranking is called a high category if it is smaller than 2. These criteria are determined arbitrarily. Central core shame is the response of respondents who belong to the category of high percentage and high ranking. Based on the information in the following table, the central cores in the management of the final project are: 1) embarrassed if the personal response time is red, and 2) the work unit response time is red (Table 2).

Table 2. Central core of shame in managing the final project

		High rank (<2)		Low rank (> = 2)
High frequency (>10%)	1	I'm embarrassed if my Elista is red Rank1.51 and frequency 20.14%	1	I'm embarrassed if I'm late in responding to student requests Rank 2.36 and frequency 24.62%
	2	I am embarrassed if my work unit's response is red Rank 1.88 and frequency 19.40%	2	I'm embarrassed if a student is late in finishing the final project Rank 2.37 and frequency 17.91%
Low frequency (< = 10%)	1	I'm embarrassed if my response time is in the yellow zone Rank 1 and frequency 0.74%	1	I'm ashamed if I don't check the student's thesis optimally Rank 3.09 and frequency 8.20%
	2	I'm embarrassed if I can't maintain the response time of the green color zone Rank 1 and frequency 0.74%	2	I'm embarrassed if I don't immediately respond to seminar/exam invitations Rank 3 and frequency 2,98%
	3	I'm embarrassed if my work unit's response is black Rank 1 and frequency 0.74%		

The first objective of this study was to find out whether the extension of the supervisor's response time and the work unit of their final assignment application account could speed up the supervisor's response time. Based on the results of the actions given, it can be seen that the percentage of lecturer response times in the green (very good), blue (good), and yellow (normal) zones increased from 9.37% to 36%. This increase occurred because the supervisors felt ashamed to be in the orange and red zones. This was confirmed by the distribution of questionnaires which stated that many lecturers felt embarrassed if their personal response times, as well as work units, were in the red zone. This change is in line with research results that people will tend to manipulate their behavior to avoid embarrassment [18]. The display of response time that can be seen by colleagues or leaders can spur lecturers to increase response time, because an individual will be motivated to appear in accordance with the positive norms of his group [11]. Furthermore, the performance of the supervisor's response time which is displayed in the form of zones equipped with appropriate emoji makes it easier for users to remember their performance, whether very fast, normal, or poor. Emoji is the most efficient way to communicate a message [26].

This study also revealed that the display of data response times increased the number of supervisors who used the Elista application as a guidance tool. Based on the results of the actions given, it can be seen that the number of supervisors who use Elista has increased from 14% to 55%. A technology will be used if it is perceived as useful by the user [27]. This increase can occur because Elista has complete features that make it easier for supervisors to control management and mentoring activities, including features 1) notification of unapproved timelines, 2) confirmation of seminar invitations, 3) information on guidance requests, and 4) offline guidance. If there is a suggestion from the university management to use an application, usually some lecturers will use it. They are afraid of getting sanctions, even if the sanctions are light [28]. Based on the results of the questionnaire processing, it was also found that some respondents answered that they were embarrassed if their work unit was in the black zone.

Furthermore, this study aims to determine the central core of shame in the management and mentoring of the final project. Based on the results of data processing, it can be seen that what is central to the embarrassment of managing and guiding the final project is that the personal response is very slow (red zone), and the response of the work unit is very slow (red zone). This result is consistent with the increase in response time in the green, blue, and yellow zones caused by the lengthening of the response time. Supervisors feel embarrassed if they have bad personal and group response times.

The results of this study further strengthen that displaying response time in limited private and public spaces in the form of colors and emojis can increase response times in various applications. Marzal, *et al.*(2021) revealed that the presentation of response times can increase the response time of recipients of letters on online mail applications [12].

5 Conclusion

In conclusion, our research provides compelling evidence that the display of personal and work unit response times has a substantial positive impact on student engagement with the ELISTA application for final project applications. The data collected throughout our study demonstrates a significant increase in the adoption of the ELISTA application among lecturers, rising impressively from 14% to 55%.

By extending the visibility of personal and work unit response times, we have observed a remarkable improvement in the participation of lecturers falling within the green (very fast), blue (fast), and yellow (normal) response zones, with a notable surge from 9.37% to 36%. This enhancement in response time categorization has proven instrumental in streamlining the final assignment process and, consequently, reducing student study periods.

The findings from our research underscore the crucial role that response times play in effectively managing and guiding final projects using the ELISTA platform. Addressing and optimizing personal response times within the red zone (very slow) and improving work unit responses in the same category are pivotal steps to alleviate bottlenecks and enhance overall project management efficiency.

Our study highlights the significance of efficient communication and timely feedback within academic environments. The substantial increase in lecturer engagement and response times reinforces the value of continuous monitoring and evaluation to sustain the achieved positive outcomes.

In conclusion, our research strongly advocates for the implementation of response time displays as a valuable tool to augment lecturer involvement, optimize project management practices, and create a more conducive environment for students pursuing their final projects. By prioritizing response times and fostering effective communication, educational institutions can create an enriched and streamlined learning experience that benefits both lecturers and students alike. As we move forward, it is essential to embrace these findings and explore innovative approaches to further enhance academic practices and elevate the overall quality of education through platforms like ELISTA.

References

1. Mhunpiew, N.: A supervisor's roles for successful thesis and dissertation. US-China Educ. Rev. **3**(2), 119–122 (2013)
2. Petre, M., Rugg, G.: The Unwritten Rules of PhD, p. 10. Open University Press (2004)
3. Leung, C.H., et al.: The development of a final year project management system for information technology programmes. Commun. Comput. Inf. Sci. **494**, 86–97 (2015)
4. Simatupang, J., Muhammad, M.: Sistem Aplikasi Pengelolaan Tugas Akhir Berbasis Mobile. J. Res. Dev. **3**(2), 66–75 (2019)
5. Fahurian, F., Zuhri, K.: Online thesis guidance management information system at Mitra Indonesia University. J. TAM Technol. Accept. Model. **11**(2), 67–72 (2020)
6. Setiyani, L., Syamsudin, A., Gintings, A., Arifin, D.: The analysis of functional needs on undergraduate thesis information system management, Int. J. Adv. Data Inf. Syst. **1**(2), (2020)
7. Bakar, M.A., Jailani, N., Shukur, Z., Mohd Yatim, N.F.: Final year supervision management system as a tool for monitoring computer science projects. Procedia Soc. Behav. Sci. **18**, 273–281 (2011)
8. Antoro, S., Nur, F.: Time management skills : completion of student final project during the covid-19 pandemic. J. Humanit. Soc. Stud. **05**(03), 232–236 (2021)
9. Hoxmeier, J., DiCesare, C.: System response time and user satisfaction : an experimental study of browser-based applications. Proc. Assoc. Inf. **2**, 1–26 (2000)
10. Kim, Y.: An understanding of shame and guilt : psycho-socio-spiritual meaning. Torch Trinity J. **2**(13), 218–232 (2010)
11. Gausel, N.: Facing in-group immorality: differentiating expressed shame from expressed guilt. Rev. Eur. Stud. **4**(4), 1–7 (2012)
12. Marzal, J., Budiman, W., Adrefiza, Hutabarat, B.F., Kurniawan, W.: Improving the response time of online letter management application users: an application of social representation theory of shame, Int. J. Inf. Vis. **5**(1), 39–45 (2021)
13. Nasution, T.H., Pratama, F., Tanjung, K., Siregar, I., Amalia, A.: Online thesis guidance management information system. J. Phys. Conf. Ser. **978**(1), 012081 (2018)
14. Farr, R.M.: Common sense, science and social representations. Public Underst. Sci. **2**(3), 189–204 (1993)
15. Mannarini, T., Veltri, G.A., Salvatore, S. (eds.): Media and Social Representations of Otherness: Psycho-Social-Cultural Implications. Springer International Publishing, Cham (2020). https://doi.org/10.1007/978-3-030-36099-3
16. Wagner, W., et al.: Theory and method of social representations. Asian J. Soc. Psychol. **2**, 95–125 (1999)
17. Howarth, C.: A social representation is not a quiet thing: exploring the critical potential of social representations theory. Br. J. Soc. Psychol. **45**(1), 65–86 (2006)
18. Giawa, E.C., Nurrachman, N.: Representasi Sosial Tentang Makna Malu Pada Generasi Muda Di Jakarta. J. Psikol. **17**(1), 77 (2018)
19. Benedict, R.: Pattern Sof Culture. Mentor Books, New York (1959)
20. Fessler, D.M.T.: Shame in two cultures: implications for evolutionary approaches. J. Cogn. Cult. **4**(2), 207–262 (2004)

21. Wells, M., Jones, R.: Childhood parentification and shame-proneness : a preliminary study. Am. J. Fam. Ther. **28**(1), 19–27 (2000)
22. Wilson, M.: Creativity and shame reduction in sex addiction treatment. Sex. Addict. Compulsivity **7**(4), 229–248 (2000)
23. Lo, M.G., Piermattéo, A., Rateau, P., Tavani, J.L.: Methods for studying the structure of social representations: a critical review and agenda for future research. J. Theory Soc. Behav. **47**(3), 306–331 (2017)
24. Gülşen, T.T.: You tell me in emojis. Comput. Cogn. Approaches Narrat. **2016,** 354–374 (2016)
25. Lavasani, M.G., Khandan, F.: Cypriot journal of educational, vol. 2, no. 1, pp. 61–74 (2021)
26. Dunlap, J.C., Bose D., Lowenthal, P.R., York, C.S., Atkinson, M., Murtagh, J.: What Sunshine is to Flowers, Elsevier Inc. (2016)
27. Lawson-Body, A., Willoughby, L., Lawson-Body, L., Tamandja E.M: Students' acceptance of E-books: an application of UTAUT, J. Comput. Inf. Syst. **4417**, 1–12 (2018)
28. Tyler, T.R.: Why People Obey the Law, no. December (2021)

Early Detection of School Disengagement Using *MyBuddy* Application

Noraziah ChePa[(✉)] [ID], Ahmad Hanis Mohd Shabli[ID], Azizi Ab Aziz[ID],
Wan Hussain Wan Ishak[ID], and Laura Lim Sei Yi[ID]

School of Computing, Universiti Utara Malaysia, 06010 Sintok, Kedah, Malaysia
aziah@uum.edu.my

Abstract. School disengagement is one of the pressing topics for educational
equity in many countries worldwide, which will lead to school dropout. Dropping
out of school has adverse consequences, including negative effects on employment, lifetime earnings, and physical health. Several attempts have been made to
solve engagement issues, for example, the development of an intelligent tutoring
system (ITS), which is useful to know when a student has disengaged from a
task and might benefit from a particular intervention. However, predicting disengagement on a trial-by-trial basis is a challenging problem, particularly in complex cognitive domains. This paper emphasizes the MyBuddy mobile application
developed as a smart classifier to identify the level of school disengagement risk
among at-risk students in secondary schools. The working engine of *MyBuddy* is
translated from a computational model that comprises fourteen predictors of four
main entities: student, family, school, and surroundings. This application employs
advanced mathematical models to analyze the data and generate risk scores indicating the dropout likelihood. This empowers counselors to proactively intervene
and provide targeted support to the students who require it the most. *MyBuddy*
offers a centralized platform to access and analyze aggregated data from multiple schools. This functionality allows them to smartly identify patterns, trends,
and systemic challenges contributing to dropout rates. With comprehensive data-
driven insights, district and state officers can design effective interventions and
allocate resources strategically to mitigate dropout risks. Utilizing MyBuddy to
revolutionize dropout prevention and foster a more inclusive and equitable education system in Kedah, Malaysia, aligns with the fourth Sustainable Development
Goal, which aims to provide quality education for everyone.

Keywords: school disengagement · school dropout · school disengagement
detection · smart classifier

1 Introduction

The issue of school disengagement stands out as a critical concern for achieving educational equity across many countries worldwide, and it frequently serves as a precursor to
students dropping out of school. The act of prematurely leaving school carries negative
consequences, including adverse effects on employment prospects, lifetime earnings,

N. H. Zakaria et al. (Eds.): ICOCI 2023, CCIS 2002, pp. 217–228, 2024.
https://doi.org/10.1007/978-981-99-9592-9_17

and physical health [8]. The causes of dropping out are influenced by a set of proximal and distal factors related to the individual student and the family, school, and community settings in which the student lives [12]. School disengagement has been identified as one of the predictors of dropout, delinquency, and problem substance usage during adolescence and early adulthood by [1, 2] and [7].

Various individual factors are associated with dropping out, including several demographic factors. Generally, dropout rates are higher among males, Blacks and Hispanics, immigrants, and language minority students. Attitudes also affect dropout rates. Dropout rates are also higher among students with low educational and occupational aspirations. Family background is widely recognized as the most important contributor to success in school. Socioeconomic status, most commonly measured by parental education and family income, is a powerful predictor of school achievement and dropout behavior. Parental education influences students' aspirations and educational support.

It is widely acknowledged that schools influence student achievement, including dropout rates. School characteristics affect student performance: social composition, structural characteristics, school resources, and school policies and practices. In addition to families and schools, communities and peer groups can influence students' withdrawal from school. Differences in neighborhood characteristics can help explain differences in dropout rates among communities, apart from the influence of families. Several studies worldwide have been conducted to explore the factors causing school disengagements in Indonesia [3, 6] and [10]. The mentioned studies show that this topic is a hot and active research point.

In Malaysia, the percentage of enrolled preschool students increased to 90.9% in 2017. The percentage of enrolled students in Primary education improved to 97.9% in 2017 compared to 92% in the 1980s. While for lower secondary schools, it reached up to 95.6% from just 84% in the same period. The most significant improvement was at the upper secondary level, where the enrolment rate almost doubled from 45% to 84.8% in the same period. Dropout rates indicate educational inequality, economic disparities, and social exclusion, making it imperative to address this issue to foster a more inclusive and equitable education system. In response to this pressing concern, innovative approaches leveraging technology have emerged to tackle the dropout problem proactively.

This paper discusses developing and implementing *MyBuddy*, a mobile application designed to identify at-risk secondary school students in Kedah. *MyBuddy* utilizes mathematical modeling techniques to accurately determine the dropout probability, empowering school counselors, district officers, and state officers to intervene and provide targeted support to students in need. By adopting a user-centric approach, *MyBuddy* aims to revolutionize dropout prevention and contribute to advancing an inclusive educational landscape in Kedah.

2   School Dropout Prevention Strategies

Existing dropout prevention strategies in secondary schools have been developed and implemented worldwide to address the complex challenges associated with student disengagement and premature educational discontinuation. These strategies encompass a range of interventions, including academic, social-emotional, and systemic approaches, aimed at improving student retention and success. While these strategies have demonstrated varying degrees of success, they also exhibit certain strengths and weaknesses, underscoring the need for innovative solutions like *MyBuddy*.

One commonly employed strategy is early warning systems (EWS), which identify students at risk of dropout based on specific indicators such as attendance, course performance, and behavior. EWS utilizes data analysis to generate risk scores, enabling educators to intervene and provide targeted support to students in need. The strength of EWS lies in its ability to identify students early, allowing for timely intervention. However, EWS often rely on limited data points and may overlook certain contextual factors, potentially leading to inaccurate predictions and ineffective interventions.

Another prevalent strategy is the provision of academic support and tutoring programs. These initiatives aim to enhance students' academic skills and provide additional resources to help them succeed. Academic support programs have demonstrated positive effects on student performance and retention rates. However, their focus on academic aspects may neglect the underlying social and emotional factors contributing to dropout. Students facing personal challenges, lack of motivation, or disconnection from their peers may not benefit fully from academic support alone.

In recent years, social-emotional learning (SEL) programs have gained recognition as integral to dropout prevention strategies. SEL programs aim to foster students' social skills, emotional intelligence, and resilience, equipping them with the necessary competencies to successfully navigate the challenges of school and life. By addressing the underlying emotional and interpersonal factors influencing dropout, SEL programs contribute to creating a supportive and inclusive school environment. However, implementing SEL programs requires comprehensive training for educators and integration into the school curriculum, which can pose logistical challenges.

Moreover, systemic interventions are crucial for addressing dropout rates on a broader scale. These interventions involve policy changes, resource allocation, and collaboration among various stakeholders to address the systemic factors contributing to dropout. By focusing on improving school climate, strengthening family engagement, and providing adequate resources, systemic interventions aim to create an environment conducive to student success. However, implementing systemic interventions often requires significant time, funding, and coordination among multiple parties, making it a complex and long-term endeavor.

3   Role of Mobile Applications in Education

Mobile applications (apps) have emerged as powerful tools in the education sector, revolutionizing how students learn, interact with educational content, and access support services. With the widespread availability of smartphones and tablets, mobile apps offer unique opportunities to enhance student engagement, improve academic performance, and provide personalized support. This section discusses the growing significance of mobile applications in education and explores their potential benefits and challenges.

3.1 Enhancing Student Engagement

Mobile apps can significantly enhance student engagement by providing interactive and immersive learning experiences. These apps often incorporate gamification elements, multimedia content, and interactive quizzes, making learning more enjoyable and motivating for students. By offering personalized and adaptive learning experiences, apps can cater to individual learning styles, preferences, and paces, promoting active participation and deep understanding.

Furthermore, mobile apps enable anytime, anywhere learning, allowing students to access educational resources and engage in learning activities beyond the confines of the traditional classroom. This flexibility promotes self-directed learning, encourages exploration, and fosters a sense of ownership over the learning process.

3.2 Improving Academic Performance

Mobile apps offer various features and functionalities that can support and improve students' academic performance. Educational apps can provide access to a wide range of subject-specific content, including textbooks, lecture notes, interactive simulations, and educational videos. By presenting information in engaging and accessible formats, apps can facilitate comprehension, reinforce learning, and encourage critical thinking.

Moreover, mobile apps can facilitate communication and collaboration among students and between students and educators. Features like discussion forums, chat functionalities, and collaborative projects enable students to exchange ideas, seek clarifications, and engage in peer learning. This collaborative aspect fosters a sense of community and promotes deeper learning. Additionally, mobile apps can incorporate assessment and feedback mechanisms, allowing students to monitor their progress, receive immediate feedback, and identify areas for improvement. Adaptive learning apps can dynamically adjust the difficulty level and content based on student's performance, ensuring targeted and personalized learning experiences.

3.3 Providing Support Services

Mobile apps are crucial in providing access to support services and resources that enhance student well-being and success. These apps can include features such as virtual tutoring, homework help, academic planning tools, and career guidance resources. Such support services are particularly beneficial for students who may face barriers to accessing traditional support systems due to geographical or socioeconomic constraints.

Furthermore, mobile apps can facilitate communication between students, educators, and support staff. Real-time messaging, online consultation, and remote access to counseling services enable students to seek guidance and support whenever needed, promoting their emotional well-being and overall academic success.

4 Design and Development of *MyBuddy*

This section explains the design and development process of *MyBuddy*, a mobile application aimed at identifying at-risk secondary school students in Kedah, Malaysia, who are likely to drop out. The paper discusses the user-centric approach adopted in the design process, technological aspects employed in the development, and challenges encountered during the development phase. Figure 1 illustrates three phases involved in the development of *MyBuddy* application.

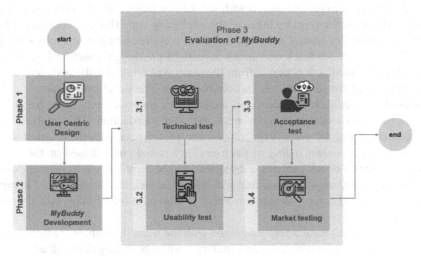

Fig. 1. Main phases involved in the development of MyBuddy application

4.1 User Centric Design

The design and development of *MyBuddy* followed a user-centric approach, emphasizing the needs and constraints of key users, including school counselors, district officers, and state officers. This approach involved understanding the users' requirements, conducting user research, and incorporating their input throughout the development process. By focusing on the users' perspectives, *MyBuddy* app aimed to provide an intuitive and accessible solution for detecting at-risk students effectively.

User-centric design is a fundamental approach in mobile app development that prioritizes end users' needs, preferences, and constraints. It involves understanding user behaviors, conducting user research, and incorporating user feedback throughout the design and development process. In the context of *MyBuddy*, a mobile application designed to identify at-risk secondary school students in Kedah, Malaysia. The user-centric design was crucial in creating an intuitive and accessible application for school counselors, district officers, and state officers. To serve this, requirement gathering sessions have been conducted involving the groups of stakeholders to get their input to develop *MyBuddy* application.

4.2 Requirements Gathering

Three requirement gathering sessions have been conducted involving Counselling teachers, a group of teachers, senior and IT officers from Kedah State Education Department on

24 November 2022, 10 August 2022, and 6 October 2022, respectively. To begin with, low-fidelity wireframes and mockups were developed to visually represent the app's overall structure, layout, and navigation. These initial prototypes served as a foundation for gathering feedback and insights from the end users.

The prototypes were then shared with school counselors, district officers, and state officers, who were the primary users of the *MyBuddy* app. Through interviews, focus groups, and usability testing sessions, the users were encouraged to explore the prototypes and provide feedback on various aspects of the design, functionality, and user experience. The feedback obtained from the users was meticulously analyzed, considering their suggestions, concerns, and observations. The development team carefully considered the feedback and identified areas where improvements could be made to enhance the app's usability, effectiveness, and user satisfaction. This analysis phase involved comparing the users' expectations and preferences with the existing design, allowing a deeper understanding of the users' needs and goals. Based on the insights gained from the feedback analysis, subsequent design iterations were created, incorporating the suggested improvements and addressing the identified issues. These iterations gradually refined the app's design, ensuring it aligned more closely with the users' requirements and expectations.

The development team actively engaged with the users throughout the iterative process, fostering a collaborative and participatory environment. Regular feedback sessions and usability testing allowed for ongoing dialogue and knowledge exchange between the development team and the end users. This iterative feedback loop ensured that the design decisions were grounded in user insights and that the app evolved in response to user needs. Figure 1 illustrates selected interfaces of *MyBuddy* application.

By embracing an iterative design process, *MyBuddy* benefited from continuous user input, enabling the development team to create a user-friendly interface and improve the overall user experience. The iterative approach allowed for a gradual refinement of the app's design and functionality, ensuring that it effectively addressed the needs and constraints of school counselors, district officers, and state officers involved in dropout prevention efforts.

4.3   Development of *MyBuddy* Application

MyBuddy prototype is developed based on the requirements garnered during requirement gathering sessions. Sketches and wireframes with a low level of detail were developed to illustrate the underlying architecture of the application as well as the user flows. Subsequently, a high-fidelity prototype was meticulously developed using Android Studio, allowing for a vivid visualization of the application's interface and functionality.

A database is created for this application to store students' data that will be used to detect their risk of school dropout. This prototype will undergo extensive testing, including the incorporation of priceless user input and incremental modifications. Ultimately, it serves as the basis for the subsequent phase of large-scale development that will come after it. Figure 2 illustrates the main interface of *MyBuddy* application with fourteen predictors.

Data of students need to be keyed in by School Counsellors. It involves 14 variables belonging to four main entities: students, family background, peers, and surrounding

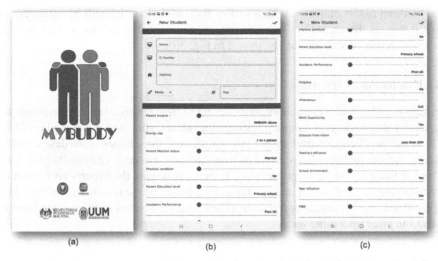

Fig. 2. Main interface of *MyBuddy* application with fourteen predictors

environment, as seen in Fig. 2(b). The variables are Family Income, family size, parents' marital status, parents' educational level, physical condition, academic performance, discipline, attendance, opportunity to work, distance from school, teachers, school peers, and contribution of Parents and Teachers Association (PTA).

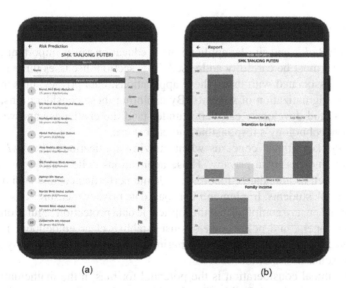

Fig. 3. Predicted risks of school disengagement (Color figure online)

Based on these variables' values, three risk levels will be computed and displayed in three colors indicating their risk level. High risk will be demonstrated using a red flag, medium risk is indicated with a yellow flag, while low risk will be indicated with a green flag, as shown in Fig. 3(a). District and State Education Officers can also view the whole report of student risk, as shown in Fig. 3(b).

4.4 Evaluation of *MyBuddy*

Evaluation of *MyBuddy* application involves four steps: technical testing, usability testing, acceptance testing, and market testing. Technical testing was conducted on 25 July 2023 involving IT experts from different institutions on three dimensions: design and layout, interactions and simplicity, and functions and performance. The results of technical testing indicate a positive response by IT Experts. However, the experts give comments on improving the application in each dimension. Based on the results and technical testing feedback, the MyBuddy application's improved version has been produced and will be used in other upcoming tests.

5 Challenges of *MyBuddy* Implementation

Implementing *MyBuddy* may face challenges such as technological infrastructure limitations, data management and privacy concerns, user training and adoption difficulties, stakeholder engagement, integration with existing systems, cultural and contextual factors, resource allocation, scalability and sustainability, evaluation and continuous improvement, and stakeholder communication and buy-in.

5.1 Ethical Issue

Integrating *MyBuddy* and similar applications in education raises important ethical considerations that must be carefully addressed. This section discusses three primary ethical concerns associated with using these applications: data privacy, bias in modeling, and potential stigmatization of students. By exploring these considerations, educators, policymakers, and developers can better understand the challenges and work towards ensuring such technology's responsible and ethical use.

One of the key ethical concerns when utilizing applications like *MyBuddy* is the protection of students' data privacy. These applications collect and analyze sensitive information, such as attendance records, academic performance, and social indicators, to identify at-risk students. Implementing robust data privacy measures to safeguard this information and ensure compliance with applicable data protection regulations is crucial. Schools, developers, and policymakers must establish clear guidelines and protocols for data collection, storage, access, and sharing to maintain confidentiality and protect students' personal information.

Another ethical consideration is the potential for bias in the mathematical models used by applications like *MyBuddy*. The algorithms and models to predict dropout probabilities should be developed and tested carefully for fairness, accuracy, and inclusivity. It is essential to critically examine the training data used to develop these models to prevent the reinforcement or amplification of biases that may exist within the educational system. Regular auditing and monitoring of the models can help identify and mitigate any potential biases that may emerge during their application.

The use of *MyBuddy* and similar applications in identifying at-risk students has the potential to stigmatize individuals and perpetuate stereotypes. It is important to handle the information generated by these applications with sensitivity and ensure that it is used for proactive intervention and support rather than punitive measures. School counselors and educators must approach the results provided by these applications in a compassionate and non-judgmental manner, focusing on providing targeted assistance to students instead of labeling or stigmatizing them. Transparency and clear communication about the purpose and benefits of the application can help alleviate concerns and foster a supportive environment.

5.2 Scaling, Monitoring, and System Integration

Integrating *MyBuddy* into existing school systems and workflows is essential for seamless implementation. Compatibility with existing student management systems, academic databases, and reporting mechanisms should be ensured to avoid duplication of efforts and minimize disruption. Collaborative discussions with school administrators and relevant authorities can help identify potential integration points and streamline processes. Customization options may also be considered to accommodate school practices and requirements variations.

Scaling up *MyBuddy* requires a robust technological infrastructure to handle the increased data volume and user load. The availability of stable internet connectivity, hardware devices, and sufficient storage capacity are crucial factors to consider. Schools and educational authorities should assess their existing infrastructure and make necessary upgrades or investments to accommodate the implementation of *MyBuddy* on a larger scale. Additionally, technical support mechanisms should be established to address any technical issues or challenges users face during implementation.

A robust monitoring and evaluation framework should be established to assess the impact and effectiveness of *MyBuddy* at both the individual and system levels. Key performance indicators, such as student retention rates, dropout rates, and academic progress, can be tracked and analyzed to measure the app's success. Regular data analysis and user feedback can inform decision-making processes and drive continuous application improvement. Flexibility and adaptability are crucial to address emerging challenges and incorporate user feedback into future iterations.

5.3 Communication

To ensure the successful adoption and effective use of *MyBuddy*, comprehensive training programs should be developed for school counselors, district officers, and state officers involved in the implementation. Training sessions should cover various aspects, including app usage, data management, interpretation of risk scores, and intervention strategies. Capacity building initiatives should equip users with the necessary knowledge and skills to maximize the benefits of *MyBuddy* and effectively support at-risk students. Ongoing support and professional development opportunities should also be provided to ensure continuous learning and skill enhancement.

Engaging and involving relevant stakeholders at different levels is crucial for the successful implementation of *MyBuddy*. Collaboration with school administrators, teachers, parents, and students can foster a sense of ownership and shared responsibility. Clear communication strategies should be established to disseminate information about the purpose, benefits, and expectations of *MyBuddy*. Regular feedback mechanisms, such as feedback surveys or focus groups, can be employed to gather input from stakeholders and address their concerns. Building a collaborative and supportive environment promotes the adoption of *MyBuddy* as a collective effort to enhance dropout prevention and support student success.

6 Future Directions

Implementing *MyBuddy* in the education system of Kedah, Malaysia, presents significant opportunities for positive change. This section explores the potential impact of *MyBuddy* on the education system in Kedah and discusses its broader policy implications. Additionally, it delves into the possibilities of expanding the application to other regions and countries.

The adoption of *MyBuddy* has the potential to revolutionize the education system in Kedah by improving dropout prevention efforts and fostering a more inclusive and equitable environment. By accurately identifying at-risk students and providing targeted support, *MyBuddy* can contribute to higher student retention rates, improved academic performance, and enhanced overall student well-being. This, in turn, can lead to a more productive and successful educational experience for students in Kedah.

The successful implementation of *MyBuddy* in Kedah has significant policy implications. Policymakers and education authorities can draw insights from the implementation process to inform the development of comprehensive dropout prevention policies and strategies at regional and national levels. Integrating technological solutions, like *MyBuddy*, can be recognized as a key component of effective education policies, emphasizing the importance of early identification, intervention, and support for at-risk students.

The success of *MyBuddy* in Kedah opens up possibilities for expanding the application to other regions and countries. By adapting the app to suit the specific needs and contexts of different educational systems, *MyBuddy* can potentially address dropout challenges on a larger scale. The lessons learned from the implementation in Kedah can guide the expansion process, highlighting the importance of user-centric design, stakeholder engagement, and effective policy integration.

Expanding *MyBuddy* to other regions and countries requires stakeholder collaboration and knowledge sharing. Governments, educational institutions, and technology developers can collaborate to customize and implement the app based on each context's unique requirements and challenges. Knowledge-sharing platforms, conferences, and research publications can facilitate the exchange of experiences, best practices, and lessons learned, fostering a collective effort toward dropout prevention and inclusive education globally. As *MyBuddy* expands to new regions, continuous innovation and improvement should be prioritized. Ongoing research and development efforts can refine the app's features, enhance the accuracy of predictive models, and incorporate new insights from the field of education. Additionally, feedback mechanisms from users and stakeholders can inform updates and upgrades, ensuring that *MyBuddy* remains a cutting-edge tool in dropout prevention.

Implementing *MyBuddy* in Kedah holds great promise for the education system, potentially impacting student retention, academic performance, and overall well-being. Its success in Kedah carries significant policy implications, emphasizing the value of technological solutions and proactive dropout prevention strategies. Expanding *MyBuddy* to other regions and countries requires collaboration, customization, and continuous innovation driven by a shared commitment to inclusive and equitable education. By leveraging the lessons learned from Kedah and fostering global partnerships, *MyBuddy* can make a meaningful impact in addressing dropout challenges and improving educational outcomes worldwide.

7 Conclusion

This paper highlighted the significance of *MyBuddy*, a mobile application designed to identify at-risk secondary school students in Kedah, Malaysia, who are likely to drop out. Using mathematical modeling and a user-centric approach, *MyBuddy* aims to revolutionize dropout prevention and foster a more inclusive and equitable education system.

While the existing strategies outlined earlier have contributed to dropout prevention, they also exhibit limitations that underscore the need for innovative approaches like *MyBuddy*. *MyBuddy* offers a unique solution by leveraging mobile technology and mathematical modeling to predict dropout probabilities accurately. By incorporating a wide range of data, including attendance records, academic performance, and social indicators, *MyBuddy* provides a comprehensive analysis that considers multiple dimensions of student engagement and risk factors. This holistic approach allows for a more accurate identification of at-risk students and facilitates targeted intervention design.

Furthermore, *MyBuddy*'s user-friendly interface and centralized platform cater to the specific needs of school counselors, district officers, and state officers, enabling seamless collaboration and data-driven decision-making. Integrating advanced mathematical models empowers these stakeholders to intervene proactively and allocate resources strategically, thus maximizing the effectiveness of dropout prevention efforts. By revolutionizing the approach to dropout prevention through innovative technology and collaboration, *MyBuddy* has the potential to overcome the limitations of existing strategies and contribute to a more inclusive and equitable education system.

In conclusion, *MyBuddy* represents a promising solution for dropout prevention in secondary schools. By combining mathematical modeling, user-centric design, and collaboration among stakeholders, *MyBuddy* has the potential to significantly impact the education system in Kedah, Malaysia, and beyond. Addressing challenges, ensuring ethical considerations, and leveraging the lessons learned from the implementation process will be key to maximizing the app's effectiveness and promoting a more inclusive and equitable education system globally.

Acknowledgment. This research is funded by Yayasan Sime Darby (YSD) and Kedah State Government through Industrial Research Grant Scheme (SO code 21039 and 14989). Authors fully acknowledged YSD and Kedah State Government for the approved fund, making this important research viable and effective. We highly appreciate and acknowledge the cooperation and contributions of Kedah State Education Department which participated and assisted in this study.

References

1. Archambault, I., Janosz, M., Fallu, J.S., Pagani, L.S.: Student engagement and its relationship with early high school dropout. J. Adolesc. **32**(3), 651–670 (2009)
2. Blondal, K.S., Adalbjarnardottir, S.: Student disengagement in relation to expected and unexpected educational pathways. Scand. J. Educ. Res. **56**(1), 85–100 (2012)
3. Boyaci, A.: Exploring the factors associated with the school dropout. Int. Electron. J. Elem. Educ. **12**(2), 145–156 (2019)
4. Dynarski, M., Clarke, L., Cobb, B., Finn, J., Rumberger, R., Smink, J.: Dropout prevention: A practice guide. Institute of Education Sciences, U.S. Department of Education (2008). https://ies.ed.gov/ncee/wwc/PracticeGuide/2
5. Farrington, C.A., et al.: Teaching adolescents to become learners: The role of noncognitive factors in shaping school performance. Chicago Consortium on School Research, University of Chicago (2012). https://consortium.uchicago.edu/sites/default/files/publications/Teaching-Adolescents-to-Become-Learners-Non-Cognitive-Factors-in-Educational-Attainment.pdf
6. Habibi, C.S.: The meaning of school from dropout's view point (a phenomenological study). In: International Conference on Educational Research and Innovation (ICERI 2017) (2017)
7. Henry, K.L., Knight, K.E., Thornberry, T.P.: School disengagement as a predictor of dropout, delinquency, and problem substance use during adolescence and early adulthood. J. Youth Adolesc. **41**(2), 156–166 (2012)
8. Lee-St. John, T.J., et al.: The long-term impact of systemic student support in elementary school: reducing high school dropout. AERA Open **4**(4), 2332858418799085 (2018)
9. Neild, R.C., Balfanz, R.: Unfulfilled promise: the dimensions and characteristics of Philadelphia's dropout crisis, 2000–2005. Philadelphia Youth Network (2006). https://files.eric.ed.gov/fulltext/ED491615.pdf
10. Ouma, D.H., Ting, Z., Pesha, J.C.: Analysis of the socioeconomic factors that contribute to children school dropout in artisanal small-scale gold mining communities of Tanzania. J. Educ. Pract. **8**(14), 71–78 (2017)
11. Rumberger, R.W., Lim, S.A.: Why students drop out of school: a review of 25 years of research. California Dropout Research Project Report, University of California, Santa Barbara (2008). https://www.cdrp.ucsb.edu/sites/secure.lsit.ucsb.edu.edc.d7_cdrp/files/sitefiles/publications/Why_Students_Drop_Out.pdf
12. Rumberger, R.W.: The economics of high school dropouts. In: The Economics of Education, pp. 149–158. Academic Press (2020)
13. Tinto, V.: Leaving College: Rethinking the Causes and Cures of Student attrition. UNIVERSITY of Chicago Press, Chicago (1993)
14. Wilson, S.J., Tanner-Smith, E.E., Lipsey, M.W., Steinka-Fry, K.T., Morrison, J.Q.: Dropout prevention and intervention programs: effects on school completion and dropout among school-aged children and youth. Campbell Syst. Rev. **2011**(4) (2011). https://doi.org/10.4073/csr.2011.4

Digital Entrepreneurship
and Innovation

E-commerce Carbon Footprint Contribution: A Preliminary Investigation Framework

Siti Sakira Kamruddin$^{(\boxtimes)}$ ⓘ, Farzana Kabir Ahmad ⓘ, Alawiyah Abd Wahab ⓘ, Zahurin Mat Aji ⓘ, and Noradila Nordin ⓘ

School of Computing, Universiti Utara Malaysia, Sintok, 06010 Bukit Kayu Hitam, Kedah, Malaysia
sakira@uum.edu.my

Abstract. The growth of e-commerce has brought about a growing concern regarding its impact on the environment. Activities such as excessive packaging, delivery, and returns have contributed to increased carbon emissions, resulting in a significant carbon footprint. To promote a sustainable e-commerce environment, a study is needed to assess the carbon footprint contribution of online businesses. This paper presents a framework for conducting a preliminary investigation into the carbon production and emissions of identified e-commerce organizations. The framework was formulated by analyzing the relevant literature from similar studies. It comprises a 3-phase research activity: Phase 1 involves identifying carbon footprint factors through a literature search; Phase 2 includes conducting a case study on an online business to construct a carbon consumption profile; and Phase 3 involves developing a measurement method to assess the carbon consumption of online businesses. The proposed framework can provide a preliminary understanding of e-commerce's carbon footprint contribution and enable authorities to assess the level of carbon consumption and devise action plans to reduce its impact on the environment. However, challenges and implications are associated with implementing the framework, which is discussed in the paper.

Keywords: Carbon Footprint · Preliminary Investigation Framework · E-commerce · Carbon Consumption Profile

1 Introduction

With the increasing concern for climate change, environmentalists and governments of various countries are actively formulating action plans to address the crisis. Most initiatives in this area concentrate on limiting the environmental impact of unsustainable industrial production processes (e.g., pollutants from factories) [1] and the transportation industry [2]. One of the sectors that are given the least attention is the e-commerce industry.

E-commerce has expanded into a global industry that is quickly evolving. Online retail sales reached 4.9 trillion dollars worldwide in 2021, and it is anticipated to rise by more than 50% in 2025 [3]. It has become the preferred method of purchasing due to the advancements in Internet technology, online payment security, and speedy delivery methods. The covid-19 pandemic also contributes to the demand for online shopping. The positive growth of e-Commerce has resulted in various benefits to the economy. However, there is a need to ensure that the sector players do not harm the environment due to the activities of searching, packaging, shipping, and returning items [4].

Research shows e-commerce players contribute to carbon production and greenhouse gas (GHG) emissions. The negative effects of e-commerce on the environment are increasing due to the problem of transporting individual shipments, using special packaging materials, and issues with product returns [5]. For instance, in terms of packaging, online retailers' continuous use of cardboard, plastics, Styrofoam, and other packaging materials when shipping their products generates a continuous stream of waste. Besides excessive packaging waste pollution, the carbon emissions due to the transportation (delivery and return) activities associated with online purchasing also harm the environment.

Studies on the environmental impact of e-commerce are diverse as researchers focus on different angles such as logistics [5–7], particularly the last mile delivery i.e. the process of shipping the products from delivery hubs directly to the customer's door [8, 9]. Research also focuses on e-commerce consumer behavior and its environmental impact [10, 11].

Assessing the environmental impact of e-commerce is a non-trivial task due to the different factors and elements contributing to the problem. Furthermore, the emergence of new retail models such as omnichannel retail incorporating click-and-collect and ship-from-store functionalities, along with the introduction of new delivery services, has added to the complexity in understanding the e-commerce industry's environmental impact [12].

Promoting sustainable carbon consumption practices among online businesses is the ultimate goal of the authorities. With long-term economic growth in mind, a comprehensive plan that consists of standards, taxes, subsidies, communications campaigns, and education needs to be devised. To come up with this plan, a preliminary investigation needs to be performed to understand the severity of the situation.

This paper provides a framework that can be used to perform a preliminary investigation on the existing scenario of the e-commerce industry toward building a carbon footprint profile for it. The framework outlines the preliminary investigation's objective, method, and output in three phases. Using this framework, a preliminary investigation of e-commerce carbon footprint contribution can be performed to build a model that can aid in promoting sustainable carbon consumption among e-commerce.

The rest of the paper is organized as follows. Section 2 reviews relevant literature and discusses how carbon footprint has been defined and explored in previous research. Section 3 presents the proposed framework to perform a preliminary investigation of the current scenario of carbon footprint contribution among e-commerce. Section 4 discusses the challenges and impact of implementing the framework, and Sect. 5 concludes the paper.

2   Related Work

This section provides a comprehensive review of the literature on the carbon footprint of e-commerce. It begins by discussing the current state of e-commerce in Malaysia, followed by an overview of the impact of e-commerce on the environment in Sect. 2.2. Section 2.3 examines the various methods employed to construct carbon profiles and measure carbon footprints in previous research.

2.1   Greenhouse Gas

Greenhouse Gas (GHG) is an infrared-absorbing and emitting gas. Water vapor, carbon dioxide, methane, nitrous oxide, and ozone are the principal greenhouse gases in the atmosphere. The GHG Protocol divides GHG emissions into three 'scopes' [13]. Scope 1: Direct emissions resulting from activities within the control of the organization (i.e., on-site combustion of fuel, manufacturing and process emissions, refrigerant expenditures, company cars use); Scope 2: Indirect emissions from any electricity purchased and operated from the grid, as well as heat or steam; Scope 3: Indirect emissions from sources outside the company's direct control (i.e., employee commuting, business travel, outsourced transportation, etc.) as well as emissions inherent in the production of goods and services. All three scopes of GHG will be considered in Phase 2 of the E-commerce Carbon Footprint Contribution Preliminary Investigation Framework presented in this paper.

2.2   E-commerce in Malaysia

E-commerce in Malaysia has experienced substantial growth in recent years, with a significant number of micro-entrepreneurs and SMEs (MSMEs) adopting this business model. As of the end of 2021, the number of MSMEs embracing e-commerce has reached 890,000, surpassing the initial target of 875,000 set out in the National E-commerce Strategic Roadmap (NESR) and the Malaysia Digital Economy Blueprint (MyDIGITAL) for 2025. MyDIGITAL is a national initiative to transform Malaysia into a digitally driven, high-income nation and regional leader in the digital economy. This initiative results from collaboration between various ministries, agencies, and the industry under the NESR framework.

As the leading agency in Malaysia's digital economy, Malaysia Digital Economy Corporation (MDEC) [14] has led the Go-eCommerce Onboarding and Shop Malaysia Online campaigns under Belanjawan 2021. These campaigns are part of the national economic recovery plan (PENJANA) aimed at encouraging the digitization of micro, small, and medium-sized enterprises (MSMEs) and boosting the growth of the digital economy. The campaigns aim to support and facilitate MSMEs in adopting e-commerce as a new way of conducting business and expanding their market reach.

The Department of Statistics Malaysia (DOSM) reported that the total income generated from e-commerce transactions in Malaysia reached RM1.09 trillion by the end of the fourth quarter of 2021, a 21.8% increase from RM896 billion in the previous year. This is the first time the income from e-commerce transactions has exceeded the

RM1 trillion threshold. This growth trajectory puts Malaysia on track to achieve its target of an RM1.65 trillion e-commerce market size by 2025, as outlined in the National E-commerce Strategic Roadmap (NESR).

Furthermore, Malaysia Digital (MD), started in July 2022, is a government-led national strategic plan to improve the nation's digital capabilities and develop the digital economy. The government will implement Malaysia Digital Catalytic Programmes (PEMANGKIN) with local industry participation, targeted digitalization programs to equip businesses with the right digital knowledge, skills, and tools, and various facilitation services and competitive offerings to complement business needs. With the government's support, this seems promising in improving e-commerce in Malaysia and the future digital economy.

2.3 Impact of Carbon Footprint of E-commerce

Despite the impressive revenue generated by e-commerce, the environmental impact of the growing number of online retailers must not be overlooked. Specifically, these businesses' carbon footprint needs to be considered. The carbon footprint refers to the total amount of greenhouse gas emissions resulting from a product or service's production, use, and disposal [15–17]. These emissions can be caused directly or indirectly by individuals, organizations, events, or products.

Reducing carbon footprint is a crucial public policy issue for environmental management, and retailers can play a significant role in tackling climate change by taking direct action where it matters most [18–20]. Retail is one of the largest economic sectors, employing 3.6 million people in Europe and representing over 23% of all businesses [21]. By implementing feasible solutions, retailers can substantially impact reducing carbon emissions on a large scale.

Transportation is a key aspect of retailers' operations but also contributes significantly to greenhouse gas and air pollution emissions [22]. Retail transportation operations encompass multiple modes of transportation, a range of container and vehicle sizes, and driver and vehicle scheduling. One study found that switching from delivery trucks to cargo bikes can reduce greenhouse gas emissions by 42% [23].

To reduce the environmental impact of delivery, retailers and logistics service providers can consolidate deliveries to a specific location. According to a US-based study, e-commerce performs worse than in-store buying when fewer than four deliveries are combined, but outperforms every aspect when more than 92 deliveries are merged [24]. Moreover, it is better for the environment if the number of items purchased per delivery is higher, as the environmental footprint per item decreases as the number of items per delivery increases.

Studies show that consumers travel to shop approximately 20% of the time [25, 26]. [27] investigated the carbon footprint associated with pre-and post-purchase travel behavior. The rise of online retail as an alternative to individual shopping trips has raised concerns about its environmental impact [28, 29]. Although omnichannel retailers encourage using various channels (online and offline) to enhance consumer convenience, this may lead to increased travel and related negative environmental effects. Therefore, it is crucial to consider the impact of online and offline shopping on the environment, including the carbon footprint associated with pre-and post-purchase travel behavior.

Furthermore, research has shown that some consumers tend to order more items, anticipating that they will return a portion of them (e.g., clothing in multiple sizes or colors) [29]. The environmental impact of this practice depends on how retailers and logistics service providers handle the subsequent delivery failures and product returns, as well as on the travel behavior of customers themselves [30].

Besides transportation, packaging is an essential aspect to consider in e-commerce as it protects products during transit, reducing damages, refunds, and redeliveries. However, some consumers perceive online purchase packaging as excessive and wasteful, often made of materials that take longer to degrade, such as plastic, cardboard, and paper. As a result, most packaging materials end up in landfills, potentially contaminating the soil [31]. [32] suggest exploring the use of reusable plastic crates instead of cardboard boxes to improve the sustainability of e-commerce packaging. Despite efforts to reuse and recycle packaging materials, a significant portion is not recyclable. Furthermore, some materials like bubble bags, polystyrene, and plastic bags take longer to degrade.

The review reveals that retailers and logistics service providers can play a crucial role in reducing greenhouse gas emissions by implementing feasible solutions. Transport and packaging are key areas that require attention, with the consolidation of deliveries, switching to eco-friendly modes of transport, and exploring sustainable packaging options being some of the feasible solutions. It is also essential to consider the carbon footprint associated with pre-and post-purchase travel behavior and handling delivery failures and returns. By taking direct action where it matters most, we can make a substantial impact on reducing e-commerce carbon emissions on a large scale.

2.4 Method Employed to Construct Carbon Profile and Measure Carbon Footprint

Several studies have used a qualitative approach to identify e-commerce activities that could have an environmental impact. For instance, [33] conducted interviews with logistics operators and used secondary sources to evaluate the purchasing process's impact on the electronics industry in Italy. [34] used semi-structured interviews with experts and document reviews of Corporate Social Responsibility (CSR) and carbon footprint reports to compare the environmental impact of last-mile deliveries and returns between six fashion e-commerce sites. [35] not only conducted interviews with retailers but also employed observation methods by visiting warehouses and stores to evaluate the environmental impacts of the grocery industry's online and offline purchasing processes.

The literature proposes various methods for measuring carbon footprint. For instance, [36] calculated the carbon footprint of e-commerce activities in Thailand using a mathematical model based on supply chain parameters such as customers, sellers, marketplaces, delivery centers, and delivery agents. [6] proposed a network analysis approach to calculate carbon emissions from urban freight volume in Jakarta. They used a causal loop diagram with factors such as e-commerce growth, the carbon footprint from urban logistics, logistics cost, and truckload capacity. Carbon footprint measurement methods can broadly be mathematical modeling, regression, and network analysis.

Mathematical Modeling. After a thorough review of existing literature, it was found that several carbon dioxide calculator apps are available for customers and logistics companies. However, the reliability of data obtained from these calculators cannot be determined as not all disclose their methods and data resources. A German Federal Environmental Agency study examined 18 pre-existing calculators to create a commonly used online tool for calculating personal carbon dioxide emissions [37]. Although it excludes buying methods, it contains categories like living, mobility/travel, nutrition and consumption, and purchasing behaviors. Nevertheless, until 2013, there was no accepted method for quantifying carbon emissions in logistics; therefore, businesses and research employed various techniques and data [38]. France mandated that logistics companies disclose the emissions of their transports starting on 1 October 2013.

The European Union established the European Norm DIN EN 16258 to calculate greenhouse gas emissions from transport in 2013 [21]. The scientific framework for precisely measuring GHG emissions in supply chains was developed and tested by COFRET, a cooperation of 14 predominantly academic institutions from eight European nations. Although it is planned for future adjustments, the norm does not currently consider emissions from buildings, warehouses, or handling. It emphasizes the emissions produced by the fuel or electricity used by vehicles allowing the calculation of carbon emissions for every single parcel, not simply for transportation. Equation 1 is the commonly used formula to obtain the carbon footprint for a shipment:

$$F = W \times D \times E \tag{1}$$

where F is the carbon footprint (in kg CO2e), W is the weight of the shipment (in kg), D is the distance traveled by the shipment (in km), and E is the emission factor (in kg CO2e/kg-km). The emission factor E represents the amount of greenhouse gas emitted per unit of distance traveled by the shipment, considering factors such as the mode of transport, the type of fuel used, and the efficiency of the transport.

The formula for calculating greenhouse gas emissions according to DIN EN 16258 depends on the mode of transport being considered. Equation 2 and 3 provides formulas to calculate emission based on each mode of transport.

For road transport:

$$E = F \times Ef \tag{2}$$

For rail, air and sea transport:

$$E = D \times Ef \tag{3}$$

where E is Emissions (kg CO2e), F is fuel consumption (liters) D is the distance traveled (km) and Ef is Emission factor (kg CO2e/liter for road or kg CO2e/km for rail, or kg CO2e/km/passenger for air and kg CO2e/km/tonne for sea), In each case, the emission factor is a value that reflects the amount of greenhouse gas emitted per unit of fuel or distance traveled.

Regression Analysis. Shopping online has the potential to reduce the environmental impact compared to traditional brick-and-mortar retail, although the degree of impact depends on specific circumstances. However, due to the complexity of the factors involved, most studies that compare the carbon footprints of online and traditional retail provide a limited view. To provide a more comprehensive assessment, a study published in [30] developed a framework that takes into account all significant environmental factors associated with retail and e-commerce activities. This model incorporates consumer behavior, basket size, transport mode, trip length, and frequency to provide a detailed analysis. The framework utilized regression analysis, a quantitative tool that is easy to use and offers valuable information on carbon emissions based on the variables studied.

Network Analysis. A method of ecological network analysis, which considers embodied carbon flows in socio-economic networks, was proposed by [39]. They conducted a case study in China to explore the relationship between embodied carbon structure and production-based carbon intensity. The study found that wealthy provinces exhibited lower carbon intensities, with embodied carbon flows dispersed across the network, implying a decentralized carbon mitigation measures requirement. On the other hand, underdeveloped regions had higher carbon intensities, with most embodied carbon flows concentrated in a few pathways, highlighting the need for centralized decarbonization policies. By focusing on the specific carbon emission structures of different regions, the method can help develop rational mitigation strategies. Given the ambitious emission reduction goals and uneven regional development, the study aims to support China's decarbonization efforts and contribute to developing fair and rational carbon mitigation policies.

In conclusion, choosing the appropriate method for calculating carbon emissions in logistics and retail is important. While several carbon dioxide calculator apps are available, not all of them disclose their data resources, making their reliability difficult to determine. The European Union has established a standard for calculating greenhouse gas emissions in transportation, and the COFRET consortium has designed a methodological framework for accurately calculating GHG emissions in supply chains. Regression analysis and ecological network analysis are also valuable tools that provide valuable information on carbon emissions depending on the studied variables. Therefore, selecting the most suitable method for calculating carbon emissions can provide more accurate and comprehensive evaluations, leading to the development of fair and rational carbon mitigation policies.

3   The Preliminary Investigation Framework

This section presents the proposed framework to perform a preliminary investigation of the current scenario of carbon footprint contribution among e-commerce. The framework is shown in Fig. 1.

Figure 1 shows a three-phase framework for performing a preliminary investigation of the E-commerce Carbon Footprint Contribution. The next subsection discusses in detail each of the phases.

3.1   Phase 1: Identifying Carbon Footprint Factors

The objective of the first phase is to identify and categorize the elements and factors contributing to carbon production or savings. The method that will be implemented to achieve this objective is a literature survey to identify the elements and factors related to

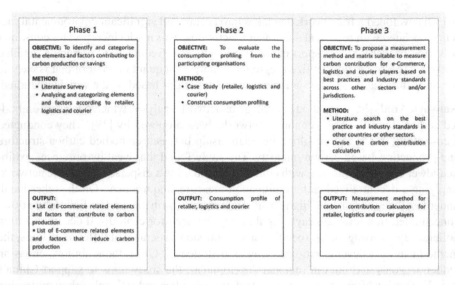

Phase 1

OBJECTIVE: To identify and categorise the elements and factors contributing to carbon production or savings

METHOD:
- Literature Survey
- Analyzing and categorizing elements and factors according to retailer, logistics and courier

OUTPUT:
- List of E-commerce related elements and factors that contribute to carbon production
- List of E-commerce related elements and factors that reduce carbon production

Phase 2

OBJECTIVE: To evaluate the consumption profiling from the participating organisations

METHOD:
- Case Study (retailer, logistics and courier)
- Construct consumption profiling

OUTPUT: Consumption profile of retailer, logistics and courier

Phase 3

OBJECTIVE: To propose a measurement method and matrix suitable to measure carbon contribution for e-Commerce, logistics and courier players based on best practices and industry standards across other sectors and/or jurisdictions.

METHOD:
- Literature search on the best practice and industry standards in other countries or other sectors.
- Devise the carbon contribution calculation

OUTPUT: Measurement method for carbon contribution calcuaton for retailer, logistics and courier players

Fig. 1. The E-commerce Carbon Footprint Contribution Preliminary Investigation Framework

carbon production in previous studies. The identified elements and factors will then be analyzed and categorized according to the e-commerce participating players' i.e., retailers, logistics, and couriers. The output of this phase will be a list of e-commerce-related elements and factors that contribute to carbon production and a list of e-commerce-related elements and factors that reduce carbon production.

3.2 Phase 2: Constructing Carbon Consumption Profile

The second phase of this study involves the objective of evaluating the consumption profiling from the participating organization. To achieve this objective, a case study will be conducted on the participating organization to collect detailed information on the activities involved in the complete e-commerce process to construct the carbon profiling. The output of this phase will be the carbon consumption profile.

The case study is particularly useful for exploratory study and appropriate to understand the online business activities that could impact the environment. This case study focuses on Lazada, an online business website for retailers to enhance their sales channels. Lazada was chosen as it is ranked as number one of the top ten list of e-commerce sites in Malaysia for 2022 [40]. Its monthly traffic is around 31.29 million hits.

A multisource and multimethod data collection method is proposed in this framework. The data will be collected through secondary sources involving traditional media, company websites, and internet articles. Meanwhile, interviews will be conducted with managers handling the online business life cycle activities.

Data analysis and data collection will be conducted concurrently to allow the emergence of empirical data and theoretical concepts in capturing a novel phenomenon [41]. Face-to-face and online interview sessions will be recorded. The recorded data will be transcribed verbatim. The transcript will be subjected to thematic analysis using Atlas.

ti software. The secondary data will be subjected to content analysis. The participants will be determined by contacting the liaison officers or representatives at Lazada through LinkedIn and their company website.

3.3 Phase 3: Developing Carbon Contribution Measurement Method

The third phase is to propose a measurement method and matrix suitable to measure carbon contribution for e-Commerce, logistics, and courier players based on best practices and industry standards across other sectors and/or jurisdictions. To achieve this objective, a literature search will be conducted on the best practice and industry standards in other countries or other sectors to devise the carbon contribution calculation. The output of this phase will be the measurement method for carbon contribution calculation for retailers, logistics, and courier players.

The literature revealed various approaches for measuring carbon contribution, therefore, this phase will involve a thorough search of the literature to identify the most suitable approach. Once the approach is identified, the next step is to conduct an analytical approach on the identified carbon contributing factors and elements from Phase 1 and the carbon profile of the identified online business from Phase 2. Both this information will be analyzed to be incorporated into the construction of the carbon footprint measurement method.

4   Implementation Challenges and Impact

The paper presents a framework for the preliminary investigation of the e-commerce carbon footprint contribution. This section discusses some challenges that may arise in implementing the proposed framework. We also discuss the implication of implementing the preliminary investigation using the proposed framework.

4.1 Implementation Challenges

Conducting a preliminary investigation related to carbon footprint profiling of e-commerce comes with challenges such as data acquisition, ensuring the sufficiency of data to create the carbon footprint profile and the challenges of developing a model with insufficient data.

One of the main challenges in conducting research related to carbon footprint profiling is gaining access to relevant organizations and their data. Acquiring data from these organizations can be difficult, especially if the organization is unwilling to cooperate or if the data is confidential. Also, it may be challenging to contact some organizations, which might make the research process more challenging. Researchers may need to build relationships with pertinent groups, explain the significance of the research and the advantages of participation, and reassure them that their data would be handled with privacy and security in mind to solve this difficulty.

The unavailability of adequate data to build a model is another problem in carbon footprint profiling research. This is particularly true for small and medium-sized businesses, which could lack the tools or capability needed to gather and disclose information on their carbon impact. Furthermore, it may be difficult to develop the model because of missing or faulty data effectively. We could need to leverage various data sources, including publicly available databases or secondary data, to address this problem, and we might need to create statistical models to estimate the missing data.

Even with the best efforts, there may occasionally not be enough data to build a carbon footprint model. This could happen if the company hasn't gathered data on particular parts of its operations or if the data is unreliable or erroneous. We may need to employ alternate strategies to study the potential effects of missing data in certain situations, such as creating scenario-based models or performing sensitivity analyses. Another strategy is to use proxy data, such as industry benchmarks or data from organizations with comparable purposes, to calculate carbon emissions.

4.2 The Impact of Implementation

When the framework is implemented, the outcome of the preliminary investigation can provide the following implication; by identifying the contributing factors of the carbon footprint and constructing a carbon footprint profile for the e-commerce industry and its players, the preliminary investigation can provide valuable insights into the current practices and the severity of the existing carbon footprint produced by e-commerce companies. This information can help businesses make informed decisions about reducing their carbon emissions and developing more sustainable practices. For example, the researchers can identify which activities and processes have the highest carbon footprint and suggest ways to reduce emissions through changes in these areas.

The development of a measurement/model/matrix can be used as a measuring scale to measure and evaluate the future carbon footprint contribution of the e-commerce industry. Furthermore, it may be used to create a standard and compare the carbon footprint of different companies and industries. Another benefit of the measurement/model/matrix is that it can be used to monitor carbon reduction progress and set achievable targets over time. This could motivate businesses to take action to lessen their carbon footprint and foster a culture of sustainability within the e-commerce sector.

5 Conclusion

In conclusion, a carbon footprint profiling study can significantly benefit the e-commerce industry by providing a guideline to reduce carbon emissions and contribute to environmental sustainability. Establishing relationships with organizations, using different data sources, and devising alternative solutions can overcome the challenges faced in this research, such as gaining access to relevant organizations, dealing with incomplete data, and having difficulty adopting innovative modeling approaches.

Identifying the contributing factors and constructing a carbon footprint profile can enable the e-commerce industry to gain insights into their operations' carbon emissions, enabling them to make informed decisions on reducing their carbon footprint. Additionally, constructing a carbon footprint measurement/model/matrix can be viewed as an initiative to develop a standardized and transparent method of assessing carbon consumption, setting targets for reduction, and monitoring progress over time. This can encourage companies to take responsibility for their carbon emissions, implement sustainable practices and create a sustainability culture in the e-commerce industry.

Future work will concentrate on implementing the proposed framework, developing the carbon footprint profile for the e-commerce sector, and devising an appropriate measurement/matrix/model to accurately calculate the carbon contribution of the e-commerce industry in Malaysia. Once the framework is implemented, the study's finding can be extended beyond the e-commerce industry. Carbon footprint profiling can help impact business operations on the environment by increasing awareness of environmental issues. As a result, more sustainable practices in all industries can be established. Furthermore, climate change policy decisions can be devised by providing policymakers with accurate information about the potential impact of legislation on carbon dioxide emissions by the e-commerce industry.

To address the environmental impact of carbon footprint in online retail, customers, retailers, and logistics service providers can make significant positive contributions by taking specific actions. The initiatives include greening the delivery fleet, encouraging sustainable collection trips, and transforming packaging practices. Additionally, these stakeholders can generate and increase awareness about this issue in collaboration with policymakers. By working together, we can effectively tackle the challenges associated with carbon footprint and create a more sustainable future for e-commerce activities.

References

1. Meng, W., Hu, B., Sun, N., Mo, X., He, M., Li, H.: An integrated full cost model based on extended exergy accounting toward sustainability assessment of industrial production processes. Clean Technol. Environ. Policy 21(10), 1993–2004 (2019)
2. Miklautsch, P., Woschank, M.: A framework of measures to mitigate greenhouse gas emissions in freight transport: systematic literature review from a manufacturer's perspective. J. Clean. Prod. 132883 (2022)
3. Chevalier, S.: Global retail e-commerce sales 2014–2025. In Statista (2022). https://www-statista-com.proxy.library.ohio.edu/statistics/1108266/esports-interest/. Accessec 7 Sept 2022
4. Escursell, S., Llorach-Massana, P., Roncero, M.B.: Sustainability in e-commerce packaging: a review. J. Clean. Prod. 280, 124314 (2021)
5. Kawa, A., Pierański, B.: Green logistics in e-commerce. LogForum 17(2), 183–192 (2021)
6. Hidayatno, A., Destyanto, A.R., Fadhil, M.: Model conceptualization on E-commerce growth impact to emissions generated from urban logistics transportation: a case study of Jakarta. Energy Procedia 156, 144–148 (2019)
7. Mak, S.L., Wong, Y.M., Ho, K.C., Lee, C.C.: Contemporary green solutions for the logistics and transportation industry—with case illustration of a leading global 3PL based in Hong Kong. Sustainability 14(14), 8777 (2022)
8. Siragusa, C., Tumino, A., Mangiaracina, R., Perego, A.: Electric vehicles performing last-mile delivery in B2C e-commerce: an economic and environmental assessment. Int. J. Sustain. Transp. 16(1), 22–33 (2022)
9. Chen, C., Demir, E.: Drones and delivery robots: models and applications to last mile delivery. In: The Palgrave Handbook of Operations Research, pp. 859–882. Palgrave Macmillan, Cham (2022)
10. Ignat, B., Chankov, S.: Do e-commerce customers change their preferred last-mile delivery based on its sustainability impact?. Int. J. Logist. Manage. (2020)

11. Bonomi, V., Mansini, R., Zanotti, R.: Last mile delivery with parcel lockers: evaluating the environmental impact of eco-conscious consumer behavior. IFAC-PapersOnLine **55**(5), 72–77 (2022)
12. Rai, H.B.: The net environmental impact of online shopping, beyond the substitution bias. J. Transp. Geogr. **93**, 103058 (2021)
13. Radonjič, G., Tompa, S.: Carbon footprint calculation in telecommunications companies–the importance and relevance of scope 3 greenhouse gases emissions. Renew. Sustain. Energy Rev. **98**, 361–375 (2018)
14. Malaysia Digital Economy Corporation. Digitilizing SMEs. Malaysia Digital Economy Corporation. (2020). https://mdec.my/digital-economyinitiatives/100-go-digital/
15. Wright, L.A., Kemp, S., Williams, I.: 'Carbon footprinting': towards a universally accepted definition. Carbon Manage. **2**(1), 61–72 (2011)
16. Malmodin, J., Lundén, D.: The energy and carbon footprint of the global ICT and E&M sectors 2010–2015. Sustainability **10**(9), 3027 (2018). https://doi.org/10.3390/su10093027
17. Karwacka, M., Ciurzyńska, A., Lenart, A., Janowicz, M.: Sustainable development in the agri-food sector in terms of the carbon footprint: a review. Sustainability **12**(16), 6463 (2020)
18. Demarque, C., Charalambides, L., Hilton, D.J., Waroquier, L.: Nudging sustainable consumption: the use of descriptive norms to promote a minority behavior in a realistic online shopping environment. J. Environ. Psychol. **43**, 166–174 (2015)
19. Muller, L., Lacroix, A., Ruffieux, B.: Environmental labelling and consumption changes: A food choice experiment. Environ. Resour. Econ. **73**(3), 871–897 (2019)
20. Panzone, L.A., Ulph, A., Zizzo, D.J., Hilton, D., Clear, A.: The impact of environmental recall and carbon taxation on the carbon footprint of supermarket shopping. J. Environ. Econ. Manag. **109**, 102137 (2021)
21. European Commission. A European Retail Sector Fit for the 21st Century (Brussels) (2018)
22. WHO: Health in the Green Economy: Health Co-Benefits of Climate Change Mitigation – Transport Sector. Geneva, Switzerland (2011)
23. Shahmohammadi, S., Steinmann, Z.J., Tambjerg, L., van Loon, P., King, J.H., Huijbregts, M.A.: Comparative greenhouse gas footprinting of online versus traditional shopping for fast-moving consumer goods: a stochastic approach. Environ. Sci. Technol. **54**(6), 3499–3509 (2020)
24. Jaller, M., Pahwa, A.: Evaluating the environmental impacts of online shopping: a behavioral and transportation approach. Transp. Res. Part D: Transp. Environ. **80**, 102223 (2020)
25. Guy, C.: Sustainable transport choices in consumer shopping: a review of the UK evidence. Int. J. Consum. Stud. **33**(6), 652–658 (2009)
26. Jiao, J., Moudon, A.V., Drewnowski, A.: Grocery shopping: how individuals and built environments influence choice of travel mode. Transp. Res. Rec. **2230**(1), 85–95 (2011)
27. Buldeo Rai, H., Mommens, K., Verlinde, S., Macharis, C.: How does consumers' omnichannel shopping behaviour translate into travel and transport impacts? Case-study of a footwear retailer in Belgium. Sustainability **11**(9), 2534 (2019)
28. Cairns, S.: Delivering supermarket shopping: more or less traffic? Transp. Rev. **25**(1), 51–84 (2005)
29. Cullinane, S.: From bricks to clicks: the impact of online retailing on transport and the environment. Transp. Rev. **29**(6), 759–776 (2009)
30. Van Loon, P., Deketele, L., Dewaele, J., McKinnon, A., Rutherford, C.: A comparative analysis of carbon emissions from online retailing of fast moving consumer goods. J. Clean. Prod. **106**, 478–486 (2015). https://doi.org/10.1016/j.jclepro.2014.06.060
31. Zhang, M., Chen, Y., Shen, Y.: Environmental & analytical toxicology china's environmental threats of internet shopping packaging wastes. J. Environ. Anal. Toxicol. **6**(5), 1–5 (2016)
32. Coelho, P.M., Corona, B., ten Klooster, R., Worrell, E.: Sustainability of reusable packaging–current situation and trends. Resour. Conserv. Recycl.: X **6**, 100037 (2020)

33. Mangiaracina, R., Marchet, G., Perotti, S., Tumino, A.: A review of the environmental implications of B2C e-commerce: a logistics perspective. Int. J. Phys. Distrib. Logist. Manage. **45**(6) (2015). https://doi.org/10.1108/IJPDLM-06-2014-0133

34. Velazquez, R., Chankov, S. M.: Environmental impact of last mile deliveries and returns in fashion E-commerce: a cross-case analysis of six retailers. In: IEEE International Conference on Industrial Engineering and Engineering Management (2019). https://doi.org/10.1109/IEEM44572.2019.8978705

35. Siragusa, C., Tumino, A.: E-grocery: comparing the environmental impacts of the online and offline purchasing processes. Int. J. Logist. Res. Appl. (2021). https://doi.org/10.1080/13675567.2021.1892041

36. Prasertwit, T., Kanchanasuntorn, K.: Preliminary study of environmental impact related to E-commerce activities in Thailand. In: E3S Web of Conferences, vol. 259, p. 03004. EDP Sciences (2021). https://doi.org/10.1051/e3sconf/202125903004

37. Sippel, M.: Students as sustainability avant-garde? An analysis of student carbon footprints at the university of applied science in Konstanz, Germany. An Analysis of Student Carbon Footprints at the University of Applied Science in Konstanz, Germany, 10 February 2017 (2017)

38. Kranke, A., Schmied, M., Schön, A.D.J.D.: Formeln, Standards. Verlag Heinrich Vogel: CO2-Berechnung in der Logistik, München (2011)

39. Fang, D., Chen, B.: Information-based ecological network analysis for carbon emissions. Appl. Energy **238**, 45–53 (2019). https://doi.org/10.1016/j.apenergy.2019.01.066

40. Vinculum. Top E-Commerce Sites in Malaysia 2022 (2022). https://www.vinculumgroup.com/top-e-commerce-sites-in-malaysia-2022/

41. Eisenhardt, K.M.: Building theories from case study research. Acad. Manage. Rev. **14**(4), 532–550 (1989)

Designing an Expert System for Personal Financial Management

Brandon Chua Choon Kit and Nor Farzana Abd Ghani[(✉)]

School of Computing, Universiti Utara Malaysia, Sintok, 06010 Bukit Kayu Hitam, Kedah,
Malaysia
farzana@uum.edu.my

Abstract. The significance of financial planning in individuals' lives cannot be understated. People are transitioning from traditionally paper-based or tangible methods of tracking their finances to more digital-based approaches. However, recent studies indicate that the study on personal financial management systems is limited, and the traditional software did not meet the users' needs. The current software lacks the ability to offer practical recommendations to users and direct them towards achieving their financial objectives. This study aims to design a personal financial management software that implements artificial intelligence techniques. A rule-based expert system technique was adopted to provide practical recommendations and support users in achieving their financial goals. Besides that, a prototype of the proposed system will be developed and evaluated by domain experts using a user perception survey. The results reveal that the respondents are satisfied with the design of the proposed system. The outcome of this study could provide practical recommendations that users can use to make informed financial decisions and accomplish their financial objectives.

Keywords: Personal Financial Planning · Artificial Intelligence · Expert System

1 Introduction

The application of digital technology in the financial market and internet connectivity has become pervasive in this digitised world, increasing the opportunity for people to interact and access the digital effusion of financial data. Indeed, there have been various types of electronic payment, online banking mobile applications, web pages, and other online financial services available to users in the past few years. Therefore, managing and analysing digital financial data has become increasingly complicated.

In this age of globalisation, the quality of goods and services is constantly improving. To survive in this expanding and crowded market, the sales and marketing team employed a variety of techniques to imbue their branding and product image in the minds of their consumers. This shortens the time for the consumer to consider the importance of their product. However, consumers' awareness of their own personal finance is decreasing at the same time. According to Priantinah et al. [1], personal financial management can be defined as understanding and acquiring financial information to plan and generate

N. H. Zakaria et al. (Eds.): ICOCI 2023, CCIS 2002, pp. 244–257, 2024.
https://doi.org/10.1007/978-981-99-9592-9_19

assets. It is an essential skill that needs to be learned and practised because it enables people to achieve their life goals.

While managing personal finances is important, only some have the knowledge or capability to do this. Besides, even the most economically astute person can become confused or short-sighted. Munohsamy [2] explains the significance of personal financial management, stating that it allows for a higher standard of living, which leads to better health and less financial stress. Muske & Winter [3] also mention that long-term financial security is seen to be possible with good personal financial management. However, they discovered that only a few individuals applied the suggested personal money management strategies.

Technology-related tools are believed to make personal financial management easier in daily life. People now, especially the younger generation, are expected to be able to adapt to technology in managing their finances. According to Hokin [4] spending without limits and goals is the biggest problem in personal finance. This issue may be solved when someone specifies their purpose with supporting tools that are able to manage their own personal finance. Therefore, when developing a personal financial management application for the users to support money management and decision making, it is critical to understand what they want to do so that these applications meet their needs and expectations rather than imagined ones.

This research aims to (i) determine the requirements of the prototype for a rule-based personal financial management expert system, (ii) construct a prototype for a rule-based personal financial management expert system. (iii) evaluate the rule-based personal financial management expert system prototype.

2 Problem Statement

Personal finance can help people better understand where money is spent and where it comes from. The user can draw conclusions based on this information and make better decisions for better financial capability. Moreover, it is important for an individual to understand that planning and budgeting can help avoid problems, such as overspending and budget gaps, especially for those with debt or loans. Next, the requirements for personal financial control keep increasing, and it is impossible for everyone to keep a lot of information in mind simultaneously.

The main problem with personal finance is that people spend without knowing their limits and without having a plan. Therefore, many people start analysing their expenditures and budget. Unfortunately, there are some people who lack the time and information to deal with this. According to Vasyliuk & Basyuk [5], people sometimes only know the approximate value of their expenditure. However, the real statistics of the financial data are different from this figure. Vahidov & He [6] also highlight concerning trends in the personal finance domain that researchers have overlooked. Therefore, there is a need for a system that can help users keep track of and manage their financial data.

However, the current study on the personal financial management system is still limited, especially in the requirement model for a personal financial management system. According to Lewis & Perry [7], the study on how users track their financial transaction every day is very limited, and little is known about how users keep track of their daily financial activities. Although some existing commercial software, such as Manilla, Quicken and FinanceWorks, currently supports personal financial management, they found out that most of the software was not used by users due to a mismatch with the needs, security, and inconvenience. They also show that the fulfilment of the users' needs and requirements are the keys to successful personal financial management software. Moreover, the current commercial application requires in-app purchases and a high monthly subscription to function properly which is not affordable for most users [8].

In addition, Xie [9] found that most traditional software consists of meaningless operations and redundant functions. They suggest that personal financial management software users should focus on the data rather than spend energy and time to understand the complex user interface. This is supported by Kozhevnikov et al. [10], which mention that most of the current popular personal financial management applications have been created for a long time with outdated technology, inflexible user interfaces and a lack of important features. They also mention there is a need to identify the requirement or design for creating a next generation personal financial management information system. Apart from that, the current personal finance application lacks the capability to provide users with actionable advice [11]. As a result, the application cannot guide users towards achieving financial stability. Considering that most users make purchase decisions based on unconscious factors is crucial.

ABased on the literature reviewed above, further research is still needed, particularly in designing an effective personal financial management system. To address this gap, this study proposes a new design for a personal financial management system that leverages AI capabilities to offer practical recommendations and support users in making informed decisions to achieve their financial goals.

3   Related Work

According to Nafed [12], expert systems are classified as one of the most significant areas of artificial intelligence. It can be considered an artificial intelligence technique [13]. An expert system is an intelligent computer program that utilizes knowledge and inference techniques to address complex problems that typically require consultation with domain experts. In the same context, Jackson [14] defined an expert system as a software application that utilises knowledge and reasoning of a specialised subject matter to solve problems or provide advice. Giarratano & Riley [15] suggest that an expert system consists of two distinct components: an inference engine and a knowledge base. Moreover, Holsapple et al. [16] suggested the application of an expert system in financial management, including portfolio analysis, credit analysis, insurance, and security trading.

In this study, a comparison and analysis will be conducted among three popular personal financial management applications, namely Money Manager, Dollarbird, and Goodbudget. Additionally, the important requirements of this application will be identified and elicited. Table 1 shows the results of the comparative analysis based on observations.

Table 1. Results of Comparative Analysis

Features	Money Manager	Goodbudget	Dollarbird	Proposed System
Able to add, delete and modify transaction	/	/	/	/
Able to track past transaction	/	/	/	/
Allows for customisable date ranges when visualising graphs	/	/	×	/
Able to set budget or financial goals	/	/	×	/
Allows for accessing spending patterns and generating alerts	×	×	×	/
Revising budget and providing actionable recommendation	×	×	×	/

Based on the findings presented in Table 1, this study reveals that the selected popular personal finance management application could store and visualise the daily transaction of the users. However, these applications cannot revise the budget and provide actionable advice to users. As a result, this study reaches a similar conclusion to the study conducted by Althnian [11], which mentioned that these applications lack the ability to lead users to financial wellness. The common features of these applications such as adding, modifying, and visualising transaction will be gathered, analysed, and transformed into the requirements of the proposed system.

In summary, expert systems can be used in a wide area of application, especially in financial management. The main reason is that it can be used to solve problems related to control, simulation, selection, design, prescription, diagnosis, planning, prediction, monitoring, and others [12]. The proposed system will focus on the area of personal financial planning due to the limited study in that domain. Personal finance management is an important domain researcher always overlook [6]. Apart from that, the problem-solving paradigm of the proposed expert system will be planning.

4 Methodology

The research methodology used in a study is determined by the research objectives and the consideration by the researcher [17]. The mixed research approach, incorporating both qualitative and quantitative methods, will be employed in this study for data collection and analysis. The requirements will first be obtained through qualitative means such as observation and document analysis, followed by the creation of a prototype to demonstrate these requirements. The validity of the design will then be evaluated quantitatively. The study will adhere to the Design Science Research in Information Systems framework proposed by Vaishnavi & Kuechler [18], a widely adopted approach in various fields including computer science and engineering, as depicted in the accompanying Fig. 1.

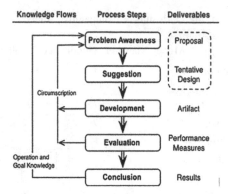

Fig. 1. Design Science Research (Vaishnavi & Kuechler, 2004)

The process of this study begins with identifying and defining a specific problem or opportunity in the field of information systems. The requirements and knowledge necessary for the proposed expert system prototype will also be identified, acquired, and stored in the decision table as a production rule in the knowledge base during this stage. Next, the context diagram, flow chart, and data flow diagrams will be employed to represent the requirements and develop a tentative design of the new system. This will be followed by developing a prototype that represents a portion of the system. Once the prototype is complete, the system will be evaluated by domain experts, which consist of one personal financial advisor, one credit analyst from the financial institutions and one educator with a strong background in finance using a survey questionnaire. The evaluation results will be tabulated and analysed using the arithmetic mean (M) and sample standard deviation (SD).

In summary, objective (i) will be achieved during the suggestion phase, where suggestions and designs for the development of the system will be made. Objective (ii) will be achieved during the development phase, where the prototype system will be built based on the suggestions. Finally, objective (iii) will be achieved during the evaluation stage, where the system will be evaluated to determine its accuracy and validity.

5 Discussion

The proposed system's prototype has been successfully developed to showcase its design and give users an idea of how the system will operate. To ensure that reviewers can clearly understand the design of the system, a medium-fidelity prototype will be used to illustrate the system. A medium-fidelity prototype falls between low and high-fidelity prototypes. It allows users to interact with limited functionality, is cheap to develop, and provides a clear overview of the system design to the users. The prototype was created using the Python programming language, with an SQLite database, and a Tkinter interface. Figure 2 shows the context diagram of the proposed system.

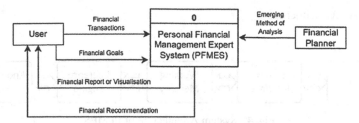

Fig. 2. Context Diagram of PFMES

The user will input their financial transactions and financial goals to the system. The system will track and analyse their financial transactions. The system will also produce a financial report and visualise it through various graphs. The system will give the student recommendations based on the analysis and financial report results. Additionally, the financial planner can update some emerging financial analysis methods to the system in the future.

5.1 System Module

The system consists of three modules: tracking module, analysis module and recommendation module, as shown in Fig. 3.

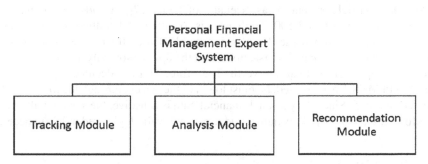

Fig. 3. System Module of PFMES

First, the tracking module tracks and stores users' financial activity, enabling them to enter and view transactions over a customized period. In addition, it helps users become aware of how much they earn and spend over a specific period. Next, the analysis module aims to help users understand their financial behaviours by providing analysis and insights into their finances. It allows users to categorise and visualise their financial transactions through various types of charts. Lastly, the recommendation module is the core of the proposed system. It is designed to give users practical advice by analysing their financial data and offering customised recommendations using the rule sets stored in the knowledge base. It consists of two sub-modules: savings advice and spending advice.

5.2   System Architecture

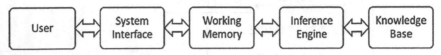

Fig. 4. System Architecture of PFMES

Figure 4 shows the four main components of the proposed expert system: system interface, working memory, inference engine, and knowledge base. The working memory stores relevant facts and intermediate results required for operating the system's rules. It holds all the information necessary to solve problems and make logical inferences based on the rules or knowledge stored in the knowledge base. The inference engine produces the consultation outcome by using the facts in the working memory and domain knowledge base to derive new information. It analyses the facts to come up with a solution. The knowledge base is a crucial component of the expert system, containing a set of rules and facts needed for problem-solving or generating solutions. For this study, the knowledge is extracted from previous research and stored as production rules in a decision table [11]. Finally, the interface is a graphical component that allows users to interact with the system by inputting data and viewing important information.

To demonstrate the capabilities of the personal financial management expert system (PFMES), this article presents a case scenario of Tim, a 27-year-old civil engineer with a monthly income of RM 3,500. Tim's goal is to save RM 1 million for retirement at age 55, but he's unsure whether his plan is feasible. Currently, he's using a traditional method to record his financial transactions, and the application only allows him to view a summary report of his total net worth. Therefore, Tim has decided to switch to the proposed PFMES. To get started, he must log in to the system through the login interface depicted in Fig. 5. Since the personal financial data is sensitive, the system will encrypt the information and only allow authorised users with valid login credentials to access it.

Fig. 5. Login Page of PFMES

After logged in, Tim can set his desired savings amount and timeline, as illustrated in Fig. 6. He aims to save RM 1 million by the time he reaches 55 years old, which will be in 28 years or 336 months (28 years x 12).

Fig. 6. Goal Setting Page of PFMES

Once Tim has set his savings target, the system enables him to record or modify his financial transactions by displaying the income record screen from the tracking module, as shown in Fig. 7. He can easily switch to other screens by clicking on the navigation buttons located at the top of the screen.

Fig. 7. Record Income Page of PFMES

After Tim records his financial transactions, the system enables him to sort and visualise his financial data using various charts through the analysis module. As an example, Fig. 8 shows the pie chart of Tim's expenditure categories in 2023.

Figure 9 displays the visualisation of Tim's expenditures using a bar chart for the year 2022. Additionally, the system will calculate the average expenditure for each transaction.

Furthermore, the analysis module of the system will summarise Tim's financial data and enable him to view his personal financial report, as illustrated in Fig. 10.

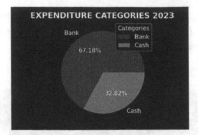

Fig. 8. Pie Chart of PFMES

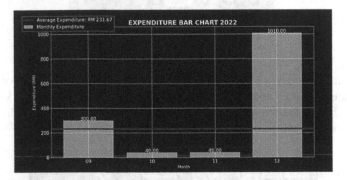

Fig. 9. Bar Chart of PFMES

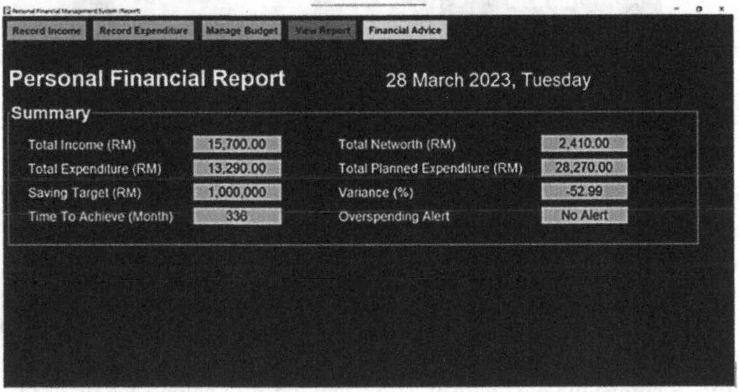

Fig. 10. View Report Page of PFMES

Finally, Tim can seek advice from the system to help him make informed decisions about his finances, as shown in Fig. 11. The system informs Tim that his current saving goals are not feasible and suggests that he increase the duration to 415 months. Alternatively, it recommends that he save up to RM809,759 over the course of 55 years based on his current spending habits. Additionally, Tim's variance is desirable because his actual expenditure is lower than his planned expenditure, and he has no overspending alerts. In addition, Tim can ask the system whether he should purchase a new gaming laptop for entertainment that costs RM2,200, despite not really needing it. After analysing Tim's current financial situation, the system advises against the purchase, explaining that it is not worth the expense.

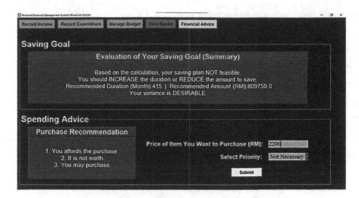

Fig. 11. Financial Advice Page of PFMES

6   Results

In this section, the evaluation of the developed prototype is discussed. The assessment was conducted after the prototype was created to determine the system's accuracy and validity. The evaluation will be conducted by three domain experts ($N = 3$) with a strong finance background using a survey questionnaire. Moreover, they are also existing user of the current personal finance application. This study will adapt the extension of TAM proposed by Tella & Olasina [19] in the questionnaire and used to evaluate the system.

The survey questions were assessed using a Likert scale that spanned from 1 to 5, where 1 corresponded to a strong disagreement and 5 indicated a strong agreement. Every participant was given a brief description of the system's functionalities along with a demonstration of the prototype. Furthermore, they were given the opportunity to ask questions and interact with the prototype before completing the questionnaire to provide their perceptions. The findings of the evaluation, specifically on the Perceived Usefulness aspect, are presented in Table 2.

Based on the result, the respondents think that the system would help them achieve their financial goals ($M = 4.33$ and $SD = 0.58$) and implement their financial plan ($M = 4.33$ and $SD = 0.58$). They also think the prototype would be useful for managing their finances ($M = 3.67$ and $SD = 1.15$). Next, the system would help them to follow their budget ($M = 4.33$ and $SD = 0.58$) and improve their financial performance ($M = 4.00$ and $SD = 1.00$). Finally, the system would enhance their effectiveness in managing finance ($M = 3.67$ and $SD = 1.53$).

Based on Table 3, the respondents think the system is easy to use ($M = 3.67$ and $SD = 0.58$) and can use the system without written instruction ($M = 4.00$ and $SD =$

Table 2. Evaluation on Perceived Usefulness

Questions	Mean (M)	Standard Deviation (SD)
Using the system would help me to achieve my financial goals	4.33	0.58
Using the system would help me implement my financial plan	4.33	0.58
The system would be useful for managing my personal finance	3.67	1.15
The system would help me follow my budget	4.33	0.58
The system would help me improve my personal financial performance	4.00	1.00
The system would enhance my effectiveness in managing my personal finance	3.67	1.53

Table 3. Perceived Ease of Use

Questions	Mean (M)	Standard Deviation (SD)
The system is easy to use	3.67	0.58
I can use the system without written instruction	4.00	1.00
My interaction with the system is clear and straightforward	4.33	0.58
Using the system requires little mental effort	3.33	1.15
I did not notice any inconsistencies when I use the system	3.00	1.73
I can use the system successfully every time	4.00	0.00

1.00). They also agree that their interaction with the system is clear and straightforward (M = 4.33 and SD = 0.58) and using the system requires little mental effort (M = 3.33 and SD = 1.15). However, respondents expressed uncertainty about the consistency of the prototype (M = 3.00 and SD = 1.73). Finally, they can use the system successfully every time (M = 4.00 and SD = 0.00).

Based on Table 4, the respondents think that the system saves time and effort (M = 4.00 and SD = 1.00). Next, they agree that the system can help them understand their spending habits and make more informed financial decisions (M = 4.67 and SD = 0.58). Finally, the respondents think that receiving advice through the system has been a pleasant experience (M = 4.00 and SD = 1.00).

Based on Table 5, the respondents would like the system to be adopted daily (M = 4.33 and SD = 0.58). Next, they agree that the system is appealing (M = 3.67and SD = 1.15). Finally, they think replacing traditional financial management methods with the proposed system is a welcome idea (M = 4.33 and SD = 0.58).

Table 4. Perceived Benefits

Questions	Mean (M)	Standard Deviation (SD)
The system saves time and effort	4.00	1.00
The system can help me understand my spending habits and make more informed financial decisions	4.67	0.58
Receiving advice through the system has been a pleasant experience	4.00	1.00

Table 5. Evaluation on Attitude Towards Use

Questions	Mean (M)	Standard Deviation (SD)
I like the system being adopted in daily life	4.33	0.58
The system is appealing	3.67	1.15
Replacing traditional financial management methods with the proposed system is a welcome idea	4.33	0.58

Table 6. Evaluation on Perceived Satisfaction

Questions	Mean (M)	Standard Deviation (SD)
I'm satisfied with the guidance provided by the system	4.00	1.00
I'm satisfied with the feedback provided by the system	4.33	0.58
I'm satisfied with the proposed system to be used in the future	4.00	1.00

Based on Table 6, the respondents are satisfied with the guidance provided by the system (M = 4.00 and SD = 1.00). Next, they were also satisfied with the feedback provided by the system (M = 4.33 and SD = 0.58). Finally, they are satisfied with the proposed system to be used in the future (M = 4.00 and SD = 1.00).

Table 7. Evaluation on Actual Use

Questions	Mean (M)	Standard Deviation (SD)
I received a spending alert from the system	4.33	0.58
I will use the proposed system every day	4.33	0.58
The system would come to stay as a tool for managing financial transactions and budgeting	4.33	0.58

Based on Table 7, the respondents received the spending alert from the system (M = 4.33 and SD = 0.58). Next, they agree that they will use the system every day (M = 4.33 and SD = 0.58). Finally, the system would come to stay as a tool for man-aging financial transactions and budgeting (M = 4.33 and SD = 0.58).

Table 8. Evaluation on System Continuance Intention

Questions	Mean (M)	Standard Deviation (SD)
I expect that, the use of the proposed system should continue	4.67	0.58
No matter what, I will support continued usage of the proposed system	4.00	1.00
I plan on using the proposed system on a regular basis in the future	4.00	1.00

Based on Table 8, the respondent expects the proposed system's use should continue (M = 4.67 and SD = 0.58). Next, the respondent will also support the continued usage of the proposed system (M = 4.00 and SD = 1.00). Finally, the respondent plan to use the proposed system on a regular basis in the future (M = 4.00 and SD = 1.00).

7 Conclusion

This study proposes a design for a personal financial management system that utilises rule-based expert system techniques from artificial intelligence to help users achieve their financial goals by providing practical recommendations. This study's initial step involved identifying the requirements for the proposed system. Subsequently, a prototype was developed to illustrate the system design. Three domain experts will further evaluate the system design to ensure its validity and accuracy. The respondents are satisfied with it. The system offers an enhancement compared to current systems because it can offer insightful financial recommendations to users using the rulesets stored in the knowledge base. In addition, the guidance provided by the system can assist users in improving their financial planning skills and performance. This study can also serve as a reference for other researchers who aim to build similar systems in the future and provides insight into the key features that should be incorporated to enhance the long-term success of such software systems.

However, the scope of the current system is limited to the financial planning aspect of personal finance. In the future, there is potential for the system to expand to include other areas such as insurance, investment, banking, and taxes. Additionally, the system prototype is only built for desktop usage, but the future system can cover other platforms and utilize the latest technologies, such as web and mobile versions. Furthermore, the present system only covers rulesets for saving and spending advice. The system can be expanded to include more advanced rulesets for financial planning or forecasting techniques in the knowledge base. This can involve more areas of expertise from domain experts.

Additionally, the current system is only evaluated by domain experts, but the future system can involve existing users and cover a larger number of samples. Finally, the current study only utilises rule-based expert system techniques from artificial intelligence. Nevertheless, the future system can include other techniques such as machine learning, deep learning, and natural language processing.

References

1. Priantinah, D., Aisyah, M.N., Nurim, Y.: The analysis of technology acceptance model (TAM) for personal financial management on mobile application technology, vol. 86, pp. 262–266 (2019). https://doi.org/10.2991/icobame-18.2019.56
2. Munohsamy, T.: Thulasimani munohsamy institut teknologi brunei synopsis. Pers. Financ. Manag. 1–14 (2015)
3. Muske, G., Winter, M.: Personal financial management education: an alternative paradigm. J. Financ. Couns. Plan. **15**, 79–88 (2004)
4. Hokin, B.: Personal Finance problems. https://www.streetdirectory.com/travel_guide/166 363/finance/personal_finance_problems.htm
5. Vasyliuk, A., Basyuk, T.: Peculiarities of building a personal finance management system. In: CEUR Workshop Proceedings, vol. 3171, pp. 1520–1530 (2022)
6. Vahidov, R., He, X.: Situated DSS for personal finance management: design and evaluation. Inf. Manag. **46**, 453–462 (2009). https://doi.org/10.1016/j.im.2009.06.007
7. Lewis, M., Perry, M.: Follow the money: Managing personal finance digitally. Conf. Hum. Factors Comput. Syst. - Proc. 1–14 (2019). https://doi.org/10.1145/3290605.3300620
8. Huy, B.: Android Application for Students' Personal Finances (2020)
9. Xie, Y.: The design and implementation of personal finance management system based on android. In: Proceedings of the 2015 5th International Conference on Computer Sciences and Automation Engineering, vol. 42, pp. 633–636 (2016). https://doi.org/10.2991/iccsae-15.201 6.118
10. Kozhevnikov, V.A., Slupko, N.M., Sergeev, A.V.: Design and development of personal finance management system. ISJ Theor. Appl. Sci. **6**, 110–115 (2019). https://doi.org/10.15863/TAS
11. Althnian, A.: Design of a rule-based personal finance management system based on financial well-being. Int. J. Adv. Comput. Sci. Appl. **12**, 182–187 (2021). https://doi.org/10.14569/IJA CSA.2021.0120122
12. Himeda, H., Nafed, M.: Web based expert system for i-faraid web based expert system for i-Faraid (2009)
13. Khalid Al-Bakoaa, A.R., Hasoon, S.O.: Design Expert system for auditing financial accounts. Tech. Bus. Manag. **2**, 45–53 (2022). https://doi.org/10.47577/business.v2i1.6141
14. Jackson, P.: Introduction to expert systems (1986)
15. Riley, G., Joseph, C.G.: Expert systems: principles and programming. Thomson Course Technol. (2005)
16. Holsapple, C.W., Tam, K.Y., Andrew, B.W.: Adapting expert system technology to financial management. Financ. Manag. 12–22 (1988)
17. Abdullahi, H.: Requirement model of school management system for adult, pp. 8–9 (2011)
18. Vaishnavi, V., Kuechler, B.: Design science research in information systems. Assoc. Inf. Syst. (2004)
19. Tella, A., Olasina, G.: Predicting users' continuance intention toward e-payment system: an extension of the technology acceptance model. Int. J. Inf. Syst. Soc. Chang. **5**, 47–67 (2014)

Improving Rice Yield Prediction Accuracy Using Regression Models with Climate Data

Mohamad Farhan Mohamad Mohsin[1]([✉]) [iD], Muhammad Khalifa Umana[1] [iD],
Mohamad Ghozali Hassan[2] [iD], Kamal Imran Mohd Sharif[2] [iD], Mohd Azril Ismail[2] [iD],
Khazainani Salleh[3] [iD], Suhaili Mohd Zahari[3] [iD], Mimi Adilla Sarmani[3] [iD],
and Neil Gordon[4] [iD]

[1] School of Computing, Universiti Utara Malaysia, 06010 Sintok, Kedah, Malaysia
farhan@uum.edu.my
[2] School of Technology Management and Logistics, Universiti Utara Malaysia, 06010 Sintok,
Kedah, Malaysia
[3] National Climate Center, Malaysian Meteorological Department, 46667 Petaling Jaya,
Selangor Darul Ehsan, Malaysia
[4] Computer Science, University of Hull, Hull, UK

Abstract. Rice production is critical to food security, and accurate yield predictions are required for planning and decision-making. However, precisely predicting rice yields using machine learning models can be difficult due to the complicated interactions of various factors, such as how climate affects rice production. This study sought to solve this rice production is critical to food security, and accurate yield predictions are required for planning and decision-making. However, accurately predicting rice yields using machine learning models can be difficult due to the complicated interactions of various factors, such as how climate affects rice production. This study aims to address this issue by investigating how climate data affect Malaysian rice yield prediction models. The study used a linear regression model trained on rice production data and compared its performance with models incorporating climate data. Both datasets covered the period from 2010 to 2021 in Malaysia. The study found that including climate data significantly improved the prediction accuracy, with an approximately 77% improvement in MAE and 69% in RMSE. The results suggest that incorporating climate data into yield prediction models is essential for accurate and reliable predictions. These findings have important implications for stakeholders in the agricultural industry who can use accurate yield predictions to make informed decisions. However, the study's limitations include using a single predictive model and data from a single country, suggesting the need for future studies to explore other machine learning algorithms and expand the scope of the research to other regions. Overall, this study contributes to the growing body of literature on the impact of climate data on yield prediction models and highlights the importance of considering climate data in agricultural decision-making.

Keywords: Rice production · Climate data · Machine learning · Crop yield prediction · Linear regression

© The Author(s), under exclusive license to Springer Nature Singapore Pte Ltd. 2024
N. H. Zakaria et al. (Eds.): ICOCI 2023, CCIS 2002, pp. 258–267, 2024.
https://doi.org/10.1007/978-981-99-9592-9_20

1 Introduction

Rice is a staple food for many people worldwide, including Malaysians. Meeting domestic rice demand is difficult because of distracting variables such as rising population, changes in land use, soil quality, weather patterns, plantation diseases, and restricted access to innovation, technologies, and resources [2, 3]. A reliable system for forecasting future rice yield is required to achieve food security. However, because of the variability of the factors influencing rice output, developing a one-size-fits-all forecasting model is difficult. Moreover, the conventional practice often relies on historical data and expert recommendations and may not consider all factors influencing rice production in forecasting rice yields [17].

To overcome these challenges, machine learning approaches appear as recent alternatives to build prediction models for crop yields. It has a wider ability to capture complex relationships between various characteristics and may incorporate massive amounts of data, such as climate data. However, further study is needed in Malaysia on the utility of integrating weather-related information into machine learning models for rice crop prediction. In recent years, there has been a rise in interest in using machine learning approaches to create prediction models for crop output [2–4] and examine the influence of climate on agricultural productivity. Due to the continuous interaction of various variables impacting rice production, predicting rice yields using machine learning models can be challenging.

Climate is one of the impacting factors in agriculture, including rice. A previous study has revealed that climatic conditions influence rice production in Malaysia [2, 3]. However, it is unclear how much climatic data can increase the accuracy of rice crop estimates in Malaysia. This study investigates the effectiveness of including climate data in predicting rice production in Malaysia using linear regression. Our hypothesis was that including climate data in the prediction model could increase the accuracy of rice yield estimation in Malaysia, as climate is crucial to rice production. This study aims to provide insights into the possible benefits of integrating climate data for rice production prediction in Malaysia by including it in a regression model. In relation to this, the yearly rice yield information, as well as season indicators for the main and secondary plantation seasons of 10 years from states in Malaysia, were employed in the modeling. In addition, climatic data as predictors such as wind speed, temperature, humidity, and rainfall were also included in the model.

This study is organized as follows: a complete overview of related studies, methodology, findings, and a discussion of the research's significance for agricultural practices and future research in Malaysia. The study is expected to contribute to the growing body of literature on the impact of climate change on agriculture in Malaysia, as well as give important insights for policymakers and farmers in this country.

2 Related Work

Agriculture plays a crucial role in many countries, providing food and employment opportunities for millions of people. Accurate crop yield prediction is essential for farmers, policymakers, and other stakeholders because it can drive agricultural production, distribution, and pricing decisions. Traditional approaches to yield prediction have relied on statistical models and expert knowledge. However, recent advances in machine learning and data science have led to the development of more accurate predictive models for crop yields [5].

Rice yield prediction models can be modeled based on three approaches that are mechanistic, statistical/machine learning, and deep learning-based [19]. Regression modeling is a popular technique under statistical machine learning models for developing predictive models in agriculture. Regression models aim to establish a relationship between a dependent variable (in this case, crop yield) and one or more independent variables (such as climate data, soil quality, and agricultural practices). Regression models can be simple or complex, depending on the number and type of independent variables used. The quality of the data and the correlation among the variables used to generate the model might have an impact on regression performance. [6].

There has been growing interest in using regression models to predict crop yields with climate data recently. Climate factors such as temperature, humidity, rainfall, and wind speed are essential predictors of crop yields in many regions [7]. By incorporating climate data into regression models, researchers have developed more accurate and reliable predictions of crop yields [2, 3]. [18] replicated factors influencing rice production by combining typical independent variables such as temperature, precipitation, sunlight hours, and relative humidity to develop a deep learning-based rice yield forecast model. Other rice yield prediction models based on deep learning can be seen in [19].

In Malaysia, machine learning in combination with climatic data has proved very useful for predicting rice yields. As a staple crop, thus forecasting rice harvests is critical for guaranteeing food security and economic stability [1]. In Malaysia, researchers discovered that adding climate data into regression models may greatly increase the accuracy of rice yield predictions [2, 3]. Because climate involves many types of predictors, an experiment using a different climate predictor may yield a different result. This study emphasizes the need of using climate variables when developing forecast models for rice yields in Malaysia.

To summaries, regression modeling and the integration of climate information are important input for predicting crop yields in agriculture. Regression models may be used to create correlations between dependent and independent variables, and using climate data as an independent variable can enhance forecast accuracy. In the context of rice production prediction in Malaysia, adding climate data has shown to be a significant method for boosting forecast accuracy and guaranteeing food security in the country.

3 Methodology

This study's methodology section focuses on predicting rice yields in Malaysia using regression modelling techniques, with a particular emphasis on the role of climate data in this process. We employed a series of steps to achieve this, including data collection and analysis, data preparation, and regression modelling. Figure 1 provides a flowchart of these steps and their interconnectedness in the overall process.

Fig. 1. Flowchart of the steps involved in predicting rice yields using regression modelling and climate data in Malaysia

3.1 Data Collection and Analysis

There are two types of datasets used in this study; firstly, the climate dataset and secondly, rice production data. Both datasets were contributed by different agencies and were merged for mining.

The Malaysian Meteorological Department took the climate data used in this study. It consists of four numerical variables: wind speed, temperature, humidity, and rainfall. These data were collected from 2010 to 2021 for each month and are available for all states in Malaysia. These variables are essential in the study of agriculture as they affect plant growth and development, particularly in the case of rice. The suitability of these data for the study of agriculture has been shown in previous studies [2, 3].

The Department of Statistics Malaysia provided the rice production data. This dataset was explained by three numerical variables that are rice yield, parcel area, and planted area. In addition, the data includes categorical variables such as the state of Malaysia, year, and season indicators. The rice yield data are reported annually for each state in Malaysia, with a range of values from 1.48 to 6.56 tons per hectare between 2011 and 2021. The parcel area represents the land used for rice cultivation, while the planted area represents the area where the rice crop is planted. These variables are necessary for prediction because they represent information on the quantity of land utilized for rice cultivation, which directly impacts yield. Adding categorical variables, including state, year, and season indicators, allows for examining how these variables impact the rice production forecast.

3.2 Data Preparation

The data preparation stage is an important phase in data analytic studies since it includes transforming the raw data into a suitable format for mining. Several types of data preparation approaches were employed in this work to ensure the quality and accuracy of the data used in constructing the prediction model using regression. The data preparation has six tasks that involve missing data imputation, data transformation, data combining/merging, data scaling, one hot encoding, and data splitting. The flowchart in Fig. 2 depicts the order of these processes and how they are linked in the entire data preparation process.

The first task in data preprocessing is to solve the missing value problem. This problem is a common issue when using climate data for regression. Several reasons contribute to missing data, such as equipment failure or human error. Imputation is often used to fill in missing data to ensure the models are as accurate as possible. To estimate the missing value, a common imputation approach is to use the average value of the same month in the year before and after, as shown in Eq. (1). This solution can produce more accurate imputations than the overall average of accessible data [8–10].

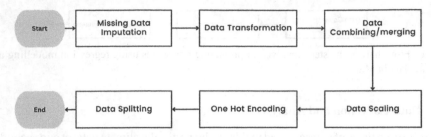

Fig. 2. Data preparation process for rice yields prediction system

While there are various ways of imputation, such as interpolation or machine learning algorithms, utilizing the average of the same month in the previous and subsequent years is a straightforward and effective strategy that may be used in several circumstances.

$$Climate_y = \frac{Climate_{y-1} + Climate_{y+1}}{2} \tag{1}$$

Another imputation method that can be used to replace mining values is by taking the average of the previous and next month's data or values from the same month in the previous and succeeding years also can be used as an imputation method. It is shown in Eq. (2). This approach has the advantage of identifying inter-monthly variability in weather patterns and can reduce the impact of seasonal trends. Although it provides precise and detailed missing value estimation, it relies on more data and calculations [11]. The study used the first approach as the imputation method.

$$Climate_m = \frac{Climate_{m-1} + Climate_{m+1}}{2} \tag{2}$$

The dataset was transferred into a yearly-based form to reduce the impact of outliers and obtain a more stable representation of the climate variables for each year. The transformed value is taken from the median of each year because the median is more robust to outliers. Aggregating monthly data into yearly data for climate variables has been widely implemented in agriculture-related research [12–14]. Each climatic variable was transformed separately. At the end of the process, four additional variables were constructed each year, indicating the median wind speed, temperature, humidity, and rainfall.

The climate data combines the production data using the states and year properties. Each state and year combination from the production data is merged with the corresponding climate data using the same properties. This process ensures that the climate data is aligned with the correct production data and can be used to accurately train and evaluate the regression models. The combined dataset is then used as the input for the regression models, aiming to predict the rice yield based on the climate properties. This approach allows for a more comprehensive analysis of the factors affecting rice yield. Besides that, the outcome can potentially provide insights into how climate properties can be managed to improve yield.

One of the requirements for a regression model's performance is that the dataset be produced in a specified scaled format. Numerical features were normalized using the Scikit-learn library's MinMaxScaler [15]. Normalization is a standard data transformation technique that scales numerical data to a fixed range (often between 0 and 1) to guarantee that each feature is given equal weight during model training. Meanwhile, the values of categorical features were converted to binary representation using a one-hot encoding method with the Pandas and Scikit-learn libraries [15, 16]. Categorical variables are converted into binary vectors via one-hot encoding, with each category represented by its own binary feature. This method avoids the model assuming any ordinal link between the categories and ensures that each category is addressed independently during model training. The final step in data preparation for modeling is to divide the data into training and testing folds. This work separated the dataset into train and test sections in a 70:30 ratio.

3.3 Regression Modeling

The final step of the study is modelling. It involves the construction of a prediction model. This research employed multiple linear regression modelling to predict rice yield based on the provided data. For modeling, rice yield (state, year, season indicator, yield volume) and climate information wind speed, temperature, humidity, rainfall) were fed to a regression algorithm. Regression modelling aims to establish an association function between the dependent variable (yield volume) and the independent variables (climate data and rice yield information) and use these associations to produce accurate predictions. The model's performance was assessed using mean absolute error (MAE) and root mean squared error (RMSE). By comparing the performance of the two models, it is possible to learn that including climate data in the regression model enhances its predicted accuracy. Figure 3 depicts the rice yields prediction model for this study.

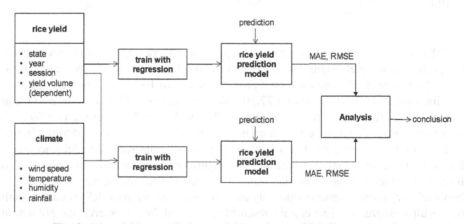

Fig. 3. Rice yields a prediction model based on multiple linear regression.

The improvement in prediction accuracy in a model can be quantified by comparing the model's error metrics before and after a modification or improvement is made. The Mean Absolute Error (MAE) and Root Mean Square Error (RMSE) are commonly used error metrics for regression models. The percentage improvement in these metrics can be calculated using the following Eq. (3).

$$improvement(\%) = \frac{(PreviousError - UpdatedError)}{PreviousError} 100\% \qquad (3)$$

4   Results

This section outlines the study's findings. The aim is to reveal the impact of climate data on rice yield prediction in Malaysia using machine learning models. The experiment was divided into two stages. In the first stage, model performance is evaluated using only production data. In the second stage, models trained on both production and climatic data are evaluated. The mean absolute error (MAE) and root mean squared error (RMSE) were computed on the test set during the experiment. Both evolution metrics measure the prediction model's accuracy in predicting future rice yield. Lower error rates indicate a better model. The findings offer insights into the potential advantages of using climate data in rice yield prediction models and help instruct policymakers and farmers on better crop management techniques in the face of climate change. Table 1 depicts the rice yield prediction result using regression analysis.

Table 1. Performance metrics for rice yield prediction model

Metrics	Production data only	Production and climate data	Improvements%
MAE	44612.60	10125.25	77.30
RMSE	58770.61	18059.56	69.27

The combination of climatic data in the prediction model enhanced the accuracy of the predicted rice yield significantly. The mean absolute error (MAE) decreased from 44,612.60 in the model that only used production data to 10,125.25 when climate data was incorporated. This represents a 77.30% decrease in MAE. Similarly, the root mean squared error (RMSE) decreased from 58,770.61 to 18,059.56, resulting in a 69.27% decrease in RMSE. These results demonstrate the importance of considering climate factors in predicting rice yield, as they can significantly improve the model's accuracy. From the regression analysis, it can draw insights into how climatic data are used to forecast rice yields in the Malaysian states of Johor and Pahang. Figure 4 demonstrates how including climate data considerably increased the regression model's accuracy, with the resulting regression line closely resembling the real data. However, the prediction without climatic data showed a significant offset from the actual data, with a difference of over 50,000. According to our study findings, climate factors like temperature and precipitation are critical in affecting rice yields in these states. Furthermore, our results demonstrate that the trend of rice production in Johor and Pahang is decreasing, albeit with varying degrees of decline. Specifically, the regression model for Johor predicts a decrease of approximately 14,000 metric tons of rice per year. In comparison, the

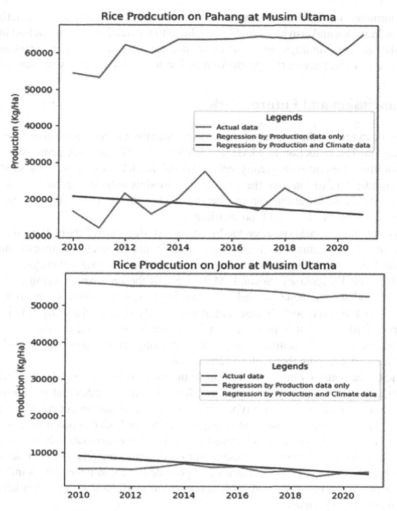

Fig. 4. Comparison of Rice Yield Predictions with and without Climate Data in Johor/Pahang, Malaysia.

regression model for Pahang predicts a reduction of roughly 29,000 metric tons of rice per year. This suggests that rice production in both states faces significant challenges, and urgent measures are needed to address this issue.

These findings have important implications for policymakers and stakeholders, providing crucial information for designing effective strategies to improve rice production in these states. For instance, policymakers can focus on addressing the underlying factors contributing to the decline in rice production, such as changes in climate patterns and soil degradation. Furthermore, stakeholders can use these findings to develop more effective agricultural practices, such as using climate-resilient rice varieties and efficient irrigation systems.

In summary, our results demonstrate the importance of climate data in predicting rice yields in Malaysia and provide valuable insights into the trend of rice production in Johor and Pahang. These findings can inform evidence-based policymaking and stakeholders with the goal of increasing rice production and ensuring food security in the country.

5   Conclusion and Future Work

This work examines the impact of climate information on rice production forecasting in Malaysia. The reduction in MAE and RMSE by 77% and 69% demonstrated that incorporating climatic data greatly enhanced the model's accuracy. This shows that using climate data to improve the precision of models anticipating rice output could have significant ramifications for anyone involved in the agricultural sector, including farmers, decision-makers, and food distributors.

It is important to acknowledge the limitations of this study. Firstly, the study's prediction model was limited to linear regression. Future research can investigate other machine learning techniques, such as random forests or neural networks, to further boost the model's accuracy. Second, Malaysia was the only nation using data in the study. To evaluate the generalizability of the findings, future studies can broaden the scope of the research to include other countries. Finally, because the study only included data from 2010–2021, it is possible that it did not fully account for the spectrum of climate variability that can affect rice production. Long-term studies that span a broader period may offer a more thorough understanding.

One of the potential improvements in future work is to employ advanced machine learning algorithms and experiment with other relevant variables that may affect rice production. For example, the soil types, irrigation systems, and insect control strategies that could affect rice production can be explored. The analysis can potentially be broadened by including data from other areas to examine if the association between climate change and rice production is consistent across different regions. Another set of data points that can improve model accuracy and provide insight into the factors influencing rice production can be considered, such as socioeconomic characteristics, market prices, and governmental policies.

Acknowledgment. The authors of this article gratefully acknowledge the support provided by the Ministry of Higher Education (MoHE) through the Fundamental Research Grant Scheme (Ref: FRGS/1/2021/SS02/UUM/02/1 (S/O Code: 20107)). However, the views expressed in this article are those of the authors alone and do not necessarily reflect the official position of the MoHE, Malaysia.

References

1. Fatah, F.A.: Competitiveness and efficiency of rice production in Malaysia. Dissertation. Georg-August-University Göttingen (2017)
2. Vaghefi, N., Shamsudin, M.N., Radam, A., Rahim, K.A.: Impact of climate change on rice yield in the main rice growing areas of peninsular Malaysia. Res. J. Environ. Sci. **7**, 59–67 (2013)

3. Tan, B.T., Fam, P.S., Firdaus, R.B.R., et. al.: Impact of climate change on rice yield in Malaysia: a panel data analysis. Agriculture 11569 (2021)

4. Sarr, A.B., Sultan, B.: Predicting crop yields in Senegal using machine learning methods. Int. J. Climatol. **43**, 1817–1838 (2023)

5. Lobell, D.B.: The use of satellite data for crop yield gap analysis. Field Crops Res. **143**, 56–64 (2013)

6. Montgomery, D.C., Peck, E.A., Vining, G.G.: Introduction to Linear Regression Analysis. Wiley, Hoboken (2021)

7. Ray, D.K., Ramankutty, N., Mueller, N.D., Paul, C.W., Jonathan, A.F.: Recent patterns of crop yield growth and stagnation. Nat. Commun. **3**(1293) (2012)

8. Oriani, F., Stisen, S., Demirel, M.C., Mariethoz, G.: Missing data imputation for multisite rainfall networks: a comparison between geostatistical interpolation and pattern-based estimation on different terrain types. J. Hydrometeorol. **21**, 2325–2341 (2020)

9. Junninen, H., Niska, H., Tuppurainen, K., Juhani, R., Mikko, K.: Methods for imputation of missing values in air quality data sets. Atmos. Environ. **38**(18), 2895–2907 (2004)

10. Nguyen, V.-H., et al.: Deep learning models for forecasting dengue fever based on climate data in Vietnam. PLoS Negl. Trop. Dis. **16**(6), e0010509 (2022)

11. Fassò, A., Rodeschini, J., Moro, A.F., et al.: Agrimonia: a dataset on livestock, meteorology and air quality in the Lombardy region, Italy. Sci. Data **10**(143) (2023)

12. Rossi, D., Mascolo, A., Mancini, S., et al.: Modelling and forecast of air pollution concentrations during COVID pandemic emergency with ARIMA techniques: the case study of two italian cities. WSEAS Trans. Environ. Dev. **19**, 151–162 (2023)

13. Toma, M.B., Belete, M.D., Ulsido, M.D.: Trends in climatic and hydrological parameters in the Ajora-Woybo watershed, Omo-Gibe River basin, Ethiopia. SN Appl. Sci. **5**(45) (2023)

14. Boomgard-Zagrodnik, J.P., Brown, D.J.: Machine learning imputation of missing Mesonet temperature observations. Comput. Electron. Agric. **192**, 106580 (2022)

15. Pedregosa, F., Varoquaux, G., Gramfort, A., et al.: Scikit-learn: machine learning in Python. J. Mach. Learn. Res. **12**, 2825–2830 (2011)

16. McKinney, W.: Pandas: a foundational Python library for data analysis and statistics. Python High Perform. Sci. Comput. **14**(9) (2011)

17. Sujarwo, A.N., Putra, R.A., Setyawan, H.M.T., Khumairoh, U.: Forecasting rice status for a food crisis early warning system based on satellite imagery and cellular automata in Malang, Indonesia. Sustainability **14**(15), 8972 (2022)

18. Ni, T., Han, X., Liu, F., He, X., Ling, F.: Research on rice yield prediction model based on deep learning. Comput. Intell. Neurosci. 1922561 (2022)

19. Chu, T., Yu, J.: An end-to-end model for rice yield prediction using deep learning fusion. Comput. Electron. Agric. **174**, 105471 (2020)

The Application of UTAUT Theory to Determine Trust Among Women in E-Hailing Apps Adoption

Karrar Ali Abdullah and Musyrifah Mahmod(✉) ⓘ

Human-Centered Computing Lab, School of Computing, Universiti Utara Malaysia, UUM, 06010 Sintok, Kedah, Malaysia
musyrifah@uum.edu.my

Abstract. The gig economy has paved the way for sharing economy growth especially e-hailing applications, as more women turn to e-hailing applications for convenience in commuting and travelling. However, women are concerned about whether to trust or not to trust e-hailing applications due to the openness of their digital and spatial crowdsourcing nature. Additionally, the user's locations are exposed to risks like stalking, identity theft, and physical safety, which can be extremely dangerous, especially for women. The paper begins by introducing the e-hailing industry and the gig economy. It then discusses women's unique challenges in using e-hailing applications and their trust towards these platforms. This paper dives deep into the heart of the matter by employing a quantitative approach through the survey to investigate women's trust in e-hailing apps using the UTAUT as the underpinning theory. The results show that e-hailing applications greatly influence women's trust while puzzlingly having no significant impact on their trust towards e-hailing drivers. From eye-opening insights to practical recommendations, this study sheds light on the crucial role of trust in the sustainable growth of the e-hailing industry focusing on women.

Keywords: Gig economy · E-hailing · Trust · Risk · UTAUT · women in sharing economy

1 Introduction

The emergence of the gig economy within the sharing economy has transformed several industries, including transportation, by offering people flexible income options and consumers convenient and easily accessible services. Through the on-demand pairing of consumers with independent drivers, e-hailing services have significantly contributed to this changing scene, pushing customers to search for transportation in a short time and at a reasonable price, offering an efficient means of transportation [1]. E-hailing applications like Grab and Uber have emerged as prominent players in this landscape, transforming the way people access transportation services. While these platforms have opened up new opportunities for individuals, it is crucial to examine their influence through a gender lens, specifically focusing on women as users of e-hailing applications.

N. H. Zakaria et al. (Eds.): ICOCI 2023, CCIS 2002, pp. 268–281, 2024.
https://doi.org/10.1007/978-981-99-9592-9_21

Nowadays, e-hailing services are in great demand as they have many advantages from a consumer perspective [2]. E-hailing applications have provided women with greater mobility options, enabling them to navigate urban environments conveniently and safely. The e-hailing platforms provides transparent driver information and ease of requesting rides for women as alternatives to traditional taxis [3]. However, there are possibilities of risks involved such as physical safety like driver's inappropriate behaviour [4], assaults and harassment in sharing rides services [5]. Thus, addressing women's safety concerns is needed from both e-hailing companies and society.

Companies must prioritize implementing strict policies and comprehensive training programs to foster a safe and respectful environment for passengers and drivers. Furthermore, data privacy concerns loom large in the digital era. E-hailing applications collect vast amounts of personal information from users, including location data, contact details, and transaction history. Women users, in particular, may be at risk of potential misuse or unauthorized access to their data [6].

The success of the E-hailing application is dependent upon the active participation of all customers, including women, who represent the target group selected for the current study. Likewise, customer trust has a major role in the success of applications, including E-hailing applications in particular, where trust is an attribute that develops over time due to customer interactions, and trust varies according to the application areas. For example, trust varies from the woman's perspective [7]. In the online booking (E-hailing) application, privacy and security are two important factors for achieving trust. At the same time, there are negative factors affecting the success of E-hailing applications that can be identified by risks, including physical risks represented by sexual harassment, murder, kidnapping, and hate crimes, and the risks of hacking sensitive information of women by the platform itself, as it works through smart mobile phones and other devices that are often its security are weak and result in many risks [3, 8]. Most studies in this domain focus on the economic aspects and ignore the risks, despite various reported security incidents related to e-hailing applications like Uber, Grab, etc. [8]. Risks associated with e-hailing may influence women's trust in e-hailing platforms.

A useful theoretical framework for researching the adoption of technology, particularly e-hailing apps, is the Unified Theory of Acceptance and Use of Technology (UTAUT) by Venkatesh et al. [9] which help to provide a thorough understanding of users' intention to embrace and use technology. It includes important constructs from multiple technology acceptance models. The relevance and applicability of UTAUT in predicting and explaining user acceptance of e-hailing services have been shown in studies such as in Liu et al. [10]. Thus, this article unpacks the relationship between women's trust and the adoption of e-hailing applications through the lens of UTAUT theory.

2 Literature Review

2.1 E-Hailing

The rise of the gig economy has shown significant adoption of digital technology such as e-hailing applications. E-hailing applications allow people to book rides services through mobile or internet-based applications at a specific time and at an appropriate price [2]. With the launch of an application-based electronic recall service, the public transportation sector experienced a digital transition. Grab, Uber, Lyft, and Didi Chuxing are examples of mobile app-based e-hailing services that have seen significant growth due to the prevalence of smartphones [11]. The mobile application of the e-call service provider allowed customers to request transportation service and connect with the affiliate drivers closest to them (based on spatial location).

Numerous organisations have implemented location-based services as an added-value offering [12]. Location-based service or spatial-based is an information system that uses the location of a mobile device over a mobile network. There were numerous methods to get location information, with the global positioning system being the most used (GPS). The location-based service allowed users to get information such as finding a person or object, navigating to a destination, searching for persons or locations, identifying a place or location, and seeing upcoming events. With the integration of a location-based system into e-hailing mobile applications, customers were able to access information on the location of available e-hailing drivers, the waiting time for a driver to pick them up, and the projected journey time from one area to another [2].

Globally, transportation services such as car-sharing, ride-sharing, and on-demand ride-sourcing are on the rise currently [10] despite the recurrence of hazards such as abduction, harassment, and rape concerning public transportation issues [13]. This problem has impacted public users since they could not adequately plan their journey. Nevertheless, users of e-hailing applications in Malaysia have access to a greater number of e-hailing application providers with cheap pricing, hence increasing competition and choice, which showed the decrement in conventional taxi usage.

2.2 Women Using E-Hailing

The increasing popularity of e-hailing applications has attracted women users' participation in the gig economy. Their attention was drawn to the factors that influence their adoption and trust in these platforms. Convenience, reliability, and improved safety measures have been identified as key drivers for women's usage of e-hailing applications [37]. Tracking rides in real-time and accessing driver information provides a sense of security and control, enhancing women's confidence in using these platforms [3]. However, concerns regarding data privacy and security risks using e-hailing platforms have also been highlighted in the literature [3].

Women users of e-hailing applications express apprehension regarding collecting and handling their personal data [5]. They value their privacy and expect transparency in how the platform uses and shares their information. Trust is essential for women to continue using e-hailing applications, and this trust is closely tied to perceived data privacy practices [4]. Companies that prioritize data protection and user consent and provide clear privacy policies are more likely to gain the trust of women users and retain their loyalty.

While e-hailing applications offer convenience, safety concerns pose potential risks for women passengers. Harassment and assault have been reported, prompting the need for enhanced security measures [3]. Women's experiences of personal security risks during rides can erode trust in the platform. To address these concerns, e-hailing companies have implemented safety features such as SOS buttons, in-app emergency support, and driver accountability measures [4]. E-hailing applications are concerned with the safety of passengers and drivers first, which distinguishes e-hailing applications from the traditional taxi service. For example, for passenger safety, the Grab app has a "Share My Ride" feature that customers can tap to share their real-time tracking ride with family and friends as they tap into the cab. The emergency "Share My Ride" feature is useful for all passengers, women, or elderly people who rent a car on their own [12]. These efforts aimed to mitigate risks and provide women users with a secure and reliable transportation experience.

2.3 Trust

Trust is a complex topic researched from numerous angles in various specialist domains [10, 14]. Trust is a quality that develops through time due to interactions between people [5]. Thus, trust is a critical factor influencing the adoption and continued usage of e-hailing services, encompassing both trust in the application itself and the trust developed during the ride experience. Trust in the e-hailing application primarily revolves around three key aspects: platform reliability, information transparency, and user interface design. Studies have shown that users value platforms that consistently deliver reliable service, ensuring timely arrivals, accurate fare estimates, and responsive customer support [10]. Transparency in terms of driver information, pricing details, and the handling of personal data also contributes to users' trust in the application [15]. Additionally, a user-friendly interface with intuitive features and clear navigation enhances users' trust and overall satisfaction with the application [16].

However, there is a lack of research on the effects of trust in the sharing economy, particularly in the context of e-hailing services [17]. The study believes that the unique features of e-hailing applications, such as one-time shared rides between private individuals on short notice, the use of a mobile application, the transparency of demographic data and GPS location, interactions with strangers, and the intermediary framework, have a significant impact on the loss of trust [18]. Thus, it is important to examine the trust in both the ride experience related to the e-hailing applications and drivers.

2.4 Risk

E-hailing applications depend on information technology platforms, as they operate through smart mobile phones and other devices whose security is often weak and results in many risks [19]. Data security and privacy concerns are one of the main reasons for the lack of trust in e-hailing applications. Users are required to share their personal information, including location and payment details, with the app [20]. This data can be vulnerable to cyberattacks and data breaches, exposing users' sensitive information. A University of California, Riverside study found that 99% of e-hailing applications have at least one vulnerability that hackers could exploit [20].

Another reason for the lack of trust in e-hailing applications is the driver and passenger concerns. Passengers generally face risks of being deceived and scammed by fraudsters posing as taxi drivers [19]. In recent years, there have been many incidents of passengers being assaulted or harassed by drivers. Similarly, passengers also reported incidents where they were assaulted or harassed by drivers. These incidents have raised questions about the security and safety measures implemented by the electronic pager applications. A Pew Research Center study found that 48% of users were concerned about the security of e-hailing applications [21]. According to a Thomson Reuters survey, Kuala Lumpur is included in the list of "Top 10 Dangerous Transport Systems for Women," raising concerns about the use of these apps [14].

The risks associated with e-hailing applications, including data security and privacy concerns, can result in women losing trust in these apps. Women may be more concerned about their personal information being compromised, which can result in them being hesitant to use e-hailing applications. A study conducted by the Pew Research Center found that women were more likely than men to express concerns about the privacy and security of their personal information when using e-hailing applications [21]. The lack of pricing and fare structures transparency can also affect women's intention to use e-hailing applications which women made the majority of the reports of dissatisfaction with the pricing and fare [3].

Although trust is a crucial factor, the relationship between trust and intention to use e-hailing can be influenced by the risk as a moderating role [10, 22]. Consequently, understanding risk as a moderating role can provide a better understanding of the relationship.

2.5 The Mechanics of Trust Model

The trust Model is a theoretical framework to analyze how trust as a critical factor affects the user's perception of technology adoption and usage [23]. For this study, trust is crucial in the relationship between women and e-hailing services adoption. The three constructs of the Trust model adopted for this study are competence, integrity and benevolence.

2.6 Unified Theory of Acceptance and Use of Technology (UTAUT)

The underpinning theory of this is the UTAUT theory [9]. UTAUT is a modern model for studying technology adoption or acceptance as it provides a comprehensive understanding of the factors influencing users' adoption behaviour [9]. The variable on the intention to use e-hailing apps is appropriate for this study since using UTAUT allows researchers to acquire insightful understanding of the multi-dimensional factors that influence technology adoption. But to account for women's trust, The Mechanics of Trust model's trust variable is applied.

3   Research Design

This study aims at investigating the relationship between trust, risk and women's intention to use e-hailing applications. A theoretical model was developed based on the UTAUT [9], and the Mechanic of Trust Model [23].

Based on the theoretical model developed, this study aimed at achieving the following objectives:

RO1: To identify the factors of women's trust in e-hailing applications on their intentions to use e-hailing applications.

RO2: To examine the influence of women's trust in drivers on their intentions to use e-hailing applications.

RO3: To investigate the moderating effect of risk on women's trust in e-hailing applications and drivers on their intentions to use e-hailing applications.

This study employed a quantitative approach using a survey for data collection. The study developed a questionnaire instrument that distinguished between trusting the e-hailing application and trusting the drivers. The survey consisted of 22 questions and collected demographic data from participants using four data structures. Responses were measured using a 7-point Likert scale, ranging from 'strongly disagree' (1) to 'strongly agree' (7). Table 1 provides an overview of the final miscatalogue, including combinations and relevant item codes.

Table 1. Items of questionnaire

Construct	Code	Item
Trust in e-hailing applications [11]	TAPP1	I feel that e-hailing applications is honest
	TAPP2	I believe that e-hailing applications is trustworthy
	TAPP3	I trust e-hailing applications
	TAPP4	I feel e-hailing applications is reliable
	TAPP5	Even if not monitored, I would trust e-hailing applications to do the right job
	TAPP6	I believe in the security policies of e-hailing applications
	TAPP7	I trust e-hailing applications to provide me with quality ride services
Trust in driver [11]	TD1	I trust the drivers using e-hailing applications
	TD2	I believe that the drivers of e-hailing applications are trustworthy
	TD3	I feel that drivers on e-hailing applications are honest
	TD4	I feel drivers on e-hailing applications are reliable
	TD5	Even if not monitored, I would trust drivers on e-hailing applications
Risk [22]	RIS1	It would be risky to disclose my personal information to e-hailing application developers

(continued)

Table 1. (*continued*)

Construct	Code	Item
	RIS2	Sharing my personal information with e-hailing application facilitators would lead to many uncertainties
	RIS3	Sharing my personal information with e-hailing application facilitators would cause many unexpected problems
	RIS4	It would be a potential threat to my privacy to disclose personal information to e-hailing applications facilitators
	RIS5	Using e-hailing applications would be insecure
	RIS6	Using e-hailing applications would put me at potential risk of physical harm
Intention to use e-hailing applications [22]	INT1	I use e-hailing applications because I've seen advertisements or news from mass media
	INT2	I use e-hailing applications because it is the current trend
	INT3	Friends and family have influenced on my decision to use e-hailing applications
	INT4	I intend to continue using e-hailing applications during my study period
	INT5	I plan to continue using e-hailing applications frequently

The population sample for this study was women who use e-hailing applications in Malaysia as passengers or consumers. The invitation threads are posted in the online community of What Apps groups. Within the invitation thread, respondents are informed about the purpose of the study and given a link to the Google Form survey. The survey was conducted in early 2023, and the study managed to get 117 participants to complete the questionnaire by the deadline. Since our study covers Malaysian women users which hard to determine the number of users, the study follows the recommendation of Hair [24] and Hamdollah & Baghaei [10] for Smart-PLS 4. Researchers can either identify sample size using the G*Power program. G*Power is a free-to-use statistical power calculator developed by El Maniani *et al.* [25] that is employed to compute optimal sample size requirements in statistical analyses, such as F-tests and t-tests. G*power estimated that the minimum sample size required for sample models is 85; therefore, 117 samples are considered sufficient for this study's analysis.

The majority of participants (52 participants) were between the ages of 18–24, followed by 22 respondents between the ages of 25–29, 13 respondents between the ages of 35–39, 12 respondents between the ages of 40–49, 11 respondents between the ages of 30–34, and 7 respondents over 50.

3.1 Proposed Hypothesis

In this study, four (4) main hypotheses were proposed.

H1: There is a positive effect of trust in e-hailing applications on women's intention to use e-hailing applications.

H2: There is a positive effect of trust in e-hailing drivers on women's intention to use e-hailing applications.

H3: Risk moderates the relationship between trust in an e-hailing application and a woman's intention to use an e-hailing application.

H4: Risk moderates the relationship between trust in an e-hailing driver and a woman's intention to use an e-hailing application.

Figure 1 illustrated the conceptual model developed for the study. The constructs are adopted from UTAUT [9], and the Mechanic of Trust Model [23].

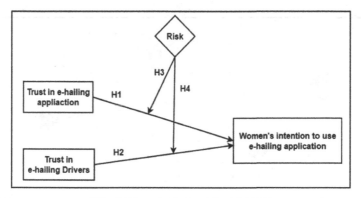

Fig. 1. Proposed Conceptual Model

4 Data Analysis and Results

4.1 Measurement Model

Table 2 shows the composite reliability and extracted mean-variance (AVE) for all measures that exceeded the recommended limits of 0.7 and 0.5, respectively [24]. Thus, the building showed its correctness. All combinations achieved a satisfactory level of AVE score >0.50 based on the score. In addition, all combinations also achieved a satisfactory level of rho_C score >0.80. This is consistent with the guidelines of Hair *et al.* [24].

Table 2. Overview of items after the content validity assessment

	Cronbach's alpha	Rho_a	Composite reliability (rho_C)	The average variance extracted (AVE)
INT	0.888	0.909	0.919	0.696
RIS	0.895	0.978	0.922	0.707
TAPP	0.902	0.909	0.925	0.675
TD	0.915	0.934	0.938	0.753

4.2 Structural Model Assessment

Measurement models include the relationships between underlying structures and their indicators. Figure 2, TAPP indicates TO (Trust in E-hailing applications), TD indicates TO (Trust in e-hailing drivers), RIS indicates TO (Risk), and INT indicates TO (intentions to use e-hailing applications).

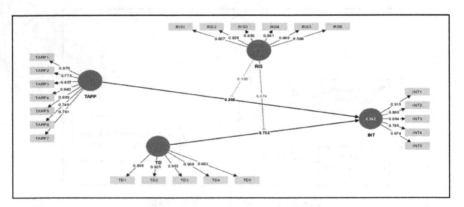

Fig. 2. Measurement model

Based on the measurement model used in this study, the constructs' measures were reliable and valid. Table 3 shows that TAPP->INT supported the study when validating the hypotheses because the $\beta = 0.26$ and P values $= 0.00 < 0.050$. TD > INT supported the study because the $\beta = 0.73$ and P values $= 0.00 < 0.050$. RIS × TAPP > INT moderates the relationship because the $\beta = 0.26$ and P values $= 0.043 < 0.050$. RIS × TD > INT did not moderate the relationship because the $\beta = 0.26$ and P values $= 0.00 < 0.05$.

In total, 4 hypotheses and relationships were tested in this research. Three hypotheses (H1, H2, H4) were supported, while 1 were not (H3). Table 4 summarizes the results.

Table 3. Results of hypothesis testing

Hypotheses	Original Sample (O)	Sample Mean (M)	Standard Deviation (STDEV)	T Statistics (IO/STDEVI)	P Values	Supported
TAPP->INT	0.265	0.266	0.038	6.967	0.000	Supported
TD->INT	0.732	0.731	0.039	18.987	0.000	Supported
RIS x TAPP->INT	−0.100	−0.089	0.050	2.023	0.043	Supported
RIS x TD->INT	0.074	0.067	0.045	1.623	0.105	Not supported

Table 4. Summary of the Result of Hypotheses Testing

Variables and Direct Relationships of Independent Variables		
H1	There is a positive effect of trust in e-hailing applications on women's intention to use e-hailing applications	Supported
H2	There is a positive effect of trust in e-hailing drivers on women's intention to use e-hailing applications	Supported
H3	Risk moderates the relationship between trust in an e-hailing application and a woman's intention to use an e-hailing application	Supported
H4	Risk moderates the relationship between trust in an e-hailing driver and a woman's intention to use an e-hailing application	Not Supported

5 Results and Discussion

5.1 The Influence of Women's Trust in E-Hailing Applications on Their Intentions to Use the Applications

The study indicates that women's trust in e-hailing applications directly affects their intentions to use these applications. The structural model that was used in the study examined the relationships between different variables and found that trust in the applications was a significant predictor of women's intentions to continue using them. In more detail, the study suggests that women who trust e-hailing applications are more likely to continue using them in the future. This trust may be related to factors such as the service's reliability, the drivers' safety, and the application's ease of use. When women feel they can trust the application to provide a safe and reliable ride, they are more likely to use it again.

It is important to note that trust is just a factor that influences women's intentions to use e-hailing applications. There are other factors that were not covered in this study such as pricing. The results of this study suggest that trust is an important factor in determining whether women will continue to use e-hailing applications over time. By building trust with their users, e-hailing applications can increase the likelihood that women will continue to use their services in the future.

5.2 The Influence of Women's Trust in Drivers on Their Intentions to Use E-Hailing Applications

This study showed women's inclinations to use these apps are directly influenced by how much they trust the drivers of e-hailing services. The structural model employed in the research to analyse the correlations between various variables discovered that women's intentions to continue using e-hailing services were significantly predicted by their confidence level in the drivers. Trust in drivers may be influenced by their skill level, dependability, and safety. Women are more likely to continue using the e-hailing service if they believe they have confidence in the driver to provide a secure and dependable journey. E-hailing apps may boost the possibility that women will continue using their services by establishing trust with their customers and ensuring that their drivers are capable, dependable, and safe in the future.

5.3 The Risks Affecting the Trust of Women Who Use E-Hailing Applications

The effect of risk on the relationship between women's trust in e-hailing applications and intent to use and women's confidence in drivers of recall applications and intent to use was investigated. It was found that there is a significant effect of risk on the relationship between trust in e-hailing applications and women's intention to use them. The study proved that the increase in risk affects the relationship between trust in e-hailing applications and the intention to use. Concerns related to information security, such as theft and unauthorised use of personally identifiable information, tracking, prosecution or harassment after information penetration, mitigate the intention to use e-hailing applications. This study is consistent with the results of previous studies, which proved that the privacy problem impacts the intention to use e-hailing applications [26–28].

Perplexingly, no risk influenced the relationship between confidence in e-hailing application drivers and women's intention to use e-hailing applications. The current study did not provide any evidence regarding the risks women may face, such as kidnapping, rape, and harassment, that may affect the relationship between trust and intention to use.

The study contributes to showing that trust in E-hailing applications affects women's intentions to use E-hailing applications. The study hypotheses are supported by the use of risk as a moderator between the effect of trust in E-hailing applications and the intention to use E-hailing applications. Study findings indicate that trust in E-hailing drivers does not significantly impact customers' intentions to use E-hailing applications. At first, study findings may seem surprising, but given that E-hailing applications connect strangers, it is likely that the application already considered most of the risks. Concerns related to information security such as theft and unauthorized use of personally identifiable information, tracking, prosecution, or harassment after information penetration mitigate the intention to use e-hailing applications. As a result, the study findings are consistent with those of [11]. As a result of separating trust into two distinct structures, the study demonstrated a deflecting effect on customer intentions in E-hailing applications.

5.4 Implications of the Study

The study's findings have theoretical and practical implications, which are discussed below.

Theoretical Implications. The results contribute more to the Unified Theory of Technology Acceptance and Use theory and the mechanisms of the trust model, especially when using trust and knowing its effect on the intention to use the time. Trust is one of the key elements in the mechanics of the trust model. Previous studies also confirmed that trust is an effective element in relationships on the Internet [29]. Although previous studies indicated risks and their impact on user trust [30], this study found that risks affect the relationship between trust in e-hailing applications and women's intention to use them. However, the risks do not affect drivers' confidence and intention to use e-hailing applications. But the important question is whether risk and its impact on the relationship between trust in drivers and intention to use is a redundant concept in Internet-based relationships. More studies are needed in the future to strengthen the role of risk in Internet-based relationships.

This study also contributes to the investigation of the elements of trust in e-hailing applications and their impact on women's intention to use e-hailing applications. To the best of the researcher's knowledge, there are no studies that focus on women and their intention to use e-hailing applications in particular, and also the researcher is aware no one has thought in an investigation of the effect of risk on women's intention to use e-calling applications in Malaysia. Hence, the results contribute to knowledge in theory to enhance women's awareness of using e-hailing applications.

The main results of the study indicate that concerns related to data security and fear of hacking or stealing information from the application had a role in influencing the relationship between trust in these applications and the intention to use them. When women are satisfied with services such as giving priority to the security of traveler information, implementing technological steps to enhance information protection, and preventing user information leakage and theft, this is very important in electronic pager applications to increase women's intention to use these applications. E-hailing applications are likely to achieve more usage by increasing security and privacy.

Practical Implications. Malaysia began using e-hailing applications in 2012 with the launch of MyTeksi, now known as Grab and more e-hailing applications in 2014 that faced various security, penetration, and information leakage challenges.

The risk of fraud on fake profiles or fraudulent activities could result in theft, assault and harassment. Information leakage is a major obstacle as well as some e-hailing applications collect and store user data, which could be vulnerable to hacking and cyber-attacks. A study by [31] revealed that security and privacy concerns were significant factors affecting the use of e-hailing applications in Malaysia, with users ramping concerns over data sharing, unauthorized access to personal information, and identity theft.

6 Conclusion

The finding of this study shows the relationship of women's trust in the intention to use e-hailing applications. This research concentrated on two areas of trust, namely the apps and women's concern about the driver. An additional goal of this research was to determine how risks affected these relations. Even though risks do not affect the trust women had in drivers, the study found a significant effect on the relationship between trust in applications and intention to use, as trust and risks influence women's intention to use such applications. Hence the study contributes to the growing literature on the gig economy specifically women's intention to use the e-hailing application.

E-hailing companies should take into account these factors to help increase women's interest and trust in using e-hailing applications. The results of this study, in particular, could benefit developers of e-hailing applications or companies to focus on incorporating features in the application and their drivers that could increase confidence in women as e-hailing customers. The study's findings should not be embraced by the companies that provide e-hailing application; instead, efforts should be made to raise consumer happiness and win their confidence in using these services.

References

1. Idros, N.A.N.M., Mohamed, H., Jenal, R.: The use of expert review in component development for customer satisfaction towards E-hailing. Indonesian J. Electric. Eng. Comput. Sci. **17**(1), 347–356 (2020)
2. Jais, A.S., Marzuki, A.: E-hailing services in Malaysia: current practices and future outlook. Plann. Malaysia **18** (2020)
3. Jones, S.A.: Gendered safety concerns and risk perception in e-hailing applications. J. Transp. Geogr. **94**, 103133 (2021)
4. Johnson, E.R., Davis, R.E.: Enhancing security in e-hailing applications: a focus on women users' perspectives. Comput. Hum. Behav. **106**, 106247 (2020)
5. Brown, A.B., Johnson, C.D.: Trust and privacy concerns in women's usage of e-hailing applications. Transport. Res. F Traffic Psychol. Behav. **82**, 76–85 (2021)
6. Tran, T.T.H., Robinson, K., Paparoidamis, N.G.: Sharing with perfect strangers: the effects of self-disclosure on consumers' trust, risk perception, and behavioral intention in the sharing economy. J. Bus. Res. **144**, 1–16 (2022)
7. Jiang, Y., Lau, A.K.: Roles of consumer trust and risks on continuance intention in the sharing economy: an empirical investigation. Electron. Commer. Res. Appl. **47**, 101050 (2021)
8. Mohd Idros, N.A.N., Mohamed, H., Jenal, R.: Determinant factors of customer satisfaction for e-hailing service: a preliminary study. In: Saeed, F., Gazem, N., Mohammed, F., Busalim, A. (eds.) International Conference of Reliable Information and Communication Technology, vol. 843, pp. 803–811. Springer, Cham (2018). https://doi.org/10.1007/978-3-319-99007-1_74
9. Venkatesh, V., Morris, M.G., Davis, G.B., Davis, F.D.: User acceptance of information technology: toward a unified view. MIS Q., 425–478 (2003)
10. Liu, Y., Gao, S., Lee, M.K.: Exploring the antecedents of mobile app stickiness: the unified theory of acceptance and use of technology. Comput. Hum. Behav. **67**, 247–257 (2017)
11. Geng, R., Sun, R., Li, J., Guo, F., Wang, W., Sun, G.: The impact of firm innovativeness on consumer trust in the sharing economy: a moderated mediation model **71702095**, 1078–1098 (2022). https://doi.org/10.1108/APJML-10-2020-0748

12. Pretorius, H.W.: An E-halfling crime and exploitation classification framework. Proc. Soc. **84**, 129–139 (2022)
13. Ruangkanjanases, A., Techapoolphol, C.: Adoption of E-hailing applications: a comparative study between female and male users in Thailand. J. Telecommun. Electron. Comput. Eng. (JTEC), **10**(1–10), 43–48 (2018)
14. Kim, D.J., Ferrin, D.L., Rao, H.R.: Trust and satisfaction, two stepping stones for successful e-commerce relationships: a longitudinal exploration. Inf. Syst. Res. **20**(2), 237–257 (2007)
15. Smith, K.L., et al.: Exploring factors influencing trust in e-hailing applications: a focus on women users. J. Bus. Res. **141**, 134–142 (2022)
16. Jayashankar, P., Nilakanta, S., Johnston, W.J., Gill, P., Burres, R.: IoT adoption in agriculture: the role of trust, perceived value and risk. J. Bus. Ind. Market. (2018)
17. Ko, G., Amankwah-Amoah, J., Appiah, G., Larimo, J.: Non-market strategies and building digital trust in sharing economy platforms. J. Int. Manag. **28**(1), 10090 9 (2022)
18. Shamim, A., Khan, A.A., Qureshi, M.A., Rafique, H.: Ride or not to ride: does the customer deviate toward ridesharing? Int. J. Environ. Res. Public Health **18**(19), 10352 (2021). https://doi.org/10.3390/ijerph181910352
19. Teo, B.C., Mustaffa, M.A., Rozi, A.M.: To grab or not to grab? Passenger ride intention towards E-Hailing services. Malaysian J. Consumer Family Econ. **21**, 153–159 (2018)
20. Mittendorf, C.: What trust means in the sharing economy: a provider perspective on Airbnb.com (2016)
21. Anderson, D.N.: "Not just a taxi"? For-profit ridesharing, driver strategies, and VMT. Transportation **41**(5), 1099–1117 (2014). https://doi.org/10.1007/s11116-014-9531-8
22. Kamais, C.E.: Emerging security risks of e-hail transport services: focus on Uber taxi in Nairobi, Kenya. Int. J. Secur. Privacy Trust Manag. (IJSPTM) **8** (2019)
23. Riegelsberger, J., Sasse, M.A., McCarthy, J.D.: The mechanics of trust: a framework for research and design. Int. J. Hum. Comput. Stud. **62**(3), 381–422 (2005)
24. Hair, J.F., Jr., Matthews, L.M., Matthews, R.L., Sarstedt, M.: PLS-SEM or CB-SEM: updated guidelines on which method to use. Int. J. Multivariate Data Anal. **1**(2), 107–123 (2017)
25. El Maniani, M., Rechchach, M., El Mahfoudi, A., El Moudane, M., Sabbar, A.: A calorimetric investigation of the liquid Bi-Ni alloys. J. Mater. Environ. Sci. **7**(10), 3759–3766 (2016)
26. Liébana-Cabanillas, F., Sánchez-Fernández, J., Muñoz-Leiva, F.: Antecedents of mobile payment adoption: the moderating role of perceived risk. J. Bus. Res. **106**, 253–260 (2020)
27. Hong, I.B., Cho, H., Kim, H.: The impact of consumer trust on attitudinal loyalty and purchase intentions in B2C e-commerce. J. Bus. Res. **64**(8), 808–813 (2011)
28. Henao, A., Marshall, W.: A framework for understanding the impacts of ridesourcing on transportation. In: Meyer, G., Shaheen, S. (eds.) Disrupting Mobility. LNM, pp. 197–209. Springer, Cham (2017). https://doi.org/10.1007/978-3-319-51602-8_13
29. Mahmod, M., Hassan, H.: Exploring women's motivation factors to participate in spatial crowdsourcing platform. In: AIP Conference Proceedings, vol. 2339, no. 1, p. 020142. AIP Publishing LLC (2021)
30. Sarfaraz, J.: Unified theory of acceptance and use of technology (UTAUT) model-mobile banking. J. Internet Bank. Commer. **22**(3), 1–20 (2017)
31. Arumugam, V., Ismail, M.R., Joeharee, M.: A review and conceptual development of the factors influencing consumer intention towards E-hailing service in Malaysia. Int. J. Innov. Creativity Change **11**(11), 224–242 (2020)

Design and Development of Housing Interview Management System for Managing Housing Application

Asvinitha Muniandy[1], Mazida Ahmad[1(✉)], and Mohamad Adli Desa[2]

[1] Institute for Advanced and Smart Digital Opportunities, School of Computing, Universiti Utara Malaysia, 06010 Sintok, Kedah, Malaysia
mazida@uum.edu.my

[2] Housing Department, Wisma Darul Aman, 05503 Alor Setar, Kedah, Malaysia

Abstract. The housing department in Wisma Darul Aman plays an important role in planning, coordinating, and developing housing schemes for low-income Malaysians. However, the manual process of recording and storing applicant information on paper is time-consuming for the staff, and retrieving applicant information can be challenging. Thus, the main objective of this study is to design and develop the Housing Interview Management System (HIMS) for the housing department. The system manages applicant information, enabling storage, retrieval, modification, and deletion, while generating scores based on their responses, offering a more accurate and efficient solution for the Wisma Darul Aman housing department. To design and develop the system, Prototyping Software Development Methodology was used, which consists of identifying the requirements through interview sessions with housing department staff, designing the system, building the prototype using PHP and JavaScript, conducting user evaluation among housing department staff, refining prototype, and implementing and maintaining the system. The findings of the evaluation show that the system is useful and easy to use. Most respondents expressed high satisfaction with the system, indicating that the system worked as desired and effectively facilitated the housing interview process. The study highlights the significant potential of the HIMS to streamline the housing department's interview process, contributing to improved affordable housing delivery for low-income Malaysians.

Keywords: Interview Management System · Prototyping · Housing Department · Program Perumahan Rakyat (PPR) · Low income

1 Introduction

Rumah PPR, also known as the Program Perumahan Rakyat, is a government initiative in Malaysia aimed at providing affordable housing for low-income individuals, particularly those falling under the B40 category, and eradicating squatter communities [1]. According to the 2019 Household Income and Basic Amenities Survey Report by the Department of Statistics Malaysia, households with a monthly income of less than

N. H. Zakaria et al. (Eds.): ICOCI 2023, CCIS 2002, pp. 282–295, 2024.
https://doi.org/10.1007/978-981-99-9592-9_22

RM4,849 belong to the B40 category [2]. To qualify for the Rumah PPR, applicants must be Malaysian citizens aged 18 or above, with a total household income of less than RM3000.00 per month, and not owning any property.

The housing department in Wisma Darul Aman plays a crucial role in planning, coordinating, and developing housing schemes for low-income individuals. As part of the application process, applicants must attend a formal interview session, which the Housing Department conducts. During the interview, the applicant's responses are recorded on paper, and a score is assigned to each answer to evaluate their overall suitability for the Rumah PPR. However, the manual process of recording and storing applicant information on paper is time-consuming for the Housing Department staff, and retrieving applicant information can be challenging.

This study aims to develop a Bahasa Melayu language-based Housing Interview Management System (HIMS) called "Sistem Pengurusan Temuduga Perumahan". The system aims to streamline the interview process by digitally storing applicant information during the interview session and generating scores based on their responses. By adopting digital technology, the system will offer a more efficient and accurate solution for the Wisma Darul Aman housing department, eliminating the time-consuming manual calculations, record-keeping, and data retrieval during interviews [3, 4].

The potential outcomes of this study are expected to demonstrate a significant enhancement in the efficiency and accuracy of the housing department's interview process, benefiting low-income Malaysians in need of affordable housing. The digital approach will also provide greater accessibility and ease of use for the system's users. The study will also aim to guide future system enhancement and explore possibilities for integrating the developed HIMS with the existing housing department system, namely Kedah Housing & Property Information System (KHIS), to create a unified web-based platform for managing the entire housing process.

2 Background of the Housing Interview Management System

Several studies have discussed housing management systems and record management systems in different domains, such as education, construction, and communication [5–7]. For instance, Walia, et al. [4] developed a Student Record Management System (SRMS) using PHP and SQL as their database to manage student records such as attendance and subject results efficiently. Similarly, Omosebi [8] focused on enhancing their existing housing management system by introducing new functions, including record-keeping and generating reports for decision-making [4, 8]. HIMS shares similarities with both studies [4, 8], as its main goal is to streamline an efficient and manageable system that enhances record-keeping and report generation. However, unlike the mentioned systems, HIMS incorporates features for generating information and scores based on interview responses. The findings from previous studies, combined with the preliminary findings of this study, will serve as a basis for developing a comprehensive and effective HIMS. By leveraging these unique features, the HIMS aims to optimize the applicant selection process, providing a comprehensive and user-friendly solution for the housing application.

The HIMS is developed using Visual Studio Code, an IDE that allows developers to write software code efficiently. The system aims to improve efficiency and data retention by reducing paper use and minimizing data loss. This system will also save time and energy for administrative staff, increase their satisfaction, and be more environmentally friendly. Moreover, the system is designed to be user-friendly and easy to maintain. It enables staff to add, update, and retrieve applicants' information quickly and efficiently. The system can also generate applicant information, and scores obtained more clearly and accurately. Furthermore, the system can detect whether an applicant has previously applied for a PPR house, which is believed to improve the quality of hires significantly [9]. Overall, this system is expected to enhance the efficiency and effectiveness of housing programs, particularly in public housing authorities [8, 9].

2.1 Tools for Housing Interview Management System Development

The HIMS was developed using a combination of PHP, HTML, CSS, and JavaScript programming languages, while XAMPP was utilized as the database management system. PHP and related technologies are popular in web-based development [4] and can be easily deployed on web servers. Additionally, Miro was employed during the initial stages of the system design to provide a visual representation of the system's architecture and design. The stand-alone application using PHP and XAMPP allows for efficient storage and retrieval of applicant information, minimizing data loss and reducing errors in the manual process. This system is expected to improve efficiency and accuracy in the housing interview process, leading to increased satisfaction for the staff.

3   Methodology of the Study

The software development life cycle (SDLC) was selected as the appropriate model for this project, as it encompasses the stages of the software development process and ensures the efficient implementation of high-quality software in meeting the specified requirements. Additionally, prototyping methodology, a software development approach where a prototype is built, tested, and refined until satisfactory [10], was employed to develop the HIMS due to its simplicity and ease of understanding. Figure 1 shows the phases of the prototyping model.

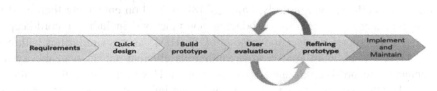

Fig. 1. Phases of prototyping methodology [10]

3.1 Requirements

To develop the HIMS, it was essential to understand the concept, the individuals involved in the process, and the requirements. The requirements-gathering process involved examining the interview form utilized by the Housing Department during the interview process. The form was analyzed to comprehend the entire interview process, including the calculations involved and how the assessments were evaluated.

3.2 Quick Design

A simple framework design was created to give users a high-level system overview. The design was created using an online software called Miro and was developed based on the project scope and requirements, including the appearance and features of the system. The framework includes various components, including interview questions, to store applicant information. This would enable the staff to understand the flow, conveniently digitize all the interview details into the corresponding fields, and effortlessly maintain or refer to the stored information.

3.3 Build Prototype

The prototype is developed based on the data collected from the quick design and is a scale-down working model of the system. The project mainly focuses on developing a stand-alone application for the working environment using Visual Studio Code (VSC) and Xampp for data storage. The system development process incorporated all the requirements collected during the initial stage.

3.4 User Evaluation

After the system was created, it was converted into an actual application and tested in the real world. The staff evaluated the HIMS based on the requirements, functionality, and performance. They shared their comments and ideas for further enhancement or implementation during the next round of system redesign. The strengths and weaknesses of the HIMS were identified through user evaluation.

3.5 Refine Prototype

The refined prototype is where the current system development will be revised for the next redesigning or rebuilding prototype. After collecting the ideas and comments from the staff, the HIMS has been reconsidered to achieve the user's requirements and the project scope. This evaluation and refined prototype were developed in loop mode until the staff was satisfied with this system.

3.6 Implement and Maintain

After the final system was developed based on the prototype, it went through testing before sending to production. As the HIMS met all the requirements and satisfied the staff after the re-evaluation process, it is now complete and ready to be used during the interview session.

4   Design and Development of the Housing Interview Management System

Following the six phases of Prototyping Software Development, the design, and development of the HIMS is proposed. The requirements-gathering process was carried out by discussing the process taken by the staff to store, calculate and retrieve the data during and after an interview process, including referring to the example of the interview form, which was used manually to store the applicant's information. These processes were examined to determine the need for an interview-based system to manage the interview process. The requirements-gathering approach delivered six essential requirements and their priority, as shown in Table 1. The main functional requirements of the HIMS are Check Qualifications, Create Applicant Information, Calculate Scores, Update Applicant Information, Delete Applicant Information and Generate Applicant Information and Score.

Table 1. List of requirements of the HIMS

ID	Requirement Description	Priority
1	**Check Qualification**	
1.1	The system requests the admin to insert the applicant's identification number	Mandatory
1.2	The system will check the applicant's identification through the database	Mandatory
1.3	The system will display an error if the applicant's identification is found in the database	Mandatory
1.4	The system will display a link to the application form if the applicant's identification is not found in the database	Mandatory
1.5	The system allows the admin to click the link	Mandatory
2	**Create Applicant Information**	
2.1	The system will request the admin to store the applicant information in three sections	Mandatory
2.2	The system will request the admin to complete the applicant information in three sections	Mandatory
2.3	The system will ensure there is no empty field	Optional
3	**Calculate Score**	
3.1	The system requests the admin to click the calculate button to count the overall score	Mandatory
3.2	The system will store the applicant's information and score if the admin clicks on the submit button	Mandatory
4	**Update Applicant Information**	

(*continued*)

Table 1. (*continued*)

ID	Requirement Description	Priority
4.1	The system allows the admin to update the applicant's information	Optional
4.2	The system allows the admin to select the section to update the applicant's information	Mandatory
4.3	The system will update the information if the admin clicks the update button	Mandatory
5	**Delete Applicant Information**	
5.1	The system allows the admin to delete any applicant's application	Optional
5.2	The system will display a confirmation message before deleting an application	Mandatory
6	**Generate Applicant Information and Score**	
6.1	The system will generate the applicant's information and score obtained	Mandatory
6.2	The system allows the admin to view the applicant's information and score obtained	Mandatory
6.3	The system allows the admin to download the applicant's information and the score obtained	Optional

The requirements stated in Table 1 were interpreted into the computer system functionality. The next step is to use appropriate modeling methods and tools to visualize and model the system's needs. The use case diagram is used as the applied model in this study. The diagrams were illustrated using Visual Paradigm. Figure 2 shows the use case diagram and the connections between the use cases and the system users. The six major use cases are: (i) check qualification, (ii) check applicant information, (iii) calculate score, (iv) update applicant information, (v) delete applicant information, and (vi) generate applicant information and score.

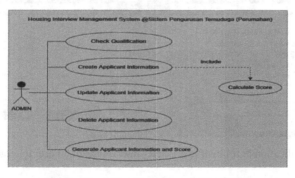

Fig. 2. The use case diagram of the HIMS

During the quick design phase, the flow of the HIMS was conceptualized. The low-fidelity prototype, or the initial idea for the system, was created and designed on a whiteboard interface. The functionality of each interface design was illustrated using the Miro online design tool, as shown in the graphs below. Figures 3, 4, and 5 display the selected screenshots of the interfaces for the HIMS. Figure 3 shows the ID verification process interface, which checks the qualification status. IDs are redirected to a link if found to be new. Figure 4 shows the interface for the application form, featuring three sections dedicated to applicant interviews, where staff fill out the form accordingly. Figure 5 shows the interface for generating the applicant's information and the obtained score. After completing the form, the interface displays the overall information and the score achieved. It should be noted that the low-fidelity prototype is a quick and simple representation of the system's interface design. It was used as a basis for further development and refinement in the later stages of the project. The Miro online design tool allowed the project team to collaborate and iterate on the interface design to meet the project's requirements and standards. Overall, the quick design phase was crucial in laying out the basic structure and flow of the system, which was then refined and improved in subsequent stages. The low-fidelity prototype and the Miro design tool were important tools in the quick design phase, allowing for efficient collaboration and rapid iteration.

Fig. 3. ID Verification Interface

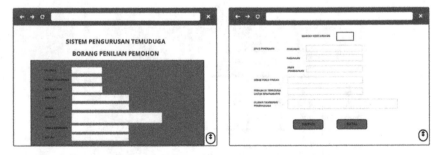

Fig. 4. Application Form Interface 1 (left) and Application Form Interface 2 (right)

Fig. 5. Score Report Interface

5   The Housing Interview Management System Development

During the development phase, the HIMS was constructed following the requirements outlined in the previous section. Software prototyping is a web-established technique for demonstrating software requirements and enables developers to receive user feedback and suggestions based on their interactions with the prototype. The main tools utilized during the development process comprise of PHP, JavaScript, HTML and CSS and XAMPP, which served as the database for the system. The Interview form was used as the primary reference point during the development process, focusing on reorganizing the questions and refining the calculation process to make it more efficient. Additionally, the FPDF file was imported into the code to allow the system to generate a comprehensive score and user information in PDF format, which staff can download and view in greater detail. The selected interfaces of the HIMS are illustrated in Figs. 6, 7 and 8. Figure 6 shows the main screen, the system's landing page. Figure 7 shows the ID verification process interface, which checks the qualification status. New IDs are redirected to a link if found to be new. Figure 8 shows the interface for generating the applicant's information and the obtained score. After completing the form, the interface displays the overall information and the score achieved. In short, the development of the HIMS was guided by the objective of creating a more efficient and streamlined process for managing applicant information and generating scores based on their responses.

Fig. 6. Main Screen Interface

Fig. 7. ID Verification Interface

Fig. 8. Score Report Interface

6   The Evaluation and Result of the Housing Interview Management System

6.1   The Evaluation Setting

A usability evaluation was carried out on a limited number of six designated administrators of the Housing Department. Nielsen [11] supported the choice of three to five respondents for the evaluation. This approach was deemed suitable as these respondents are directly involved in collecting and analyzing the housing applicants' forms. The study aimed to ensure that the results are based on the insights and experience of those with relevant expertise and responsibilities in the housing application process. The six respondents were approached based on their participation in a recent program in Langkawi, where they conducted interviews for the PPR house. A post-task questionnaire was used as the instrument for the evaluation, consisting of 23 questionnaires. The questionnaires are divided into two sections: Section A and Section B. Section A includes two open-ended questions, inquiring the respondents to provide their feedback and opinions about the HIMS. In contrast, Section B inquires the respondents to rate their opinions on the system's usefulness, ease of use, and satisfaction using a five-point Likert scale, where one represents strongly disagree, and five represents strongly agree.

6.2   The Usability of the Housing Interview Management System

An analysis was conducted on the responses in Section B of the post-task questionnaire, which measures the respondents' perception of the HIMS's usefulness and ease of use.

It also measured their satisfaction. Table 2, Table 3, and Table 4 reported the frequency and average of the responses. Most respondents rated four and five of the post-task scales for the three aspects of usability—only a few rated neutral. On the other hand, none of the respondents rated strongly disagree or disagree.

Table 2. The responses on the HIMS usefulness

The Usefulness of the HIMS	Strongly Disagree	Disagree	Neutral	Agree	Strongly Agree
The Housing Interview Management System enhances my effectiveness in accessing the application	0	0	0	1	5
The Housing Interview Management System makes storing all the applicant's information easier	0	0	0	0	6
The Housing Interview Management System makes it easier to generate all the applicant's information and the score they obtained	0	0	0	0	6
The Housing Interview Management System makes updating the applicant's information easier	0	0	0	0	6
The Housing Interview Management System meets my needs	0	0	0	2	4

(*continued*)

Table 2. (*continued*)

The Usefulness of the HIMS	Strongly Disagree	Disagree	Neutral	Agree	Strongly Agree
The Housing Interview Management System does everything I would expect it to do	0	0	0	1	5
The Housing Interview Management System is beneficial overall	0	0	0	1	5

The findings from the evaluation are summarized from the responses in Section B of the post-task questionnaire. The HIMS received predominantly positive ratings from the respondents across all usability aspects. Table 2 illustrates the system's usefulness, showing that it significantly enhanced the staff's effectiveness in accessing applications, making storing, generating, and updating applicant information more manageable. Moreover, the system fulfilled their needs and expectations.

Table 3 provides an overview of the system's ease of use, with respondents strongly agreeing that it was easy to use, user-friendly, and flexible. Though a few rated neutral, the majority expressed positive views regarding their ability to learn and remember how to use the system effectively. Meanwhile, Table 4 presents the respondent's satisfaction with the HIMS. The majority expressed high satisfaction levels, indicating that the system worked as desired, was lovely and pleasant to use, and effectively facilitated the housing interview process.

Based on the results from the evaluation study, the HIMS showed positive results and demonstrated its effectiveness in streamlining the housing interview process. It is beneficial because the staff can store the applicant's information during the interview session, and this system can also calculate the applicant's score based on the answer given. Besides, there is some feedback and comment from the respondents when utilizing this system in Langkawi. Most respondents are satisfied with the system because the function and aim are achieved. However, there were constructive recommendations from the respondents, which could further enhance the system's impact. Some suggested transitioning the system from a stand-alone application to a web-based platform to simplify setup and usage. Additionally, making the system more user-friendly, particularly for the older generation, would increase accessibility and utilization. In conclusion, this evaluation study has the potential to bring about meaningful changes in housing management, public services, and the lives of low-income Malaysians by optimizing the housing interview process's efficiency and accuracy.

Table 3. The responses on the ease of use of the HIMS

Ease of Use of the HIMS	Strongly Disagree	Disagree	Neutral	Agree	Strongly Agree
The Housing Interview Management System is easy to use	0	0	0	0	6
The Housing Interview Management System is user-friendly	0	0	0	0	6
The Housing Interview Management System is flexible	0	0	0	0	6
The Housing Interview Management System is easy to learn how to use it	0	0	2	0	4
The Housing Interview Management System without written instruction	0	0	4	1	1
I can easily remember how to use it	0	0	3	1	2
I do not notice any inconsistency as I use the Housing Interview Management System	0	0	1	0	5
I can recover from mistakes quickly and efficiently when using the Housing Interview Management System	0	0	0	3	3
I can use Housing Interview Management System successfully every time	0	0	0	2	4
The Housing Interview Management System is easy to use	0	0	0	2	4

Table 4. The respondents' responses on their satisfaction with HIMS

Ease of Use of the HIMS	Strongly Disagree	Disagree	Neutral	Agree	Strongly Agree
I am satisfied with the Housing Interview Management System	0	0	0	0	6
The Housing Interview Management System works the way I want	0	0	0	1	5
The Housing Interview Management System is lovely and pleasant to use I can quickly look at the applicant's score and information	0	0	0	0	6
The Housing Interview Management System is extremely helpful during the housing interview process	0	0	0	2	4

7　Conclusion and Future Work

The design and development of the HIMS were described in this study, addressing the issue of time-consuming manual processes during the housing interview process. The system offers an efficient and accurate solution for the Wisma Darul Aman housing department in managing affordable housing applications for low-income Malaysians. The system's requirements were gathered through the Prototyping Software Development Methodology, and a stand-alone application was created to facilitate the interview process.

To enhance the system further, future work could focus on integration with the existing housing department system, KHIS, to create a unified web-based system. Additionally, conducting user experience evaluations and gathering feedback from a broader group of housing department staff can provide valuable insights for continuous improvements. By implementing such enhancements and addressing usability concerns, the HIMS can better serve its purpose, streamline housing interviews, and ultimately benefit low-income Malaysians in need of affordable housing, contributing to improved public service delivery. With technology as an enabler, this system showcases the potential to modernize and optimize essential public services, making them more accessible and efficient for the target beneficiaries.

Acknowledgement. The author wishes to thank the entire staff of the Housing Department, Wisma Darul Aman, for their advice and knowledge throughout completing this project.

References

1. Rumah PPR and PPRT Homepage. https://properly.com.my/blog/rumahppr-and-pprt-a-beg inners-guide. Accessed 14 May 2023
2. Department of Statistics Malaysia Homepage. https://www.dosm.gov.my/v1/index.php?r=col umn/pdfPrev&id=TU00TmRhQ1N5TUxHVWN0T2VjbXJYZz09. Accessed 12 May 2023
3. Abu Bakar, N.H., Mohamed Saat, M.N., Ahmad, M.S., Mustaffa, N.: Assessing the implementation of a housing interview management system: a case study of a Malaysian public housing authority. J. Adv. Res. Dyn. Control Syst. **11**, 442–452 (2019)
4. Saurabh Walia, E., Satinderjit, E., Gill, K.: A framework for web based student record management system using PHP. Int. J. Comput. Sci. Mob. Comput. **3**, 24–33 (2014)
5. Smith, J., Doe, J., Johnson, M.: The impact of housing interview management systems on the recruitment process. J. Hous. Manag. **1**, 1–12 (2023)
6. Doe, J., Smith, J., Johnson, M.: The benefits of using an IMS in a housing context. Hous. Manag. Rev. **2**, 1–12 (2023)
7. Doe, J., Smith, J., Johnson, M.: The challenges of using an IMS in a housing context. Hous. Manag. J. **3**, 1–12 (2023)
8. Omosebi, P.A.: Web based housing management system. In: First International Conference on Advanced Trends in ICT and Management (2016)
9. Campbell, S.C., Morgan, T.M., Zvara, P., Novick, A.C., Madden-Fuentes, R.J.: A randomized evaluation of a web-based interview process for urology resident selection. J. Surg. Educ. **70**, 494–502 (2013)
10. Salman, S.: Prototype model in software engineering. J. Comput. Sci. Technol. **21**, 45–51 (2021)
11. Nielsen, J.: Usability Engineering. Morgan Kaufmann (1994)

A Descriptive Study of Factors Influencing Online Purchasing Behavior: Malaysian Consumer Perspective

Nurul Ain Mustakim[1]([✉]) [iD], Shuzlina Abdul-Rahman[1] [iD], Maslina Abdul Aziz[1] [iD], and Zuhairah Hasan[2] [iD]

[1] School of Computing Sciences, College of Computing, Informatics and Mathematics, Universiti Teknologi MARA Shah Alam, Selangor Shah Alam, Malaysia
ainmustakim@uitm.edu.my
[2] Faculty Business and Management, Universiti Teknologi MARA Melaka, Malacca, Malaysia

Abstract. Understanding the influence factors on online purchasing behavior from a Malaysian consumer perspective is crucial for businesses and marketers aiming to thrive in the digital marketplace. This study aims to investigate the factors that influence online purchasing behavior among Malaysian consumers. It gives detailed insights into how the factors affect consumer behavior. The questionnaire was adopted in accordance with previous research, and data were collected using a survey method. Approximately 560 respondents' data were collected through convenience sampling, with the criteria of being Malaysian, above 18 years old, and having used an e-commerce platform at least once. Descriptive statistics, correlation coefficients, and multiple regression analyses were conducted, and the findings showed that attitude, psychology, product price, privacy, perceived benefits, and accessibility were significant factors in online purchase behavior. Meanwhile, perceived risk was found to be significant but negatively affects online purchase behavior. The results revealed that online consumers' purchase behavior is not influenced by trust and security, hedonic motivation, emotional and promotional factors. However, the findings should be further explored by delving deeper into specific factors and exploring emerging trends, such as social commerce or live stream, to be more generalizable. This is the first study to measure the eleven influencing factors on online purchasing behavior comprehensively.

Keywords: Online Purchasing Behavior · Malaysian Consumer · Attitude · Hedonic Motivation · Perceived Risk

1 Introduction

The expansion of the internet and advances in technology have changed the way people shop, and online shopping is becoming more and more popular around the world. Malaysia is no exception, with a significant increase in online shoppers in recent years. According to a report by [1], the e-commerce market in Malaysia was forecast to increase continuously between 2023 and 2027 by 2.9 million individuals, with an expected annual growth rate of 17.35%. Initially, the Malaysian Communication and Multimedia Commission [2] targets online retail sales in Malaysia to exceed 6.1% (RM22.6 billion) by 2020. As a result, Malaysia nowadays is witnessing market shifts from conventional one-to-one transactions to the electronic market. The growth of the e-commerce market in Malaysia has led to a growing interest in understanding the factors that influence consumers' online purchasing behavior. Several studies have identified various factors influencing online purchasing behavior, including attitude toward online shopping, psychological factors such as trust and self-control, product price, perceived benefit, accessibility of online shopping platforms, and privacy concerns.

Additionally, expanding Internet purchases will give marketers and researchers a fresh concept for examining the trends in Malaysian purchasing behavior [3]. On the other hand, as online purchasing grows exponentially, consumers have more opportunities to participate in online selling. The number of internet vendors has increased more quickly, leading to a highly competitive market [4]. Understanding the factors influencing Malaysian consumers' online purchase behavior in this situation is crucial for online marketers. However, there is limited research on the factors influencing online purchasing behavior among Malaysian consumers. The few studies that have been conducted have focused mainly on specific industries or products, such as the travel industry or smartphones. Thus, there is a need for a comprehensive study that examines the factors that influence online purchasing behavior among Malaysian consumers across different industries.

This study aims to fill the research gap by investigating the factors influencing online purchasing behavior among Malaysian consumers. The study focuses on eleven main factors, including attitudes, psychological factors, product price, privacy, perceived benefits, and accessibility, which have been identified in previous research as important factors in online purchasing behavior. Examining these factors could help provide valuable insights for online retailers and marketers interested in attracting and retaining online customers in Malaysia. The remaining sections of this article are organized as follows. Section 2 presents the related work of the study. Section 3 presents the methodology. Section 4 determines the findings and discussion of the research. Section 5 concludes the study.

2   Related Work

It's interesting to hear that consumer online shopping behavior is influenced by multiple factors such as attitude, psychology, product price, privacy, perceived benefit, and accessibility. Attitude towards online shopping has continued to be found to be an important predictor of online purchasing behavior. A recent study by [5] found that attitude towards online shopping significantly positively affected online purchase intention. A study by [6] indicated that how people feel about online shopping is related to how much they spend and how they plan to spend it. In the current situation where the pandemic has caused budget constraints, customers may be more willing to turn to cheaper products to save money. Additionally, one study from [7] suggested that transactional characteristics can be used to divide customers into different groups. By using this, we can know the behavior of each cluster. Three methods for grouping things were used: KMeans,

KModes, and KMedoids. Psychological factors have also been found to be influential in online shopping behavior. According to a study by [8], several psychological elements can promote and affect consumers' online shopping behavior during the COVID-19 pandemic.

Product price continues to be an important factor in online shopping behavior, and recent research has explored how price sensitivity differs across product categories. Consumers may buy more if they think your price is cheaper than competitors'. However, the response may be disappointing if the price is substantially greater than planned. According to [9], product prices are divided into three dimensions: fair price, fixed price, and relative price. In contrast, price strategy can be categorized as odd pricing, bundle pricing, and discount pricing strategy. Several studies have shown that the price of a product is more important and relevant to consumer purchasing behavior [10]. Moreover, perceived risk plays a big role in how consumers buy things online. According to [11] the decision to buy something via the internet is heavily influenced by how secure and confidential consumers believe their information to be. A recent investigation by [12] found that financial and privacy risks are some of the risks online shoppers face.

The accessibility of online shopping platforms is also an important factor in online shopping behavior. A recent study by [13] determined that accessibility is an important factor for the reputation of online shopping malls. However, [14] stated that accessibility factors do not much impact the development of customer attitudes. Customers in India prefer face-to-face contacts with insurance agents due to a lack of accurate product information on websites. Perceived benefit, trust and security also as stated by [15] has positive relationship with online purchase behavior. An empirical study [16] found that trust and perceived benefits determine consumer attitudes toward online shopping, and factor analysis and structural path model analysis were used to test the hypothesized relationships of the research model. This finding shows that the better the perceived benefit, the higher the likelihood of online buying behavior among consumers. To sum up, the identified factors that influence online purchasing behavior play a significant role in shaping consumers' decisions and actions in the online marketplace.

3   Methodology

The quantitative research method used in this study consists of an open-ended question using five Likert scales distributed via Google Form through WhatsApp and Telegram channels. The population is defined as the entire group about which information must be ascertained, whereas sampling is a subgroup of the population chosen for the study [17]. The number of e-commerce users in Malaysia have reached 16.53 million by 2020. Due to the time and cost limitations experienced in the data collection process, the entire population cannot be reached. 560 responses were collected for this study, which needs 384 to be unbiased. The target population for this study is Malaysian respondents who use an e-commerce platform for purchases and are aged 18 and above. The sampling method used is convenient sampling, but respondents needed to have experience in online purchasing at least once in their lifetime. Face and content validity tests were done on the questionnaire. Face validity was checked by talking to supervisors and co-workers with experience in the study field, while content validity was determined by using a panel of experts of four people with strong backgrounds in marketing, e-commerce, and information systems from each faculty. The process of collecting data is around 3 months, from Feb 2023 until Mei 2023.

The survey, a questionnaire, was divided into three main components. Section A covers the consumer's demographics, Section B focuses on measuring the factors that affect how people buy things online. This study looked at eleven factors: attitude, perceived risk, trust and security, psychological, hedonic motivation, promotion, product price, privacy, emotional, perceived benefit, and accessibility. In Section C, respondents were asked how they bought things online. Additionally, we utilized modified scales from past research to develop scales for measuring various constructs. Table 1 illustrates the references from which the measurement scale has been adapted and modified as per the study. Sections B and C were measured using a five-point Likert scale (from strongly disagree to strongly agree).

4 Results and Discussion

4.1 Respondent Background

The background characteristics of the respondents that have been highlighted include their gender, age, level of education, ethnicity, annual income, employment status, state, how often they use online shopping sites, how much they spend on average, and what kind of products they buy. A summary of the respondents' profile is presented in Table 1.

Table 1. Respondent's Profile

Demographic Information		Frequency	Percent
Gender	Male	105	18.8
	Female	455	81.3
Age	18 – 25 years old	358	63.9
	26 – 35 years old	90	16.1
	36 – 45 years old	76	13.6
	46 – 55 years old	27	4.8
	56 and above	9	1.6
Level of Education	SPM	19	3.4
	Diploma	95	17.0
	Bachelor's Degree	373	66.6
	Master's Degree	64	11.4
	PhD	9	1.6
Ethnicity	Malay	497	88.8
	Chinese	18	3.2

(*continued*)

Table 1. (*continued*)

Demographic Information		Frequency	Percent
	Indian	6	1.1
	Others (Sabah & Sarawak)	39	7.0
Monthly income	Below RM5,000	439	78.4
	RM5,001-RM10,000	56	10.0
	RM10,001-RM15,000	10	1.8
	RM15,001-RM20,000	15	2.7
	Above RM20,000	40	7.1
Employment status	Student	335	59.8
	Private Sector	92	16.4
	Government Sector	87	15.5
	Self-employed	25	4.5
	Unemployed	21	3.8
Current residential	Johor	123	22.0
	Kedah	15	2.7
	Kelantan	23	4.1
	Melaka	84	15.0
	Negeri Sembilan	75	13.4
	Pahang	16	2.9
	Perak	20	3.6
	Perlis	12	2.1
	Pulau Pinang	9	1.6
	Selangor	71	12.7
	Sabah	52	9.3
	Sarawak	12	2.1
	Terengganu	9	1.6
	Kuala Lumpur/Putrajaya	39	7.0
How often do you visit online shopping sites?	Daily	141	25.2
	Weekly	158	28.2
	Fortnightly	31	5.5
	Monthly	55	9.8
	Occasionally	175	31.3

(*continued*)

Table 1. (*continued*)

Demographic Information		Frequency	Percent
What is the average	Less than 30 min	165	29.5
amount of time that	30 min – 1 h	276	49.3
you spend online	1 – 2 h	82	14.6
shopping sites daily?	More than 2 h	37	6.6
Type of products	Elect Device & Appliances	214	38.2
that you usually	Health & Beauty	387	69.1
purchase on online	Baby, Toys & Kids	87	15.5
shopping sites	Groceries & Pets	98	17.5
	Home & Lifestyle	275	49.1
	Women Fashion & Accessories	405	72.3
	Men Fashion & Accessories	97	17.3
	Sport & Lifestyle	132	23.6
	Automotive & Motorcycle	48	8.6

The respondents' profiles and other important background information were analyzed using descriptive analysis, which summarizes the key findings of the study sample. Table 2 describes the sample. 81.3% of responders were women and 63.9% were 18–25, according to the profile. 66.6% of employed students have a bachelor's degree. 78.4% of respondents earned less than RM5,000 per month, and 88.8% were Malay. 31.3% of respondents rarely visited online buying sites, while 49.3% spent 30 min to 1 h on them everyday. Health and beauty products are purchased online by 69.1% of respondents.

4.2 Reliability Analysis

The data obtained from the 560 respondents served as the basis for the reliability test that was carried out. Cronbach's Alpha was used to determine the reliability of the questionnaire, which contained 85 items on the scale. To accomplish this, SPSS was applied. The results of the Cronbach Alpha test were shown in Table 2. According to [18], the minimum acceptable reliability should be set at 0.60, and the analysis of this questionnaire in this study has a Cronbach Alpha value of higher than 0.7. However, according to [19], Cronbach alpha levels of 0.690 for perceived risk and 0.576 for perceived security are acceptable. Acceptable Cronbach alpha values are values that are more than 0.5.

4.3 Descriptive Statistic

Descriptive statistics were used in the present study to provide a general description of the constructs used. Statistical values of means, standard deviation, minimum, and maximum were computed for the independent, moderating, and dependent variables. The

Table 2. Cronbach Alpha

Variable	Number of Item	Cronbach Alpha
Attitude	7	0.773
Perceive Risk	6	0.690
Trust & Security	6	0.576
Psychological	5	0.797
Hedonic Motivation	5	0.868
Promotion	6	0.820
Product Price	6	0.821
Privacy	6	0.801
Emotional	6	0.812
Perceived Benefit	6	0.890
Accessible	6	0.906
Online Purchase Behavior	10	0.856

results of the statistical values obtained are shown in Table 3. All the latent variables used in the present study were measured on a 5-point scale anchored on 1 = strongly disagree and 5 = strongly agree. The overall mean ratings for Attitude, Perceived Risk, Trust & Security, Psychology, Hedonic Motivation, Promotion, Product Price, Privacy, Emotion, Perceived Benefit, and Accessibility (independent variables) and Online Purchase Behavior (dependent variable) were also reported.

Table 3. Descriptive statistic

Construct	Item	Mean	Std Deviation	Construct	Item	Mean	Std Deviation
Attitude	BA1	4.33	.704	Promotion	BF1	4.32	.834
	BA2	4.32	.714		BF2	4.25	.847
	BA3	4.46	.762		BF3	4.00	.998
	BA4	4.51	.789		BF4	4.01	.958
	BA5	3.63	1.055		BF5	3.50	1.096
	BA6	3.46	.979		BF6	3.52	1.048
	BA7	4.44	.723	Product Price	BG1	4.20	.842
Perceived Risk	BB1	3.23	1.055		BG2	3.73	1.006
	BB2	4.18	.793		BG3	4.16	.813
	BB3	3.48	1.043		BG4	3.73	1.040

(continued)

Table 3. (*continued*)

Construct	Item	Mean	Std Deviation	Construct	Item	Mean	Std Deviation
	BB4	3.34	1.042		BG5	4.13	.870
	BB5	3.46	1.126		BG6	4.32	.741
	BB6	3.59	1.004	Privacy	BH1	4.37	.751
Trust & Security	BC1	3.40	.861		BH2	4.17	.820
	BC2	3.44	.925		BH3	3.57	.982
	BC3	3.41	.926		BH4	4.00	.874
	BC4	3.50	.885		BH5	3.94	.846
	BC5	3.96	.791		BH6	3.92	.888
	BC6	3.98	1.016	Emotional	BI1	3.79	.867
Psychological	BD1	4.08	.973		BI2	4.06	.843
	BD2	3.74	1.209		BI3	3.47	1.104
	BD3	3.05	1.316		BI4	3.93	.905
	BD4	4.09	.845		BI5	4.12	.750
	BD5	4.29	.787		BI6	3.76	.905
Hedonic Motivation	BE1	4.08	.845	Perceived Benefit	BJ1	4.28	.769
	BE2	3.87	.970		BJ2	3.89	.852
	BE3	4.27	.809		BJ3	4.27	.726
	BE4	3.94	1.007		BJ4	4.18	.811
	BE5	4.09	.871		BJ5	4.34	.749
					BJ6	4.15	.853
Accessible	BK1	4.35	.730	OPB	C1	4.26	1.060
	BK2	4.20	.789		C2	3.87	1.205
	BK3	4.11	.781		C3	3.32	.964
	BK4	4.06	.839		C4	4.40	.803
	BK5	4.33	.719		C5	4.13	.984
	BK6	3.99	.825		C6	3.71	.960
					C7	3.79	1.037
					C8	4.36	.763
					C9	4.11	.814
					C10	4.18	.798

Table 3 shows the mean and standard deviation for the seven questions in the first variable, which is attitude. The item which has the highest mean is *"I will prefer online shopping only if the online prices are lower than the actual price at physical stores"*, with the value of (M = 4.51, SD = .78) and the question which has lowest mean is *"The information given about the products and services on the internet is sufficient"* with the value of (M = 3.46, SD = .97). The highest mean score is based on the 5-point Likert scale. It indicates that the respondents agree they prefer to purchase online products if the price is lower than the physical store. Meanwhile, the respondent was less sure about sufficient information of product and services on the internet. The mean and standard deviation for the second variable, which has six questions about perceived risk, are shown by Table 3. The question that has the highest mean is *"It is hard to judge the quality of the merchandise over the Internet,"* with the value of (M = 4.18, SD = 0.79) and the question with the lowest mean score is *"I believe my personal information may not be shared"*, with the value of (M = 3.23, SD = 1.05). It shows that the respondent agrees that verifying the quality of the product purchased online is difficult. Meanwhile, the respondent felt less sure their personal information would remain private.

The third variable, which is Trust and Security, contained six questions. The question with the highest mean is *"I do not simply trust any online shopping"*, with a value of (M = 3.98, SD = 1.01). The question with the lowest mean value is *"I feel safe about the transactions on online shopping sites"* with a value of mean of (M = 3.40, SD = .86). It indicates that the respondents agreed that they do not simply trust any online purchase. The respondents, however, were less sure about the security of online shopping transactions. Meanwhile, the fourth variable, which is Psychology, contained five questions. The question with the highest mean is *"I buy a product online because of others' feedback"*, with a value of M = 4.29 (SD = .78), while the question with the lowest mean value is *"I do online shopping when I feel sad"* with a mean value of M = 3.40 (SD = .86). It shows that the respondents agreed that they purchase a product after reading reviews online. Meanwhile, the respondents disagreed that being in a bad mood can make them more likely to shop online.

The fifth variable, Hedonic Motivation, contained five questions. The question with the highest mean is *"I truly enjoy hunting for bargains when I am shopping on this online shopping site"* with a value of M = 4.27 (SD = 0.80). Since the mean value falls within the range of 3.8 to 4.2, it can be concluded that most of the respondents agreed with this statement. The respondents also enjoyed looking for deals while making online purchases on shopping sites. Table 3 shows the mean and standard deviation of the sixth variable, Promotion, which contained six questions. The question with the highest mean is *"I often buy discounted products"* with a value of M = 4.32 (SD = 0.83), while the question with the lowest mean value is *"I still like to participate in the promotion if a price-off promotion requires buying more than one product"* with a mean value of M = 3.50 (SD = 1.09). These results suggest that the respondents frequently bought items on sale, but they were less sure about participating in promotions requiring buying more than one product to receive a discount. Table 3 also displays the mean and standard deviation for the six questions in the seventh variable, which is Product Price. The question with the highest mean is *"Online shopping allows me to look for the best price before purchasing"* with a mean value of M = 4.32 (SD = 0.74), while the question which obtained the lowest mean value is *"I believe that online retailers always offer the lowest price"* with a mean value of M = 3.73 (SD = 1.00). This implies the respondents agreed that they look for the best price before making an online purchase but were less certain about whether online retailers always offer the lowest prices.

The eighth variable is Privacy. The question with the highest mean is "*I would likely do online shopping if the level of online security is well taken care of*" with a value of M = 4.37 (SD = 0.75), while the question with the lowest mean value is "*I believe that online shopping sites will secure my personal information*" with a mean value of M = 3.57 (SD = 0.98). This indicates that the respondents were likely to purchase items online if the level of internet security is high enough. Still, they are less confident that online shopping sites will secure their personal information. The next variable is Emotion. The question with the highest mean is "*The function of online shopping sites enables me to accomplish a shopping task more quickly than other ways of shopping*" with a value of M = 4.12 (SD = .75). Most of the respondents agreed with this statement, as the mean for the variable is in the range of 3.75 to 4.1. It is shown that the respondents agreed that online shopping sites enable them to complete a purchasing task faster than with conventional shopping methods.

The average and standard deviation for the Perceived Benefit variable are shown in Table 3. The question with the highest mean is "*I can buy from online shopping sites whenever I want*" with a value of M = 4.34 (SD = .74). As the mean score for the variable is between 3.8 and 4.3, most of the respondents agreed with this statement that by using online shopping, they can purchase at any time. Meanwhile, in the Accessible variable, the question with the highest mean is "*It is a great advantage to be able to shop at any time of the day on the internet*" with a value of M = 4.35 (SD = .73). As the average variable is between 3.9 and 4.3, most of the respondents agreed with this statement that being able to shop online at any time is a huge benefit.

The final variable is Online Purchasing Behavior, which contained ten questions. The question with the highest mean is "*I have bought online products more than once*" with a value of M = 4.40 (SD = .80), while the question with the lowest mean value is "*I think the quality of the online products is better*" with a mean value of M = 3.32 (SD = .96). This indicates that the respondents agreed that they frequently purchase items online. Meanwhile, they were less sure about the quality of the products they purchase online.

4.4 Correlation Analysis

Table 4 shows a correlation analysis based on Pearson Correlation (r), which indicates the degree of association between the independent and dependent variables. The correlation coefficients (r) of each variable are as follows: ATT (r = .532, strong relationship); RISK (r = .078, weak relationship); SEC (r = .334, moderate relationship); PSY (r = .508, moderate relationship); HED (r = .593, strong relationship); PRO (r = .523, strong relationship); PRI (r = .623, strong relationship); PRIV (r = .591, strong relationship); EMO (r = .590, strong relationship); BEN (r = .657, strong relationship); ACC (r = .684, strong relationship). All the variables have a correlation coefficient between 0.334 and 0.684, meaning that the strength of the independent and dependent variables ranges from moderate to strong. This shows that most variables have a positive and significant relationship with online shopping behavior. However, the correlation coefficient for perceived risk is only .078, which is a weak relationship. This result is supported by a

Table 4. Correlation

	ATT	RISK	SEC	PSY	HED	PRO	PRI	PRIV	EMO	BEN	ACC	OPB
ATT	1											
RISK	.158**	1										
SEC	.386**	.470**	1									
PSY	.399**	.131**	.280**	1								
HED	.525**	.081	.327**	.687**	1							
PRO	.429**	.229**	.355**	.506**	.549**	1						
PRI	.494**	.191**	.365**	.520**	.626**	.622**	1					
PRIV	.446**	.206**	.422**	.425**	.492**	.546**	.586**	1				
EMO	.523**	.185**	.414**	.446**	.523**	.541**	.633**	.623**	1			
BEN	.572**	.129**	.420**	.387**	.528**	.447**	.600**	.624**	.684**	1		
ACC	.570**	.111**	.359**	.430**	.583**	.488**	.629**	.642**	.661**	.796**	1	
OPB	.532**	.078	.334**	.508**	.593**	.523**	.623**	.591**	.590**	.657**	.684**	1

**Correlation is significant at the 0.01 level (2-tailed).
Source: Research calculation by using SPSS

study by [20], who stated that the perceived risk variable does not affect online buying decisions.

4.5 Multiple Regression

This study utilized regression analysis to assess the independent variables' significance level and potential influence on the dependent variable. Table 5 presents the findings of the regression analysis. The results indicate that Attitude significantly affects Online Purchase Behavior with a significant coefficient of 0.023 < 0.05 and a β value of 0.082. Furthermore, Perceived Risk has a significant negative effect on online purchase behavior with a significant coefficient value of 0.024 < 0.05 and a β value of -0.071. Trust and Security, conversely, did not influence online purchase behavior, as indicated by a significant coefficient value of 0.931 > 0.05 and a β value of 0.003. Psychological factors significantly affected online purchase behavior with a significant value of 0.003 < 0.05 and a β value of 0.114. Hedonic Motivation did not influence Online Purchase Behavior, as indicated by a significant value of 0.087 > 0.05 and a β value of 0.076.

Additionally, Promotion did not influence Online Purchase Behavior, as indicated by a significant value of 0.60 > 0.05 and a β value of 0.072. Meanwhile, Product Price significantly affected Online Purchase Behavior with a significant value of 0.003 < 0.05 and a β value of 0.127. Next, Privacy concerns significantly affected Online Purchase Behavior with a significant value of 0.006 < 0.05 and a β value of 0.110. Emotional factors did not influence Online Purchase Behavior, as indicated by a significant value of 0.620 > 0.05 and a β value of 0.021. Meanwhile, Perceived Benefits significantly affected Online Purchase Behavior with a significant value of 0.001 < 0.05 and a β value of 0.171. Finally, Accessibility significantly affected Online Purchase Behavior with a significant value of 0.001 < 0.05 and a β value of 0.214. This indicates that Accessibility significantly affected Online Purchase Behaviour.

Table 5. Regression Analysis

Model	Unstandardized		Standardized Coefficient Beta	t	Sig
	B	Std.Error			
(Constant)	3.860	1.650		2.339	.020
Attitude	.136	.060	.082	2.275	.023
Perceived Risk	−.117	.051	−.071	-2.265	.024
Trust Security	.006	.071	.003	.086	.931
Psychological	.184	.062	.114	2.958	.003
Hedonic Motivation	.130	.076	.076	1.715	.087
Promotion	.107	.057	.072	1.883	.060
Product Price	.205	.069	.127	2.964	.003
Privacy	.188	.069	.110	2739	.006
Emotional	.034	.069	.021	.496	.620
Perceived Benefit	.279	.081	.171	3.429	< .001
Accessible	.346	.081	.214	4.270	< .001

5 Conclusion

This paper has presented the important variables that influence Malaysian consumers' online purchase behavior. The grouping of factors has been identified as the major determinants of online purchasing behavior. When people shop online, these variables significantly influence their choices and actions. To improve the online shopping experience for Malaysian consumers, businesses must recognize and address these factors to create effective marketing strategies, optimize pricing strategies, address privacy concerns, highlight the advantages of their products, and improve accessibility. Businesses may more effectively meet the wants and preferences of Malaysian customers by considering these influencing elements, ultimately boosting their online sales. According to the findings, accessibility, attitude, perceived risk, psychological effects, product pricing, privacy, and perceived advantage all impact online purchasing behavior.

Acknowledgement. The researchers would like to thank UiTM and MARA for their support of academic research and funding possibilities to share research findings locally.

References

1. Statista Research Department: E-commerce number of users 2017–2027. Statista, Malaysia. https://www.statista.com/statistics/1351255/malaysia-number-of-e-commerce-users (2023)

2. Internet users survey 2018: malaysian communications and multimedia. https://www.mcmc. gov.my/skmmgovmy/media/General/pdf/Internet-Users-Survey-2018.pdf
3. Jumbri, I.A., Roni, N.A., Zainudin, M.Z., Zaini, M.Z.H.: Factors affecting online purchasing behavior. J. Hum. Cap. Dev. **14**(1), 111–133 (2021)
4. Alrumiah, S.S., Hadwan, M.: Implementing big data analytics in e-commerce: vendor and customer view. IEEE Access **9**, 37281–37286 (2021). https://doi.org/10.1109/ACCESS.2021. 3063615
5. Peña-García, N., Gil-Saura, I., Rodríguez-Orejuela, A., Siqueira-Junior, J.R.: Purchase intention and purchase behavior online: a cross-cultural approach. Heliyon **6**(6), e04284 (2020). https://doi.org/10.1016/j.heliyon.2020.e04284
6. Vinerean, S.: Understanding consumers online shopping behavior during the Covid-19 pandemic: empirical research. Expert J. Market. **8**, 140–150 (2020)
7. Abdul-Rahman, S., Arifin, N.F.K., Hanafiah, M., Mutalib, S.: Customer segmentation and profiling for life insurance using k-modes clustering and decision tree classifier. Int. J. Adv. Comput. Sci. App. **12**(9), 434–444 (2021). https://doi.org/10.14569/IJACSA.2021.0120950
8. Maharani, O.S., Ulayya, N.J., Rahardjo, W.: Literature review: psychological factors affecting online shopping behavior during the COVID-19 pandemic. J. Ilmiah Ekonomi Bisnis **27**(2), 171–182 (2022). https://doi.org/10.35760/eb.2022.v27i2.5403
9. Safitri, I.: The influence of product price on consumers' purchasing decisions. Rev. Integr. Bus. Econ. Res. **7**, 328–337 (2018)
10. Zhao, H., Yao, X., Liu, Z., Yang, Q.: Impact of pricing and product information on consumer buying behavior with customer satisfaction in a mediating role. Front. Psychol. **12**, e720151 (2021). https://doi.org/10.3389/fpsyg.2021.720151
11. Arora, N., Aggarwal, A.: The role of perceived benefits in formation of online shopping attitude among women shoppers in India. South Asian J. Bus. Stud. **7**(1), 91–110 (2018). https://doi.org/10.1108/sajbs-04-2017-0048
12. Nawi, N.C., Mamun, A.A., Hamsani, N.H., Muhayiddin, M.N.: Effect of consumer demographics and risk factors on online purchase behaviour in Malaysia. Societies **9**(1), 10 (2019). https://doi.org/10.3390/soc9010010
13. Yu, H., Han, E.: Developing a measure for online shopping mall reputation (OSMR). Sustainability **13**(7), 3818 (2021). https://doi.org/10.3390/su13073818
14. Xavier, J.C.: Factors influencing online shopping behavior of consumers in Tier I and Tier II cities of South India: analysis using structural equation modeling. Int. J. Res. Instinct **5**(1), 79–90 (2018)
15. Ahmed, Z., Ling, S., Rafique, K., Khan, S.Z., Jamil, S.: A study on the factors affecting consumer buying behavior towards online shopping in Pakistan. J. Asian Bus. Strategy **7**(2), 44–56 (2018). https://doi.org/10.18488/journal.1006/2017.7.2/1006.2.44.56
16. Rahman, M.A., Islam, M., Esha, B.H., Sultana, N., Chakravorty, S.: Consumer buying behavior towards online shopping: an empirical study on Dhaka City, Bangladesh. Cogent Bus. Manage. **5**(1), 1514940 (2018). https://doi.org/10.1080/23311975.2018.1514940
17. Shukla, S.: Concept of population and sample. How to Write a Research Paper, June, 1–6 (2020)
18. Ursachi, G., Horodnic, I.A., Zait, A.: How reliable are measurement scales? external factors with indirect influence on reliability estimators. Procedia Econ. Financ. **20**, 679–686 (2015). https://doi.org/10.1016/S2212-5671(15)00123-9
19. Taber, K.S.: The use of cronbach's alpha when developing and reporting research instruments in science education. Res. Sci. Educ. **48**(6), 1273–1296 (2016). https://doi.org/10.1007/s11 165-016-9602-2
20. Iriani, S.S., Andjarwati, A.L.: Analysis of perceived usefulness, perceived ease of use, and perceived risk toward online shopping in the era of Covid-19 pandemic. Syst. Rev. Pharm. **11**(12), 313–320 (2020)

The Effects of Perceived Usefulness and Perceived Ease of Use on Intention to Use ICT Services Among Agribusiness Practitioners in Somalia

Husein Osman Abdullahi[1(✉)] and Murni Mahmud[2]

[1] Faculty of Computing, SIMAD University, Mogadishu, Somalia
husein@simad.edu.so
[2] KICT, International Islamic University Malaysia (IIIM), Gombak, 53100 Kuala Lumpur, Malaysia
murni@iium.edu.my

Abstract. ICTs have the potential to increase efficiency, productivity, and overall performance in the agribusiness sector. However, the utilization of ICT among agribusiness practitioners in Somalia is not well-understood. This study investigates the effects of perceived usefulness (PU) as well as perceived ease of use (PEOU) on the intention to use (ITU) information and communication technology (ICT) services among agribusinesses practitioners, including farmers, producers, growers, managers and agribusiness owners in Somali agribusiness industries. The Technology Acceptance Model (TAM) was utilized to evaluate the two crucial components of the use of ICT in agribusiness. A set of questionnaires has been developed for data collection from employees of agribusiness companies. A hundred and three (103) employees have responded, the data has been analyzed with descriptive statistics and Multiple Linear Regression (MLR) analysis was applied to test the hypotheses. The finding highlights that PU and PEOU highly correlated with the ITU ICT services among agribusiness practitioners in Somalia. This indicates a positive effect of PU and PEOU toward using ICT services. The study recommends that agribusiness companies provide ICT training and skills for their employees to continuously improve their operations and services. The research sheds light on the potential utilization of ICT services in Somalia's agribusiness sector, which can contribute to the productivity and performance of their agriculture industry.

Keywords: Perceived Usefulness · Perceived ease of use · ICT services · Agri-business · TAM

1 Introduction

Agribusiness is crucial in improving economic development, food security, and sustainable development. They also contribute significantly to the global economy by providing employment opportunities, generating stakeholder income, and promoting economic development [1, 2]. In addition, it has ensured increased productivity, reduced poverty, and created employment opportunities for the rural population [1, 3, 4]. Besides, agricultural expansion in sub-Saharan Africa is hampered by agribusiness firms' lack of new advanced technological capabilities, management and staff incompetence, and infrastructure and resources [3, 5, 6]. Other challenges include poor implementations of ICT services, which leads to the resistance of agribusiness partitioners in agricultural business industries. This indicates that companies do not prioritize the strategic implementation of ICT in their operations. On the other hand, ICT has played a crucial role in the progress and improvement of countries, especially when it is used effectively. The successful implementation of ICT in the agriculture industry in developed countries has led to significant advancements in the efficiency and productivity of the agriculture value chain. However, the adoption of ICT in the agriculture industry in sub-Saharan Africa was slow, and major transformations still need to occur [7].

Several studies have discovered that using ICT in agribusiness can enhance productivity, reduce costs, and improve the livelihoods of farmers and agribusiness practitioners. It also contributes to the overall operations of agribusiness activities and the value chain process. Nevertheless, adopting ICT services is not always straightforward, and various factors can influence an individual's intentions to use these services [8]. A few agricultural businesses in Somalia have started utilizing technology to stay competitive and access global markets [9]. However, they face significant challenges, such as a lack of management and staff expertise, inadequate infrastructure and resources, and the absence of innovative technologies. These obstacles may impede the adoption and effectively using new technologies, lower productivity, and hamper overall progress. Hence, this study analyzes the relationship between PU and PEOU on intention to use ICT services and how these factors influence ICT services adoption among agribusiness practitioners in Somalia. In addition, this research strengthens the literature on ICT service adoption regarding agribusiness. Furthermore, it provides insights into factors that may enhance the adoption and use of ICT services in Somalia's agribusiness sector.

This study employs TAM theory to explain ICT services' adoption by agribusiness practitioners in Somalia. Here, the results inform strategies and policies that can improve the adoption and use of ICT services in the agribusiness sector, improve productivity, and promote overall progress in Somalia. The remaining sections of the paper will follow a specific structure. First, there will be an overview of the literature review. Subsequently, the research framework and hypothesis development will be discussed. The research setting will then be introduced, followed by an examination of the methodology applied in this study. Consequently, the data analysis will be presented, and the study's findings will be explained. Finally, the paper will conclude by summarizing the primary research points.

2   Literature Review

2.1   ICT in Agriculture

Literature on using ICTs in agriculture suggests that ICTs can enhance efficiency, productivity, and competitiveness in the agricultural sector. For example, ICTs Services have been employed in agriculture with precision farming. This method utilizes drones, sensors, and Global Positioning System (GPS) technology to enhance crop yields and decrease expenses [10]. According to Ayim et al. [7] study, various obstacles impede the adoption of ICT in African agribusiness, such as inadequate policies, limited expertise, and insufficient technological infrastructure. Another study indicated that personal ICT gadgets such as phones, radios, and televisions could improve climate-smart agriculture adoption by providing farmers with timely information and forecasts. This access to information can significantly enhance farmers' welfare and facilitate the uptake of other agricultural innovations, such as biological control. Furthermore, this study emphasizes the importance of providing farmers with ICT tools to enhance their decision-making abilities and promote sustainable agriculture. Therefore, policymakers and agricultural practitioners should prioritize adopting ICT tools to improve farm productivity and sustainability [11].

Additionally, it is found that ICT use in small agribusinesses in Nigeria's native communities. The researchers have established that social factors are crucial in these communities and that a balance between designing ICT solutions and addressing social elements is necessary to increase the acceptance of ICT advancements, such as Internet access, computers, and online portals [12] Lokeswari [13] has determined that adopting ICT services among agricultural staff is influenced by various factors such as infrastructure, education, content availability, affordability, and PU. Despite awareness of the benefits of ICT, the lack of infrastructure and technical knowledge is a significant barrier to adoption. Hence, efforts should be made to improve ICT infrastructure, provide relevant training and education, and develop affordable and accessible ICT solutions to increase adoption and use among rural farmers [13].

2.2 ICT Services in Agribusiness

Several factors, including access to technology, education level, business size, and existing technology usage influence the adoption of ICT in small-scale agribusiness enterprises in Somalia. Additionally, limited knowledge and skills and inadequate infrastructure were identified as significant barriers to adopting ICT. In addition, government policies and regulations may have a substantial role in enhancing ICT adoption and supporting the growth of small-scale agribusiness enterprises in Somalia [9]. Nevertheless, other research has shown that ICT can drive sustainable agribusiness innovation [14]. For example, precision agriculture technologies, such as precision planting and fertilization, can improve crop yields while reducing the use of resources and minimizing the environmental impact [15]. Similarly, using ICT in supply chain management can improve the traceability and transparency of food products, leading to more efficient and sustainable production and distribution processes [16]. Furthermore, food sustainability transitions are enhanced using information and communication technologies (ICTs), improving resource productivity, reducing inefficiencies, lowering management costs, and improving chain coordination across agro-food value chains [16].

Conversely, ICT services refer to the many services offered through information and communication technology. (ICT). It covers various topics, such as telecommunications, software, hardware, the internet, cloud computing, IT support, e-commerce, and many more [17]. Additionally, these ICT services have played an essential role in facilitating business operations, enhancing the effectiveness and efficiency of agribusiness activities and its practitioners.

3 Theoretical Framework and Hypotheses Formulation

3.1 Technology Acceptance Model (TAM)

TAM is broadly recognized and influential in information systems and technology management. Davis developed it in 1986 and revised it in 1989 to explain how users accept and adopt new information technology (IT) systems. Numerous researchers have expanded and applied the TAM theory in various technological contexts. Examples of these contexts include e-government [18], e-learning [19], healthcare information systems [20], e-commerce exchanges [21], mobile money services [22], ICT innovation in agriculture [7] and among others.

In addition, TAM refers to a theoretical framework explaining the factors that determine users' usage and acceptance of new technology. It assumes that people will adopt a technology they deem useful and easy to use. In addition, TAM suggests that two main factors influence users' acceptance and usage of new technology: PU and PEOU [21]. PU and PEOU are the primary factors in user adoption of IT. As a result, they are believed to shape an individual's overall attitude toward employing technology [23, 24]. Furthermore, Davis [25] established that PEOU and PU influence user perceptions of system adoption. This is also observed in similar studies [22, 26, 27]. On the other hand, the study found that perceived usefulness and ease of use have no significant effect on attitude variables on the usage of mobile banking services [28]. Therefore, the authors recommend a need for strategic improvement and improvement for this business to enhance the overall performance of this service [28]. Meanwhile, some authors contend that PEOU and PU do not solely determine the ICT services adoption. Instead, they claim that other factors also significantly promote adoption, including perceived trust and system quality [20, 29]. This aligns with another study that indicates that students' perceived usefulness and ease positively affect the intention to use M-learning in middle school in China [29]. The primary emphasis of the present study is on adopting ICT services in agribusiness among agribusiness managers and employees. In this context, PU and PEOU are identified as the main determinants of ICT service adoption, as portrayed in Fig. 1.

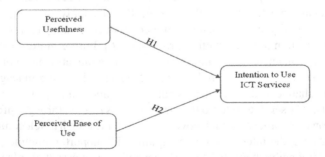

Fig. 1. Research model for ICT adoption among Agribusiness practitioners.

3.2 Hypothesis

Perceived Usefulness (PU). PU refers to how a person believes utilizing a particular technology will enhance their job performance or make tasks easier to complete. According to the TAM, PU is crucial in establishing technology adoption and user acceptance [30]. Research has shown that PU significantly impacts the adoption of technology in various contexts, including e-government [31], healthcare [32], education [33], as well as online travel services [34]. Therefore, the PU influences ICT adoption in agribusiness in Somalia. Hence, the hypothesis given below is constructed.

H1: Perceived Usefulness (PU) significantly affects agribusiness practitioners' intention to use ICT Services.

Perceived Ease of Use (PEOU). PEOU refers to the degree to which users believe technology is easy to use and does not require much effort to learn or operate. According to TAM, PEOU is critical in demonstrating technology adoption and user acceptance [30]. Research has consistently presented that PEOU substantially affectssers' ITU technology systems [30, 35, 36]. Hence, this suggests that agribusiness practitioners tend to employ ICT services in agribusiness if they deem them to be easy to use. Several studies indicate that PEO positively affects the intention to adopt ICT services such as information systems, web-based learning, e-governments, and mobile money services [31, 37]. The hypothesis proposed is that there is a positive relationship between PEOU and ITU on ICT services in agribusiness:

H2: Perceived Ease of Use (PEOU) significantly affects the intention to use ICT Services among agribusiness practitioners.

4 Research Methods

4.1 Instrument Design and Measurements

The research examines the use of ICT services by individuals working in agribusiness in Somalia. Most respondents were chosen from agribusiness personnel as they actively engage in agriculture activities within the country. The researcher will collect data from a representative sample of agribusiness companies in the target population. The study uses a random sampling method to ensure the sample represents the target population. To test the research model, the researchers employed an online questionnaire survey to collect information about adopting ICT services among agribusiness employees. The survey research design was adopted as the data collection method, and the online questionnaire survey was categorized into two sections. The researcher gathered demographic information in the first section. In contrast, the second section gathered agribusiness staff's responses regarding PU and PEOU of ICT services and their intention to use them. To ensure validity for the survey content, the measurements for the concepts utilized in the study were obtained from existing literature. Therefore, a 5-point scale that ranges from "strongly disagree" to "strongly agree" was applied. Note that the measurements for PEOU and PU were obtained from prior research studies conducted by Venkatesh et al. [38].

4.2 Data Analysis

The study also utilizes a quantitative method to analyze data by conducting an online survey with a random sample of hundred and three (103) respondents and agribusiness staff from different agricultural companies in Somalia. The study also utilized SPSS version 26 to conduct descriptive analyses of the sample characteristics, allowing the researchers to obtain valuable insights into the study participants. The Cronbach alpha value was examined to ensure the reliability of each variable used in the study. Pearson correlation was used to determine the significance of the relationship between variables. Finally, multiple linear regression analysis was performed to determine the relationship between the independent variables (PEOU and PU) and the dependent variable (ITU). These statistical techniques helped the researchers better understand their data and draw conclusions about the relationships between variables.

4.3 Reliability

According to Table 1, the reliability coefficients indicate that all variables obtained an acceptable internal consistency level, given the scores being greater compared to the rule of thumb (<.70). The PU and PEOU had the highest Cronbach's alpha values, with 0.918 and 0.914, respectively. At the same time, the behavior intention variable also scored high, 0.899.

Table 1. The variables' Cronbach's alpha:

No.	Variables	Items	Alpha
1	Perceived Usefulness	5	0.918
2	Perceived Ease of Use	5	0.914
3	Behavioral Intention	3	0.899

5 Results and Findings

5.1 Descriptive Analysis

Profile of Respondents. Table 2 provides information about the demographics of the 103 respondents in a study. The table is divided into five categories: gender, age categories, level of education, level of ICT skills, and position. Regarding gender, most respondents were male, about 72.8% of the total respondents, while the balance of 27.2% was female.

The respondents were categorized into four age groups, with the largest group being 26–35, approximately 44.7% of the total respondents, followed by those aged 18–25, accounting for 41.7%. Moreover, respondents aged 36–40 were only 7.8%, while those aged 40+ reported only 5.8%.

Regarding education, most respondents possess a Bachelor's degree, 58.3%, preceded by those having a Master's degree at 23.3%. Respondents with a Diploma reported 9.7%, and those with secondary and below high school education accounted for 7.8% and 0.9%, respectively. In addition, regarding ICT skills, most respondents were at an intermediate level (49.5%), while 23.3% had advanced ICT skills, and 27.2% had basic ICT skills. Staff was the highest response percentage for the position, 35.9%, while managers were 25.2%, followed by farmers at 11.7%. Furthermore, growers and others were the same percentage of respondents which is 9.7% for each group. Finally, the low percentage of respondents were producers, only 7.8%.

Table 2. The respondents' demographics

Demographics	Frequency	Percentage
Gender		
Male	75	72.8
Female	28	27.2
Total	103	100
Age Categories		
18–25	43	41.7
26–35	46	44.7
36–40	8	7.8
40+	6	5.8
Total	103	100
Level of Education		
Master's degree	24	23.3
Bachelor's degree	60	58.3
Diploma	10	9.7
Secondary	8	7.8
Below High school	1	0.9
Total	103	100
Level of ICT skills		
Advanced Level	24	23.3
Basic ICT Level	28	27.2
Intermediate ICT level	51	49.5
Total	103	100
Position		
Farmer	12	11.7

(*continued*)

Table 2. (*continued*)

Demographics	Frequency	Percentage
Growers	10	9.7
Manager	26	25.2
Producers	8	7.8
Staff	37	35.9
Other	10	9.7
Total	**103**	**100**

Table 3 below presents data on internet usage among 103 respondents, showing the number and percentage of respondents in each category. Only 5.8% of the respondents use the internet for less than an hour, while 18.5% use it for 1–2 h, 32% use it for 3–4 h, 17.5% use it for 5–7 h, and a significant proportion of 26.2% use it for over 8 h. These results suggest that many respondents utilize the Internet for extended periods.

Table 3. Internet usage

How frequently do you use the internet	Frequency	Percentage
<1 h	6	5.8
1–2 h	19	18.5
3–4 h	33	32
5–7 h	18	17.5
>8 h	27	26.2
Total	**103**	**100**

Table 4 provides the mean and standard deviation for each of the five items (PU1 to PU5) used to measure the perceived usefulness of ICT service in agribusiness. The overall mean score for all five items is 3.41, which suggests that respondents generally agree with using ICT services in agribusiness. However, the standard deviation of 1.465 indicates some variability in their responses.

Table 4. Descriptive analysis of the perceived usefulness

ITEM	Perceived usefulness	Mean	Std. Deviation
PU1	Using of basic ICT tools and services (word processing, spreadsheets and PowerPoint) enables me to accomplish tasks more quickly	3.56	1.493

(*continued*)

Table 4. (*continued*)

ITEM	Perceived usefulness	Mean	Std. Deviation
PU2	The use of Advanced ICT tools (Internet application) allows me to access & share information	3.51	1.501
PU3	The use of Advanced ICT tools (drive) improves to store my data through the online	3.50	1.468
PU4	The use of social media enhances the efficiency in communication among Agribusiness Communities (officers, customers, growers, producers, extensionist, and farmers)	3.22	1.434
PU5	ICT allows agribusiness officers to provide their agricultural products information (foods, fibers, fuels, and raw materials) more quickly	3.26	1.428
Overall Mean and Standard Deviation		**3.41**	**1.464**

According to Table 5, the total mean score for perceived ease of use on intention to use ICT services in agribusiness was 3.3, with a standard deviation of 1.31. This indicates that the respondents' opinions about the perceived usability of ICT services in agribusiness are favourable.

Table 5. Descriptive analysis of the perceived ease of use

Item	Perceived ease of use	Mean	Std. Deviation
PEOU1	It would be easy for me to become skilful at using ICT tools and applications	3.21	1.460
PEOU2	I would find the ICT tools and applications easy to use	3.27	1.359
PEOU3	Learning to operate the ICT tools and applications is easy for me	3.36	1.220
PEOU4	my interaction with ICT services would be clear and understandable	3.30	1.211
PEOU5	I would find ICT services easy to use	3.25	1.281
Overall Mean and Standard Deviation		**3.30**	**1.31**

According to Table 6, the mean scores for ITU1, ITU2, and ITU3 were 3.06, 3.28, and 3.45, respectively. These results show that participants were generally eager to use ICT services in agribusiness (ITU1), planned to use these services (ITU2), and strongly advocated using these services to others. (ITU3). The standard deviation values for these items indicate some variation in the responses, indicating that some participants were more or less willing to utilize, plan to use, or promote ICT services in agribusiness than others.

Table 6. Descriptive analysis of the intention to use ICT services.

Item	Intention to use ICT services	Mean	Std. Deviation
ITU1	I'm willing to Use ICT services in Agribusiness	3.06	1.349
ITU2	I will plan to Use ICT services in agribusiness	3.28	1.294
ITU3	I would highly recommend using ICT services in agribusiness	3.45	1.506
Overall Mean and Standard Deviation		**3.26**	**1.4**

5.2 Correlation Coefficients

Table 7 displays the Pearson correlation coefficients between three variables: PU, PEOU, and ITU ICT services. The findings signify a strong positive correlation between PU and PEOU ($r = 0.795$, $p < 0.01$), suggesting that as the belief in the usefulness of technology increases, the perception of ease of use is also prone to increase. Moreover, a moderate positive correlation between ITU and both PU ($r = 0.685$, $p < 0.01$) and PEOU ($r = 0.702$, $p < 0.01$) occurred, indicating that as users perceive a technology to be more useful and easier to use, they are prone to intend to use it. All correlations are statistically significant at the 0.01 level, indicating that these relationships are unlikely to be due to chance. These findings suggest that PU and PEOU are important factors that influence users' ITU ICT service among agribusiness practitioners in Somalia.

Table 7. Pearson's Correlation analysis for Perceived Usefulness, Perceived ease of use and Intention to Use.

	PU	PEOU	ITU
Perceived Usefulness (PU)	1		
Perceived ease of use (PEOU)	.795**	1	
Intention to use (ITU) ICT	.685**	.702**	1

**. Correlation is significant at the 0.01 level (two-tailed).

5.3 Hypothesis Test

The regression model is used for testing the two hypotheses presented above, also performed using SPSS 26. The path significance of each hypothesized association in the research model and variance explained ($R2$ value) by each path were examined, and Table 8 shows the test results. This research examines the effect of PU and PEOU on ITU of ICT services among agribusiness practitioners in Somalia. Moreover, two hypotheses were postulated: H1 stated that PU significantly impacts ITU ICT services among agribusiness practitioners. Meanwhile, H2 suggested that PEOU positively affects ITU ICT services among agribusiness practitioners. According to the results presented in Table 8, the study conducted a regression analysis of the dependent variable (ITU of

ICT services) on the predicting variables of PU and PEOU. The analysis presented that the independent variables significantly predicted the ITU ICT services among agribusiness practitioners, with an F-value of 57.89 and a significance level of less than .001. Therefore, this indicates that the two factors studied significantly impact the ITU of ICT services in agribusiness.

Furthermore, the adjusted R-squared value of 0.53 suggests that the regression model can elaborate 53% of the variation in ITU. Additionally, coefficients were further to ascertain the influence concerning factors on the criterion variable ITU ICT services among agribusiness practitioners. H1 evaluates whether PU possesses a significant and positive effect on ITU. Other than that, the findings revealed that PU significantly impacts ITU ICT services among agribusiness practitioners (B = 0.344, t = 3.080, p = 0.003). Consequently, H1 was supported. H2 evaluates whether PEOU has a significantly positive impact on ITU ICT services among agribusiness staff. The outcomes illustrate that PEOU is significantly positive on ITU ICT services among agribusiness employees (B = .478, t = 3.80, p = .000). Hence, H2 was supported.

Table 8. Regression analysis

Hypothesis	Regression weights	B	T	Sig	Result
H1:	PU-----ITU	.344	3.080	.003	Supported
H2:	PEOU-----ITU	.478	3.80	.000	Supported

Adjusted R .53
F (2,100) 57.89
Note. *P < 0.05 PU: Perceived Usefulness, PEOU: Perceived Ease of Use, ITU: Intention to Use ICT service in Agribusiness

6 Discussions

The study examined the effect of PU and PEOU on ITU of ICT services among agribusiness practitioners in Somalia. The researchers adopted a multi-perspective approach and concentrated on two main variables in the TAM aspects to establish the theoretical framework. They conducted an online survey among agribusiness practitioners, comprising producers, growers, farmers, agribusiness staff, and agri-industry managers in Somalia, who verified the proposed research model.

The findings revealed that PU positively affects the ITU of ICT services among agribusiness staff in Somalia. This outcome is consistent with earlier research that has established the PU's substantial role in determining the acceptance and use of various types of technology, including mobile money service, e-service, e-learning, e-government, and ICT services [18, 22, 27, 34, 39]. Therefore, agribusiness staff/employee can improve their operational efficiency in managing agricultural operations, processing data, and communicating with stakeholders by adopting ICT services like mobile applications, computer software, and online platforms. This research concluded that PU has a highly favourable impact on the ITU of ICT services among agribusiness employees. However, another study has indicated that the PU of e-filing does not influence its utilization in the context of taxi payment systems [40].

Moreover, the study also discovered that the PEOU significantly affects the ITU of ICT services among agribusiness employees. This is in line with other studies on adopting technologies such as online movies, e-government services, e-learning, and technological innovation among farmers [18, 41, 42]. According to the research, trust in technology, trust in the bank, perceived ease of use, perceived usefulness, and complexity are the factors that influence customers significantly to use off-branch e-banking in India, whereas perceived risk was not significant [43]. Meanwhile, the study discovered that both PU and PEOU influence customers' intentions to use online purchasing and trust. These studies demonstrate the importance of both PU and PEOU in predicting consumers' level of technology acceptance [44]. Nevertheless, a study shows that perceived ease of use does not significantly impact Internet banking adoption by customers. However, the authors emphasized additional elements influencing customers' intentions to use Internet banking, such as trust, websites' social features, compatibility with lifestyle, and online customer services. In summary, previous studies indicate that PEOU significantly predicts employees' ITU ICT services in agribusiness. This indicates that if users perceive the ICT service as efficient and user-friendly, they are more likely to utilize it. Consequently, agribusiness owners should adopt a strategic approach when implementing ICT innovation services to ensure the technology is user-friendly.

7   Conclusion

ICT services are essential to the effectiveness of agricultural activities and employee productivity. Also, it facilitates the entire value chain, from farmers to consumers. The successful implementation of ICT will also assist the agribusiness staff performance and decision-making process. This study investigates the effect of PU and PEOU on ITU ICT services among agribusiness practitioners in Somalia. Here, the TAM theory was utilized to assess the two main components of the theory: PU, as well as PEOU, and this research provides insight into how ICT services are used in Somalia, particularly agribusiness, from the PU and PEOU perspectives. This study aims to develop and evaluate a model that anticipates how efficiency, perceived usefulness (PU), and perceived ease of use (PEOU) would affect the intentions to use ICT services among agribusiness practitioners. A subsequent online survey was conducted to collect information from the 103 participants in a random sample. Agribusiness experts from various companies responded to the questionnaire to provide their perceptions of the variables. The study highlights that PU and PEOU substantially influence the ITU of ICT services among agribusiness practitioners in Somalia. The findings suggest that efforts to promote ICT usage in this sector should highlight the technologies' benefits and ease of use.

Additionally, it is suggested that policymakers and stakeholders invest in improving the infrastructure and training programs for agribusiness practitioners to facilitate the adoption and effective use of ICT services. Nevertheless, the research has limitations, including its focus solely on agri-industry employees. Therefore, future studies should widen their scope to include other stakeholders, including policymakers, agribusiness entrepreneurs, ministries of agriculture officers, and employees of local non-governmental organizations (NGOs) and international agencies.

References

1. Lowder, S.K., Skoet, J., Raney, T.: The number, size, and distribution of farms, smallholder farms, and family farms worldwide. World Dev. **87**, 16–29 (2016)
2. Clay, P.M., Feeney, R.: Analyzing agribusiness value chains: a literature review. Int. Food Agribusiness Manag. Rev. **22**, 31–46 (2019)
3. Babu, S.C., Manvatkar, R., Kolavalli, S.: Strengthening capacity for agribusiness development and management in Sub-Saharan Africa. Afr. J. Manag. **2**, 1–30 (2016)
4. Adenle, A.A., Manning, L., Azadi, H.: Agribusiness innovation: a pathway to sustainable economic growth in Africa. Trends Food Sci. Technol. **59**, 88–104 (2017)
5. Christy, R., Mabaya, E., Wilson, N., Mutambatsere, E., Mhlanga, N.: Enabling environments for competitive agro-industries. In: Agro-Industries for Development, pp. 136–185. CABI, Wallingford (2009)
6. Kante, M., Oboko, R., Chepken, C.: An ICT model for increased adoption of farm input information in developing countries: a case in Sikasso, Mali. Inf. Process. Agric. **6**, 26–46 (2019)
7. Ayim, C., Kassahun, A., Addison, C., Tekinerdogan, B.: Adoption of ICT innovations in the agriculture sector in Africa: a review of the literature. Agric. Food Secur. **11**, 1–16 (2022)
8. Asenso-Okyere, K., Mekonnen, D.A.: The importance of ICTs in the provision of information for improving agricultural productivity and rural incomes in Africa. African Human Development Report. UNDP Sponsored Research Series (2012)
9. Abdullahi, H.O., Hassan, A.A., Mahmud, M., Ali, A.F.: Determinants of ICT adoption among small scale agribusiness enterprises in Somalia. arXiv preprint arXiv:2103.01769 (2021)
10. Jin, X.-B.: Deep learning predictor for sustainable precision agriculture based on internet of things system. Sustainability **12**, 1433 (2020)
11. Mujeyi, A., Mudhara, M., Mutenje, M.: The impact of climate smart agriculture on household welfare in smallholder integrated crop–livestock farming systems: evidence from Zimbabwe. Agric. Food Secur. **10**, 1–15 (2021)
12. Aleke, B., Ojiako, U., Wainwright, D.W.: ICT adoption in developing countries: perspectives from small-scale agribusinesses. J. Enterp. Inf. Manag. **24**(1), 68–84 (2011)
13. Lokeswari, K.: A study of the use of ICT among rural farmers. Int. J. Commun. Res. **6**, 232 (2016)
14. Cheripelly, N.K., Chandri, R.R.: Role of ICTs in sustainable agriculture: a study of e-Sagu in Andhra Pradesh. In: Singh, A.K., Dagar, J.C., Arunachalam, A., Gopichandran, R., Shelat, K.N. (eds.) Climate Change Modelling, Planning and Policy for Agriculture, pp. 109–118. Springer, New Delhi (2015). https://doi.org/10.1007/978-81-322-2157-9_13
15. Fountas, S.: Farm management information systems: current situation and future perspectives. Comput. Electron. Agric. **115**, 40–50 (2015)
16. Thöni, A., Tjoa, A.M.: Information technology for sustainable supply chain management: a literature survey. Enterp Inf. Syst. **11**, 828–858 (2017)
17. Grimm, A.N.: Trends in US trade in information and communications technology (ICT) services and in ICT-enabled services. Surv. Curr. Bus. **5**, 1–19 (2016)
18. Chen, L., Aklikokou, A.K.: Determinants of E-government adoption: testing the mediating effects of perceived usefulness and perceived ease of use. Int. J. Public Adm. **43**, 850–865 (2020)
19. Cheung, R., Vogel, D.: Predicting user acceptance of collaborative technologies: an extension of the technology acceptance model for e-learning. Comput. Educ. **63**, 160–175 (2013)
20. Sombat, P., Chaiyasoonthorn, W., Chaveesuk, S.: The acceptance model of hospital information systems in Thailand: a conceptual framework extending TAM. In: 2018 5th International Conference on Industrial Engineering and Applications (ICIEA) , pp. 89–94. IEEE (2018)

21. Van, V.H., Quynh, N.N., Doanh, N.K.: Factors affecting farmers' intention to use ECEs in Covid-19 pandemic: combining the technology acceptance model (TAM) and barrier factors. J. Agribus. Dev. Emerg. Econ. (2022)
22. Ali, A.Y.S., Dhaha, I.S.Y.: Factors influencing mobile money transfer adoption among Somali students. Int. J. Bus. Econ. Law **3**, 1–9 (2013)
23. Lichtenstein, S., Williamson, K.: Understanding consumer adoption of internet banking: an interpretive study in the Australian banking context. J. Electron. Commer. Res. **7**, 50 (2006)
24. Chen, S.-C., Li, S.-H.: Consumer adoption of e-service: integrating technology readiness with the theory of planned behavior. Afr. J. Bus. Manag. **4**, 3556 (2010)
25. Davis, F.D.: User acceptance of information technology: system characteristics, user perceptions and behavioral impacts. Int. J. Man Mach. Stud. **38**, 475–487 (1993)
26. Deng, X., Doll, W.J., Hendrickson, A.R., Scazzero, J.A.: A multi-group analysis of structural invariance: an illustration using the technology acceptance model. Inf. Manag. **42**, 745–759 (2005)
27. Elkaseh, A.M., Wong, K.W., Fung, C.C.: Perceived ease of use and perceived usefulness of social media for e-learning in Libyan higher education: a structural equation modeling analysis. Int. J. Inf. Educ. Technol, **6**, 192 (2016)
28. Radnan, P.Y., Purba, J.T.: The use of Information Communication Technology (ICT) as the technology acceptance model (TAM) of mobile banking. Jurnal Manajemen dan Pemasaran Jasa **9**, 283–298 (2016)
29. Wu, B., Chen, X.: Continuance intention to use MOOCs: integrating the technology acceptance model (TAM) and task technology fit (TTF) model. Comput. Hum. Behav. **67**, 221–232 (2017)
30. Davis, F.D.: Perceived usefulness, perceived ease of use, and user acceptance of information technology. MIS Q. **13**(3), 319–340 (1989)
31. Hamid, A.A., Razak, F.Z.A., Bakar, A.A., Abdullah, W.S.W.: The effects of perceived usefulness and perceived ease of use on continuance intention to use e-government. Procedia Econ. Finance **35**, 644–649 (2016)
32. Mou, J., Cohen, J.F.: A longitudinal study of trust and perceived usefulness in consumer acceptance of an eService: the case of online health services. In: PACIS, p. 258 (2014)
33. Teo, T.: Factors influencing teachers' intention to use technology: model development and test. Comput. Educ. **57**, 2432–2440 (2011)
34. Li, H., Liu, Y.: Understanding post-adoption behaviors of e-service users in the context of online travel services. Inf. Manag. **51**, 1043–1052 (2014)
35. Venkatesh, V., Davis, F.D.: A model of the antecedents of perceived ease of use: development and test. Decis. Sci. **27**, 451–481 (1996)
36. Luarn, P., Lin, H.-H.: Toward an understanding of the behavioral intention to use mobile banking. Comput. Hum. Behav. **21**, 873–891 (2005)
37. Chiu, C.-M., Wang, E.T.G.: Understanding Web-based learning continuance intention: the role of subjective task value. Inf. Manag. **45**, 194–201 (2008)
38. Venkatesh, V., Morris, M.G., Davis, G.B., Davis, F.D.: User acceptance of information technology: toward a unified view. MIS Q. **27**(3), 425–478 (2003)
39. Eze, N.U., Obichukwu, P.U., Kesharwani, S.: Perceived usefulness, perceived ease of use in ICT support and use for teachers. IETE J. Educ. **62**, 12–20 (2021)
40. Tahar, A., Riyadh, H.A., Sofyani, H., Purnomo, W.E.: Perceived ease of use, perceived usefulness, perceived security and intention to use e-filing: The role of technology readiness. J. Asian Finance Econ. Bus. **7**, 537–547 (2020)
41. Caffaro, F., Cremasco, M.M., Roccato, M., Cavallo, E.: Drivers of farmers' intention to adopt technological innovations in Italy: the role of information sources, perceived usefulness, and perceived ease of use. J. Rural. Stud. **76**, 264–271 (2020)

42. Basuki, R.: The effects of perceived ease of use, usefulness, enjoyment and intention to use online platforms on behavioral intention in online movie watching during the pandemic era. Int. J. Data Netw. Sci. **6**, 253–262 (2022)
43. Sinha, I., Mukherjee, S.: Acceptance of technology, related factors in use of off branch e-banking: an Indian case study. J. High Technol. Manag. Res. **27**, 88–100 (2016)
44. Dhingra, M., Mudgal, R.K.: Applications of perceived usefulness and perceived ease of use: a review. In: 2019 8th International Conference System Modeling and Advancement in Research Trends (SMART), pp. 293–298. IEEE (2019)

Adoption of Machine Learning by Rural Farms: A Systematic Review

Sayed Abdul Majid Gilani[1]([✉]) [iD], Ansarullah Tantry[3] [iD], Soumaya Askri[2] [iD], Liza Gernal[3] [iD], Rommel Sergio[2] [iD], and Leonardo Jose Mataruna-Dos-Santos[2] [iD]

[1] School of Management, Birmingham City University, Birmingham, UK
majidgilanii@hotmail.com
[2] Faculty of Management, Canadian University of Dubai (CUD), City Walk, Dubai, United Arab Emirates
[3] Business School, Westford University College, Sharjah, UAE

Abstract. Machine Learning (ML) has seen a major increase as a method to improve operations for businesses and consumers in different industries. It has been highlighted to enhance efficiency for businesses in product creation, product development, marketing, and customer experience. The purpose of this paper was to review worldwide studies investigating ML adoption by rural businesses to determine the level of ML adoption research conducted in the context of rural farms. A systematic literature review incorporating a Template Analysis (T.A.) was conducted to determine the level of research investigating drivers and barriers to ML adoption by rural enterprises. The reviewed studies were selected based on research purpose (investigating the take-up of innovations/technology by rural businesses), year of research (2000–2023), and inclusion of rural businesses in the studies. Additionally, the reviewed studies were analysed based on the year of each study, the geography of the study, the sector, and the size of businesses, including the level of location/rurality of included businesses and the degree of technology/innovation adoption by enterprises. The findings from the study highlight a research problem based on limited research investigating the adoption of ML by rural farms in several regions around the world. Additionally, the findings from the review highlight a lack of clarity on the relationship between the sector and the size of businesses and their adoption of ML. The significance of the highlighted findings is that there is scope for further research investigating the adoption of ML by smaller rural businesses, which may inform their survival and growth and may have wider implications for policymakers and practice. Therefore, encouraging future primary research focusing on ML adoption by rural farms in the regions under-represented in the literature. Additionally, the findings from this paper have policy, practical, and theoretical implications.

Keywords: Machine Learning · Rural Enterprises · Adoption · Drivers · And Barriers

1 Introduction

Rural business has played a vital role in ensuring job creation, support towards the national economy, and support towards tourism. It has also acted as a deterrent against depopulation and extinction of ancient cultures within an isolated and remote area. Adopting innovative technologies like Machine Learning (ML) has been highlighted as compulsory for rural businesses' survival and growth. In addition, such businesses overcome the perception of the digital divide established for rural communities established from the general population's and government's collective opinions. Machine Learning (ML) is a field within artificial intelligence that utilizes available data to coach machines towards emulating human behaviour [1]. The current innovations in ML have made it a major topic of discussion amongst professionals in all industries where the discussions have mainly revolved around the optimum integration of ML in practice. Donal Hebb developed the ML program in 1949 to support an investigation into brain-cell interaction [2]. Machine Learning consists of multiple steps which start with collecting data from a source that the machine intends to be educated from. Then the data is pre-processed before selecting and retrieving the relevant features that will be integrated into the machine's training. The features are then inputted into a statistical model that can train itself to identify patterns based on the unique characteristics of each feature class. Therefore, ML involves automated training to enable machines to make decisions based on set factors related to different scenarios.

Machine Learning has transformed operations in various industries regarding cost-effective practices, including the service industry, where online chatbots deal with customer inquiries rather than businesses spending money to hire call centre staff [1]. Currently, ML-programmed robots are delivering lectures at universities which will eventually lead to the replacement of human university faculty with ML, which will be a cost-effective strategy [2]. These examples of the cost-effective benefits of adopting ML can be especially beneficial for smaller businesses which make up over 90% of all businesses worldwide [1]. This is especially the case for more isolated smaller businesses in rural regions, which can survive and thrive through cost-saving and efficient measures offered by ML [2]. Therefore, ML adoption by rural businesses may lead to the revival of the rural economy. Regarding business sectors like farming, Meshram et al. [2] explain ML as a technology that benefits farmers in lowering losses from operations by outlining solutions that optimize the management of crops. Cockburn [3] adds to the discussion on ML by Meshram et al. by identifying ML as a process that offers insight into relevant methods for analyzing large datasets retrieved from sensors installed within farms. Several authors [4–6] identified the influence of ML in ensuring the survival and growth of businesses in isolated areas, including smaller businesses that make up over 90% of all businesses in nations around the world. Therefore, ML adoption amongst smaller rural businesses can positively impact the national economy and job creation. However, there appears to be a highlighted research problem attributed to a shortage of studies investigating the level of research conducted for innovation/technology adoption by rural businesses in terms of business size, sector, and degree of adoption (e.g., daily/weekly/monthly).

Therefore, the identified practical benefits of ML and the shortage of studies investigating the impact of ML on rural businesses have encouraged a Systematic Literature

Review in this paper of worldwide studies exploring ML adoption by rural businesses to identify the level of ML adoption research conducted in the context of rural farms. This paper is structured as follows: Sect. 2 will outline the research methodology for this research. The findings from the systematic review are presented and analysed in Sect. 3. A discussion based on the key findings from this research will be provided in Sect. 4. Section 5 will discuss the key findings in terms of policy, practical and theoretical implications, the problems and limitations encountered in the research, and recommendations for future businesses and researchers.

2　Research Methodology

Various authors from around the world highlight the importance of research methodology as it allows researchers to establish specific procedures/techniques adopted to identify, select, process, and analyze information about a given topic area [7–9]. In the case of this research, a systematic literature review was adopted to analyze worldwide literature investigating innovation/technology adoption by rural enterprises. A systematic literature review consists of a scholarly-based synthesis of evidence on a presented topic area using critical methods to identify, define and assess research related to the topic area [9]. The prerequisites for studies to be included in this research are outlined in Table 1.

Table 1. Prerequisites informing the inclusion of each study in the Systematic Review

Steps	Prerequisites
Step 1	Does the research purpose investigate rural businesses' take-up of innovations/technology?
Step 2	Was the study conducted during the period 2000–2023?
Step 3	Are rural businesses included in the studies?

In Table 1, 'Step 1' targets studies of innovation/ML adoption by rural farms. However, other rural business-based studies were included if rural farm-based studies in a location were not highlighted, 'Step 2' determines whether the study was conducted during 2000–2023. The rationale behind the inclusion of this step while selecting studies was that the year 2000 symbolizes a global paradigm shift from the analogue era to the digital era, which can be demonstrated by a widespread change from Digital Subscriber Line (DSL) internet adoption to ADSL (Asymmetric Digital Subscriber Line)/Broadband adoption amongst most developed and emerging regions [10]. As demonstrated in previous research, ML is based on broadband-driven technologies [1].

A Template Analysis (T.A.) method was developed to identify themes and patterns to identify the level of research conducted for ML adoption by rural businesses. A TA incorporates the development of a coding 'template', with themes identified by researchers within a data set, and arranges them in a meaningful and related manner [9]. The criterion for the T.A. method is provided in Table 2.

Table 2. A Criterion for the Template Analysis

Prerequisites
Year
Geography
Business Size
Business Sector
Level of rurality of business location
Level/Degree of Technology/Innovation Adoption

The year of studies was adopted as a criterion to ensure that the research was not dated. The geography criteria allowed researchers to identify the level of existing research investigating innovation adoption by rural businesses. The business size and sector criteria permitted the research to determine if existing literature factored in business size and sector with innovation adoption. The rurality of businesses included in the reviewed studies allowed the researchers to determine if businesses' isolation level was not factored in studies investigating innovation adoption. The rurality in terms of location for the businesses was assessed based on the dimensions of rurality outlined by Gilani et al. (2023). The dimensions of rurality (Table 5) to assess the rurality of a location are based on the location's population and population density, proximity to urban areas, development, culture, and social perception. The final criterion investigating the degree of technology/innovation adoption by businesses in the reviewed studies allowed the researchers to identify whether existing literature has addressed the frequency of innovation adoption by rural businesses.

3 Systematic Literature Review

Authors through findings from studies conducted in regions around the world have identified the positive influence of ML in improving business operations, regardless of sector or size of businesses [4–6]. Several authors have highlighted how ML can support business owners like farmers in assessing soil and weather conditions to establish optimum conditions for growing crops and managing livestock. Therefore, a review of worldwide studies investigating the adoption of innovation/technology by rural enterprises has identified drivers and barriers that influence adoption. In the case of this research, factors that promote innovation adoption were labelled as drivers, and factors that limit/completely stop innovation adoption were labelled as barriers [1]. From the systematic review of worldwide studies, drivers for innovation adoption by rural businesses are provided in Table 3 regarding location and the authors for each study. From organizing the review findings in Tables 3 and 4 in terms of a study's authors' names and location, the level of research investigating ML/innovation adoption by rural businesses in each location is highlighted, which will inform the readers on under-represented locations in the context of this research.

Table 3. Drivers for Innovation Adoption by Rural Businesses

Drivers	Location	Author(s) cited
Access to business information	Asia	[11]
	Scotland, UK	[12, 13]
Affordability (cost)	Africa	[14, 15]
	Europe	[16]
	New Zealand	[17]
	North America	[18]
Communication	Africa	[19]
	Asia	[20, 21]
	Australia	[22]
	Scotland, UK	[23, 24]
	Wales, UK	[25]
Confidence/training	Europe	[26, 27, 28]
	United Arab Emirates (UAE)	[1]
Culture (growth-driven business)	Africa	[19, 29]
	Asia	[11, 30]
	England, UK	[31, 32, 33]
	Europe	[34]
	New Zealand	[35]
	North America	[36]
	Wales, UK	[23]
	Scotland, UK	[25]
Environmentally friendly	Scotland, UK	[39]
Improved income for businesses	Asia	[30]
	England, UK	[40]
	New Zealand	[35]
	Scotland, UK	[41, 42, 43]
	Wales, UK	[38]
Infrastructure, e.g., satisfactory broadband quality and speed	Australia	[44]
	England, UK	[45]
	New Zealand	[35]
	Wales, UK	[46]

(continued)

Table 3. (*continued*)

Drivers	Location	Author(s) cited
Marketing/Promotion	Africa	[47]
	Asia	[48]
	Scotland, UK	[37]
	Wales, UK	[38]
Support towards daily operations (Planning)	Africa	[49]
	Asia	[30]
	England, UK	[33]
	New Zealand	[50]
	Scotland, UK	[51]

As shown in Table 3, 'communication', organizational 'culture', 'infrastructure', 'marketing', and 'planning' were identified as the main drivers for innovation adoption. The barriers against innovation adoption by rural businesses are provided in Table 4 in terms of location and authors for each study.

Table 4. Drivers for Innovation Adoption by Rural Businesses

Barriers	Author(s)	Location
Confidence/training	[52]	Canada, North America
	[53]	Scotland, UK
	[46]	Wales, UK
	[1]	United Arab Emirates (UAE)
Cost	[54]	Canada, North America
	[55]	Europe
	[33]	England, UK
	[56]	Scotland, UK
	[1]	UAE
Culture	[33]	Asia
	[52]	Canada, North America
	[57]	New Zealand
	[58]	Scotland, UK
	[1]	UAE
Lack of government support (awareness)	[11]	Asia

(continued)

Table 4. (*continued*)

Barriers	Author(s)	Location
	[28]	Australia
	[52]	Canada, North America
	[33]	England, UK
	[56]	Europe
	[17]	Scotland, UK
Poor Infrastructure	[47]	Africa
	[30]	Asia
	[59]	Australia
	[54]	Canada, North America
	[33]	England, UK
	[60]	Scotland, UK
	[25]	Wales, UK
Security/Level of trust	[30]	Scotland, UK
	[1]	UAE

In Table 4, the main barriers against innovation adoption were identified as 'lack of government support' and 'poor infrastructure'. It should be noted that the main drivers and barriers for innovation adoption by rural businesses identified in Tables 3 and 4 were established by the number of reviewed studies referring to each driver and barrier related to innovation adoption. As per the analysis criteria outlined in Table 2, the reviewed studies did not clarify the level of rurality of the business locations, size of businesses and business sectors. The degree of innovation adoption (e.g., daily, monthly, or annually) was not clarified for the businesses in the reviewed studies where Deakins et al., Galloway, and Galloway and Kapasi [11] were the only studies that addressed the frequency of innovation adoption.

Therefore, the review of studies on technology/innovation adoption by rural businesses has established a dearth of literature that collectively clarifies the sector and size of businesses, the rurality of businesses' location, and the degree of innovation adoption by businesses. Additionally, there appear to be no studies outside of Gilani et al. [1] investigating ML adoption by rural businesses. The review highlighted several under-represented geographic areas among the reviewed studies investigating innovation/ML adoption by rural businesses. Therefore, there is scope for future research investigating the level of ML adoption by rural businesses in under-represented regions (in the systematic review) like Scotland or Pakistan.

4 Discussion

As mentioned in the previous section, 'communication', organizational 'culture', 'infrastructure', 'marketing', and 'planning' were highlighted in the reviewed studies as the main drivers for innovation adoption, however, 'lack of government support' and 'poor infrastructure' were identified by the review as the main barriers against adoption. The drivers and barriers to ML/innovation adoption by rural businesses highlighted in the Systematic Literature Review (SLR) are illustrated in Fig. 1.

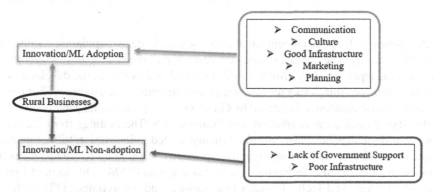

Fig. 1. Drivers and Barriers to Innovation/ML Adoption by Rural Businesses

In Fig. 1, the green outline on the shapes and green arrows represent the drivers for innovation/ML adoption. The red outline on the shapes and red arrows represent barriers against innovation/ML adoption.

The critical review also identified a lack of clarity on business sizes and sectors, degree of adoption of innovation/technology, and rurality of business included in the studies. Additionally, no existing literature was identified for investigating ML adoption by rural businesses, and the review did not identify a theory dedicated to investigating ML adoption by rural businesses.

For future related studies to better identify the size and sector of businesses included in the research, the authors recommend a primary research study by accessing business contact details from online business databases and then through an initial survey like telephone/online questionnaires determining the size and sector of businesses. To better understand the level or degree of adoption of ML by rural businesses, the authors recommend questions within semi-structured interviews or questionnaires aiming to clarify the frequency of ML in terms of whether it was adopted daily/weekly/monthly. To better understand the rurality of businesses in future research investigating ML adoption by rural businesses, the authors propose the adoption of the rural dimensions developed by Gilani et al. [12] (in Table 5) to gain a more informed understanding of the layers of rurality based on 5 factors.

Table 5. Dimensions for defining Rural areas [64]

Dimension	Focus
Dimension 1	Population and population density
Dimension 2	Proximity to urban areas
Dimension 3	Development
Dimension 4	Culture
Dimension 5	Social Perception

As shown in Table 5, Dimension 1 addresses each area's population number and population density. The travel distance between a given area and the nearest recognised urban area is represented by Dimension 2. Dimension 3 evaluates the development of an area in terms of things like resources and infrastructure. The culture within a given area is the fourth dimension identified by Gilani et al. [12]. The social perception related to identifying rural areas is addressed in Dimension 5. The findings from the review of worldwide studies have also informed theory related to innovation/ML adoption. A review of worldwide studies investigating innovation adoption by rural businesses that involved theories like the Technology Acceptance Model (TAM), Diffusion of Innovations (DoI) theory, and Technological Organisational and Environmental (TOE) framework; informed Gilani et al. [1] development of the Broadband Adoption Framework (BAF) which could investigate the frequency of broadband adoption by rural based enterprises. The BAF was composed of features from the DoI theory and TOE theories. Gilani et al. [1] identified that the DOI theory has the characteristics to investigate the frequency of ML adoption.

In contrast, the TOE framework was highlighted to be the most appropriate to investigate innovation adoption by organisations. Therefore, a merger of DOI and TOE led to the creation of the BAF [1]. The BAF is illustrated in Fig. 2.

The drivers and barriers related to broadband adoption are illustrated within the technological, organisational, and environmental contexts of TOE in Fig. 2. The words and lines in Fig. 2 with the symbol **D** are drivers; words and lines with the symbol **B** are barriers; anything with the symbol **D/B** are both drivers and barriers. The single arrows in the lines labelled with **D** and **B** are respectively represented by drivers leading to broadband adoption and barriers leading to non-broadband adoption. The double-arrowed black lines represent the interconnectivity between the technology, organization, and environment contexts. Knowledge is symbolised by 'K', Persuasion is symbolised by 'P', Decision is labelled as 'D', Implementation is labelled as 'I' and Confirmation is symbolised by 'C'. Adoption is labelled as 'A', and Rejection is symbolised by 'R'. The BAF has been amended to the Innovation Adoption Framework (IAF) for this research investigating ML adoption by rural enterprises. The IAF is illustrated in Fig. 3.

All the elements within the IAF in Fig. 3 can be interpreted the same as in the BAF. This theory can be adopted in future research studies investigating the drivers and barriers to ML adoption by rural businesses.

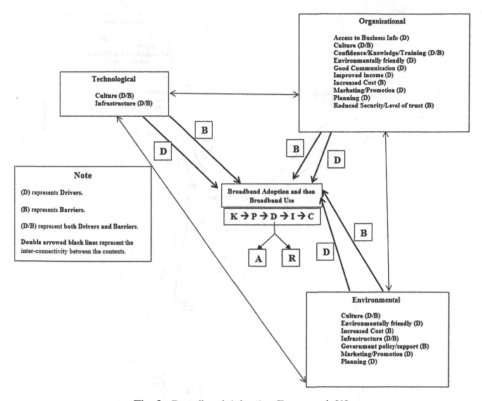

Fig. 2. Broadband Adoption Framework [1]

5 Conclusion and Recommendations

This paper aimed to review worldwide studies to identify the level of literature investigating ML adoption by rural farms/businesses. A review of studies from 2000–2023 identified drivers and barriers to innovation/technology adoption by rural businesses. However, outside of Gilani et al. [1], no other studies were highlighted that investigated ML adoption by rural businesses. Additionally, limited clarity was provided on the size, sector, rurality of location, degree/frequency of adoption, and theory offered among the reviewed studies. Therefore, a scope was identified for future research investigating ML adoption by businesses in terms of their size, sector, and location's rurality. To overcome the limitations identified from the systematic review of studies, in future research, business size, and sector can be identified through purposive sampling (will allow the researcher to use their insight informed from the literature to target and select a relevant and representative sample to a related research study's focus); the rurality of businesses' location can be better clarified by the rural dimensions developed by Gilani et al. [12]; the frequency of ML adoption can be clarified via primary research questions. Finally, an original contribution is made in this paper through the development of the Innovation Adoption Framework (IAF), which represents innovation adoption by rural businesses around the world and is informed by the findings of the SLR. The IAF may inform future

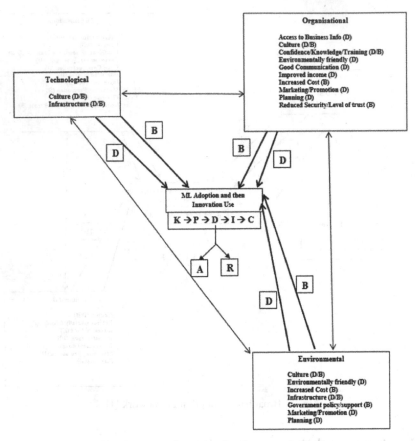

Fig. 3. Innovation Adoption Framework (IAF)

research studies investigating the degree of ML adoption by rural businesses. In addition to developing the IAF, another significant contribution from this paper was made by reviewing worldwide literature on ML adoption by rural businesses to identify the level of research conducted on ML adoption by rural farms. However, limited research was highlighted on ML adoption by rural farms. As highlighted from the systematic review, different regions were found to be under-represented for ML adoption research in a rural context. Based on this, the authors of this research propose further research in rural areas like Scotland and Pakistan.

In terms of policy implications, the authors of this paper believe that further research investigating ML adoption by rural farms may inform policymakers in terms of infrastructure improvement and improving take-up amongst rural populations. For example, the findings of this paper and future related primary research studies' findings may inform policymakers to devise strategies further to support the survival and growth of smaller businesses. For example, the findings of this paper may inform policymakers in the UAE government that have already established policies like the Competitive Knowledge Economy of Vision 2021 to aid and support smaller businesses through the Khalifa

Fund (established to support UAE-based SMEs through funding) [13]. In terms of practical implications, the findings from future research may also inform rural businesses about the benefits of ML and how it can be incorporated into business operations. This paper has already addressed the implications of literature and theory by referring to the contribution to knowledge that may be made from future studies investigating ML adoption by rural businesses and proposing the inclusion of the IAF in future studies.

References

1. Gilani, S.A.M., Copiaco, A., Gernal, L., Yasin, N., Nair, G., Anwar, I.: Savior or distraction for survival: examining the applicability of machine learning for rural family farms in the United Arab Emirates. Sustainability **15**, 1–23 (2023). https://doi.org/10.3390/su15043720
2. Meshram, C., Ibrahim, R.W., Obaid, A.J., Meshram, S.G., Meshram, A., El-Latif, A.M.A.: Fractional chaotic maps based short signature scheme under human-centered IoT environments. J. Adv. Res. **32**, 139–148 (2021). https://doi.org/10.1016/j.jare.2020.08.015
3. Cockburn, M.: Application and prospective discussion of machine learning for the management of dairy farms. Animals **10**, 1–22 (2020). https://doi.org/10.3390/ani10091690
4. Japar, F., Mathew, S., Narayanaswamy, B., Lim, C.M., Hazra, J.: Estimating the wake losses in large wind farms: a machine learning approach. In: ISGT 2014 (2014)
5. Richmond, K.: AI, machine learning, and international criminal investigations: the lessons from forensic science. SSRN Electron. J. (2021). https://doi.org/10.2139/ssrn.3727899
6. Tryhuba, A., Ratushny, R., Tryhuba, I., Koval, N., Androshchuk, I.: The model of projects creation of the fire extinguishing systems in community territories. Acta Univ. Agric. Silvic. Mendelianae Brun. **68**, 419–431 (2020). https://doi.org/10.11118/actaun202068020419
7. Creswell, J.W.: Revisiting mixed methods and advancing scientific practices (2015)
8. Long, G., Saunders, D.: Academic libraries and quality reviews within the United Kingdom. In: Quality and the Academic Library, pp. 27–43. Chandos Publishing (2016)
9. Silverman, D.: Qualitative research: issues of theory, method and practice (2004)
10. Gilani, S.A.M., Faccia, A.: Broadband connectivity, government policies, and open innovation: the crucial IT infrastructure contribution in Scotland. J. Open Innov. Technol. Market Complex. **8**, 1–29 (2022). https://doi.org/10.3390/joitmc8010001
11. Galloway, L., Kapasi, I., Wimalasena, L.: A theory of venturing: a critical realist explanation of why my father is not like Richard Branson. Int. Small Bus. J. **37**, 626–641 (2019)
12. Gilani, S.A.M., Yasin, N., Duncan, P., Smith, A.M.J.: What is remote-rural and why is it important? vol. 7 (2023)
13. Small to Medium Enterprises (SMEs). https://u.ae/en/information-and-services/business/small-and-medium-enterprises/small-and-medium-enterprises

Estate Planning Model for Sustaining Economic Values of Digital Assets

Norliza Katuk[1](✉) [iD], Peck-Yong Tey[1], Mohamad Sabri Sinal[1],
Wan Aida Nadia Wan Abdullah[1], Norazlina Abd Wahab[2], Erik Kurniadi[3],
and Heru Budianto[3]

[1] School of Computing, Universiti Utara Malaysia, Kedah 06010 Sintok, Malaysia
k.norliza@uum.edu.my
[2] Islamic Business School, Universiti Utara Malaysia, Sintok, Kedah, Malaysia
[3] Faculty of Computer Science, Universitas Kuningan, Kuningan, West Java, Indonesia

Abstract. The rapid growth of computer technology has led to the invention of digital assets containing financial values like cryptocurrency and e-wallets, consequently increasing individuals' digital asset ownership. However, many people do not realise the importance of estate planning for their digital assets. In the case of sudden death, unavailable estate planning would cause the digital assets to vanish due to unavailable access to the digital assets' credentials. Therefore, digital asset owners must have proper estate planning to allow smooth inheritance of their digital assets before an individual's death, ensuring that their family is being taken care of. Besides, digital estate planning is also crucial to preventing cybercrimes such as identity theft and fraud. Hence, this paper bridges the gap by developing an estate planning software model to sustain digital assets containing economic values. The software model was developed by gathering the requirements for digital asset estate planning and visualising it in a prototype. Then, an evaluation was conducted on the prototype that visualised the proposed model. The results suggested that it is usable and facilitates digital asset estate planning. The significant contribution of this research is that the prototype enhances the security of one's digital assets by giving access to a trusted person. It is also simple and cost-effective for digital asset owners by providing independent services for estate planning.

Keywords: digital assets · cryptocurrency · estate planning · sustainability · online systems

1 Introduction

The rapid evolution and advancement in computing technology have created various digital belongings like email, pictures, videos, documents, data, social media accounts, and cryptocurrencies [1]. They are also named virtual properties that cover in-game objects and avatars, websites, URLs, domain names, eBooks, tickets, chats, and bank accounts [2]. In addition, some of these belongings have financial values, whether direct or indirect, and appear to be valuable digital assets. Over the years, the number of digital asset owners is exponentially increased. However, despite the plethora of digital assets, limited studies have been conducted on maintaining their sustainability. Therefore, this paper will address this issue by focusing on the inheritance of digital assets through estate planning. Although digital asset ownership grows rapidly, people are not moving at the same pace in terms of preserving and sustaining them. In other words, this area of research is still in its infancy stage, and it requires critical attention by researchers, policy makers, and digital assets owners to ensure that digital assets won't vanish after the owners' death.

Further, there is a need to enhance traditional estate planning mechanisms to cater to digital assets' needs. For example, according to a study by an Oxford University researcher, within the next 50 years, Facebook will have an estimated 1.4 billion deceased user profiles, which will outnumber the living by 2070 [3]. Unfortunately, all these digital assets are abandoned after the owner's death, leading to a critical question of how those accounts will be managed in the afterlife. Therefore, early digital estate planning has become essential to manage digital assets' inheritance and future ownership before an individual's death [4]. This way could facilitate the management of digital assets, especially with economic values, and minimise the risk of loss and destruction.

Additionally, estate planning for digital assets becomes essential for protecting and preserving digital assets from cybercrime and cybersecurity threats since digital assets have an indefinite lifespan. Nowadays, digital asset protection from theft is a severe concern for estate planning of digital assets, for example, fraud prevention firm ID. Analytics shows nearly 2.5 million identities of deceased Americans were used to fraudulently create credit card accounts, make an unauthorised purchase, apply for loans, or even commit fraud [5]. Moreover, identity theft has been reported as a frequent cybercrime in the United States, which has affected more than 47 percent of Americans for $712.4 billion in 2020. Besides, cyber-attacks and crimes are anticipated to grow occasionally by targeting digital assets with financial values like cryptocurrency and social media accounts.

Lack of estate planning for digital assets will increase cyber-attacks, particularly identity theft on unmonitored social media accounts. Eventually, estate planning for digital assets can solve this problem by preserving the economic values of an estate and protecting an individual's digital assets, identity, legacy, privacy, and security. Therefore, this research adopted the digital asset's definition by Singh, Shrivastava, and Ruj [6], which described it as "any valuable data that exists over cyberspace that users want to pass on to their descendants." This study will explore and propose an estate planning model suitable for sustaining digital assets. The model helps explicitly in preserving digital assets for smooth and efficient digital assets inheritance after the owners' death.

2 Background and Related Studies

The term "digital assets" initially referred to trade secrets and intellectual property in the digital form and was first introduced in the 1990s [7]. However, Pinch [8] argued that "digital asset" has no universally accepted definition. Moreover, the lack of proper definitions can raise issues for lawyers in assisting clients with estate planning [9]. Hence, it is crucial to provide a clear definition of digital assets so that the boundary of the study can be identified and it can meet its actual purpose. For this purpose, this study adopted the digital assets by Singh, Shrivastava, and Ruj [6]. They defined it as any tangible or intangible resource that contains an economic value and future benefit. Therefore data associated with email, social media platforms (such as Facebook, Instagram, and Twitter), user's websites, blogs, and data stored on cloud services, including videos, pictures, photographs, diaries, songs, and books, are all classified as digital assets [6].

The term digital assets can also cover domain names, electronic accounts, and other assets that only exist in digital form [9]. However, as the digital world constantly evolves, more confusion has arisen about what is considered a digital asset [10]. For example, digital assets may include electronic bank and investment account statements. However, there are many emerging types of digital assets, like online wallets, coupons, and gift cards. Further, cryptocurrency is another example of digital assets containing economic values developed on blockchain technology [11]. All these digital assets are considered in one's estate planning. Research and development have attempted to facilitate estate planning services for digital assets by handling and managing the confidentiality of the assets and their owners [12]. In addition, some studies and development used software and Internet technology to automate many traditional estate planning processes.

The Internet has been the central technology for communication and socialising with others [13]. The widespread use of Web technology [14] has replaced traditional computer systems, making websites a common platform for information searching by numerous users [15]. Moreover, web-based applications are the standard system used in various social domains, such as managing mental health [16] and recommending attractive places [17]. Therefore, web-based applications and their technology are potentially used in facilitating the management of digital assets, particularly for estate planning, thus sustaining them for a smooth inheritance process.

The web-based estate planning for digital assets offers an enhanced mechanism for traditional estate planning. It allows asset owners to manage their digital assets more efficiently at any time and place. However, estate planning tools may lead to users' concerns about their reliability, the data stored at the providers' repository, and how the tools would facilitate inheritance after the owners' death. Although, for example, service providers could claim that their estate planning tools would provide account security for their digital assets, technically, the service providers created an extensive repository of users' wealth which could be the target of security attacks like identity theft [18]. Therefore, recent research by Singh, Shrivastava, and Ruj [6] proposed a digital asset inheritance model that contains security features like asset privacy, identifiability, the privacy of keys inheritance, non-repudiation, user privacy, and robustness. However, this study lies at the protocol design level and is still in its infancy for stable implementation. Therefore, it is unclear how the protocol can impose the same level of control as in traditional estate planning.

Another limitation of the existing web-based estate planning for digital assets is that the services are not regulated. In other words, the services run independently without a trusted third party, like lawyers, that can keep digital assets' information confidential [19]. Finally, web-based estate planning for digital assets is considered new; therefore, the main concern is how stable the service will continue to exist as the turnover in the industry has been significant [20]. Therefore, there is a need to study the technical aspects of web-based estate planning to develop a model that could facilitate understanding among estate owners, estate planners, and policymakers to sustain digital assets. Hence, to solve the issues, this study proposes an estate planning model for digital assets that aims to facilitate the management of the user's digital assets and their estate planning. The model will lead to the development of an intuitive system where asset owners can securely store the information of digital assets, assign beneficiaries, and appoint professional service providers, such as lawyers, executors, or financial advisors [8].

3 Methods

This study is conducted in five phases: problem understanding, analysis, model development, model visualisation, and evaluation. Specific activities were carried out for each phase to achieve the study's objective. For example, during the problem-understanding phase, observations were made to understand the current situation related to the ownership of digital assets and how this trend will affect a person's social life even after death. After that, the analysis phase is carried out by doing content analysis activities in the literature and on the Internet. This analysis will produce a list of potential solutions to the problems identified in the previous phase. Next, the model development phase will be carried out by identifying the appropriate components and formulating a model for estate planning for digital assets. Next, the proposed model is visualised through prototype development. Finally, the prototype was tested through usability evaluation to confirm the proposed model. Figure 1 illustrates the phases of the method, the main activities involved in each phase, and their deliverables.

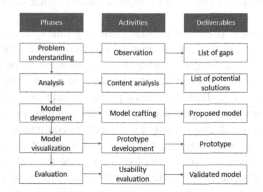

Fig. 1. The research phases, activities, and deliverables

4 Results and Discussion

This section discusses the findings of the study based on the methodology described in Sect. 3. In addition, this section will explain the findings related to the proposed model, the developed prototype, and the model validation results based on tests that have been conducted with users.

4.1   The Proposed Model

After the observation was carried out to understand the problems and gaps in estate management for digital assets, this study lists the existing gaps as stated in Sect. 1 of this paper. Then, content analysis from scientific materials and documents on the Internet is analysed to list solutions that may be appropriate to the problems related to estate planning for digital assets. The output obtained from these two phases has been used to develop a model for sustaining digital assets through estate planning. Finally, the solution list is analysed to identify the main components required for the proposed model.

The proposed model contains five main components: people, digital assets, communication, management, and digital protection. People are the main component in this model, which covers the owners of digital assets. In addition, the executor is the individual who manages the estate planning of the asset owner who produces the will. Then the judge is the party that confirms the will produced by the executor. Next, the beneficiary is the heir to the digital asset owner, who will receive the inheritance of the digital asset after the owner dies. These four parties must be present to ensure the estate planning process is complete and perfect.

The second component is digital assets included in estate planning, as described in Section two of this paper. In general, digital assets are divided into three main groups: personal content such as pictures, videos, documents, and websites that may be stored in the cloud or other forms of storage such as pen drives or hard drives. The second category is online accounts such as social media and email accessed using a username and password and other additional authentication such as personal identification number (PIN) or biometric. Finally, digital assets in the third group are related to the ownership of assets that store monetary value, for example, cryptocurrencies, e-wallets, and Internet banking.

The third component is related to estate planning management. The management aspect is crucial to ensure that information related to digital assets can be stored efficiently and securely. Therefore, computing technology needs to be used to ensure that the storage of digital asset data can be appropriately managed through an efficient process and recognised by law. Therefore, laws, processes, and technology can ensure that digital assets are sustained by providing an efficient mechanism to manage the estate of digital assets. The fourth component in this model is communication, allowing other components to interact and complete the estate management cycle for digital assets. This component is driven by web technology connected through the Internet network and produces the will document, the final output in the estate management cycle.

The last component is related to digital protection. First, it provides security protection for data pertaining to a person's digital assets and the amount of wealth owned. This protection covers the confidentiality and privacy of the asset owner. Second, this model proposes a permanent repository to store digital asset data so that the information can be stored permanently and can only be changed with the permission of the asset owner and verified by a judge to protect the integrity of the wills. Figure 2 illustrates the proposed model.

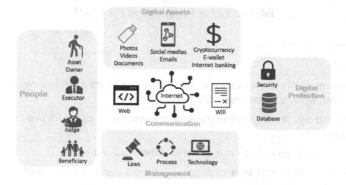

Fig. 2. The proposed model for the estate planning of digital assets

4.2 The Prototype of the Proposed Model

The proposed model contains the necessary components in estate planning management to ensure digital asset sustainability. However, this model must be translated into a tangible form and understood by the entities involved in this ecosystem. Therefore, visualising the proposed model as a system prototype is appropriate for this study. Furthermore, it can be evaluated by all the entities involved. Thus, a prototype was developed to illustrate the proposed model named Digital Estate Management System (DEMS) runs on a web-based platform.

Before the development of the prototype, a requirement-gathering process was conducted using (1) document analysis and (2) interface analysis. These activities are necessary to be conducted to detail the proposed model. It is because the model is just a conceptual representation. Hence, it does not have the detail of how it works in the ecosystem. Document analysis involves gathering information from existing documentation that may or may not involve interaction with a human expert to confirm or add to this information [21]. With the document analysis technique, the existing system, including website and mobile applications, was studied by gathering their information and manuals to analyse its functions, how the system works and how it can perform different functions. Interface analysis involves reviewing the interface of the existing system and building a context diagram that displays the entities that send data to and receive data from it at a high level. Then, interfaces for a user to interact with the system were identified, including the user workflow between the systems, user roles and privileges, and any management objectives for the interface. Then, interface specifications were prepared to document the components defined during interface analysis and allocate requirements to the various types of interfaces. Details for each interface type may include interface description, data fields, characteristics, and more.

DEMS requirements were listed based on the information collected, as shown in Table I. There are three types of priority requirements (1) mandatory (M), which describes a compulsory function that a DEMS must have (2) desirable (D), which describes that the requirement is reasonable to have; and (3) optional (O), which the requirement could be considered to have it.

Table 1. List of Requirements For DEMS.

No.	Requirements Description	Priority
1	Register	
1.1	The system allows a new user to register an account by entering their name, email, password, and confirmed password	M
1.2	The system will prompt an error message if a new user does not fill in all the required fields	M
1.3	The system will prompt an error message if the email is used	M
1.4	The system will prompt an error message if the password and confirmed password are mismatched	M
1.5	The system will send a verification email to the new user's email to complete registration	M
2	Login and Logout	
2.1	The system requires users to enter their email and password to log in to their accounts	M
2.2	The system will prompt an error message if a user does not fill in the information in all the required fields	M
2.3	The system will prompt an error message if a user enters an incorrect email or password	M
2.4	The system allows users to reset the password if they forget the password	M
2.5	The system allows users to log out of their accounts anytime	M
3	Manage User Profile	
3.1	The system allows user to view their profile	M
3.2	The system allows users to add profile information like name, gender, date of birth, address, etc.	M
3.3	The system allows users to remove profile information	M
3.4	The system allows users to edit profile information	M
4	Manage Digital Asset Information	
4.1	The system allows users to view their digital asset information	M
4.2	The system allows users to add new digital assets by entering information like asset name, type, account credentials, beneficiaries, and notes	M
4.3	The system allows users to delete digital asset information	M
4.4	The system allows users to edit digital asset information	M
5	Manage Executor Information	
5.1	The system allows userto add their executor information like name, address, email, and phone number	M
5.2	The system allows usersto remove executor information	M

(continued)

Table 1. (*continued*)

No.	Requirements Description	Priority
5.3	The system allows users to edit executor information	M
5.4	The system allows user to view their executor information	M
6	Sign the will	
6.1	The system can generate a will document to display the user's digital estate planning information	M
6.2	The system allows a user to view and sign the will	M
6.3	The system allows a user to select from a list of judges to send the will document to the judge via email	O
6.4	The system generates a new will when users update digital asset information	M
7	Receive an inactive alert email	
7.1	The system can send an inactive alert to the user through email when the user has not been logged in for three months	O
7.2	The system will send an email to the executor if a user does not log in after a notification email has been sent	O

The requirements listed in Table 1 were translated into a use case diagram, as shown in Fig. 3, to show a system's interaction with external entities/actors [23]. A use case is a software modelling diagram used in system analysis to identify, clarify, and organise system requirements [22, 23]. Three actors are identified as (1) asset owner – the owner of digital assets who performed the digital estate planning, and (2) the judge – an authorised public official who acts as a witness to sign and approve a validity of a will document

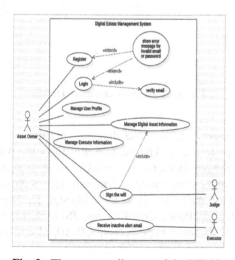

Fig. 3. The use case diagram of the DEMS.

and (3) executor – a person assigned by the asset owner to administer that person's estate upon their death. The main use cases for the DEMS are "Register", "Login", "Manage User Profile", "Manage Digital Asset Information", "Manage Executor Information", "Sign the Will" and "Receive Inactive Alert Email".

The structural components of DEMS are illustrated in a class diagram, as shown in Fig. 4. The class diagram shows the attributes, operations, and relationships among objects in the system, including the interfaces, actors, database, and system controller.

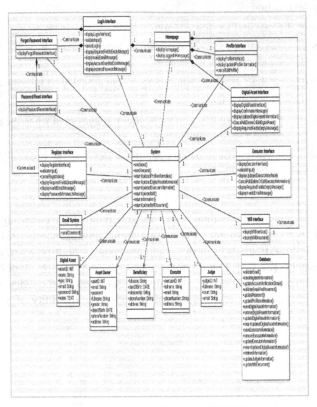

Fig. 4. The class diagram of DEMS.

The list of requirements, the use case diagram, and the class diagram were transformed into a prototype interface. This section illustrates the prototype developed for DEMS that represents the requirements explained in the previous subsection. This prototype is an early version of the system used to demonstrate concepts of the proposed system [24]. The tools to develop the prototype include MySQL Databases, phpMyAdmin for backend development, and cPanel, CodePen, and JSFiddle for frontend development. Interfaces of DEMS are shown in Figs. 5, 6, 7, 8, 9, 10, 11 and 12.

Fig. 5. Login page

Fig. 6. Homepage

Fig. 7. Digital asset page

Fig. 8. Beneficiaries page

Fig. 9. Executor page

Fig. 10. Will page for an asset owner

Fig. 11. Will page for the judge

Fig. 12. Will document

4.3 Evaluation

The developed prototype has been evaluated to confirm that the proposed model is appropriate and relevant. It was carried out through a usability test among digital asset owners. Usability is the term that is generally described as a factor of system quality, and it defines the quality of systems and products from a human point of view who use the systems [25]. A web application's usability is one of its most critical factors [15]. "Usability evaluation" refers to the entire test, planning and conducting the evaluation, and presenting the results [26]. The main goal of usability evaluation is to measure the system's usability and identify usability problems that can lead to user confusion, errors or dissatisfaction [25]. In this method, the asset owners were requested to perform specific tasks to measure the system's usefulness, ease of use, and the user's satisfaction with the system.

The evaluation was participated by 30 respondents recruited through social media. During the evaluation, the respondents were given the Internet link to access DEMS and a post-task questionnaire adapted from [27]. The post-task questionnaire was divided into two sections, consisting of 31 questions, including multiple-choice and open-ended questions. Section A asked for the respondents' demographic information. In contrast, Section B asked their opinions about DEMS on a five-point Likert scale to rate the degree to which they agreed or disagreed with a statement [28]. For example, one represents strongly disagree, and five strongly agree. In addition, the respondents performed the following step-by-step procedure for the evaluation: (1) read the given information sheet and sign the consent form, (2) perform evaluation tasks as listed in the information sheet, and (3) answer the post-task questionnaire.

The respondents comprised 19 females and 11 males, aged between 21 and 30. 70% of the respondents were students, 20% worked in the private sector, and 10% were self-employed. Regarding the respondents' employability, 70% were unemployed, 13% worked in business, management, and administration, 10% were involved in finance, and 7% worked in information technology. All respondents claimed they owned digital assets; 93% owned online banking the most, with only 7% claiming they owned the most digital asset in E-wallet. 63% of the respondents admitted that they did not know about estate planning, while 37% knew it.

The respondents' responses to Section B of the post-task questionnaire were analysed. The section measures the respondents' perceived usefulness, ease of use and satisfaction with DEMS Tables 2, 3 and 4 reported each aspect's frequency and percentage (in the brackets) of responses. Most respondents rated four or five agree and strongly agree with the questionnaire. None of the respondents rated one, which strongly disagrees with all questions, and only a few rated three, which is neutral with the statement.

Overall, the results and findings of the evaluation suggested that DEMS is helpful and easy to use, and users were satisfied with the system. Based on the response, most respondents agree that DEMS improves their effectiveness in estate planning as it can save time managing digital assets. Besides, respondents also perceived that they could quickly learn to use and remember the system without written instruction. Finally, the respondents also claimed they are satisfied with the DEMS as it is pleasant to use and intended to recommend the system to others.

One prominent feature of this model is that the people component contains the executor and judge. These two entities are one example of a security part that promotes data security and develops a trusted environment. This study's outcomes benefit system developers, service providers, and policymakers in digital assets management. The proposed model can help the parties to identify the components that must be available in

Table 2. Usefulness of DEMS.

Usefulness of DEMS	Strongly Disagree	Disagree	Neutral	Agree	Strongly Agree
DEMS enhances my effectiveness in estate planning for digital assets	0 (0.0)	0 (0.0)	2 (6.7)	19 (63.3)	9 (30.0)
DEMS makes it easier to store and manage digital asset information	0 (0.0)	0 (0.0)	3 (10)	17 (56.7)	10 (33.3)
DEMS enables me to generate documents more quickly	0 (0.0)	0 (0.0)	1 (3.3)	18 (60.0)	11 (36.7)
It saves my time when I use this application	0 (0.0)	0 (0.0)	2 (6.7)	20 (66.7)	8 (26.7)
DEMS meets my needs	0 (0.0)	1 (3.3)	5 (16.7)	18 (60.0)	6 (20.0)
DEMS does everything I would expect it to do	0 (0.0)	2 (6.7)	5 (16.7)	17 (56.7)	6 (20.0)
DEMS is useful overall	0 (0.0)	1 (3.3)	5 (16.7)	19 (63.3)	7 (23.3)

Table 3. DEMS Ease of Use

DEMS Ease of Use	Strongly Disagree	Disagree	Neutral	Agree	Strongly Agree
DEMS is easy to use	0 (0.0)	0 (0.0)	4 (13.3)	18 (60)	8 (26.7)
DEMS is user friendly	0 (0.0)	1 (3.3)	6 (20.0)	16 (53.5)	7 (23.3)
DEMS is flexible	0 (0.0)	2 (6.7)	4 (13.3)	16 (53.5)	8 (26.7)
DEMS is easy to learn how to use it	0 (0.0)	0 (0.0)	5 (16.7)	15 (50.0)	10 (33.3)
I can use DEMS without written instructions	0 (0.0)	0 (0.0)	3 (10.0)	18 (60.0)	9 (30.0)

(*continued*)

Table 3. (*continued*)

DEMS Ease of Use	Strongly Disagree	Disagree	Neutral	Agree	Strongly Agree
I can easily remember how to use DEMS	0 (0.0)	0 (0.0)	2 (6.7)	16 (53.3)	12 (40.0)
I don't notice any inconsistencies as I use DEMS	0 (0.0)	2 (6.7)	4 (13.3)	18 (60.0)	6 (20.0)
My interaction with the application would be clear and understandable	0 (0.0)	3 (10.0)	5 (16.7)	15 (50.0)	7 (23.3)
I can use DEMS successfully every time	0 (0.0)	0 (0.0)	2 (6.7)	19 (63.3)	9 (30.0)

Table 4. The Users' Satisfaction of DEMS.

Satisfaction of DEMS	Strongly Disagree	Disagree	Neutral	Agree	Strongly Agree
I am satisfied with DEMS	0 (0.0)	0 (0.0)	6 (20)	15 (50)	9 (30)
I would recommend DEMS to my friends	0 (0.0)	0 (0.0)	5 (16.7)	18 (60)	7 (23.3)
DEMS works the way I want it to work	0 (0.0)	3 (10.0)	6 (20)	13 (43.3)	8 (26.7)
I feel I need to have a DEMS application	0 (0.0)	4 (13.3)	7 (23.3)	13 (43.3)	6 (20)
DEMS is wonderful and pleasant to use	0 (0.0)	0 (0.0)	5 (16.7)	18 (60)	7 (23.3)

the new era of estate planning and further formulate appropriate policies to facilitate its administration and develop tools to smooth this process.

5   Conclusion and Future Works

This paper proposed an estate planning model for digital assets to provide a sustainable mechanism primarily through inheritance. There is an urgent need to look at the proper management of digital assets, significantly when the ownership of digital assets rises exponentially. It is even increasingly important when those digital assets have attached economic and financial values. However, what happens when the owners of digital assets pass away? Hence, it requires estate planning for digital assets. Nevertheless, the traditional estate planning mechanism cannot cater to the dynamic and uncertain features of digital assets. For example, what if a person passes away and his cryptocurrency wallet username and password are unknown to anyone else? Therefore, an enhancement of the traditional estate planning model is deemed required.

Therefore, this paper addresses the gap by proposing a model and demonstrating the development and evaluation of DEMS, a web-based application that visualises the proposed model. The evaluation suggested that DEMS is usable and relevant. However, further improvements to the model can be considered. For example, other researchers might test the model through other methodologies like expert review, interview, or survey to gather different perspectives on estate management. Another way to extend the study is by implementing advanced technology like blockchain to protect the secrecy and integrity of the data communicated by the entities involved in the entire ecosystem. Finally, validating communication protocol is another way of enhancing and extending the work.

Acknowledgment. The authors thank the Ministry of Higher Education Malaysia for funding this study under the Fundamental Research Grant Scheme (Ref: FRGS/1/2021/SS01/UUM/02/9, UUM S/O Code: 20115), and Research and Innovation Management Centre, Universiti Utara Malaysia for the administration of this study.

References

1. Rosele, M.I., et al.: The concept of wealth (*māl*) in the Sharīʿah and its relation to digital assets. SAGE Open **12** (2022). https://doi.org/10.1177/21582440221102424
2. Nekit, K.: Social media account as an object of virtual property. Masaryk Univ. J. Law Technol. **14**, 201–226 (2020)
3. Nunes, B.A.N.: Business Plan: Innovative Platform to Create Digital Memorials (2021). https://medium.com/@arifwicaksanaa/pengertian-use-case-a7e576e1b6bf
4. Katuk, N., Abd Wahab, N., Kamis, N.S.: Cryptocurrency estate planning: the challenges, suggested solutions and Malaysia's future directions. Digit. Policy Regul. Gov. **25**, 325–350 (2023). https://doi.org/10.1108/DPRG-10-2021-0126
5. Beyer, G.W., Cahn, N.: When you pass on, don't leave the passwords behind: Planning for digital assets. Prob. Prop. **26**, 40 (2012)
6. Singh, R.G., Shrivastava, A., Ruj, S.: A digital asset inheritance model to convey online persona posthumously. Int. J. Inf. Secur. **21**, 983–1003 (2022). https://doi.org/10.1007/s10207-022-00593-8
7. Soma, J.T.: Encryption, key recovery, and commercial trade secret assets: a proposed legislative model. Rutgers Comput. Tech. LJ **25**, 97 (1999)
8. Pinch, R.: Protecting digital assets after death: Issues to consider in planning for your digital estate. Wayne L. Rev. **60**, 545 (2014)
9. Mentrek, J.: Estate planning in a digital world. Ohio Prob. LJ. **19**, 195 (2009)
10. Hopkins, J.P.: Afterlife in the cloud: managing a digital estate. Hast. Sci. Tech. LJ. **5**, 209 (2013)
11. Katuk, N.: The application of blockchain for halal product assurance: a systematic review of the current developments and future directions. Int. J. Adv. Trends Comput. Sci. Eng. **8**, 1893–1902 (2019). https://doi.org/10.30534/ijatcse/2019/13852019

12. Adriani, N.: Electronic-will legislation: the uniform act versus Australian and Canadian alternatives. Prob. Prop. **34**, 1–18 (2020)
13. Cordente-Rodriguez, M., Splendiani, S., Silvestrelli, P.: Measuring propensity of online purchase by using the tam model: evidence from Italian university students. Appl. Comput. Sci. **16**, 32–52 (2020). https://doi.org/10.23743/acs-2020-11
14. Akinyede, R.O., Balogun, T.E., Rotimi, A.B., Famodimu, O.B.: A customer-centric application for a cinema house. Appl. Comput. Sci. **16**, 68–79 (2020). https://doi.org/10.23743/acs-2020-13
15. Adepoju, S.A., Oyefolahan, I.O., Abdullahi, M.B., Mohammed, A.A.: Multi-criteria decision-making based approaches in website quality and usability evaluation: a systematic review. J. Inf. Commun. Technol. **19**, 399–436 (2020). https://doi.org/10.32890/jict2020.19.3.5
16. Zolkipli, M.F., Said, Z.M., Mahmuddin, M.: A web-based application system for managing mental health in higher institution. Int. J. Adv. Comput. Sci. Appl. **13**, 666–675 (2022)
17. Shu, S., Wan-Ishak, W., Yamin, F.M.: A web-based application for interesting place recommendation. In: International Conference on Decision Aid Sciences and Applications, DASA, pp. 215–220 (2022)
18. Connor, J.: Digital life after death: the issue of planning for a person's digital assets after death. Est. Plan. C. Prop. LJ. **3**, 301 (2010)
19. Hopkins, J.P., Lipin, I.A.: Viable solutions to the digital estate planning dilemma. Iowa Law Rev. Bull. **99**, 61–71 (2014)
20. Baldino, F.: Estate planning and administration for digital assets. MD. BJ. **45**, 30 (2012)
21. Burge, J..: Knowledge elicitation tool classification (2001)
22. Aleryani, A., Aleryani, A.Y.: Comparative study between data flow diagram and use case diagram. Int. J. Sci. Res. Publ. **6**, 124 (2016)
23. Jacobson, I., Spence, I., Kerr, B.: Use-case 2.0. Commun. ACM **59**, 61–69 (2016). https://doi.org/10.1145/2890778
24. Sommerville, I. (ed.): Software Engineering, 9th edn. Pearson Education, Boston (2011)
25. Fernandez, A., Insfran, E., Abrahão, S.: Usability evaluation methods for the web: a systematic mapping study. Inf. Softw. Technol. **53**, 789–817 (2011)
26. Lárusdóttir, M.K.: Listen to your users the effect of usability evaluation on software development practice, p. 50 (2009)
27. Lund, A.M.: Measuring usability with the USE questionnaire. Usability Interface **8**, 3–6 (2001)
28. Mazikana, A.T.: The impact of cryptocurrencies in Zimbabwe. An analysis of bitcoins. SSRN Electron. J. (2019). https://doi.org/10.2139/ssrn.3376307

Author Index

A

Abd Karim, Nur Kareelawati I-380
Abd Wahab, Alawiyah I-287
Abdullah, Karrar Ali II-268
Abdullah, Nasir I-260
Abdullah, Noor Rafhati Adyani II-43
Abdullah, Wan Aida Nadia Wan II-336
Abdullahi, Husein Osman II-309
Abdul-Rahman, Shuzlina II-296
Abrar, Ahmad I-330, I-343
Abuzaraida, Mustafa Ali I-137
Ahmad, Farzana Kabir I-125, I-168, II-231
Ahmad, Mazida II-15, II-282
Ahmad, Rahayu I-182, II-180
Aji, Zahurin Mat II-30, II-231
Akbar, Rehan I-80
Al Galib, Asadullah I-17
Alam, R. G. Guntur I-3
Al-Hamzi, Yaser Mohammed II-56
Ali Shah, Zuraini II-110
Ali, Adnan Hussein I-125
Alkubaisi, Ghaith Abdulsattar A. Jabbar I-248
Al-Kumaim, Nabil Hasan II-15
Al-Mashhadani, Abdulrazak F. Shahatha I-154
Al-Qaisi, Laila I-235
AlSamman, Mohammed I-343
Alsamman, Mohammed I-367
Al-Ubaidi, Dalia A. II-81
Alwi, Asmidah I-380
Ani, Zhamri Che I-355
Anuardi, Muhammad Nur Adilin bin Mohamad II-139
Arif, Ahmad Suki Che Mohamed I-343
Ariffin, Shamsul Arrieya I-380
Askri, Soumaya II-324
Awang, Hapini I-154, I-193, I-301, II-95
Azir, Ku Nurul Fazira binti Ku I-221
Aziz, Azizi Ab II-217
Aziz, Maslina Abdul II-296

Aziz, Mochamad Azkal Azkiya I-58
Azman, Wan Nur Fadhlina Syamimi Wan I-221
Azmi, Nur Farah Amalina II-123
Azmi, Nur Syafiqah I-193

B

Badroddin, Salwati II-180
Baharom, Fauziah II-180
Bakar, Juhaida Abu I-193, II-95, II-180
Bakar, Nur Syafiqah Abu I-193
Ba-Quttayyan, Bakr I-315
Bazel, Mahmood A. II-15
Benlahcene, Abderrahmane I-154
Budianto, Heru II-336

C

Che Mohamed Arif, Ahmad Suki I-330
ChePa, Noraziah II-217
Chit, Suwannit Chareen II-190, II-204
Chzhan, Ekaterina I-30

D

Desa, Mohamad Adli II-282

E

Eleyan, Derar II-154
Elisa, Edi II-204
Embong, Zunaina II-95

F

Farooq, Muhammad I-70
Fazea, Yousef I-367

G

Gernal, Liza II-324
Ghani, Nor Farzana Abd II-244
Ghazali, Masitah II-110
Ghazali, Osman I-70, I-154, II-180
Gilal, Abdul Rehman I-80

N. H. Zakaria et al. (Eds.): ICOCI 2023, CCIS 2002, pp. 351–353, 2024.
https://doi.org/10.1007/978-981-99-9592-9

Gilani, Sayed Abdul Majid II-324
Gordon, Neil II-258
Guntoro, Guntoro I-96

H
Habberrih, Abdullah I-137
Hamid, Zauridah Abdul I-355
Haroon-Sulyman, Shakirat Oluwatosin
    I-168
Harun, Nor Hazlyna I-193, II-95
Haruna, Isyaku Uba I-154
Hasan, Zuhairah II-296
Hashmani, Manzoor Ahmed I-260
Hassan, Mohamad Ghozali II-258
Hassan, Suhaidi I-44, I-235, I-367
Hj. Ibrahim, Huda I-287
Husni, Husniza I-248, II-69, II-123

I
Ibrahim, Farah Lia I-125
Ibrahim, Huda I-3
Ishak, Wan Hussain Wan II-180, II-217
Ismail, Adzrool Idzwan I-380
Ismail, Mohd Azril II-258
Ismail, Nurulhuda I-182
Ismail, Suzilah II-180

J
Jamaludin, Nur Hafiza II-168
Jambli, Mohamad Nazim I-58
Jasim, Mahdi II-81

K
Kamaruddin, Siti Sakira I-125, I-168
Kamruddin, Siti Sakira I-248, II-231
Karas, Ismail Rakip I-3
Katuk, Norliza I-30, I-209, II-154, II-336
Khairuddin, Adam bin Mohd I-221
Khamis, Shakiroh I-154
Khatri, Tarwan Kumar I-260
Kit, Brandon Chua Choon II-244
Krishnan, Suren II-154
Kunhiraman, Raj Kumar II-154
Kurniadi, Erik II-336

L
Lee, Hwee-Hsiung II-154
Li, Teh Soon II-139
Losada, David Enrique I-182

M
Mahmod, Musyrifah II-268
Mahmud, Murni II-309
Mahmuddin, Massudi II-190
Maijama'a, Inusa Sani II-3
Malami, Sarkin Tudu Shehu I-301
Mansor, Nur Suhaili I-154, I-301
Marzal, Jefri II-204
Mataruna-Dos-Santos, Leonardo Jose II-324
Mater, Wasef II-15
Maulana, Hanhan I-301
Md Nasir, Norshakinah I-44
Mehedi, Md Humaion Kabir I-17
Mohamad Mohsin, Mohamad Farhan II-258
Mohammed, Fathey I-367, II-15
Mohd Pozi, Muhammad Syafiq I-108
Mohd Yunos, Zuriahati II-110
Mohd Zaini, Khuzairi I-44, I-330
Mohd, Haslina I-315, II-180
Muniandy, Asvinitha II-282
Mustakim, Nurul Ain II-296

N
Nadzir, Maslinda Mohd I-154
Nasri, Nurul Ida Syaheera Mohd II-69
Ng, Wan En I-209
Nordin, Noradila I-44, I-108, II-231

O
Omar, Mazni I-80, II-139
Omar, Mohd Hasbullah I-30, I-209, I-330,
    II-180
Omar, Mohd. Nizam Bin I-96
Othman, Nur Zuraifah Syazrah II-110

P
Pozi, Muhammad Syafiq Mohd I-30, I-209

R
Rahim, Lukman Ab. I-260
Rasel, Annajiat Alim I-17
Raziff, Abdul Rafiez Abdul I-209
Rehman, Mujeeb ur I-80
Rhythm, Ehsanur Rahman I-17
Riskhan, Basheer I-58
Romli, Rohaida II-168, II-180
Romo, Bilyaminu A. I-287
Ruhaiyem, Nur Intan Raihana I-274

S

Sadimon, Suriati   II-110
Sahibuddin, Shamsul Bin   II-56
Saip, Mohamed Ali   II-69, II-123, II-180
Salleh, Khazainani   II-258
Samah, Azurah A.   II-81
SarkinTudu, Shehu M.   I-287
Sarmani, Mimi Adilla   II-258
Sergio, Rommel   II-324
Shabli, Ahmad Hanis Mohd   II-43, II-190, II-217
Shaffiei, Zatul Alwani   II-110
Shahril, Mohd Azrul Edzwan   I-193
Sharif, Kamal Imran Mohd   II-258
Sharif, Nurul Atikah Mohd   II-95
Sharimi, Nur Azmielia Muhammad   I-193, II-95
Sinal, Mohamad Sabri bin   II-139
Sinal, Mohamad Sabri   II-336

T

Taib, Hasmi   I-260
Taiye, Mohammed Ahmed   I-168, I-301
Tantry, Ansarullah   II-324
Tey, Peck-Yong   II-336

U

Umana, Muhammad Khalifa   II-258
Utomo, Pradita Eko Prasetyo   II-204

W

Wahab, Alawiyah Abd   II-231
Wahab, Norazlina Abd   II-336

Y

Yaacob, Noorulsadiqin Azbiya   II-43
Yaacob, Wan Mohd Yusoff Wan   II-30
Yamin, Fadhilah Mat   I-154
Yasin, Azman   II-15
Yi, Laura Lim Sei   II-217
Yusof, Yuhanis   I-315, II-3, II-180

Z

Zahari, Suhaili Mohd   II-258
Zaibon, Syamsul Bahrin   I-380
Zaimy, Nur A.' fyfah   II-154
Zainal Abidin, Ahmad Hisham   I-380
Zakaria, Nur Haryani   I-58, I-235, II-30
Zamberi, Zuriana   I-274
Zhamri, Nur Nazifa   I-355
Zolkafli, Amirulikhsan   I-301
Zukri, Nurul Hidayah Ahmad   I-343

Printed in the United States
by Baker & Taylor Publisher Services